# Developing Musicianship through Aural Skills

*Developing Musicianship through Aural Skills* is a comprehensive method for learning to hear, sing, understand, and use the foundations of music as a part of an integrated and holistic curriculum for training professional musicians.

Each chapter is organized to take advantage of how our minds and instincts naturally hear and understand music, and presents a variety of exercises for practicing and integrating the structure into your musical vocabulary. *Developing Musicianship through Aural Skills* will provide you with the musical terms, progressions, resolutions, and devices that you will be able to draw upon as a functional and usable musical vocabulary. Ear training exercises on the companion website reinforce both discrete structures (intervals, chords, etc.) as well as all rhythmic and melodic material, and sections are provided to open discussion and reflection on the skills and attitudes professional musicians need to be successful.

**Features:**

**Easy to Understand Explanations:** Topics are logically ordered and explained to help the student make connections to their theory instruction and common usage.

**A Complete Method:** Detailed instructions are given for singing and hearing structures as they most commonly appear in music, providing students with a proven, reliable process for creating and discerning musical structures.

**Exercises:** Ideas for drill, pitch patterns, rhythms, melodies, duets, self-accompanied melodies, and examples from the literature help the student to integrate each chapter's material.

**Reflections:** Discussions of topics that help students to develop as a person, a professional, and an artist, and to integrate aural skills into their musical education.

**Ear Training Tools and Video Demonstrations** can be found on the companion website.

**Kent D. Cleland** is Associate Professor and Chair of the Department of Music Theory at the Baldwin-Wallace College Conservatory of Music. He holds degrees from Ohio University, Indiana University, and the University of Cincinnati, and he has taught at the University of Cincinnati and Oberlin College.

**Mary Dobrea-Grindahl** holds the Diplôme Jaques-Dalcroze from the Institute Jaques-Dalcroze in Geneva, Switzerland. She is Associate Professor of Piano and Chair of the Keyboard Department at the Baldwin-Wallace College Conservatory of Music, where she teaches private piano, pedagogy, Eurhythmics, and solfège.

# Developing Musicianship through Aural Skills

## A Holistic Approach to Sight Singing and Ear Training

*Kent D. Cleland and Mary Dobrea-Grindahl*

Routledge
Taylor & Francis Group
NEW YORK AND LONDON

Please visit the companion website at
www.routledge.com/textbooks/developingmusicianship

Senior Editor: Constance Ditzel
Senior Development Editor: Nicole Solano
Senior Editorial Assistant: Denny Tek
Production Editor: Sarah Stone
Project Manager: Maggie Lindsey-Jones, Keystroke
Marketing Manager: Chris Bowers
Text Design: Karl Hunt, Keystroke
Copy Editor: Ruth Jeavons
Proofreader: Ann King
Cover Designer: Jayne Varney
Composition: Keystroke
Companion Website Designer: Leon Nolan, Jr.

First published 2010
by Routledge
270 Madison Ave, New York, NY 10016

Simultaneously published in the UK
by Routledge
2 Park Square, Milton Park, Abingdon, Oxon OX14 4RN

*Routledge is an imprint of the Taylor & Francis Group, an informa business*



Typeset in ACaslon by Keystroke, Tettenhall, Wolverhampton
Printed and bound in the United States of America on acid-free paper by
Edwards Brothers, Inc.



*Library of Congress Cataloging-in-Publication Data*
Cleland, Kent D.
Developing musicianship through aural skills : a holistic approach to sight singing and ear training / Kent D. Cleland. – 1st ed.
p. cm.
1. Sight-singing. 2. Ear training. I. Dobrea-Grindahl, Mary. II. Title.
MT870.C58 2010

ISBN10: 0–415–80243–1 (hbk)
ISBN10: 0–415–80244–X (pbk)
ISBN10: 0–203–86156–6 (ebk)

ISBN13: 978–0–415–80243–7 (hbk)
ISBN13: 978–0–415–80244–4 (pbk)
ISBN13: 978–0–203–86156–1 (ebk)

For Eric

Karen, Larkin, and Chloe

Our families, for their love and patience.

To Larry Hartzell and Allyn Reilly, colleagues, mentors and friends.

To our students, from whom we have learned so much.

# Contents

# Preface

*Developing Musicianship through Aural Skills* is a comprehensive method for learning to hear, sing, understand, and use the basic materials of music.

Aural skills are an essential part of every musician's education. Just as authors need to be readers and artists need to have a discerning eye, musicians must have a developed musical ear. This allows us to understand the language we use in our careers on a musical and aesthetic level, and converse with other musicians both about and through music. Having a trained musical ear includes the ability to discriminate between different types of musical sounds, to sense and understand their natural tendencies, and to effectively translate these tendencies into performance. Aural skills are the ability to hear what you see and to see what you hear, and to communicate about and through music.

After studying aural skills, you should have a mental catalog of standard musical progressions, terms, resolutions, and devices that you will be able to draw upon as a functional and usable musical vocabulary.

## How to Use this Text

This text is based on the premise that whenever we hear a musical sound, we 1) identify a tonal center, 2) hear that musical sound in relation to that tonal center, and 3) place a label on that sound. Musical sounds are heard and understood as combinations of scale degrees in a key.

Each chapter is organized to take advantage of how our minds naturally hear and understand music. Each chapter begins with "Facts You Should Know": a listing of theoretical and practical information about that structure that helps you develop the vocabulary to place the correct label on the sounds you hear. The "facts" describe the characteristics of the structure and give information about how that sound most commonly appears in tonal music. Look for the "flag up" icon as each topic is introduced.

Next, detailed instructions are given about how to hear that particular sound as it commonly appears in tonal music. In most cases, pitched structures are presented as combinations of scale degrees in the major mode. Rhythmic structures are presented as they commonly appear in metric and tonal music. Look for the "hearing" icon.

Detailed instructions are then given for singing the structure both outside of a melodic context and as it most commonly appears melodically. Look for the "singing" icon.

Each chapter provides a variety of exercises for practicing and integrating the structure into your musical vocabulary: "Assignments for Practice" give some ideas for becoming more familiar and comfortable with the chapter's subject.

Most chapters on pitched materials also contain pitch patterns—patterns of scale degrees that include the chapter's topic sound embedded within them. The method this book uses stresses the singing and recognition of scale degrees as the most accurate and reliable way to hear and sing musical structures; thus, these exercises give practice in hearing and singing structures as scale degrees. These are to be sung in an isorhythmic manner, utilizing a given rhythmic figure. The student should sing the pattern in the given rhythm until he or she can find a logical and intuitive way to cadence.

Next come a series of melodies, duets, self-accompanied melodies, and examples from the literature that feature the chapter's topic structure as it most commonly appears and in other contexts.

Several chapters focus on improvisation through recognizing harmonic function. Some melodies throughout the text contain blank measures in which the student is expected to improvise a logical and appropriate musical figure.

The text is organized into twelve units, each of which should take approximately five weeks for an average undergraduate class to cover. Each unit contains a variety of topics with their own exercises, followed by integrating examples from the literature. The units move from basic, diatonic material, through chromatic material, and into twentieth-century and atonal material, providing a variety of strategies for how to deal with music that doesn't adhere to tonal expectations.

This text's companion website is an important tool for learning and practicing the material in the text. Look for materials to practice identifying and writing each structure both out of context and within melodies and harmonic progressions. Additional practice melodies are included for most structures, as are videos of students demonstrating this text's method for performing each topic. Look for the "website" icon throughout the text. You can find the companion website at: **www.routledge.com/textbooks/ developingmusicianship.** Visit the website for additional rhythms for this topic.

Because becoming a professional musician requires the ability to integrate aural skills throughout your education, each unit discusses topics related to developing as a person, a professional, and an artist. Let those chapters become a starting point for your development as a whole musician, and for living a rich life in music.

Together with its companion website, *Developing Aural Skills* is designed to start you on a path of discovery about how you hear, understand, and learn music while developing as an artist. The study of aural skills is a lifelong pursuit, and learning to approach it methodically and with artistry, passion, and joy is essential for your continued development as a musician. Read, learn, sing, and enjoy speaking the language of music.

We would like to express our appreciation to all of the people at Routledge who helped to make this project a reality, including Constance Ditzel for her belief in the book from the beginning, Nicole Solano, Denny Tek, Sarah Stone, Chris Bowers, and Jayne Varney - thank you. Without their patience, guidance, and wisdom, this project would still be just an idea. We would also like to thank the project management team at Keystroke including, Maggie Lindsey-Jones, Ruth Jeavons, Ann King, Karl Hunt and Emma Wood.

# Chapter 1

# Simple Meter, Rests and Phrases; The Major Mode, Major Triads and Tonic Function

## 1.1 Beats, their First Divisons and Multiples, and Simple Meters

### Note Values

#### Facts You Need to Know

Durational values are indicated using a system of visual symbols that show the relationships of notes to each other. Rhythmic values are set up in a binary numeric system, which means that each value is equal to one half of the next larger value and twice the next smallest value. The following symbols are the standard note durations: the system continues indefinitely, with each successively smaller note value adding one flag (or beam) and being one half of the next larger value and twice the next smallest value.

**EXAMPLE 1.1.1**

| *Note Value* | *Note Name* | *Equivalent Rest* |
|---|---|---|
| 𝅜 | Double Whole Note or Breve | 𝄺 |
| 𝅝 | Whole Note | 𝄻 |
| 𝅗𝅥 or 𝅗𝅥 | Half Note | 𝄼 |
| 𝅘𝅥 or 𝅘𝅥 | Quarter Note | 𝄽 |
| 𝅘𝅥𝅮 or 𝅘𝅥𝅮 | Eighth Note | 𝄾 |
| 𝅘𝅥𝅯 or 𝅘𝅥𝅯 | Sixteenth Note | 𝄿 |
| 𝅘𝅥𝅰 or 𝅘𝅥𝅰 | Thirty-second Note | 𝅀 |

## Simple Beats

### Facts You Need to Know

The fundamental rhythmic structure of Western music composed between 1600 and 1900 is based on what we refer to as a beat or pulse, that is, a steady, continuous unit of time that occurs at regular intervals. The frequency at which we perceive a beat to recur is the tempo. We recognize beats instinctively; even young children are able to listen to a piece of music and clap along with its basic rhythmic impulse.

Beats are divisible into any number of smaller units, most commonly into groups of two or three. When a beat is divided into two parts, we refer to it as a simple beat or simple beat structure. Simple beats produce a two-to-one relationship between rhythmic values; this is true whether you are dealing with the first division of the beat (twice as fast, or the diminution of the beat) or the first multiple of the beat (twice as slow, or the augmentation of the beat). Refer to the chart below:

**EXAMPLE 1.1.2**

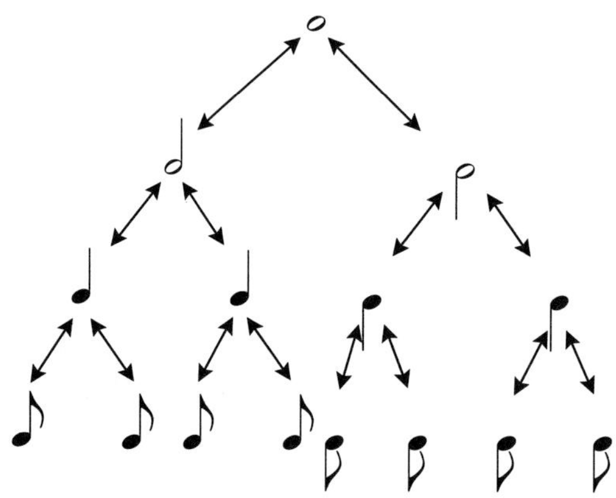

## Simple Meters

### Facts You Need to Know

Meter is created when beats organize themselves into recurring units, the most common of which are groups of two, three, or four. Groups of beats are organized into measures, delineated by a vertical line (called a bar line) at the end of each grouping. Meters are created and perceived through the interaction of several elements, including harmonic usage, tempo, melodic contour, and articulation.

Meters are defined by two characteristics: the number of beats in a measure, and the number of divisions in each beat. A measure with two beats is a duple meter, with three beats, a triple meter, and with four beats, a quadruple meter. A measure in which the beats are divided into two parts is a simple meter. For example, a meter with two simple beats is a simple duple meter.

When we listen to music, we tend to define our listening experience by the number of beats we hear; we might say, "Oh, this is in a meter of four," whereas when we read music, the meter is indicated with a time signature, the numeric symbol found at the beginning of a work. The top number of a time signature indicates the number of beats in a measure and, in simple meters, the bottom number indicates what kind of note gets a beat.

The three tables below show examples of simple duple, triple, and quadruple meters. Notice that in each example, there is a two-to-one relationship between the beat note and its division.

## Simple Duple Meters

**EXAMPLE 1.1.3**

| *Time Signature* | *Beat Note Value* | *Beat Division* | *Beats per Measure* |
|---|---|---|---|
| 2/4 | ♩ | ♪ | 2 |
| 2/2 or ¢ | 𝅗𝅥 | ♩ | 2 |
| 2/8 | ♪ | 𝅘𝅥𝅯 | 2 |

Or, as notated:

**EXAMPLE 1.1.4**

## Simple Quadruple Meters

**EXAMPLE 1.1.5**

| *Time Signature* | *Beat Note Value* | *Beat Division* | *Beats per Measure* |
|---|---|---|---|
| 4/4 or C | ♩ | ♪ | 4 |
| 4/2 | 𝅗𝅥 | ♩ | 4 |
| 4/8 | ♪ | 𝅘𝅥𝅯 | 4 |

Or, as notated:

**EXAMPLE 1.1.6**

Duple and quadruple meters are very closely related; at times, it can be nearly impossible to ascertain whether a piece is written in duple or quadruple meter. This is because quadruple meters divide themselves naturally into two parts, and have a secondary stress on the third beat of the measure.

## Simple Triple Meters

**EXAMPLE 1.1.7**

| *Time Signature* | *Beat Note Value* | *Beat Division* | *Beats per Measure* |
|---|---|---|---|
| 3/4 | ♩ | ♪ | 3 |
| 3/2 | 𝅗𝅥 | ♩ | 3 |
| 3/8 | ♪ | 𝅘𝅥𝅯 | 3 |

Or, as notated:

**EXAMPLE 1.1.8**

The elements of rhythm, harmony, melody, tempo, and articulation all combine to create meter; the character of a meter is built into the music. The stress we hear at the beginning of a measure happens because of the way these elements interact, not because one note is played louder than the others every two, three, or four beats.

Just as every interval has a distinct quality of sound, each meter has a different personality. Even a simple rhythm takes on a different meaning depending on whether it is in a duple, triple, or quadruple meter. Look at the short–short–long rhythm below; conduct and articulate each measure, and notice how the character of the rhythm changes from meter to meter.

**EXAMPLE 1.1.9**

The rhythm above completely fills the measure, so it has a natural sense of cadence, but not a sense of breadth.

**EXAMPLE 1.1.10**

The rhythm above has a strong sense of suspension because it does not divide naturally into two parts in this meter; the short notes lead to the long note in dramatic fashion.

**EXAMPLE 1.1.11**

In the rhythm above, the pattern has more weight because the meter itself, with more beats, has more breadth.

## Rhythm Reading

### Reading Rhythms in Simple Duple Meter

The exercises below use the beat and its first division and multiple in simple duple and quadruple meter. Practice each in two ways: first by clapping the beat while articulating the rhythm (using a neutral syllable like "ta"), then by conducting and articulating. Use a variety of tempi and dynamics. Two of the most common patterns in simple duple and quadruple meters are "short–short–long" and "long–short–short." Find and circle other occurrences of those patterns in the rhythms below; learning to "see" music in groups helps you develop your sight-reading skills.

**RHYTHM 1.1.1**

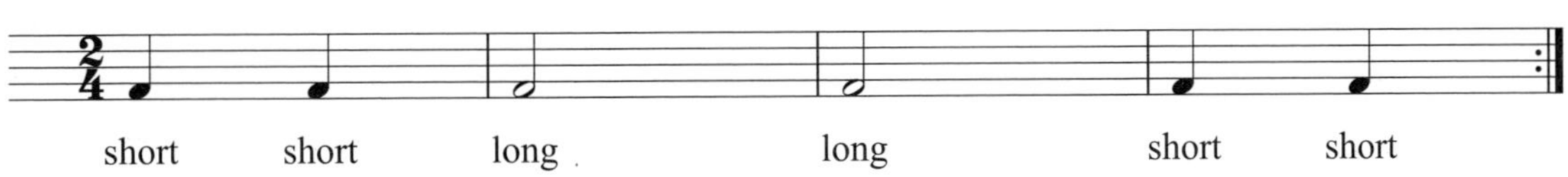


**RHYTHM 1.1.2**

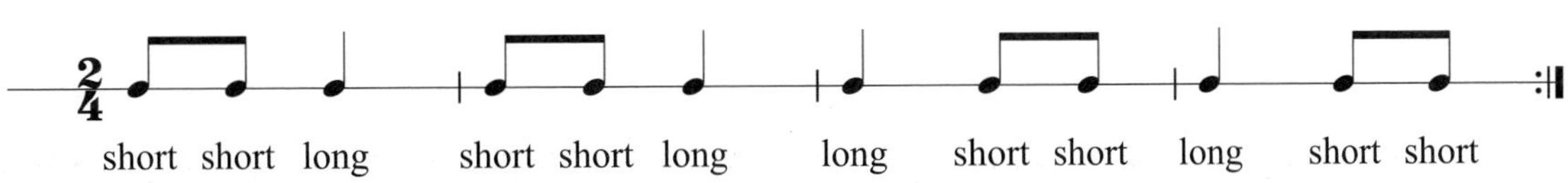

**RHYTHM 1.1.3**

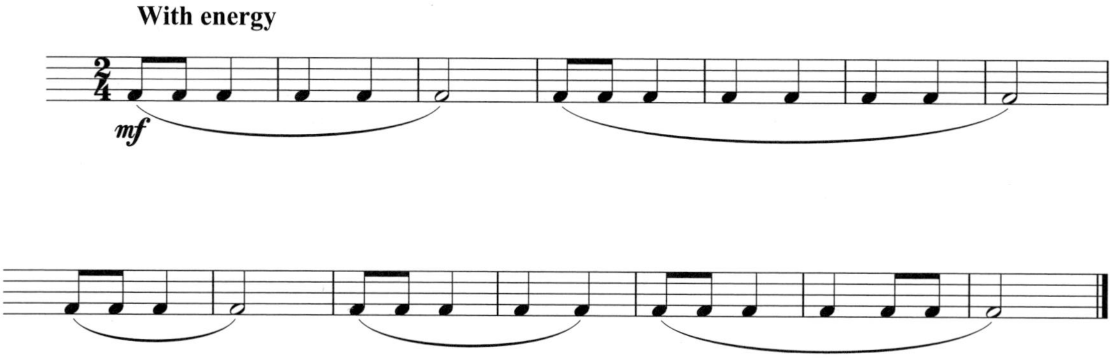


**RHYTHM 1.1.4**

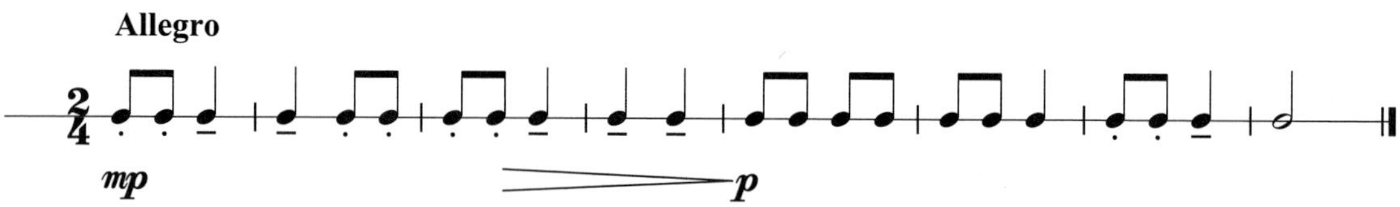


**RHYTHM 1.1.5**

**RHYTHM 1.1.6**

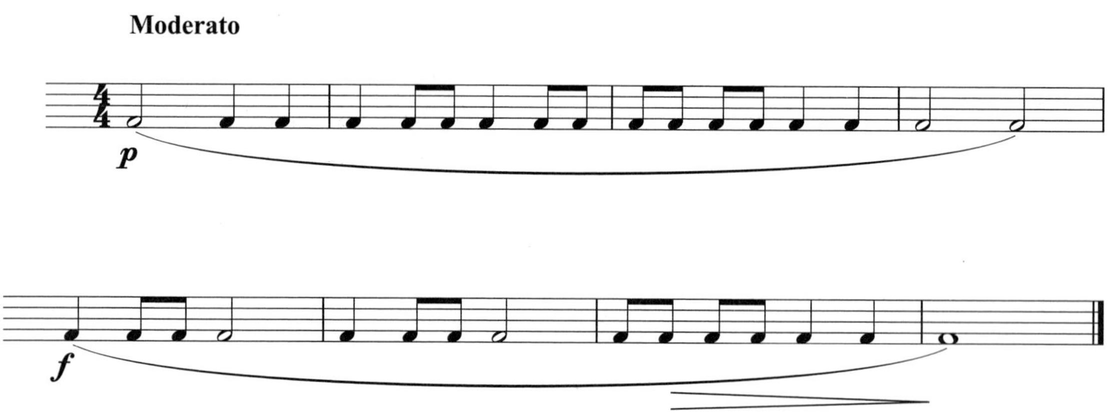


The rhythm below uses notes placed on various lines and spaces of the staff. Focus on reading only the rhythm.

**RHYTHM 1.1.7**

## Reading in Simple Triple Meter

When reading rhythms in simple triple meter, work to "see" the entire measure at once, rather than reading beat by beat.

**RHYTHM 1.1.8**

**RHYTHM 1.1.9**

**RHYTHM 1.1.10**

**RHYTHM 1.1.11**

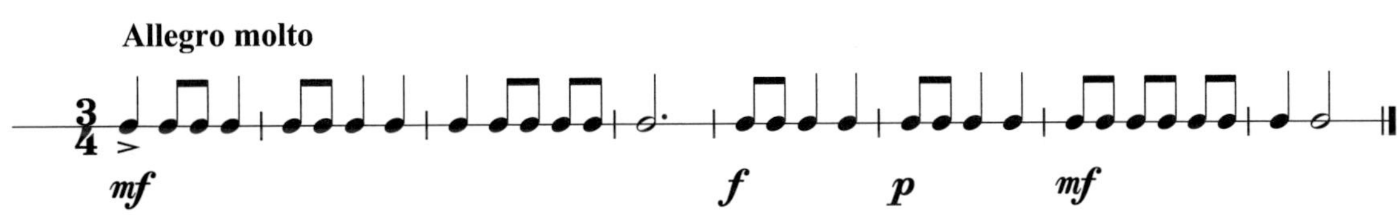


**RHYTHM 1.1.12**

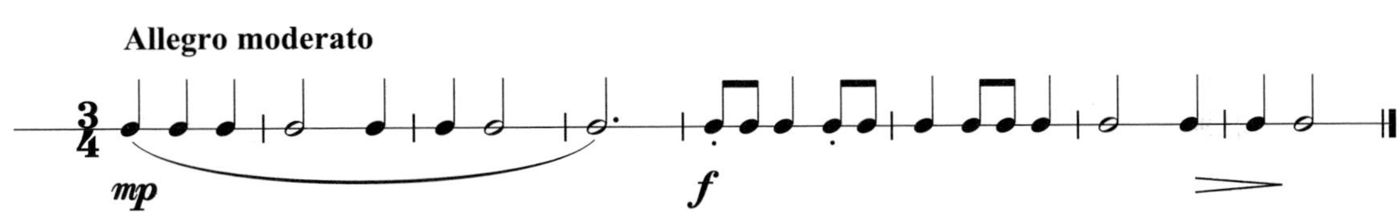

### Two-part Rhythms

Practice each part individually, then put them together by clapping the bottom voice while articulating the top voice on a neutral syllable like "ta". You may also try tapping the two parts with your hands, making sure each voice has a different sound. Finally, you may work with a friend to perform these.

**TWO-PART RHYTHM 1.1.1**

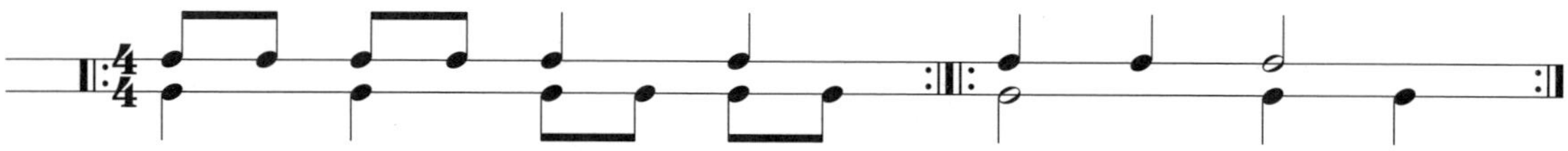

**TWO-PART RHYTHM 1.1.2**

### Three-part Rhythm

Learn to scan the entire score from the bottom voice up. Perform them using three different sounds (for example, clapping, tapping, and articulating) or with one or two friends.

**THREE-PART RHYTHM 1.1.1**

## 1.2 Second Division and Second Multiple of the Beat in Simple Meter

As you know, simple beats are binary structures because they divide and multiply naturally by two, resulting in a 2:1 relationship between manifestations of the beat. When beats are divided or multiplied twice, the result is the second division (subdivision) or second multiple of the beat. Utilizing second division or multiple results in a 4:1 relationship to the original beat. Refer to the charts opposite:

**EXAMPLE 1.2.1**

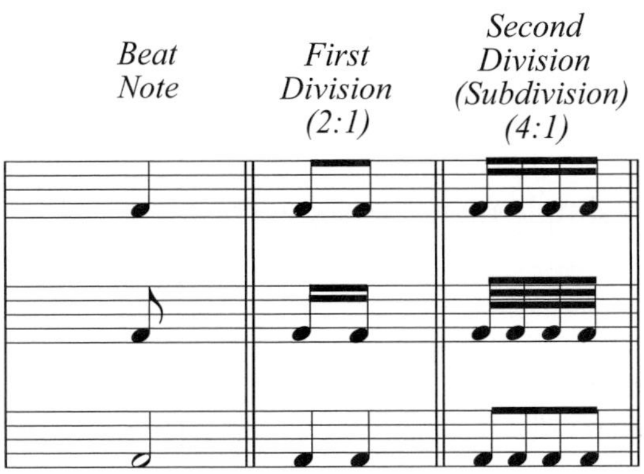


**EXAMPLE 1.2.2**

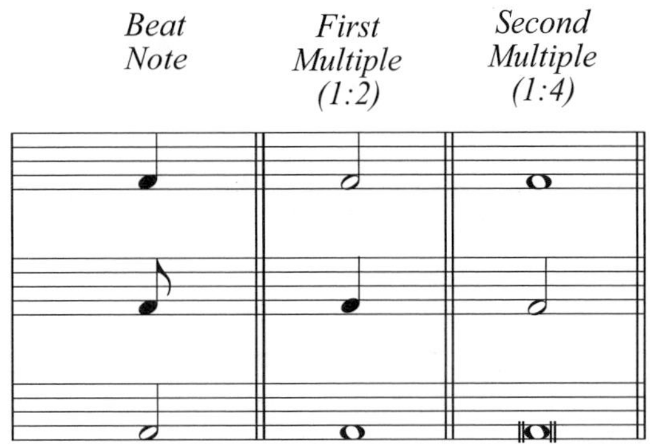


When the second division of the beat is employed, the rhythmic complexity of a piece seems to increase significantly. That complexity, however, may be more a visual phenomenon than an actual one, since at its most fundamental level, the 2:1 relationship between note values still exists. (For example, two eighth notes equal a quarter note; similarly, two sixteenths equal an eighth—the relationship between note values is the same.)

In order to be both accurate and musical when reading rhythms, use a consistent, trustworthy process, just as you do when singing intervals or other musical structures. Count eighth notes with +s, like this:

**EXAMPLE 1.2.3**

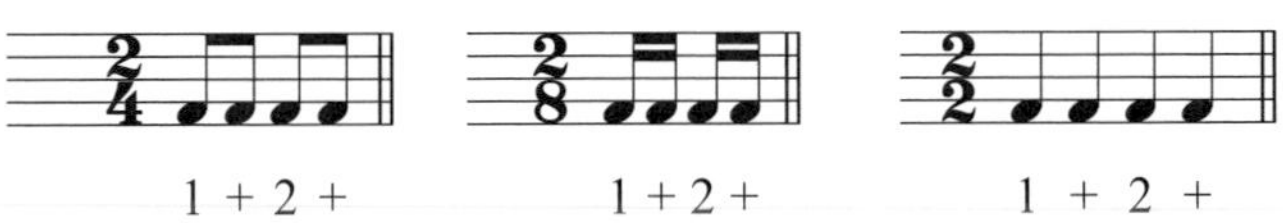


*(Say "and" on the "+" symbol.)*

The most traditional means of counting rhythms that use the second division of the beat is to add the sounds "e" and "a" to represent each part of the beat, as shown below. Notice that the "+" at the midway point of the beat is still intact. Another way to count subdivisions is to use numbers, which is less cumbersome and more precise:

**EXAMPLE 1.2.4**

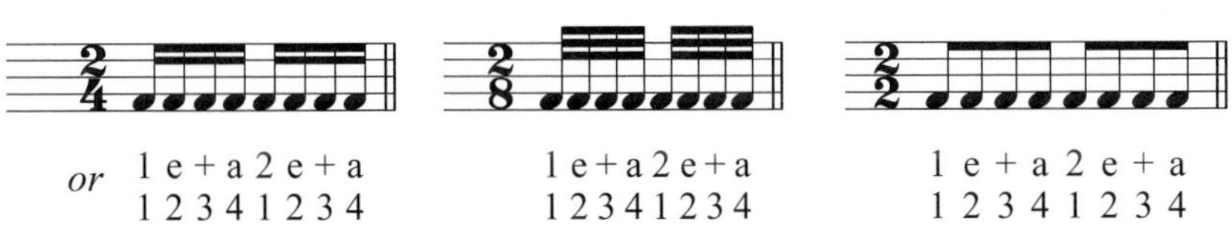


If you can feel the relationship of an eighth note to a quarter note, you can figure out a rhythm by maintaining an eighth-note pulse and relying on the two-to-one relationship, like this:

**EXAMPLE 1.2.5**

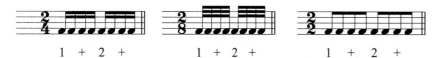

1 + 2 + 1 + 2 + 1 + 2 +

Any of the above methods can be used when reading patterns in simple meter, as shown below:

**EXAMPLE 1.2.6**

1 e +(a)2 e +(a) 1 2 3(4)1 2 3(4) 1 + 2 +

1(e)+ a 2(e)+ a 1(2)3 4 1(2)3 4 1 + 2 +

## Assignments for Practice

As before, practice each rhythm below by clapping the beat and articulating the rhythm.

**RHYTHM 1.2.1**

**Moderato**

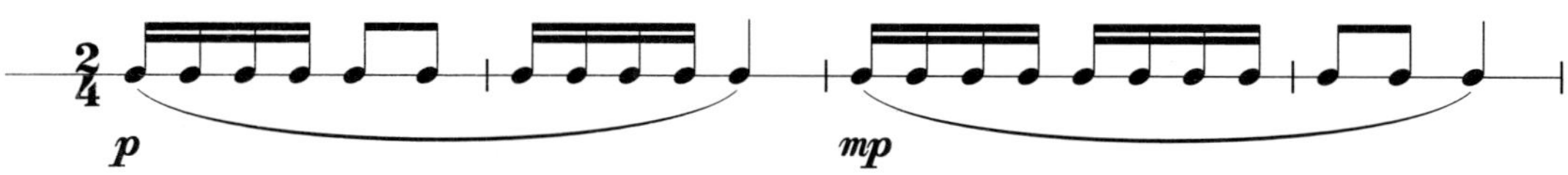


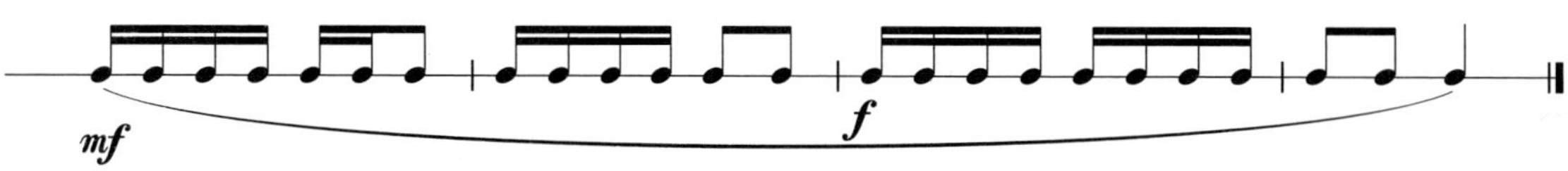


**RHYTHM 1.2.2**

**Vivace**

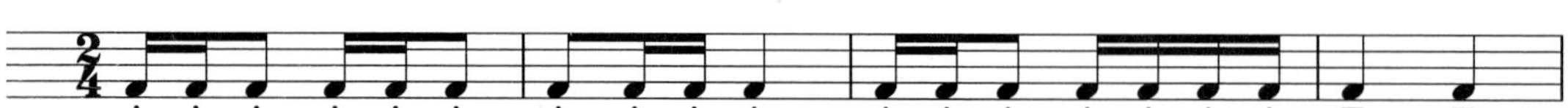

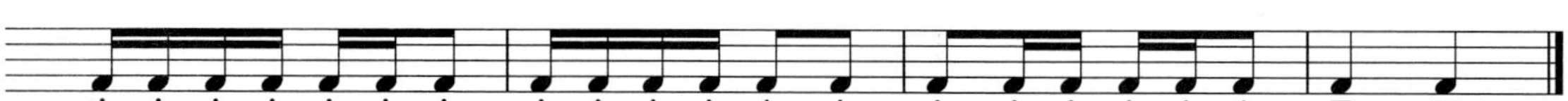

### RHYTHM 1.2.3

**Adagio**

### RHYTHM 1.2.4

**Lento**

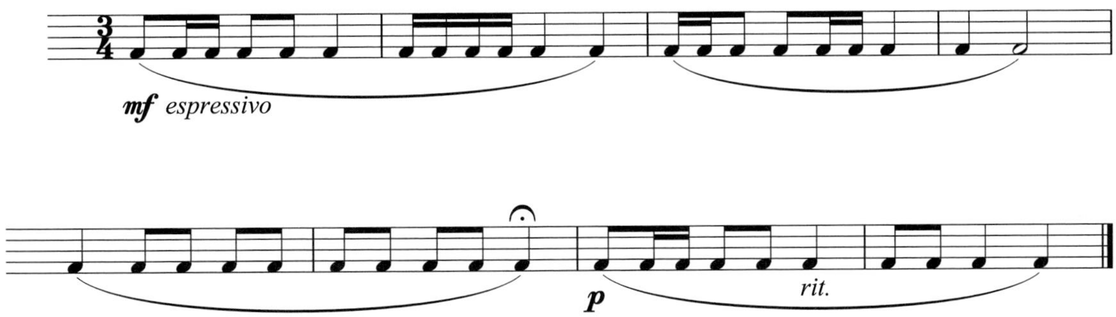


### RHYTHM 1.2.5

**Presto**

### RHYTHM 1.2.6

**Andante**

### RHYTHM 1.2.7

### RHYTHM 1.2.8

### RHYTHM 1.2.9

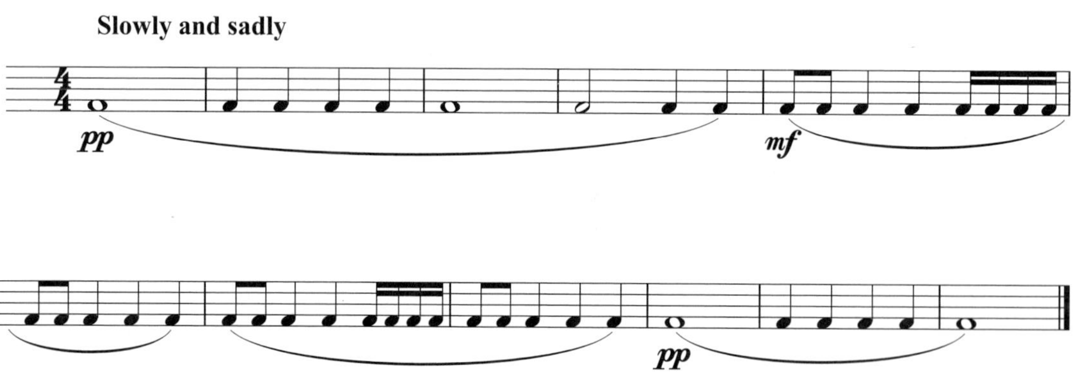


### RHYTHM 1.2.10

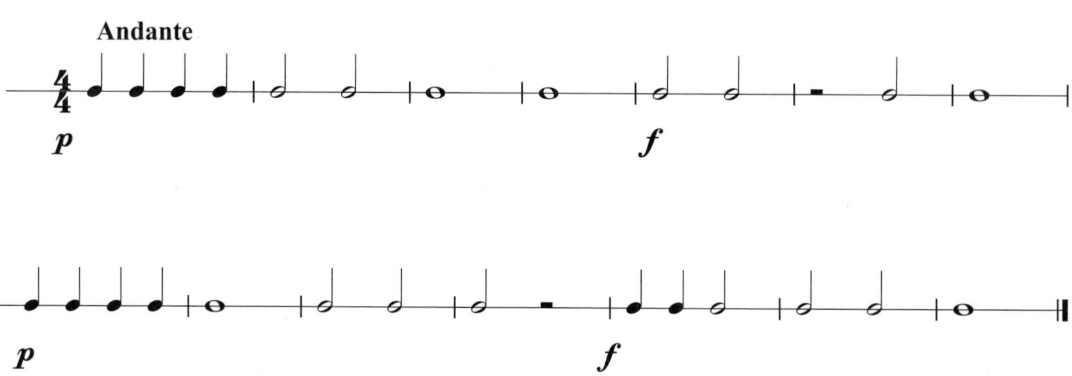

#### RHYTHM 1.2.11

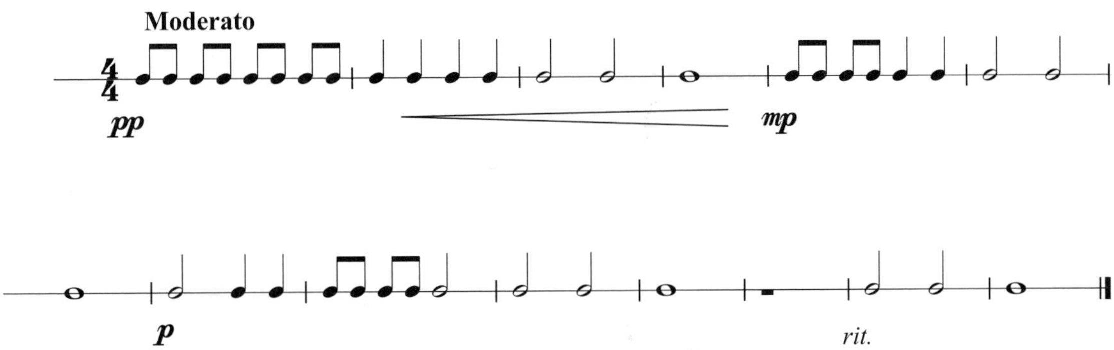


#### RHYTHM 1.2.12

### Two-part Rhythms

#### TWO-PART RHYTHM 1.2.1

#### TWO-PART RHYTHM 1.2.2

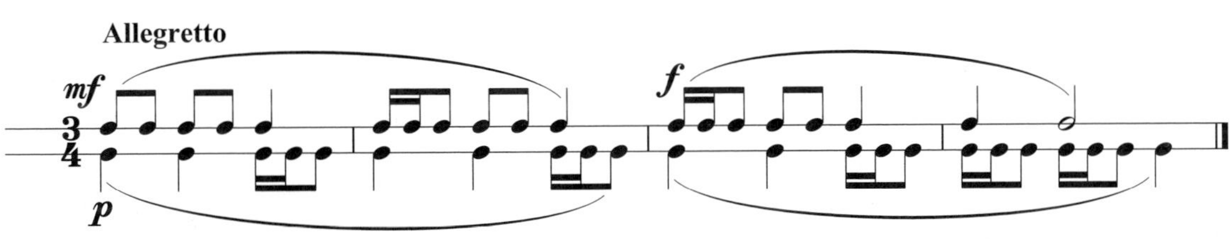

TWO-PART RHYTHM 1.2.3

## Three-part Rhythm

THREE-PART RHYTHM 1.2

## 1.3 Rests

### Facts You Need to Know

Rests are symbols used to indicate silence in music; every note value has a corresponding rest, as indicated in the chart below:

**EXAMPLE 1.3.1**

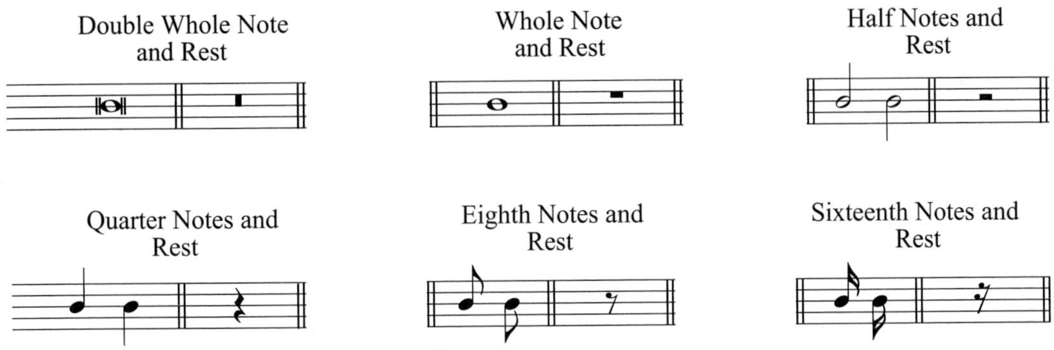


*Just as we add an additional flag for each smaller note value from the eighth note on, we add an additional "flag" on each successively smaller rest value.*

The exception to this rule is the whole rest: in addition to being equal to a whole note, it can also indicate a silence that lasts through an entire measure, regardless of the number of beats in it.

On their most complex level, rests are musical entities that help to give music space, influence phrasing, create drama, provide rhythmic energy, wreak havoc with metric impulses, add humor, or create ambiguity in music.

### Reading Rests

To read rests accurately and fluently, learn to listen to and internalize the duration of the silence. Recognize that:

1. Reading rests requires you to become knowledgeable and comfortable with the way rests are notated on the printed page. In particular, eighth-note (and smaller value) rests can "fool" the eye. The first measure of the illustration below shows rests on the second half of each beat; the second measure shows rests placed on the beat. Whether flagged or beamed, the two examples look very similar. Thus, it is necessary to define the difference between the two.

**EXAMPLE 1.3.2**

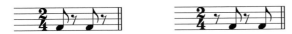

2. By rule, the way rests are notated in order to delineate metric structure can confuse the eye. In the example below, there are two eighth-note rests in succession rather than a quarter note because the

eighth notes belong to different beats. Always take time to determine where the beats fall in order to ensure reading accuracy.

**EXAMPLE 1.3.3**

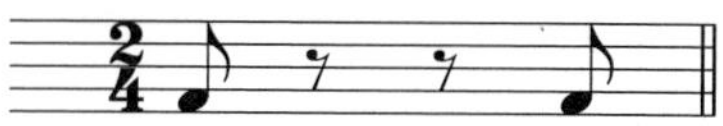

3. To overcome the natural tendency to rush rests in performance, practice two ways:
   Use a metronome during practice. (Remember, the metronome is an aid to practice—a means to an end and not an end in itself—so always repeat the exercise without the metronome.) You can also learn to avoid rushing through rests by adding a sound when you practice. A clap, "tongue-click" or sniff during a rest helps inhibit the desire to rush. As with metronome practice, always repeat this technique practicing without the claps while focusing on "hearing" the silence in your inner ear.

**EXAMPLE 1.3.4**

1 *clap clap* and   1 *clap clap* and   1

## Rhythms

Determine whether the rests are on the beat or the division of the beat before you begin each rhythm. Perform these in two ways: clapping the beat and articulating the rhythm, and articulating the rhythm and clapping the rests.

**RHYTHM 1.3.1**

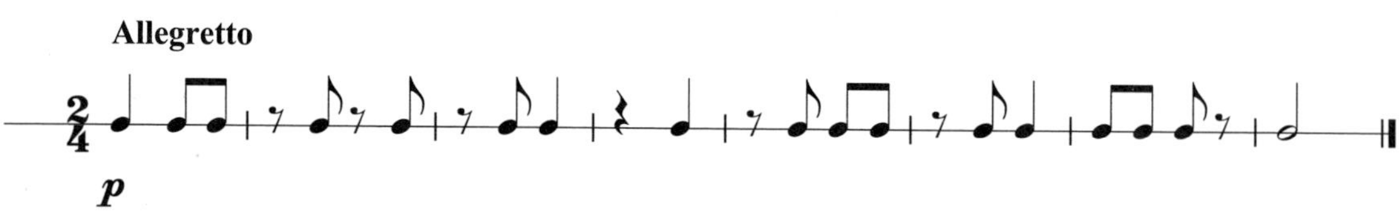


**RHYTHM 1.3.2**

### RHYTHM 1.3.3

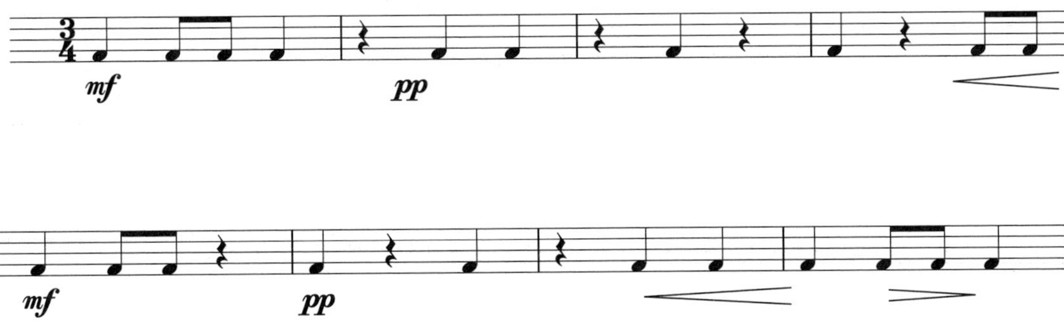


### RHYTHM 1.3.4

Vif

### RHYTHM 1.3.5

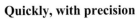

Quickly, with precision

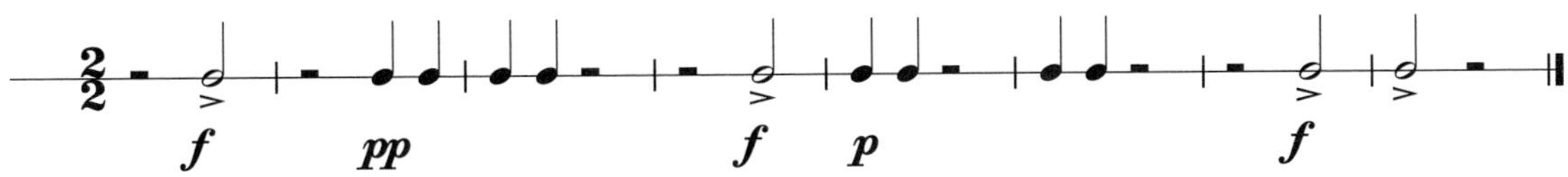


### RHYTHM 1.3.6

Vivace

**RHYTHM 1.3.7**

**RHYTHM 1.3.8**

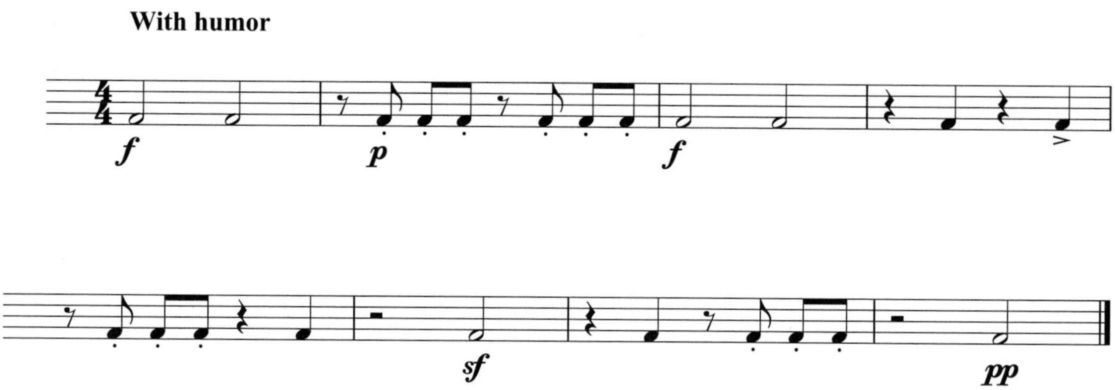


Pay attention to articulation in the following rhythm.

**RHYTHM 1.3.9**

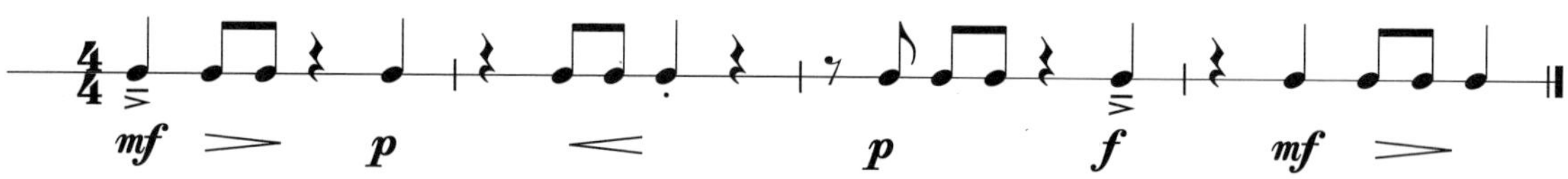


**RHYTHM 1.3.10**

RHYTHM 1.3.11

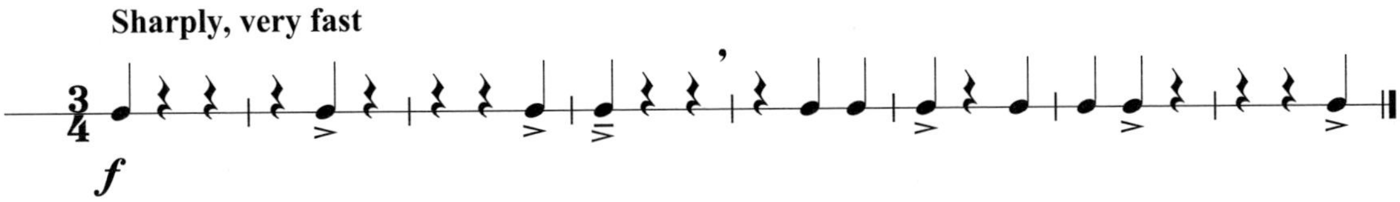


## Two-part Rhythms

TWO-PART RHYTHM 1.3.1

TWO-PART RHYTHM 1.3.2

TWO-PART RHYTHM 1.3.3

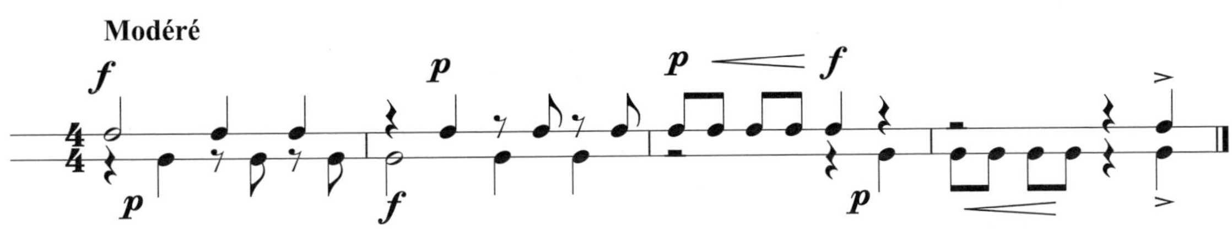

### Three-part Rhythm

**THREE-PART RHYTHM 1.3**

## 1.4 The Phrase

### Facts You Need to Know

The terms crusis, metacrusis, and anacrusis are used in two contexts: to assign a name to individual beats in a measure and to describe the three parts of a phrase.

The first beat of a measure is the crusis, the last beat is the anacrusis, and any remaining beats, the metacruses (or, singular, metacrusis).

A phrase is crusic if it begins on the first beat of a measure; it is anacrusic if it begins on any other beat or partial of the beat.

In a phrase, the crusis is the moment of sound that has the highest amount of temporal weight; it occurs most often at the ictus of the first beat of the measure. The anacrusis is the part of the phrase that directly precedes the crusis; its length is variable. The metacrusis, the length of which is in direct proportion to the length of the anacrusis, is the entire portion of the phrase between the crusis and anacrusis.

The example opposite illustrates the three parts of the phrase:

**EXAMPLE 1.4.1**

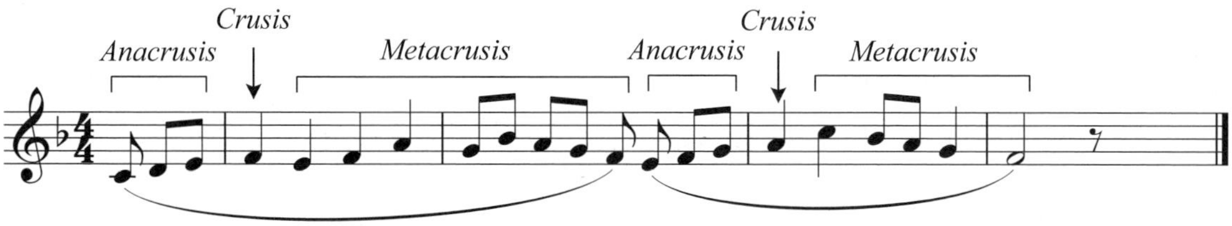
Crusis
Anacrusis
Metacrusis
Crusis
Anacrusis
Metacrusis

Examine the beaming in m. 3 of the example; notice that although the F and E belong to the same beat, they are not beamed. Those pitches belong to different phrases, and are therefore written with flags instead of beams in order to show the phrase structure. The application of this rule of notation allows a composer to be very clear about his or her intentions.

Often in music, the crusis of the measure is referred to as a "downbeat," the anacrusis, the "upbeat." These labels have become commonplace because of our visual perception; we see a conductor's baton travel down to get to beat one, but ensemble members will begin to play only after the conductor's baton changes direction; the crusic beat lifts.

This idea of directionality of beats is significant when you translate its effect on music. The crusis of a measure or a phrase is a beginning; it propels sound and energy forward, so the sound needs to lift and have forward motion to create a sense of direction. The anacrusis leads to the crusis, but doesn't have the same "explosion" of sound; it serves as a preparation for the crusis. The metacrusis takes the energy of the crusis and sustains it as it travels to the anacrusis, when the whole process begins again.

One important consideration in the performance of an anacrusis is the placement of stressed and unstressed notes. Sing the well-known children's song, "Baa Baa Black Sheep" in your head; notice that its phrase structure is crusic. Notated, it looks like this:

**EXAMPLE 1.4.2**

Baa baa black sheep have you a - ny wool? Yes, sir! Yes, sir! Three bags full.

Imagine "Baa Baa Black Sheep" if it were performed as if the phrase structure were anacrusic, like this:

**EXAMPLE 1.4.3**

Baa baa black sheep have you a - ny wool? Yes, sir! Yes, sir! Three bags full.

"Baa Baa" simply doesn't make musical sense as an anacrusic melody. Starting on the anacrusis creates false accents, which disrupt the flow of a phrase and create unintended ambiguity in performance. It is imperative to observe the stresses that occur naturally as a result of the phrase structure.

## Rhythm Reading

Conduct or clap as you perform these rhythms. Notice how the beaming of groups of notes helps you to understand which part of the measure is anacrusic.

**RHYTHM 1.4.1**

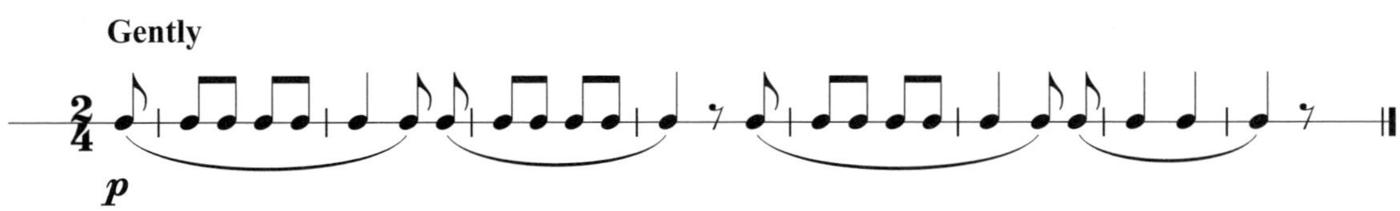


**RHYTHM 1.4.2**

**RHYTHM 1.4.3**

Add your own dynamics and phrasing to the following rhythm:

**RHYTHM 1.4.4**

**RHYTHM 1.4.5**

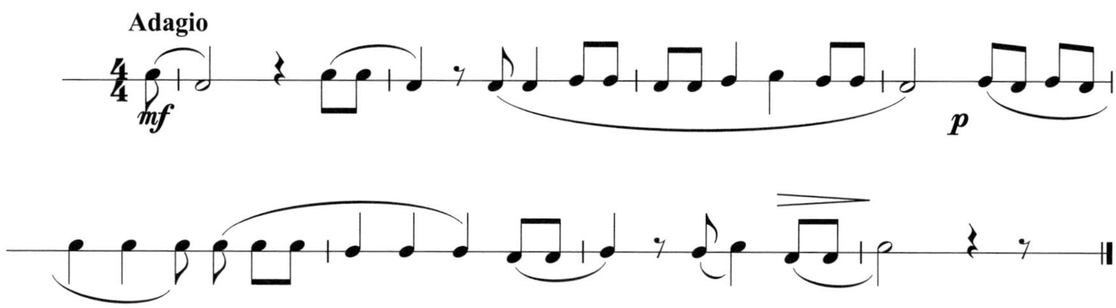


**RHYTHM 1.4.6**

**RHYTHM 1.4.7**

**RHYTHM 1.4.8**

### RHYTHM 1.4.9

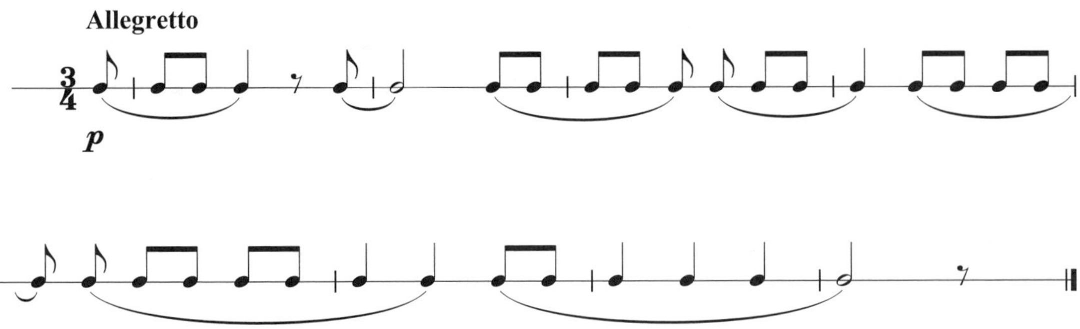


### RHYTHM 1.4.10

## Two-part Rhythms

### TWO-PART RHYTHM 1.4.1

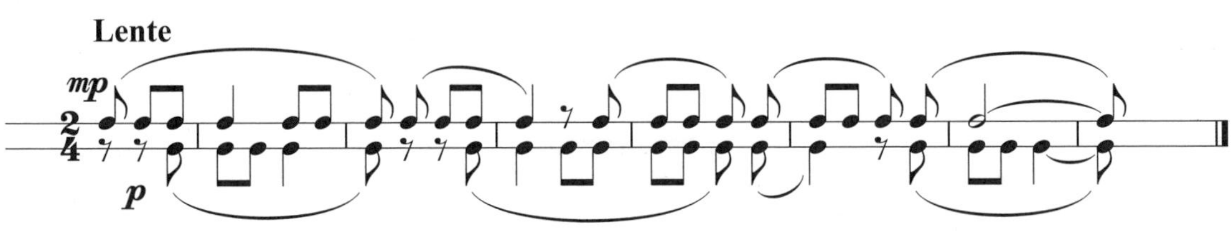


### TWO-PART RHYTHM 1.4.2

## Three-part Rhythm

### THREE-PART RHYTHM 1.4

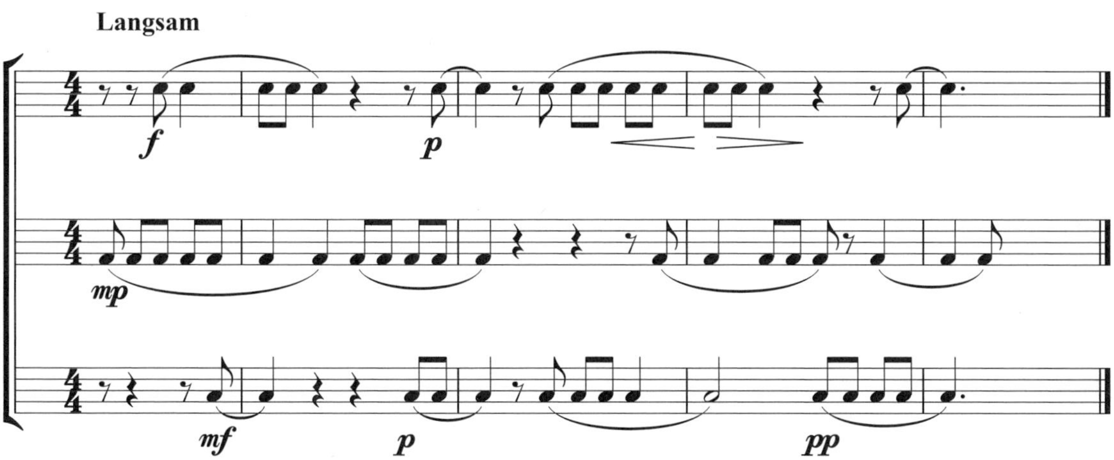


---

## 1.5 Treble and Bass Clefs

### Facts You Need to Know

The primary way musical pitches are notated is through the use of staves: parallel lines onto which dots representing notes are placed to indicate relative highness or lowness.

Clefs are symbols placed at the beginning of each staff to indicate the location of a particular pitch. Once one pitch is identified, you can figure out the location of all pitches.

Our notational system uses three clefs:

The G-clef, indicating that G4 (the G above middle C) is located on the line where the curve ends.

The F-clef, indicating that F3 (the F below middle C) is located on the line where the curve begins and between the two dots.

The C-clef, indicating that C4 (middle C) is located where the two arcs meet.

#### EXAMPLE 1.5.1

| *G-clef* | *F-clef* | *C-clef* |
|---|---|---|
|  |  |  |
| The end of the curve indicates line for G4 (the G above middle C). | The beginning of the curve and the line between the dots indicate F3 (the F below middle C). | The line that runs between the two arcs indicates C4 (middle C). |

Vertically, the lines denote the relative height or depth of pitches. Each line represents a third (or two notes) above the previous line, and pitches (represented by "dots" or note heads) can be placed either directly on or in the spaces between lines. Staff lines and spaces are numbered from the bottom up.

**EXAMPLE 1.5.2**

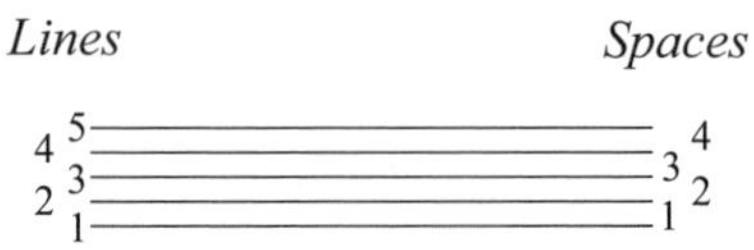


Ledger lines are used to indicate the location of pitches beyond the range of the five-line staff.

**EXAMPLE 1.5.3**

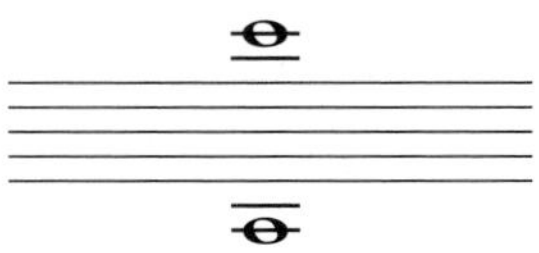

Horizontally, music is read from left to right. Events happening before others appear to the left of events to the right. Regular units of time are marked using vertical barlines, and rhythmic symbols indicate the specific placement of musical events in time.

When the G-clef is placed so that G4 is on the second line of the staff, it is called the treble clef. The placement of notes on the treble staff appears below:

**EXAMPLE 1.5.4**

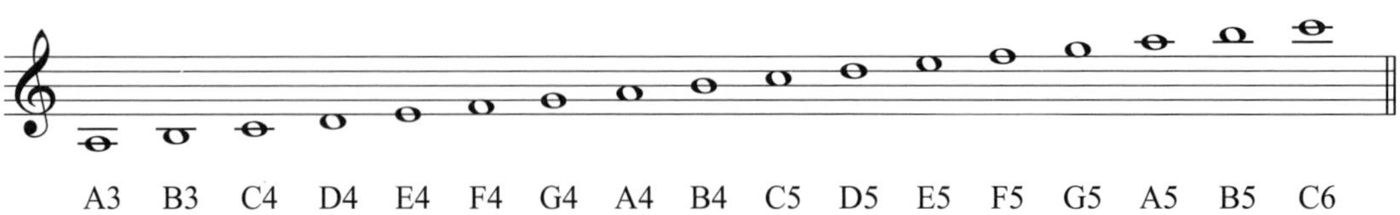


When the F-clef is placed so that F3 is on the fourth line of the staff, it is called the bass clef. The placement of notes on the bass staff appears below:

**EXAMPLE 1.5.5**

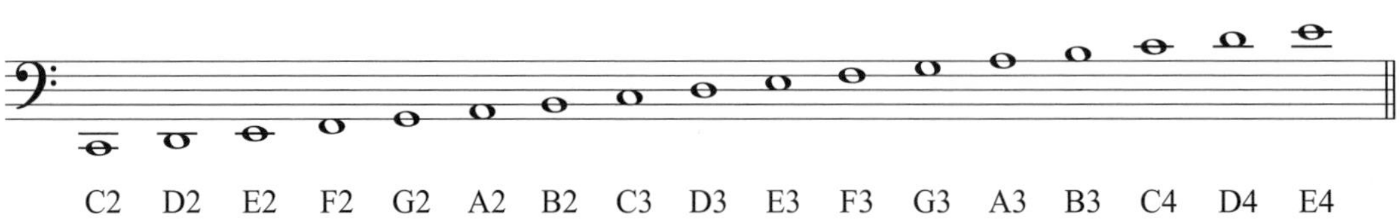

### Reading in the Treble and Bass Clefs

Begin to develop reading fluency by selecting two lines to use as "reference points" on the staff: second line G and fourth line D are good choices for the treble staff, and the second space C and fourth line F are good choices for the bass staff. By using these notes as your reference points, you can quickly figure out a note you do not recognize by relating it to one of these two lines on the staff.

Scan the notes in each exercise before you begin, looking for large leaps, and relating them to your established points of reference. You will find that these exercises require enormous concentration if you are not yet fluent in reading either clef.

The only way to effectively master this skill is to do it. Devote some time each day to reading clefs until you are fluent with both.

## Exercises

The staff you see has no clef, which means that at this moment, you can choose which clef to use for reading practice. Notice, too, that you see only stepwise motion, which means that notes will always follow an alphabetical sequence backwards or forwards. Proceed as follows:

1. Establish the tempo by clapping the beat.
2. Determine the letter name of the first pitch, based on the clef you have chosen to use. Speak the letter names of the notes, in tempo.
3. Gradually increase the tempo. In doing so, you will have less time to think and analyze, and, instead, will begin to teach yourself to simply react to what you see on the page.
4. Apply the rhythmic figure found at the end of the pitch pattern. Say the letter names in rhythm and in tempo. Work for accuracy and speed.
5. Repeat the rhythmic and pitch pattern until you arrive at a place where both rhythm and pitch create a comfortable cadence or ending.

The pitch pattern that appears to the left is realized on the right.

**PITCH PATTERN 1.5.1**

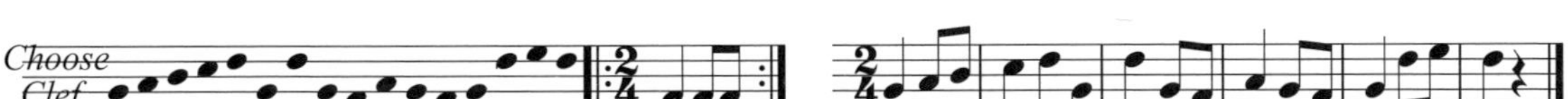


| | | | | | | |
|---|---|---|---|---|---|---|
| *Treble:* | G A B | C D G | D G F | A G F | G D E | D |
| *Bass:* | B C D | E F B | F B A | C B A | B F G | F |

Practice each of the following in both the treble and bass clefs. Make sure you spend extra time practicing your weaker clef!

**PITCH PATTERN 1.5.2**

**PITCH PATTERN 1.5.3**

**PITCH PATTERN 1.5.4**

**PITCH PATTERN 1.5.5**

**PITCH PATTERN 1.5.6**

Watch for larger leaps and ledger lines in the remaining pitch patterns. Remember to use "waypoints" to make your reading faster and more accurate.

**PITCH PATTERN 1.5.7**

**PITCH PATTERN 1.5.8**

**PITCH PATTERN 1.5.9**

**PITCH PATTERN 1.5.10**

## 1.6 Major Scales and Major Scale Degrees

### Facts You Need to Know

A scale is a collection of pitches from which a tonal composition is constructed. The majority of Western music composed between 1600 and 1900 utilizes either the major or minor scale. This chapter will examine the major scale.

The distance between most of the pitches in a tonal scale is a major second. Two pairs of pitches, however, are separated by a minor second: scale degrees 3 to 4 and 7 to 1.

**EXAMPLE 1.6.1**

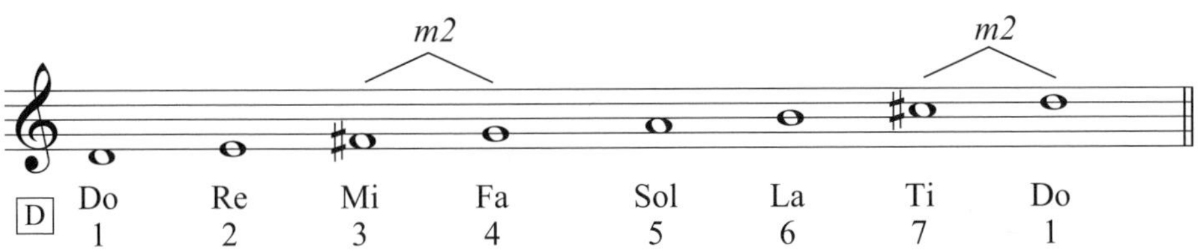


Minor seconds serve as identification points for our ears. We recognize the location of a pitch in a scale based on its relationship to one of the minor seconds.

Most people hear music as combinations of scale degrees.

Each scale degree has a unique sound that results from its energy and desire toward resolution. Memorizing the unique sound of each scale degree is essential for learning how to hear and sing musical structures.

The musical patterns that appear below are effective ways for memorizing the unique sound of each scale degree. Notice that some scale degrees have more than one pattern associated with them. In these cases, learn to use all of them.

Begin by establishing a key by playing or hearing a chord progression or scale. For now, we will learn all of the scale degrees in the key of D major. Be aware, however, that changing keys does not alter the relationship between a scale degree and its tonic pitch. A supertonic (or second) scale degree behaves the same way whether in the key of D major or in any of the eleven other major keys.

**EXAMPLE 1.6.2**

## Hearing

The major scale is often described as having a "bright, "clear," and "happy" sound when contrasted with its opposite, the minor scale.

Listen specifically for the brightness of scale degrees 3 and 6.

Listen for the relative closeness between scale degrees 3 to 4 and 7 to 1.

## Singing

Practice singing scales, chords, and melodies not as a succession of intervals but instead as scale degrees. This will improve both your accuracy and intonation. To make sure you are doing this, try the following exercises.

1. Give yourself a pitch and treat it as tonic. Sing each scale degree pattern in order. The following demonstrates this in the key of D Major:

**EXAMPLE 1.6.3**

2. Sing each scale degree in order, hearing but not singing the pattern that returns it to tonic in your head.
3. Leave out one or more scale degrees in the scale, and then checking the accuracy of the following pitch. For example, here is the D major scale with scale degrees 4 and 6 removed.

**EXAMPLE 1.6.4**

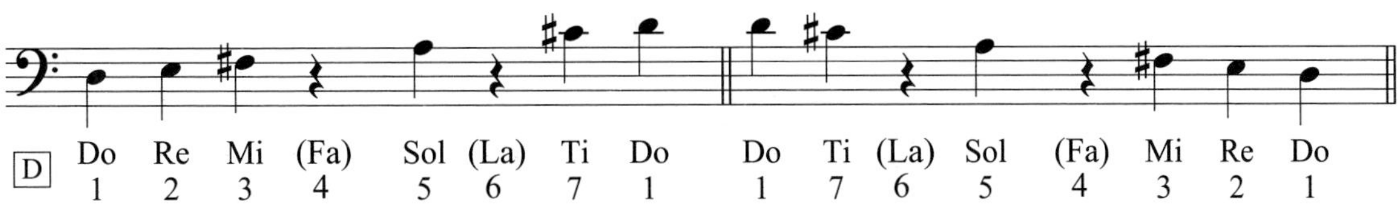


## Assignments for Practice

Developing the ability to sing and identify any scale degree (once you know where tonic is) is the most essential skill you need to develop in order to understand the music that you hear. Here are some other suggestions for singing and recognizing scale degrees:

1. Sing the scale degree patterns in a random order, always returning to the same tonic pitch.
2. With a practice partner, have one person establish a key at the piano and then play or sing random scale degrees within that key. The other person should try to identify each scale degree by singing its pattern. (If practicing alone, put yourself in the key of C major at the piano, close your eyes and play random "white key" pitches.)
3. Given a pitch, be able to sing any of the scale degree patterns from it to find the tonic pitch.
4. Practice singing major scales beginning on any scale degree. For example, sing a major scale from scale degree 2 up to scale degree 2 and back down.

Once you start to sing major scales beginning on any pitch, begin to pay attention to how each key, although it utilizes the same progression of major and minor seconds, has a unique sound. For example, musicians often describe the E major scale as having a "brighter" sound than its neighbor, E-flat major.

### Pitch Patterns

See the section on reading treble and bass clefs for instructions on performing these pitch patterns.

### PITCH PATTERN 1.6.1

### PITCH PATTERN 1.6.2

## Melodies

As you sing the following melodies, make sure that you are singing scale degrees and not intervals up or down from the previous note. Check yourself by randomly pausing to sing the scale degree pattern for a pitch you just sang. Listen also for the musical focus of each melody. Try to communicate it using at least two different musical techniques (phrasing, dynamics, etc.).

### MELODY 1.6.1

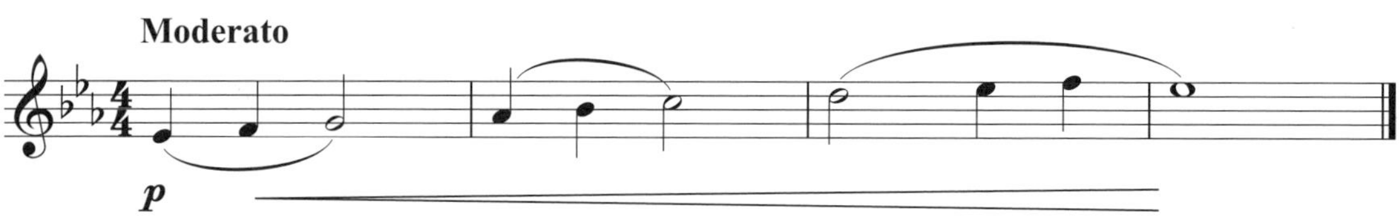


### MELODY 1.6.2

Pay attention to the articulation markings in the following melody. How do they help to tell a musical story?

### MELODY 1.6.3

### MELODY 1.6.4

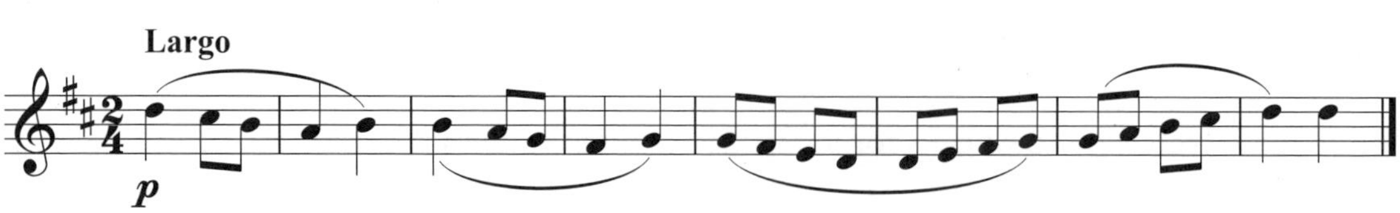

How do dynamics create a story in this melody?

**MELODY 1.6.5**

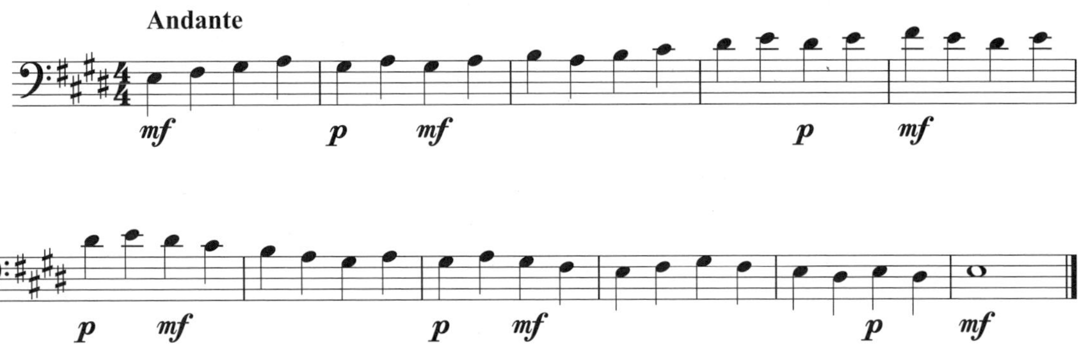


**MELODY 1.6.6**

**MELODY 1.6.7**

**MELODY 1.6.8**

### MELODY 1.6.9

### MELODY 1.6.10

Work to make all of the notes even in attack and length in the following melody.

### MELODY 1.6.11

### MELODY 1.6.12

## Duets

Which voice creates stability in this duet? How is this achieved?

### DUET 1.6.1

### DUET 1.6.2

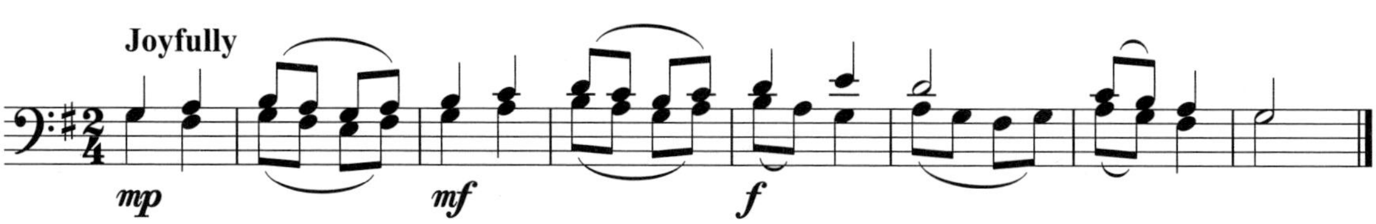

DUET 1.6.3

## Chorale

Pay attention to intonation and blend as you sing this. Take turns practicing all four voices.

CHORALE 1.6

## Self-Accompanied Melody

Sing the top line while playing the bottom part on a piano. Learn to perform the following by yourself with a steady tempo and musicality.

SELF-ACCOMPANIED MELODY 1.6

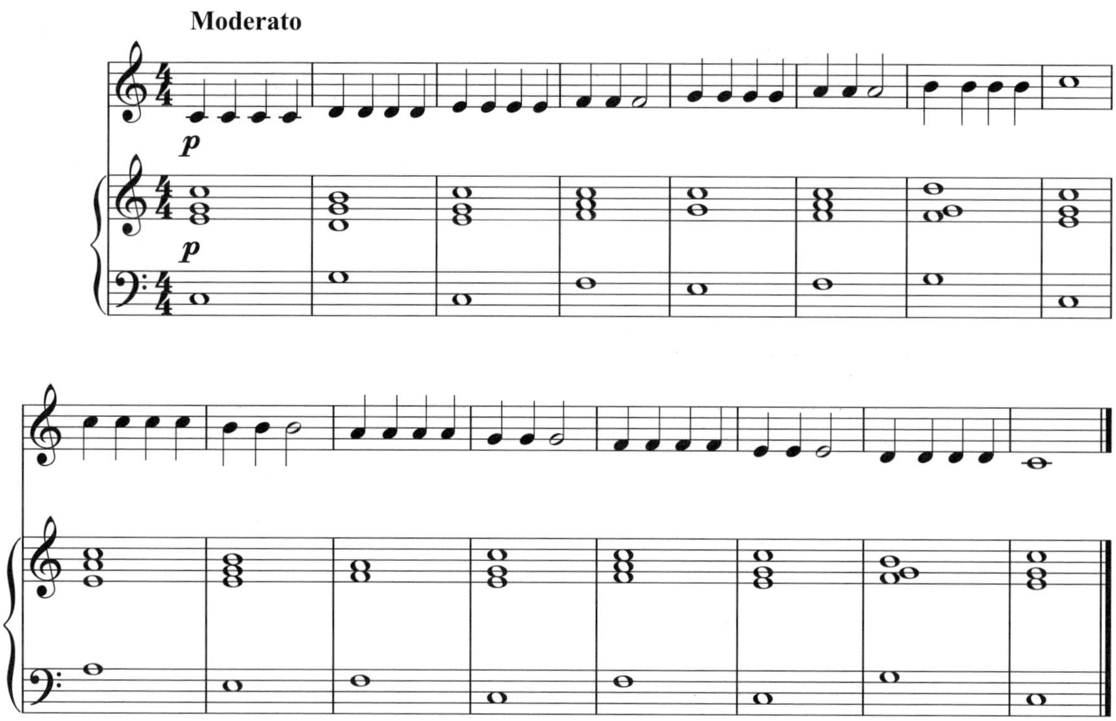


## 1.7 Major and Minor Seconds

### Major Seconds

#### Facts You Need to Know

Major seconds are created by two pitches that are separated by a single note. For example, D to E have the pitch D♯ or E♭ between them.

Major seconds occur in five places in the major scale:

1. Between scale degrees 1 and 2
2. Between scale degrees 2 and 3
3. Between scale degrees 4 and 5
4. Between scale degrees 5 and 6
5. Between scale degrees 6 and 7

**EXAMPLE 1.7.1**

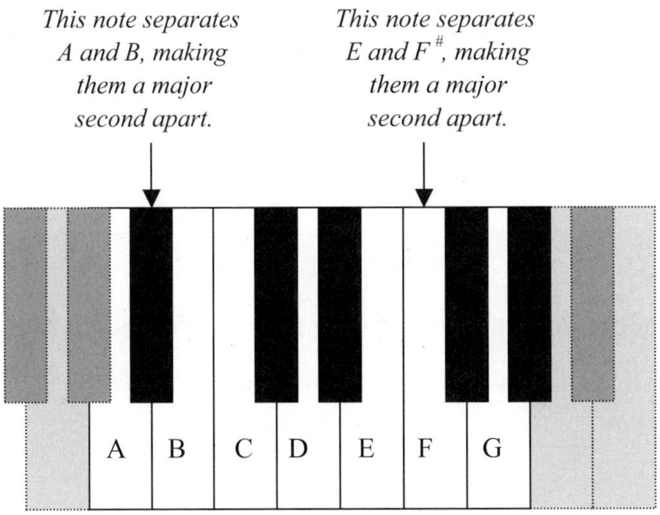
This note separates A and B, making them a major second apart.
This note separates E and F#, making them a major second apart.
A
B
C
D
E
F
G

Major seconds occur in seven places in the minor scale:

1. Between scale degrees 1 and 2
2. Between scale degrees 3 and 4
3. Between scale degrees 4 and 5
4. Between scale degrees 5 and ♯6
5. Between scale degrees ♭6 and ♭7
6. Between scale degrees ♯6 and ♯7
7. Between scale degrees ♭7 and 1

Major seconds are dissonant intervals.

## Hearing

Upon hearing a musical sound, your ear goes through the process of 1) figuring out where it hears tonic, 2) assigning scale degrees to the components of the musical sound, and 3) hearing those scale degrees in relation to the tonic it hears. The problem most untrained and beginning musicians have isn't in hearing and understanding what they hear, it is in being able to place labels on the sounds they hear. Most people can hear when music sounds "right" or "wrong" because their ear understands how music should sound. An important goal of your musical training is to learn how to attach labels to the sounds that your ear already understands. That is the dual process of hearing *and understanding* the music that you hear. Learning to recognize intervals is an early step in being able to recognize larger musical structures. The steps below describe hearing major and minor seconds, but they apply to any interval or chord. Pay close attention to how these steps are used throughout this text to recognize and label the tremendous variety of structures found in music.

1. Listen for the relative stability of the two pitches. The lower pitch should sound more stable and the upper pitch more active.

2. Hear the lower pitch as tonic. Hear the strong pull of the upper pitch, scale degree 2, wanting to resolve down by step to scale degree 1, like the last two notes of a descending major scale.

**EXAMPLE 1.7.2**

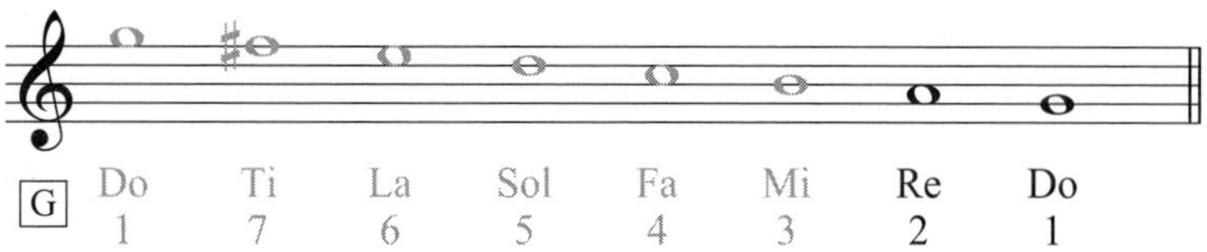


3. When listening to a harmonic major second, hear the dissonant sound and narrowness of the interval.
4. Listen for the lower pitch wanting to resolve down to a more consonant minor third. In this case, you are really hearing scale degrees 4 up to 5 in the major mode. You might recognize this sound as the first notes of the popular song "Chopsticks."

**EXAMPLE 1.7.3**

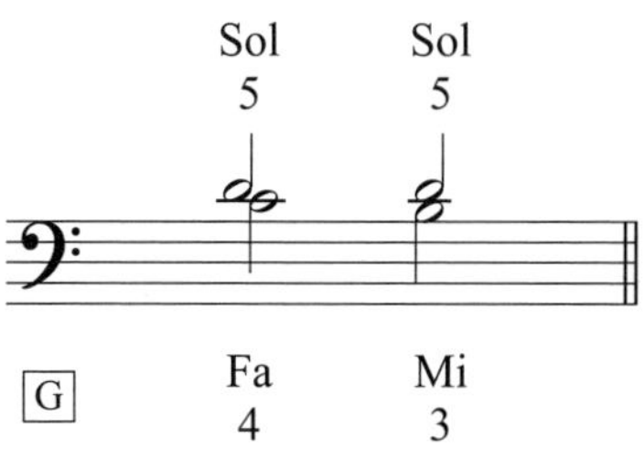


## Singing

1. Use scale degrees 1 up to 2 in the major scale as your point of reference.
2. When singing an ascending major second, hear the given pitch as tonic. From this pitch, sing all of the scale degree patterns to firmly establish this pitch as tonic.

**EXAMPLE 1.7.4**

3. Pay particular attention to the pattern for scale degree 2. Sing from scale degree 1 up to scale degree 2.

**EXAMPLE 1.7.5**

4. When singing a descending major second, hear the given pitch as scale degree 2. Find the tonic by singing the scale degree pattern for scale degree 2. If you have trouble hearing this, try singing up to scale degree 4 then down to scale degree 1.

**EXAMPLE 1.7.6**

5. If necessary, orient yourself around this tonic by singing all of the scale degree patterns from this pitch.
6. Sing scale degree 2 down to 1.

**EXAMPLE 1.7.7**

## Minor Seconds

### Facts You Need to Know

Minor seconds consist of two pitches with consecutive letter names that are adjacent to each other on the piano keyboard.

**EXAMPLE 1.7.8**

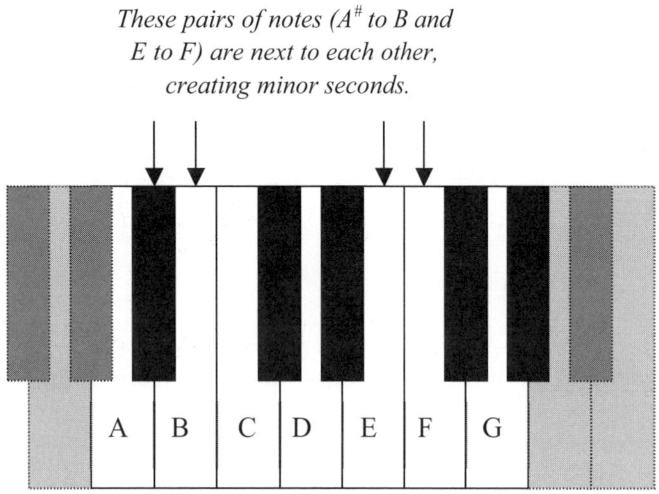
These pairs of notes (A# to B and
E to F) are next to each other,
creating minor seconds.
A
B
C
D
E
F
G

Minor seconds occur in the following places in the major scale:

1. Between scale degrees 3 and 4
2. Between scale degrees 7 and 1

Minor seconds occur in the following places in the minor scale:

1. Between scale degrees 2 and 3
2. Between scale degrees 5 and ♭6
3. Between scale degrees ♯7 and 1

Minor seconds are the defining sounds that tell our ears where a pitch is within a scale. They serve as the intervals that point to the location of tonic. Minor seconds are very strong, biting, and close dissonances.

## Hearing

1. Listen for the relative stability of the two pitches. The higher pitch should sound far more stable, and the lower should sound far more active.
2. Hear the higher pitch as tonic and the lower pitch as scale degree 7. Confirm this by singing the pattern for scale degree 7 from the lower pitch to the higher pitch. Make sure all of your pitches match the pitches you were given.

**EXAMPLE 1.7.9**

3. Harmonically, listen for a very intense and biting dissonance.

## Singing

1. Use scale degrees 7 up to 1 in the major mode as your point of reference.
2. If singing an ascending minor second, hear the given pitch as scale degree 7. Sing the pattern for this scale degree to find tonic. Sing both scale degrees.

**EXAMPLE 1.7.10**

3. If singing a descending minor second, hear the given pitch as scale degree 1. Orient yourself around this tonic by singing through all of the scale degree patterns.

**EXAMPLE 1.7.11**

4. Sing scale degree 1 and scale degree 7.

**EXAMPLE 1.7.12**

## Assignments for Practice

1. Give yourself a pitch and sing a melodic minor second above it. Once you have sung that correctly, sing a melodic minor second below that same pitch. After that, sing melodic major seconds above and below that same pitch. Be sure to follow your procedures for singing melodic intervals.
2. With a friend (or with the piano if you are practicing alone), sing harmonic minor and major seconds above and below selected pitches. Work for good tuning and blend.

### Pitch Patterns

**PITCH PATTERN 1.7.1**

**PITCH PATTERN 1.7.2**

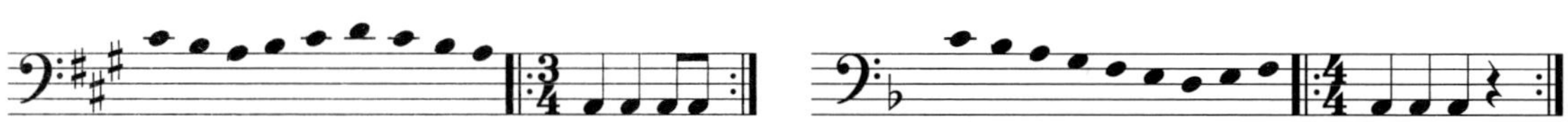

### Melodies

**MELODY 1.7.1**

**MELODY 1.7.2**

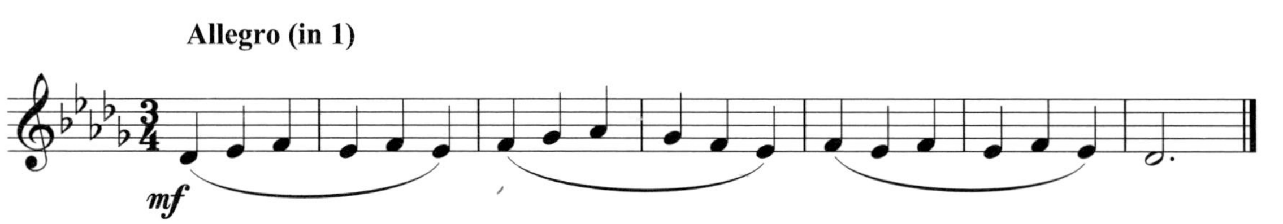


**MELODY 1.7.3**

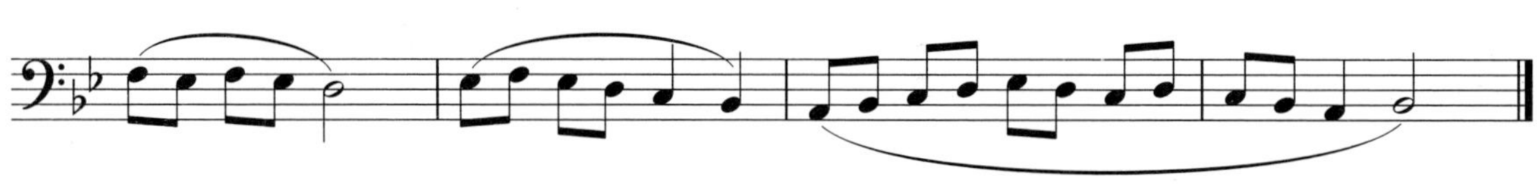

MELODY 1.7.4

MELODY 1.7.5

MELODY 1.7.6

Pay attention to articulation markings in this melody.

MELODY 1.7.7

MELODY 1.7.8

**MELODY 1.7.9**

**MELODY 1.7.10**

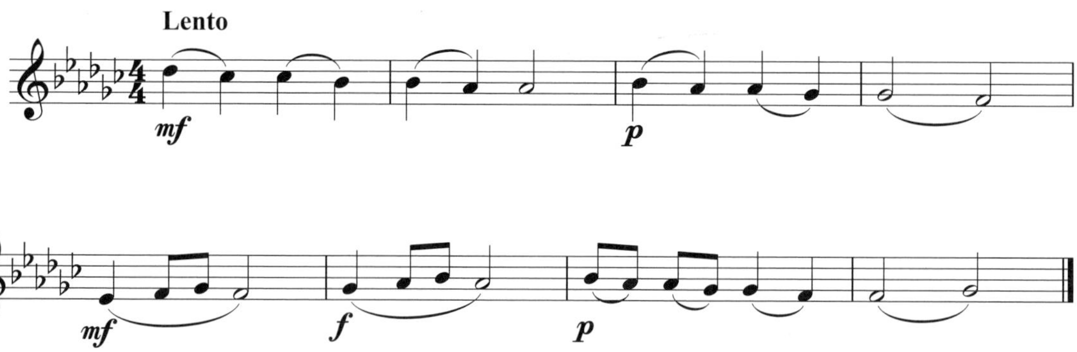


**MELODY 1.7.11**

**MELODY 1.7.12**

## Duets

Sing the harmonic seconds in the following duets with confidence. Crescendo into a dissonant interval and then decrescendo into its resolution; this can be an effective performance technique.

### DUET 1.7.1

### DUET 1.7.2

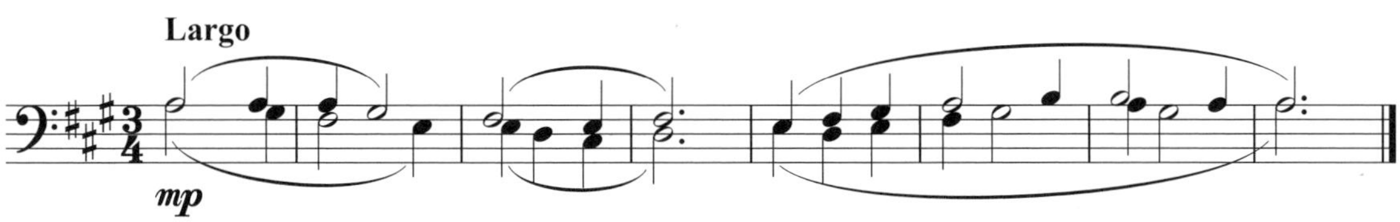


### DUET 1.7.3

## Chorale

Focus on the melodic goal of your individual line. Don't be afraid of a little dissonance!

### CHORALE 1.7

### Self-Accompanied Melody

**SELF-ACCOMPANIED MELODY 1.7**

## 1.8 Major and Minor Thirds

### Major Thirds

**Facts You Need to Know**

Thirds are a consonant interval, often described as having a "pleasing" or "pretty" sound.

Major thirds occur in the following places in a major scale:

1. Between scale degrees 1 and 3
2. Between scale degrees 4 and 6
3. Between scale degrees 5 and 7

The places where major thirds occur is significant because they represent the root and third of the tonic, subdominant, and dominant triads. This will be important to keep in mind as you develop your sight-singing skills. Major thirds occur in the following places in the minor scale:

1. Between scale degrees 3 and 5
2. Between scale degrees 4 and ♯6
3. Between scale degrees 5 and ♯7
4. Between scale degrees ♭6 and 1
5. Between scale degrees ♭7 and 2

Major thirds are imperfect consonances, meaning they have a complex yet pleasing and bright sound.

## Hearing

Remember that your ear understands intervals as scale degrees around an implied tonic pitch. Your challenge is to identify, understand, and label the sound that your ear already knows. To hear major thirds, follow these steps:

1. Listen first for the relative stability of the two pitches. The lower pitch usually has the much more stable sound of tonic, while the higher pitch usually sounds like it wants to resolve down from scale degree 3, through scale degree 2, and down to tonic.

**EXAMPLE 1.8.1**

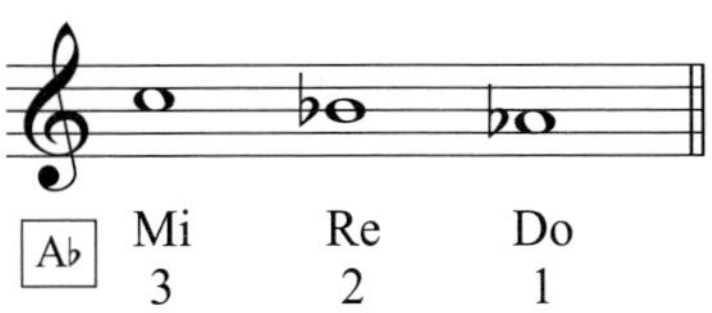


2. Note that you are hearing scale degrees 1 and 3 in the major scale, and use your knowledge of harmony to identify that interval as a major third. (We can't always control how we hear a musical sound. You may hear a major third as one of the other combinations of scale degrees listed above. Be aware of 1) your internal sense of tonic, and 2) the component scale degrees of the sound that you hear. Use your knowledge of the major or minor scale to figure out the interval that separates the scale degrees you hear.)
3. Harmonic major thirds are a narrow imperfect consonance, meaning the pitches are relatively close together and they have a complex and pleasing sound. Listen for the bright sound of the interval.

## Singing

Use scale degrees 1 to 3 to sing a major third.

1. To sing an ascending M3, hear your given pitch as scale degree 1, and orient yourself around it by singing all of the scale degree patterns to set up the key.

**EXAMPLE 1.8.2**

2. As you orient yourself around the tonic, isolate scale degrees 1 up to 3—that's an ascending M3.

**EXAMPLE 1.8.3**

To sing a descending major third:

1. Hear the given pitch as scale degree 3. Sing the pattern for scale degree 3 to find tonic. If you have trouble, try singing up to scale degree 4 and then down to tonic.

**EXAMPLE 1.8.4**

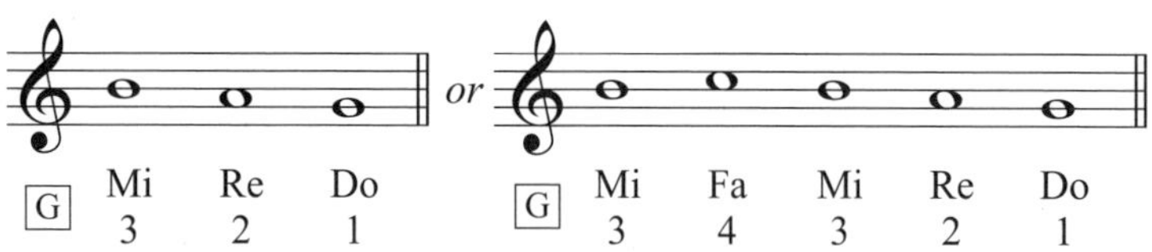


2. Isolate the outer pitches—you have sung a descending M3.

**EXAMPLE 1.8.5**

### Minor Thirds

#### Facts You Need to Know

Minor thirds occur in the following places in the major scale:

1. Between scale degrees 3 and 5
2. Between scale degrees 2 and 4
3. Between scale degrees 6 and 1
4. Between scale degrees 7 and 2

Minor thirds occur in the following places in the minor scale:

1. Between scale degrees 1 and 3
2. Between scale degrees 2 and 4
3. Between scale degrees 4 and ♭6
4. Between scale degrees 5 and ♭7
5. Between scale degrees ♯6 and 1
6. Between scale degrees ♯7 and 2

Minor thirds are imperfect consonants intervals with a darker, less stable sound than major thirds.

## Hearing

1. Use scale degrees 3 and 5 as your point of reference for minor thirds. Notice that this interval requires you to hear a tonic pitch that is not part of the interval—it is a third below the lower pitch.

2. The top pitch will sound like scale degree 5 wanting to move to tonic through scale degree 3. The bottom pitch will sound like scale degree 3 wanting to move stepwise to tonic.

**EXAMPLE 1.8.6**

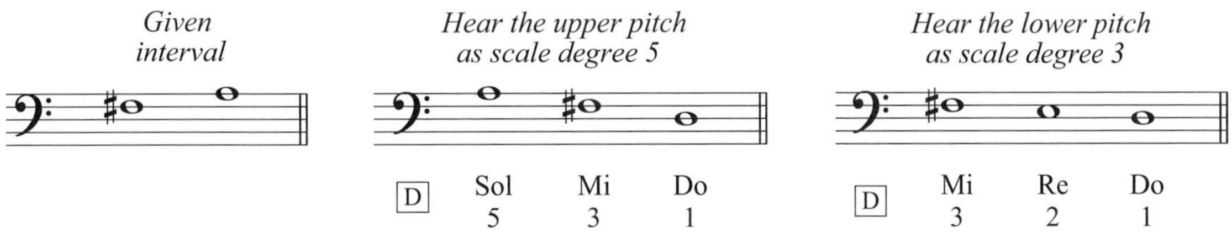


3. You might also hear this as the top two pitches of a major triad. Hear the "melody" formed by this interval as continuing to that tonic pitch.

**EXAMPLE 1.8.7**

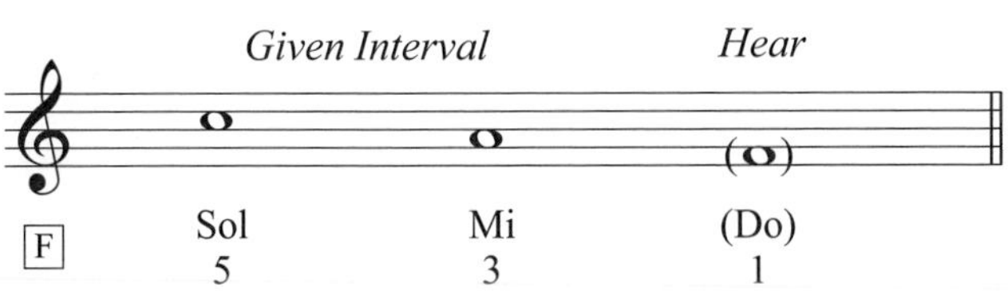


## Singing

1. To sing an ascending m3, hear the given pitch as scale degree 3. Find tonic by singing the pattern for scale degree 3, then orient yourself in the key by singing scale degree patterns, like this:

**EXAMPLE 1.8.8**

2. Isolate scale degrees 3 and 5—you will be singing an ascending m3.

**EXAMPLE 1.8.9**

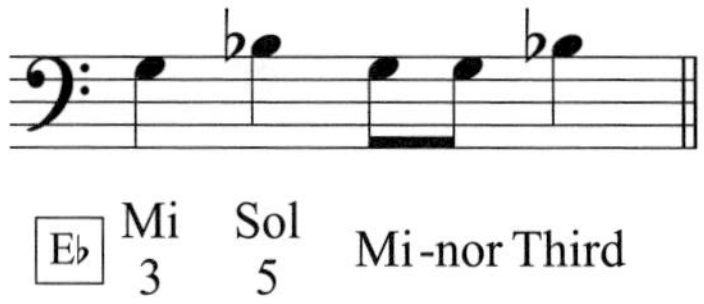


3. Use the same process to sing a descending minor third. Hear the given pitch as scale degree 5, sing tonic by singing the pattern for 5, then sing scale degrees 5 to 3, a minor third.

**EXAMPLE 1.8.10**

You can also use scale degrees 7 and 2 to sing minor thirds. For some, this might be easier because of the close proximity of 2 and 7 to tonic. If you choose this method, orient yourself in the key by singing the pattern for scale degrees 1, 2, and 7, and follow the established process.

## Assignments for Practice

1. Give yourself a pitch and practice singing major and minor thirds above and below it. Work for stellar intonation.
2. Practice singing a major scale in thirds, two ways, as shown:

**EXAMPLE 1.8.11**

Clap on the crusis of each measure while you sing. Be mindful of and focus on your intonation as you perform these exercises. Start slowly, and gradually increase your tempo, making sure you stay in tune as the tempo increases. Sing with numbers first, then repeat using syllables.

These exercises will help you to hear thirds harmonically as well as help you to sing in tune:

1. Sing thirds with a friend. Choose a pitch on the piano; you sing that pitch while your friend sings the major or minor third above it, then below it. Change roles.
2. Sing a scale in thirds with the piano. Start singing the scale on tonic and begin playing on the third scale degree, then reverse the procedure. You will be singing thirds harmonically with the piano.
3. Use the same idea of singing in thirds, but this time, sing in canon with the piano. Start by playing the scale on the piano; when the piano reaches the third scale degree, begin singing the scale on tonic. Ascend and descend, not repeating the upper tonic.

## Pitch Patterns

### PITCH PATTERN 1.8.1

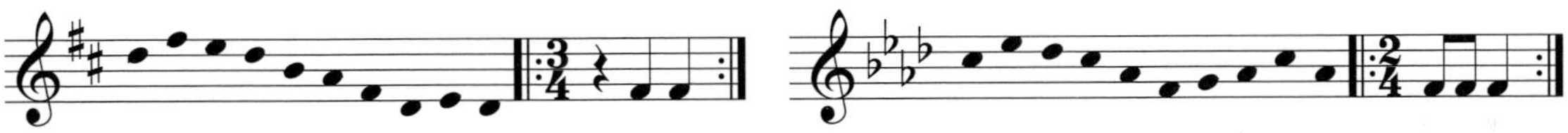

### PITCH PATTERN 1.8.2

## Melodies

When singing skips, don't "guess" at the second pitch. Maintain the integrity of the interval by hearing and singing both pitches as scale degrees in the key.

### MELODY 1.8.1

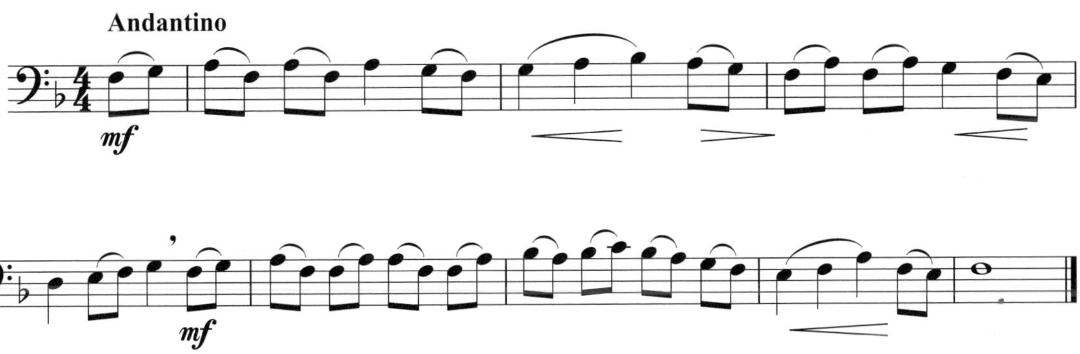


### MELODY 1.8.2

### MELODY 1.8.3

**MELODY 1.8.4**

Pay attention to articulation markings in the following melody. How do they create a musical story?

**MELODY 1.8.5**

**MELODY 1.8.6**

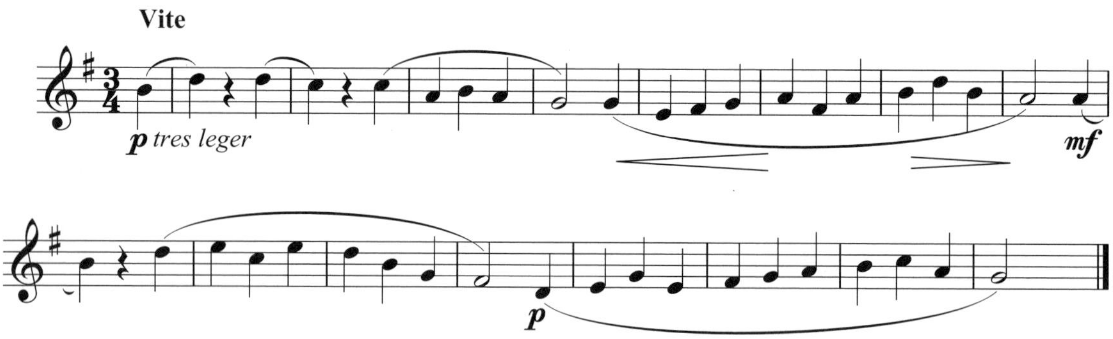


Sing the major scale in thirds before attempting this melody. How does it relate to what is happening in the melody?

**MELODY 1.8.7**

MELODY 1.8.8

What makes holding onto tonic somewhat tricky in the following melody?

MELODY 1.8.9

MELODY 1.8.10

MELODY 1.8.11

**MELODY 1.8.12**

**MELODY 1.8.13**

Notice the beaming in the following melody. What does this mean for performance?

**MELODY 1.8.14**

**MELODY 1.8.15**

## Duets

### DUET 1.8.1

### DUET 1.8.2

### DUET 1.8.3

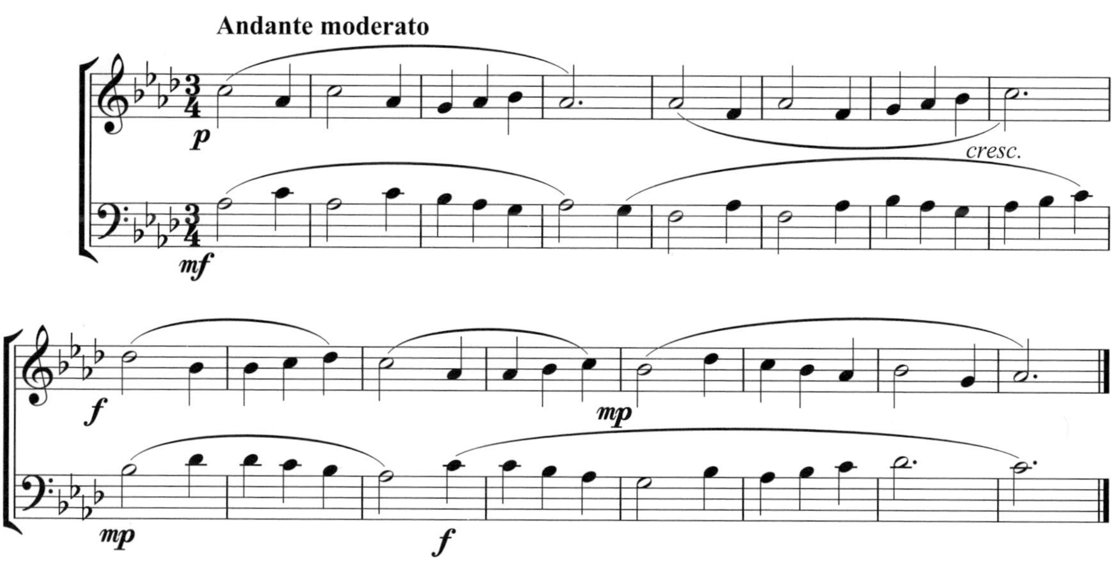

## Chorale

### CHORALE 1.8

## Self-Accompanied Melody

### SELF-ACCOMPANIED MELODY 1.8

# 1.9 Perfect Fifths and Octaves

## Perfect Fifths

### Facts You Need to Know

Perfect fifths are one of the most defining intervals in tonal music. They serve as the basis for the strongest and most frequent type of chord motion.

Perfect fifths occur in six places in the major scale:

1. Between scale degrees 1 and 5
2. Between scale degrees 2 and 6
3. Between scale degrees 3 and 7
4. Between scale degrees 4 and 1
5. Between scale degrees 5 and 2
6. Between scale degrees 6 and 3

Perfect fifths occur in six places in the minor scale:

1. Between scale degrees 1 and 5
2. Between scale degrees 3 and ♭7
3. Between scale degrees 4 and 1
4. Between scale degrees 5 and 2
5. Between scale degrees ♭6 and 3
6. Between scale degrees ♭7 and 4

Perfect fifths are perfect consonances. They are often described as having a "hollow," "open," or "ringing" sound.

## Hearing

1. When hearing melodic perfect fifths, the lower pitch usually has the more stable sound of tonic, while the upper pitch has the more active sound of scale degree 5.

**EXAMPLE 1.9.1**

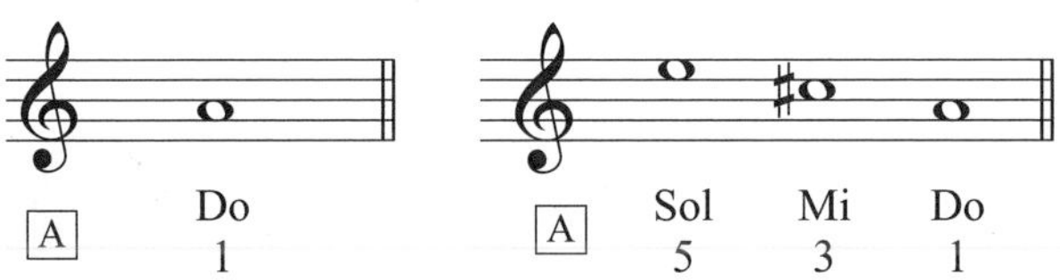


2. When hearing harmonic perfect fifths, listen for the characteristic "perfect" quality—a hollow, open, and ringing sound. Listen for how the top pitch has a strong desire to resolve down to the bottom pitch.

## Singing

1. Use scale degrees 1 to 5 in the major mode as your point of reference.
2. When singing an ascending perfect fifth, hear your given pitch as tonic. Orient yourself around this tonic by singing through the scale degree patterns for this key.
3. Find scale degree 5 above tonic. Sing the scale degrees and interval quality and size.

**EXAMPLE 1.9.2**

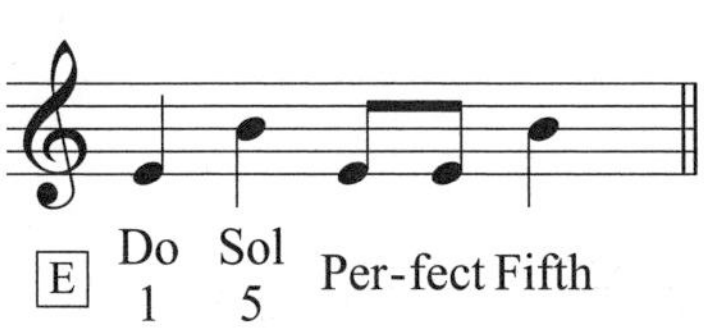

4. When singing a descending perfect fifth, hear the given pitch as scale degree 5. Sing the pattern for this scale degree or a descending scale to find tonic.
5. If necessary, orient yourself around this tonic by singing scale degree patterns.
6. Sing the scale degrees and interval quality and size.

**EXAMPLE 1.9.3**

### Perfect Octaves

#### Facts You Need to Know

Perfect octaves are perfect consonances. They have an even more pure and open sound than perfect fifths. Often, the higher pitch seems to "disappear" into the sound of the lower pitch. Perfect octaves occur on all scale degrees in the major and minor scale.

## Hearing

1. Listen for a wide consonance. Listen also for the scale degree of each pitch. If the scale degrees are the same, but in different registers, then you are hearing a perfect octave.
2. If played harmonically, listen for a very pure and open sound that is wider than a perfect fifth and in which the upper pitch seems to blend very easily into the sound of the lower pitch.

## Singing

1. Use scale degree 1 up to 1 in the major mode as your point of reference.
2. Hear the given pitch as tonic. Orient yourself around this tonic by singing the scale degree patterns.
3. Pay particular attention to the pattern and resolution of scale degree 7 in both octaves. Also, you may find arpeggiating through the pitches of the tonic triad to be helpful.

**EXAMPLE 1.9.4**

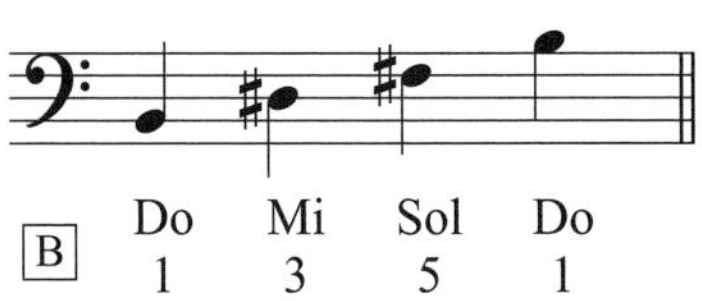

4. Sing the scale degrees and interval quality and size.

**EXAMPLE 1.9.5**

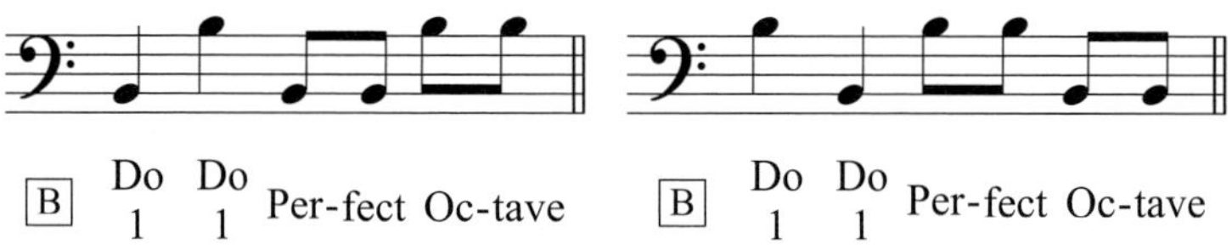


## Assignments for Practice

1. Practice giving yourself a pitch and singing a perfect fifth above it. Once that is in tune, sing a perfect fifth below it with good intonation.
2. Learn the major scale in fifths that appears below. Be aware that one dyad (pair of notes) ascending and one dyad descending (those from scale degrees 4 to 7) create a diminished fifth or tritone. For now, just sing those intervals as their respective scale degrees and notice how they sound different than the perfect fifths.

**EXAMPLE 1.9.6**

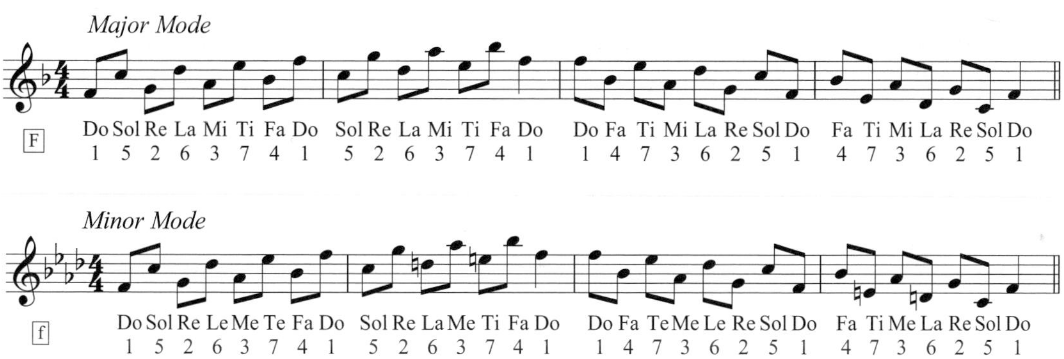


3. Listen for and identify perfect fifths in music that you hear, sing, or practice.

### Pitch Patterns

**PITCH PATTERN 1.9.1**

**PITCH PATTERN 1.9.2**

## Melodies

Remember to sing skips as combinations of scale degrees as you work through these melodies.

### MELODY 1.9.1

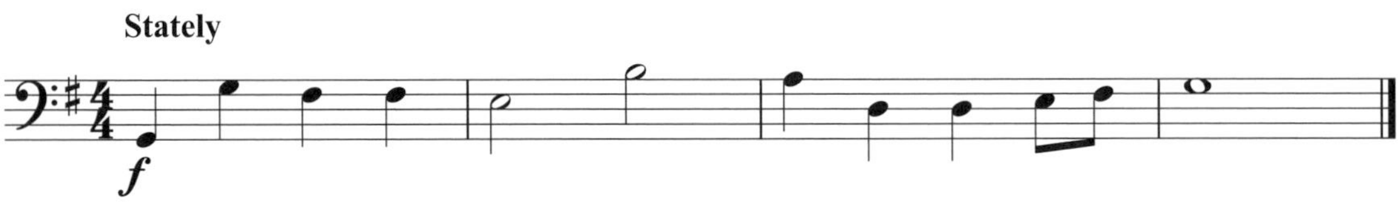


### MELODY 1.9.2

### MELODY 1.9.3

### MELODY 1.9.4

MELODY 1.9.5

MELODY 1.9.6

Divide this melody into an upper and lower line before singing. How is each line constructed?

MELODY 1.9.7

MELODY 1.9.8

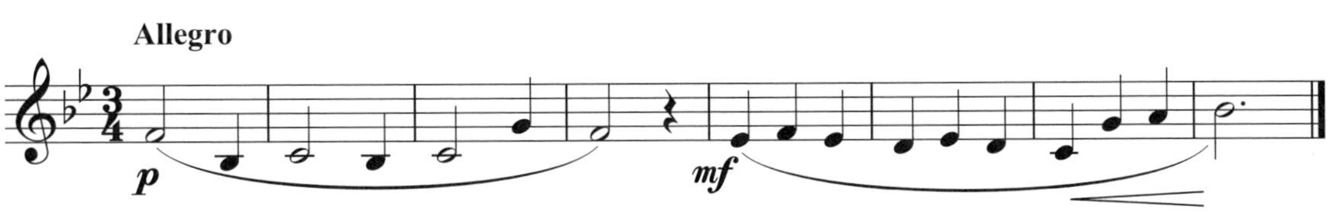

**MELODY 1.9.9**

How many phrases are in this melody, and what do the rests do to your sense of musical continuity?

**MELODY 1.9.10**

**MELODY 1.9.11**

Divide this melody into two lines before singing. Compare it to melody 1.9.7.

**MELODY 1.9.12**

**MELODY 1.9.13**

**MELODY 1.9.14**

**MELODY 1.9.15**

## Duets

Provide your own tempo and style marking for this duet.

**DUET 1.9.1**

**DUET 1.9.2**

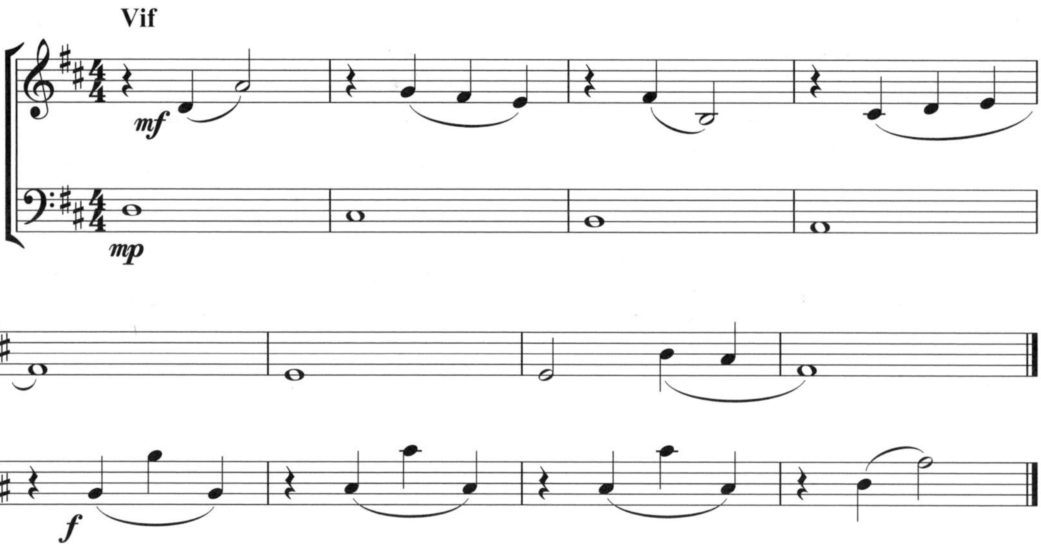


**DUET 1.9.3**

## Chorale

**CHORALE 1.9**

## Self-Accompanied Melody

### SELF-ACCOMPANIED MELODY 1.9

## 1.10 Major Triads in Root Position

### Facts You Need to Know

Triads are three-note chords. Major triads are generally described as having a "bright," "happy," and stable sound. They consist of a major third between the root and third, a minor third between the third and fifth, and a perfect fifth between the root and fifth.

**EXAMPLE 1.10.1**

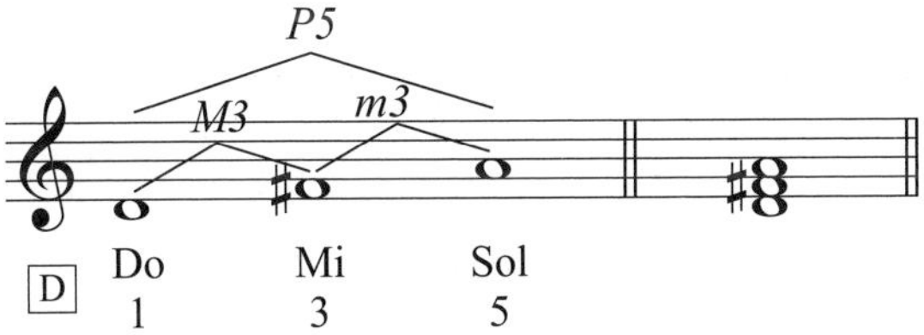


Major triads occur in three places in the major scale:

1. As the tonic (I) triad, consisting of scale degrees 1, 3, and 5.
2. As the subdominant (IV) triad, consisting of scale degrees 4, 6, and 1.
3. As the dominant (V) triad, consisting of scale degrees 5, 7, and 2.

Major triads occur in four places in the minor scale:

1. As the mediant (III) triad, consisting of scale degrees 3, 5, and ♭7.
2. As the dominant (V) triad, consisting of scale degrees 5, ♯7, and 2.
3. As the submediant (VI) triad, consisting of scale degrees ♭6, 1, and 3.
4. As the subtonic (♭VII) triad, consisting of scale degrees ♭7, 2, and 4.

## Hearing

1. Listen for the bright, happy, and stable sound of the chord.
2. Listen for the component scale degrees, usually 1, 3, and 5 in the major mode. Be aware that you may hear one of the other possibilities above.

## Singing

1. Use the tonic (I) triad, consisting of scale degrees 1, 3, and 5, as your point of reference.
2. Hear your given pitch as either scale degree 1, 3, or 5, depending on the requested ordering. If necessary, sing the scale degree pattern for this pitch to set up the key.

**EXAMPLE 1.10.2**

*Sing this pattern to find tonic if your given pitch is the...*

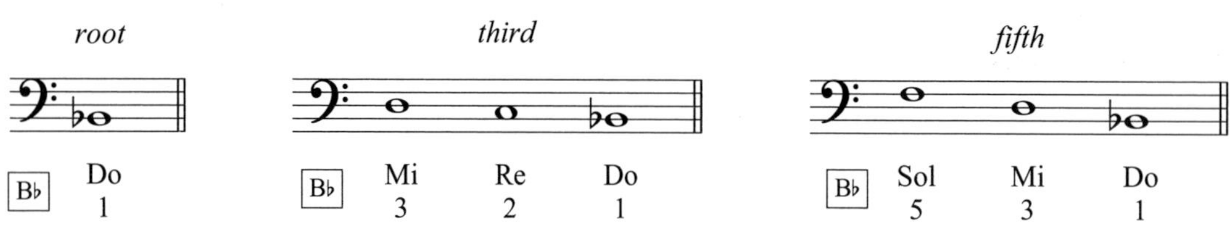


3. Sing the component scale degrees in the correct order.

**EXAMPLE 1.10.3**

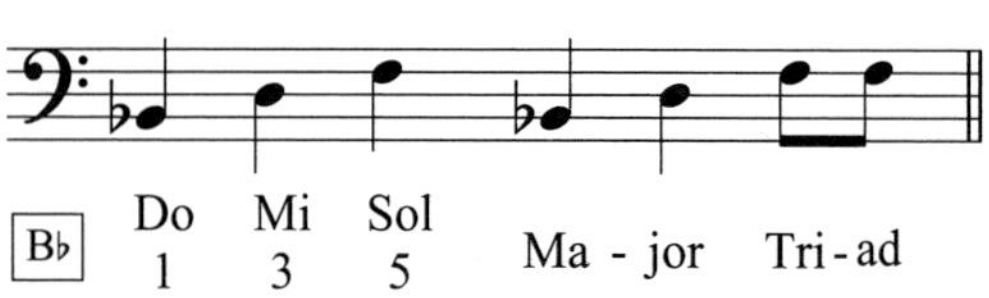

## Assignments for Practice

1. Be able to sing a major triad from any given pitch.
2. From the given pitch, figure out how to hear each triad as the subdominant in the key or the dominant in the key. This will involve finding a different tonic pitch than the one you would use when hearing the triad as tonic. Once you have sung each triad, find a logical resolution to the tonic pitch and arpeggiate through the tonic triad to establish the stability of the key.
3. Treat your given pitch as the third or fifth of the triad. From this, sing the correct scale degree pattern to find tonic before singing the triad.
4. Rearrange the order of the pitches for your major triad. Notice that there are only six ways to arrange the pitches in a three-note set such as a triad.

**EXAMPLE 1.10.4**

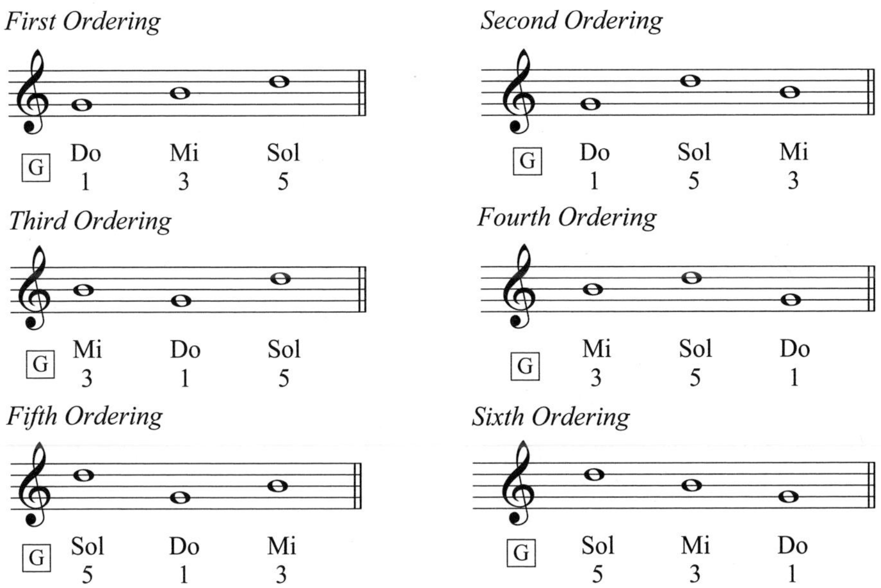


### Pitch Patterns

**PITCH PATTERN 1.10.1**

**PITCH PATTERN 1.10.2**

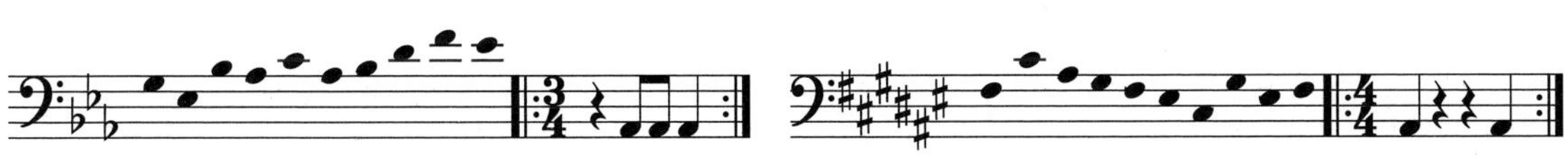

### Melodies

Look for examples of major triads in each melody you sing. Be aware that sometimes the triads will be arranged into different orderings.

MELODY 1.10.1

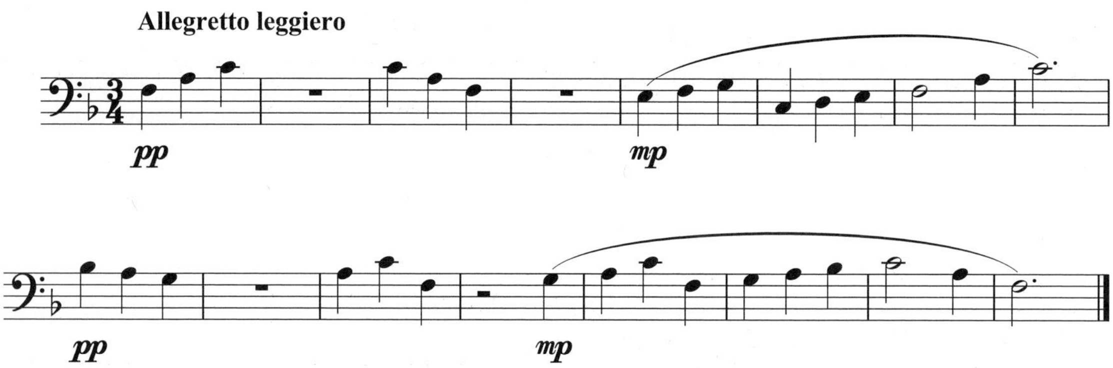


MELODY 1.10.2

MELODY 1.10.3

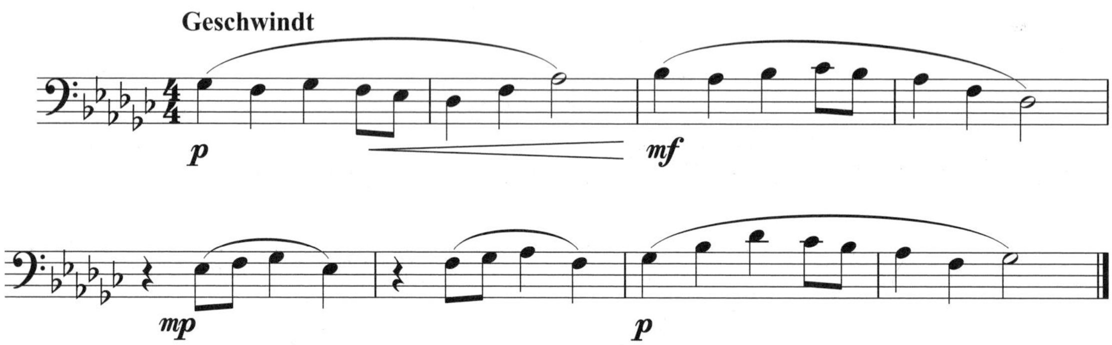


MELODY 1.10.4

MELODY 1.10.5

MELODY 1.10.6

MELODY 1.10.7

MELODY 1.10.8

MELODY 1.10.9

**MELODY 1.10.10**

**MELODY 1.10.11**

**MELODY 1.10.12**

What effect do the rests in the next melody have on the musical line? How can you maintain the integrity of the phrase across the rests?

**MELODY 1.10.13**

**MELODY 1.10.14**

**MELODY 1.10.15**

## Duets

### DUET 1.10.1

### DUET 1.10.2

### DUET 1.10.3

### Chorale

**CHORALE 1.10**

### Self-Accompanied Melody

**SELF-ACCOMPANIED MELODY 1.10**

## 1.11 Improvision I: Tonic Function

### Facts You Need to Know

Tonic function is the most stable function in tonal music. The desire to return to tonic is built into the tonal musical system. Tonic function is carried by the tonic chord (I in major, i in minor). Sometimes the submediant chord (vi and VI) or the mediant chord (iii and III) act like they carry tonic function. Note that all of these chords contain scale degree 1, which gives this chord class its stability, and scale degree three, which establishes major or minor modality.

When improvising tonic function, focus on singing scale degrees 1, 3, and 5 as your primary tones.

To improvise in tonic, use the following techniques:

1. **Repetition**: repeat a scale degree in the tonic triad.

**EXAMPLE 1.11.1**

2. **Arpeggiation**: jump between scale degrees in the tonic triad.

**EXAMPLE 1.11.2**

3. **Connected arpeggiation**: fill in the jumps between the members of the tonic triad.

**EXAMPLE 1.11.3**

When improvising, pay attention to the amount of time you have to fill. Keep counting!

Make your improvisation fit with the rest of the music by using motives and rhythms found elsewhere in the melody.

Improvision happens frequently in some styles of music (jazz and popular), but can be needed at any time, such as when an instrument malfunctions, the wind blows a page of music off the stand, or your memory leaves you under the stress of live performance.

## Singing

Below is a demonstration of how to approach a melody that requires improvisation of tonic function:

**EXAMPLE 1.11.4**

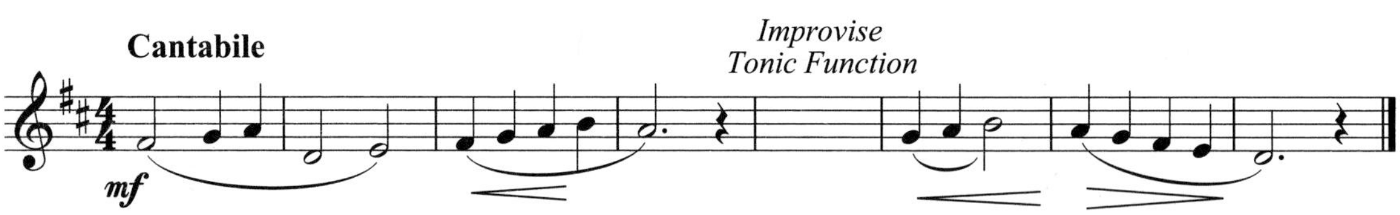


1. Notice the blank measure and instruction to improvise tonic function. Sing through the notated measures, leaving a space or singing scale degree 1 in the blank measure. Notice rhythmic or melodic elements that you may be able to imitate. Notice the general level of rhythmic activity and whether the melody tends to leap or step. Remember that you want your improvisation to sound like it fits with the rest of the music.
2. Plan your improvisation. Notice that the last written note before the improvisation is scale degree 5, and the first note after it is scale degree 4. You may want to start and end on scale degree 5 and end on scale degree 1 to make the transition in and out of the improvisation smoother and easier.
3. Internalize the meter; be aware of the crusis of the measure.

4. Try out a few ideas using the three techniques above (repetition, arpeggiation, connected arpeggiation).

**EXAMPLE 1.11.5**

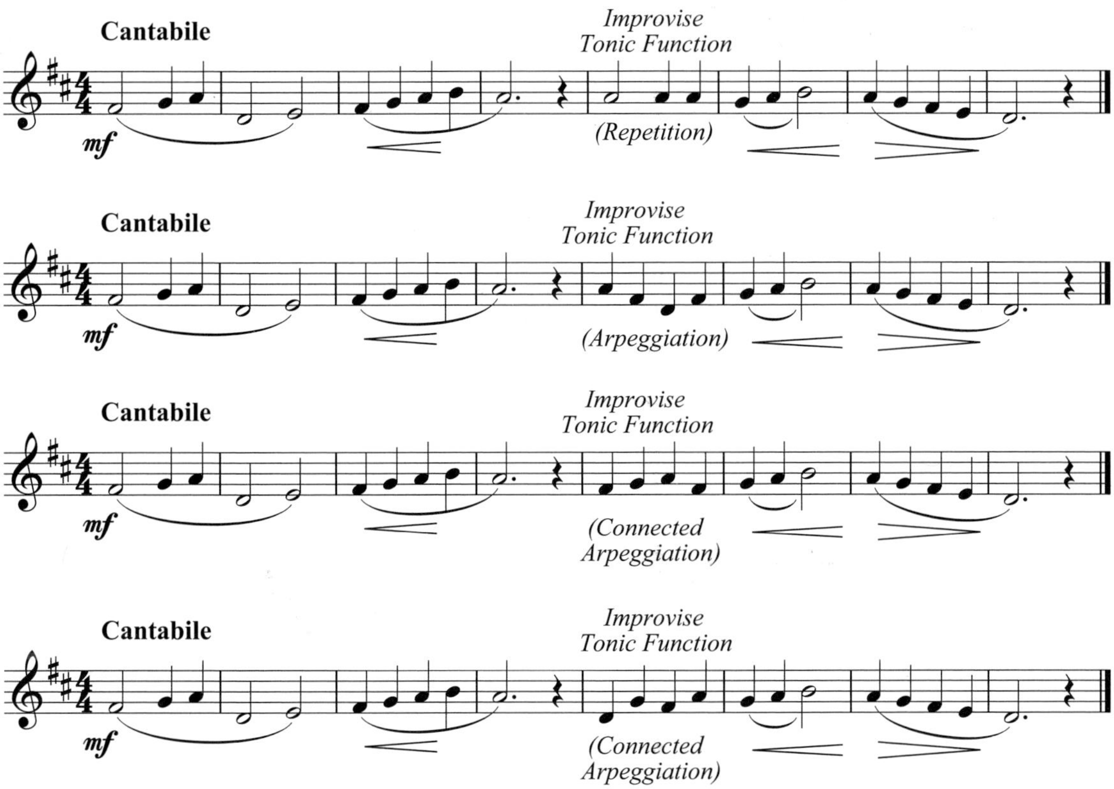


5. Sing the melody, inserting ideas that you liked in the blank measure.

## Assignments for Practice

1. Set yourself up in a key and repeat a tonic function chord in time. Improvise tonic function over it. Ask a friend to join you to improvise a duet.
2. Experiment with using other scale degrees in tonic function improvisation. Listen for how they affect the sound and shape of your improvisation.

### Melodies

Improvise tonic function in the blank measures of the melodies below. Be sure to make your rhythm fit with the rest of the melody:

**MELODY 1.11.1**

MELODY 1.11.2

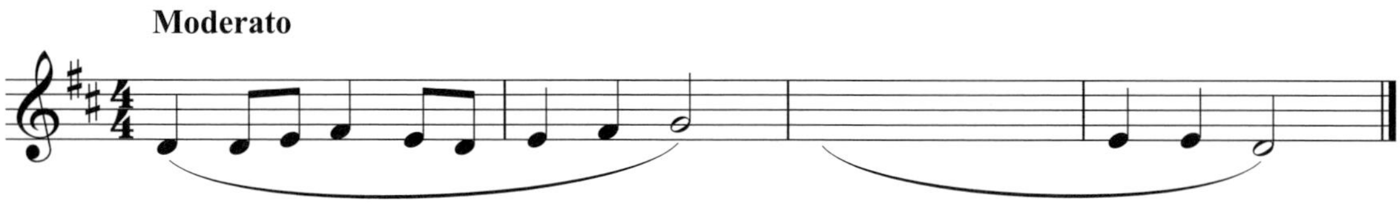


MELODY 1.11.3

MELODY 1.11.4

MELODY 1.11.5

MELODY 1.11.6

MELODY 1.11.7

MELODY 1.11.8

MELODY 1.11.9

MELODY 1.11.10

## Duets

### DUET 1.11.1

## Self-Accompanied Melody

### SELF-ACCOMPANIED MELODY 1.11

## 1.12 Music from the Literature

The following melodies are part of the standard repertoire. Find out what you can about each melody, its composer, and the musical and stylistic context in which it should be performed. Be aware that sometimes the key signature is not an indicator of the key center. Look for a variety of indicators (first and last pitch, high and low pitch, key signature and accidentals) to determine the key before starting.

**EXAMPLE 1.12.1**

*An Wasserflussen Babylon*

J.S. Bach

**EXAMPLE 1.12.2**

"Jesu Leiden, Pein und Tod," from the *St. John Passion*

J.S. Bach

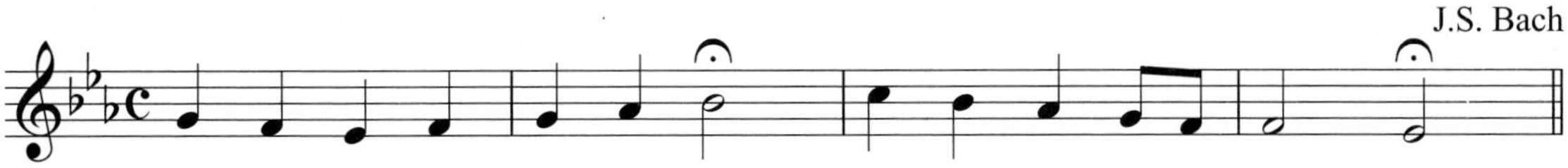

**EXAMPLE 1.12.3**

*Sonatina in C Major*, Tarantella, Op. 157, No. 1, II

m. 25-32

**Vivace**

Spindler

**EXAMPLE 1.12.4**

*Minuet*

**Moderato**

James Hook

Sing this melody in your most comfortable vocal range.

**EXAMPLE 1.12.5**

*Sonatina in C Major*, Op. 36, No. 3, II

m. 13–16

**Un poco adagio**

Clementi

Take some time to work out the rhythms in the following example. Despite the "short" note values, it moves slowly. Where skips occur, find the second note by hearing its scale degree. Notice how each musical fragment begins on the same pitch. Retain this pitch in your memory as you sing each melodic fragment.

**EXAMPLE 1.12.6**

*Symphony No. 1 in C Major,*
Op. 21, Fourth movement

violin 1

Beethoven

Sing the leaps in the following melody by hearing the scale degree that goes with each pitch. Notice the underlying stepwise motion that holds the melody together.

**EXAMPLE 1.12.7**

*String Quartet No. 80,*
Op. 76, No. 6, Second movement

m. 1–8

Haydn

**EXAMPLE 1.12.8**

British Folk Song

**EXAMPLE 1.12.9**

*Echoing*, Op. 218

Louis Kohler

**EXAMPLE 1.12.10**

*Salti di terza*

**Andantino**

Nicola Vaccai

**EXAMPLE 1.12.11**

m. 4–8

*Allegro*

**Allegro**

W.F. Bach

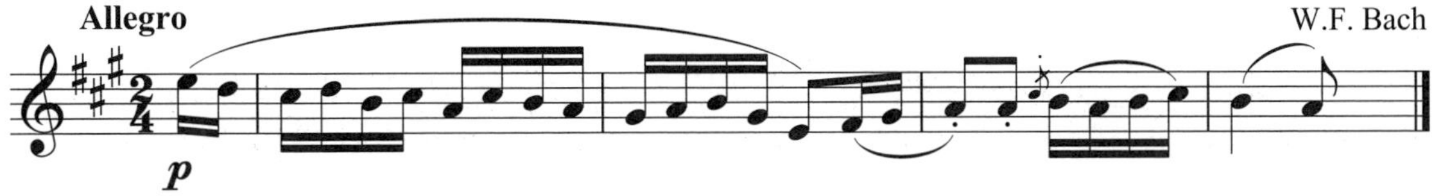


**EXAMPLE 1.12.12**

*Little Sonata*

I. Moderato

C.H. Wilton

**EXAMPLE 1.12.13**

**Allegretto**

French Folk Song

**EXAMPLE 1.12.14**

*Stepping Dance*

**Allegro**

Smetana

**EXAMPLE 1.12.15**

*Piano Sonata in G Major*,
Op. 49, No. 2, First movement

m. 20–28

**Allegro, ma non troppo**

Beethoven

**EXAMPLE 1.12.16**

*Vittoria, mio core!*

**Allegro con brio** Giacomo Carissimi

**EXAMPLE 1.12.17**

*Se Florindo e fedele*

m. 17–30

**Allegretto grazioso, moderato assai** A. Scarlatti

**EXAMPLE 1.12.18**

*Symphony No. 35, "Haffner,"*
K.385, First movement

m. 1–5

**Allegro** Mozart

## Reflections: Why Study Solfège?

A well-conceived solfège course teaches four essential skills: inner hearing, professional behavior, sensitivity to sound, and the ability to think and communicate *in* music.

Just as authors need to be readers and artists need to have a discerning eye, musicians must have well-developed *inner hearing*. It gives us the ability to "see what we hear," or to understand the nature, properties, and significance of the musical sounds we hear, and the ability to "hear what we see," or to know how the images used to represent musical sound on the printed page will sound when performed.

Solfège class is also a rehearsal for your career as a professional musician. In addition to hearing and performing skills, a well-crafted solfège class also begins to build good habits for preparation, practice, musical and professional interaction with peers, and strategies for taking care of one's body, mind, and spirit. These skills often make the difference between a very talented musician who lives from job to job and a less talented but hard-working musician who maintains a long and steady career.

Most musical instruments (including the voice) are capable of creating a tremendous variety of sounds. Skilled musicians learn how to manipulate these sounds with tremendous subtlety in order to communicate musical meaning. Musicians must be open to and aware of extremely fine shadings of all of the components of music (pitch, timbre, tempo, dynamics, etc.) for the purposes of understanding better how this affects musical meaning and for the enhancement of performance.

Perhaps the most important goal of solfège class is the ability to think in music. This ability transforms the activity of music making from simply the performance of something someone else has created to an active collaboration between the composer, the performer, and the audience. When revered professional musicians talk about the passion and joy they have for music, they often mention how individual compositions constantly challenge them. The ability to address music on its own terms and in its own language and to be a co-partner in the process of artistic creation is what transforms musicianship from a job consisting of mechanical repetition of performance skills to a joyous lifelong pursuit. It gives music students the greatest gift they can acquire—the ability to make joyful, passionate music on one's own.

For most students, solfège presents a dramatically new way of thinking about and experiencing music as well as a type of educational experience that is unlike any course they've ever taken. It is skill-based, which means that improvement and eventual mastery of the material can only come through effective daily practice. Furthermore, solfège is a lifelong skill that requires an ongoing commitment to practice. In the end, the skills taught in a well-designed solfège class are a starting point for a lifelong relationship with music.

## 1.13 Dictation Materials

@

### I. Identification of Major Scale Degrees

Your teacher will establish a key and then play its scale degrees in random order or as a specific pitch in a melody (by number—first, second, last, or by position—high or low). Identify each by writing its number in the appropriate space.

*Date:* . . . . . . . . . . . . . .

1. ____ 2. ____ 3. ____ 4. ____ 5. ____ 6. ____ 7. ____ 8. ____

*Date:* . . . . . . . . . . . . . .

1. ____ 2. ____ 3. ____ 4. ____ 5. ____ 6. ____ 7. ____ 8. ____

*Date:* . . . . . . . . . . . . . .

1. ____ 2. ____ 3. ____ 4. ____ 5. ____ 6. ____ 7. ____ 8. ____

*Date:* . . . . . . . . . . . . . .

1. ____ 2. ____ 3. ____ 4. ____ 5. ____ 6. ____ 7. ____ 8. ____

*Date:* . . . . . . . . . . . . . .

1. ____ 2. ____ 3. ____ 4. ____ 5. ____ 6. ____ 7. ____ 8. ____

## II. Interval Identification

Your teacher will play several intervals. Identify their quality and size as one of the following:

M2 = Major second
m2 = Minor second
X = Other
M3 = Major third
m3 = Minor third
P5 = Perfect fifth
P8 = Perfect octave

Be sure to make a clear difference between your capital and lower-case Ms.

*Date:* . . . . . . . . . . . . . .

1. ____ 2. ____ 3. ____ 4. ____ 5. ____ 6. ____ 7. ____ 8. ____

*Date:* . . . . . . . . . . . . . .

1. ____ 2. ____ 3. ____ 4. ____ 5. ____ 6. ____ 7. ____ 8. ____

*Date:* . . . . . . . . . . . . . .

1. ____ 2. ____ 3. ____ 4. ____ 5. ____ 6. ____ 7. ____ 8. ____

*Date:* . . . . . . . . . . . . . .

1. ____ 2. ____ 3. ____ 4. ____ 5. ____ 6. ____ 7. ____ 8. ____

*Date:* . . . . . . . . . . . . . .

1. ____ 2. ____ 3. ____ 4. ____ 5. ____ 6. ____ 7. ____ 8. ____

## III. Meter Identification

Your teacher will play several melodies. Listen for the metric division and number. Write a logical meter signature for each example. Possible answers are $\begin{smallmatrix}2\\4\end{smallmatrix}$, $\begin{smallmatrix}3\\4\end{smallmatrix}$, $\begin{smallmatrix}4\\4\end{smallmatrix}$, $\begin{smallmatrix}2\\2\end{smallmatrix}$, or "X" for other.

*Date:* . . . . . . . . . . . . . .

1. ____ 2. ____ 3. ____ 4. ____ 5. ____ 6. ____ 7. ____ 8. ____

*Date:* . . . . . . . . . . . . . .

1. ____ 2. ____ 3. ____ 4. ____ 5. ____ 6. ____ 7. ____ 8. ____

*Date:* . . . . . . . . . . . . . .

1. ____ 2. ____ 3. ____ 4. ____ 5. ____ 6. ____ 7. ____ 8. ____

*Date:* . . . . . . . . . . . . . .

1. ____ 2. ____ 3. ____ 4. ____ 5. ____ 6. ____ 7. ____ 8. ____

*Date:* . . . . . . . . . . . . . .

1. ____ 2. ____ 3. ____ 4. ____ 5. ____ 6. ____ 7. ____ 8. ____

## IV. Melodic and Rhythmic Dictation

Your teacher will play a short melody or rhythm. Notate it on the staves below. To do this, follow these steps:

1. Listen first (without writing). Learn what you can about the sound of the melody, its modality (major or minor), meter, shape, and register. Try to memorize what you can.
2. First notate the rhythm above the staff.
3. Determine the scale degree of pitches that sound more important (such as the first, last, highest, lowest, or first of each measure). Write those numbers above their corresponding note in the rhythm.
4. Figure out how those "structural" pitches are approached, left, and connected to one another.
5. Notate the pitches on the staff.
6. Add in articulation, dynamic, or other musical indicators.

Remember that clef, key signature and meter signature appear on the first line of music (in that order) and that only clef and key signature appear on all other lines.

*Date:* . . . . . . . . . . . . . .

*Date:* . . . . . . . . . . . . . .

*Date:* . . . . . . . . . . . . . .

*Date:* . . . . . . . . . . . . . .

## Chapter 2

# Compound Meters, Ties and Dots; The Minor Mode and Inverted Triads

## 2.1 Compound Meters

### Facts You Need to Know

Meters are defined by the number of beats in a measure and the number of parts into which each beat is divided. In compound meter, the beat is divided into three parts; and can be duple, triple, or quadruple, as indicated in the charts below:

### Compound Duple Meters

**EXAMPLE 2.1.1**

| *Time Signature* | *Beat Note Value* | *Beat Division* | *Beats per Measure* |
|---|---|---|---|
| 6/8 | ♩. | ♪ | 2 |
| 6/16 | ♪. | 𝅘𝅥𝅯 | 2 |
| 6/4 | 𝅗𝅥. | ♩ | 2 |

Or, as notated:

**EXAMPLE 2.1.2**

## Compound Triple Meters

**EXAMPLE 2.1.3**

| *Time Signature* | *Beat Note Value* | *Beat Division* | *Beats per Measure* |
|---|---|---|---|
| 9/8 | 𝅘𝅥. | 𝅘𝅥𝅮 | 3 |
| 9/16 | 𝅘𝅥𝅮. | 𝅘𝅥𝅯 | 3 |
| 9/4 | 𝅗𝅥. | 𝅘𝅥 | 3 |

Or, as notated:

**EXAMPLE 2.1.4**

## Compound Quadruple Meters

**EXAMPLE 2.1.5**

| *Time Signature* | *Beat Note Value* | *Beat Division* | *Beats per Measure* |
|---|---|---|---|
| 12/8 | 𝅘𝅥. | 𝅘𝅥𝅮 | 4 |
| 12/16 | 𝅘𝅥𝅮. | 𝅘𝅥𝅯 | 4 |
| 12/4 | 𝅗𝅥. | 𝅘𝅥 | 4 |

Or, as notated:

**EXAMPLE 2.1.6**

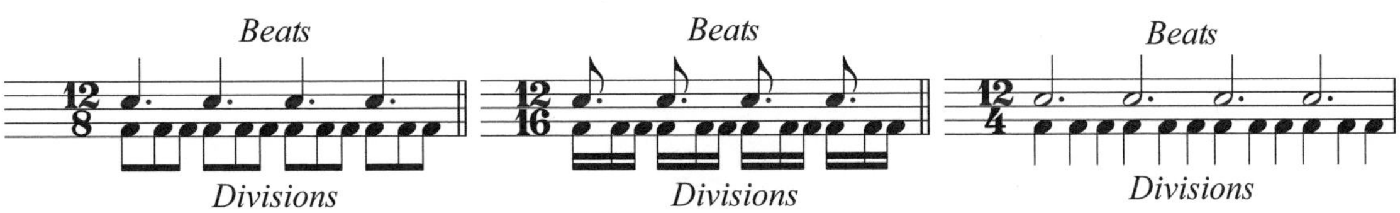


The division of the beat into three parts in compound meter creates the defining characteristic of the meter. Where simple meter tends to be square and angular, compound meter is circular. Why? Think in physical terms: if you were to step the two divisions of simple meter, you might look like a soldier marching. When you step the three divisions in compound meter, each beat begins on the opposite side of your body, creating a sense of sway or rocking motion; it's circular.

Traditionally, the top number of a time signature indicates the number of beats in each measure, and the bottom number indicates what kind of note gets a beat. In addition, the rules of notation state that notes belonging to the same beats are always beamed. If both those statements are true, the musical example below is contradictory. The time signature indicates that there are six beats in the measure, but the beaming suggests that there are only two beats.

**EXAMPLE 2.1.7**

6
8

In compound meter, the beat-note value is not the eighth note, as the time signature suggests, but the dotted quarter note, so the eighth notes are beamed in groups of three. It is accepted practice to consider the beat-note value of a compound meter to be a dotted quarter, dotted eighth, or dotted half note. The time signature tells only half of the truth.

Any time signature can be written using note values in conjunction with traditional Arabic numbers, as shown below.

**EXAMPLE 2.1.8**

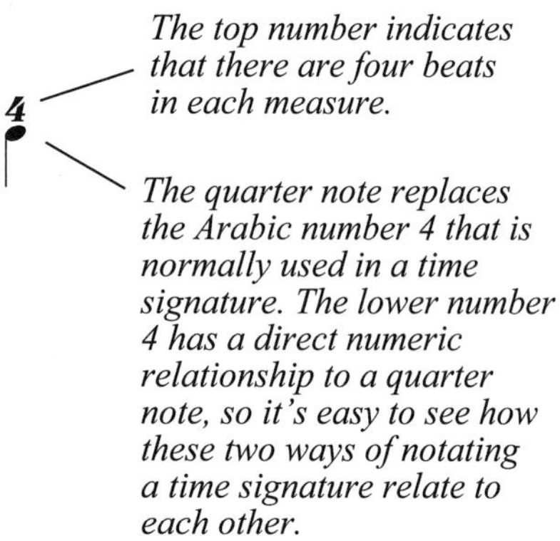
4
*The top number indicates that there are four beats in each measure.*
*The quarter note replaces the Arabic number 4 that is normally used in a time signature. The lower number 4 has a direct numeric relationship to a quarter note, so it's easy to see how these two ways of notating a time signature relate to each other.*

Utilizing the same approach in compound meter, this time signature would indicate compound duple meter:

**EXAMPLE 2.1.9**

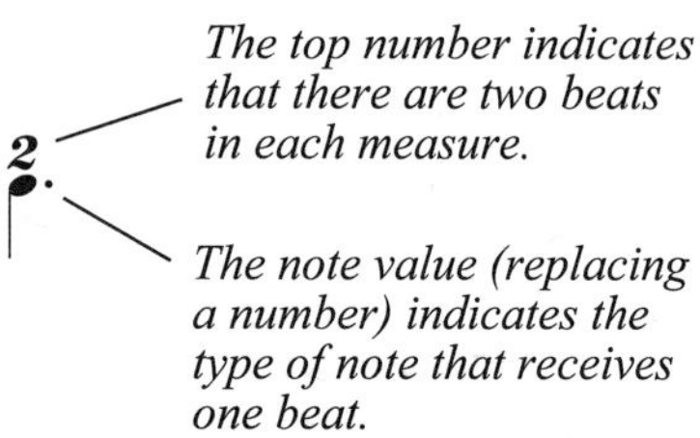
2
*The top number indicates that there are two beats in each measure.*
*The note value (replacing a number) indicates the type of note that receives one beat.*

It is not possible to translate the dotted quarter to a numerical equivalent. Many possibilities come to mind—6, or a $1\frac{1}{2}$ or a $4\frac{1}{2}$—but though they are logical choices, they don't work. Therefore, we use the symbol $\frac{6}{8}$ because there is not a single number to indicate the value of the dotted quarter—not because there are six beats in the measure.

### Common Patterns in Compound Meter

**EXAMPLE 2.1.10**

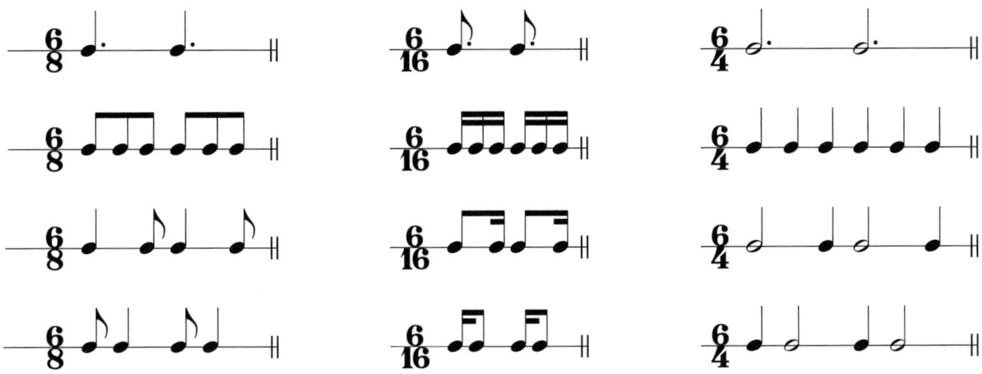

## Rhythms

For the rhythms below, clap the beat and articulate the rhythm. Figure out challenging rhythms by clapping the division of the beat.

**RHYTHM 2.1.1**

**RHYTHM 2.1.2**

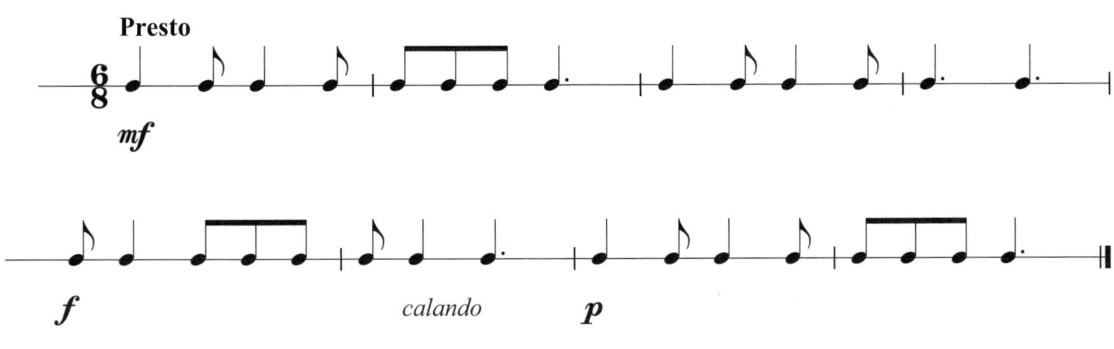

Figure out the rhythm in measure 3 before you begin. Be sure to place the second eighth note on the beat.

**RHYTHM 2.1.3**

**RHYTHM 2.1.4**

**RHYTHM 2.1.5**

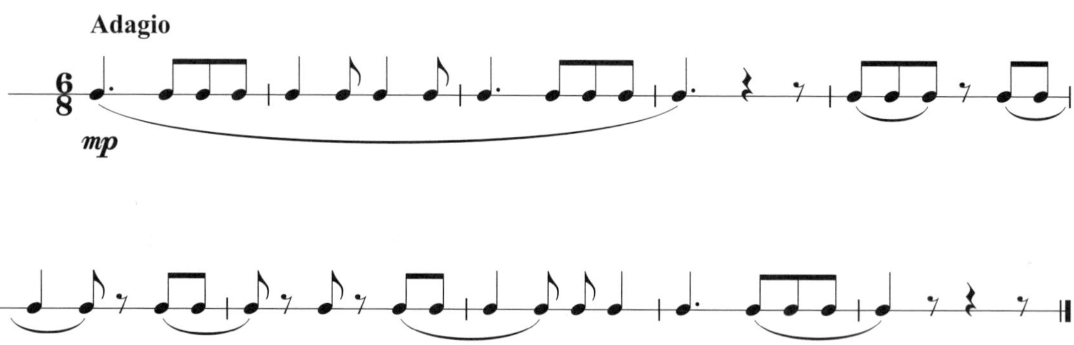


**RHYTHM 2.1.6**

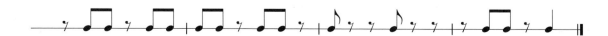

**RHYTHM 2.1.7**

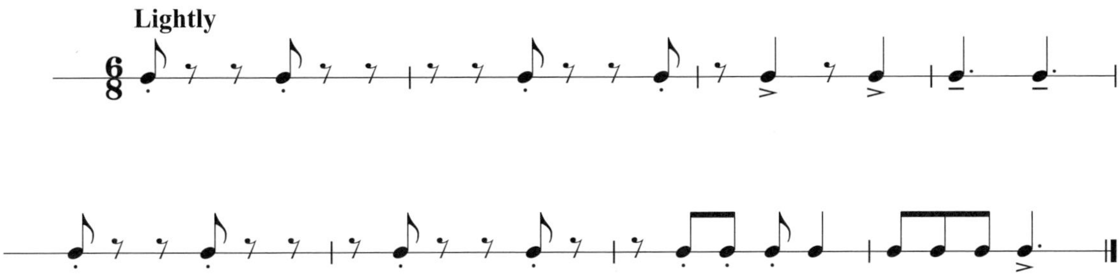


Provide your own tempo and style indicator for the following rhythm.

**RHYTHM 2.1.8**

**RHYTHM 2.1.9**

**RHYTHM 2.1.10**

### RHYTHM 2.1.11

## Two-part Rhythms

### TWO-PART RHYTHM 2.1.1

### TWO-PART RHYTHM 2.1.2

### TWO-PART RHYTHM 2.1.3

## Three-part Rhythm

### THREE-PART RHYTHM 2.1

## 2.2 Ties and Dotted Rhythms in Simple Meter

### Facts You Need to Know

Rhythmic patterns that use ties and the dotted rhythms derived from them serve to add interest and tension to music.

Notes of any value can be dotted. A dot adds half the value of the note to the note. Thus, in $\frac{4}{4}$, a dotted quarter gets one and a half beats, a dotted eighth is equal to ¾ of a beat, etc. A second dot adds half the value of the first dot to the note. (For example, a double dotted half note in $\frac{4}{4}$ gets 2 beats + 1 beat + a half beat)

A tie is a curved line used to rhythmically join together two notes on the same line or space of a staff. The two notes become one, the length of which is determined by adding the two note values together. Ties can be used both within and between measures:

**EXAMPLE 2.2.1**

but are not used within beats:

**EXAMPLE 2.2.2**

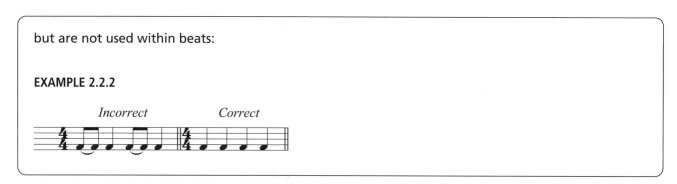

Clap the beat and articulate the following rhythms:

**EXAMPLE 2.2.3**

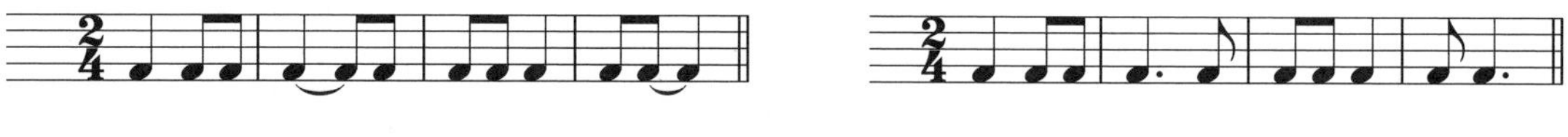

The two rhythms are identical; one is written with ties, the other with dots. Regardless of the style of notation, measures 2 and 4 are problematic; the second beat seems to be "missing" because the sound is tied over from the previous beat, creating rhythmic tension. That missing beat creates one of the challenges associated with the performance of these rhythms: the tendency to rush.

If you have difficulty performing this—or any—rhythm with ties, use this method:

1. Clap the beat and articulate the rhythm, omitting the ties completely.
2. Repeat immediately, adding the ties in again, but consciously inhale on the second beat of the measure where the tie is located. This will replace the "missing" beat with a sound to help you hear the rhythm completely and avoid rushing.
3. Perform as written.
4. Note: If you have difficulty figuring out this rhythm as written, clap eighth notes instead of the beat while you articulate; it will help you to "line up" the notes in the measure.

The dotted-eighth–sixteenth rhythm pattern (and its reverse) tends to be even more difficult to perform accurately and musically. It is essential that you hear all four sixteenth notes to avoid the tendency of "rounding" the rhythm and performing it as if it were a compound meter rhythm.

The counting methods described in 1.2, "Second Division and Second Multiple of the Beat," can be applied to performing the dotted-eighth–sixteenth pattern as well, as shown in the example opposite:

**EXAMPLE 2.2.4**

Practice both rhythms below. The first measure is in simple meter, the second, an example of the rhythm in the incorrect, "rounded" version. Learn to discriminate between the two manifestations of the rhythm.

**EXAMPLE 2.2.5**

One general principle you can apply to the natural impulse of rhythm is that short notes lead to long notes. Except for very specific stylistic examples of the opposite tendency in music of the Renaissance, you will find this maxim to be true. There may not be a better example of the impetus for a short note to resolve itself to a long note than in these dotted and tied rhythms. The impulse is so strong, in fact, that it is easy to hear the rhythm as anacrusic rather than crusic.

The same rhythmic impulse of the short note resolving to the long exists when the rhythm is turned around (eighth-dotted quarter). In this case, the short note is stressed because it falls on a beat, and the rhythm remains convincingly crusic. The short note again resolves to the long note, but the character of the long note is different; there is a sense of suspension as the duration passes "through" the missing beat.

## Rhythms

**RHYTHM 2.2.1**

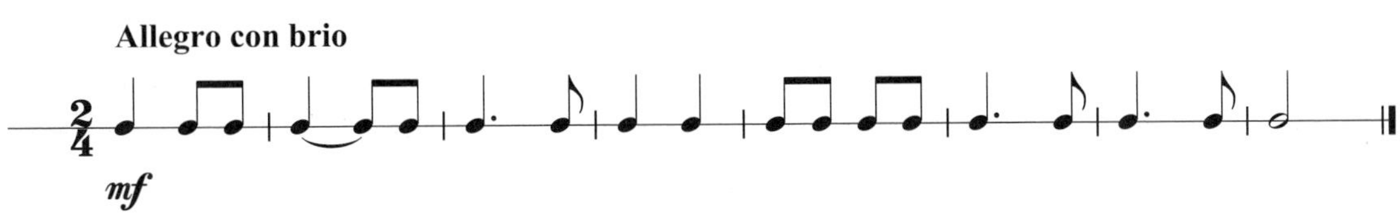

### RHYTHM 2.2.2

### RHYTHM 2.2.3

Pay particular attention to dynamics in the following rhythm.

### RHYTHM 2.2.4

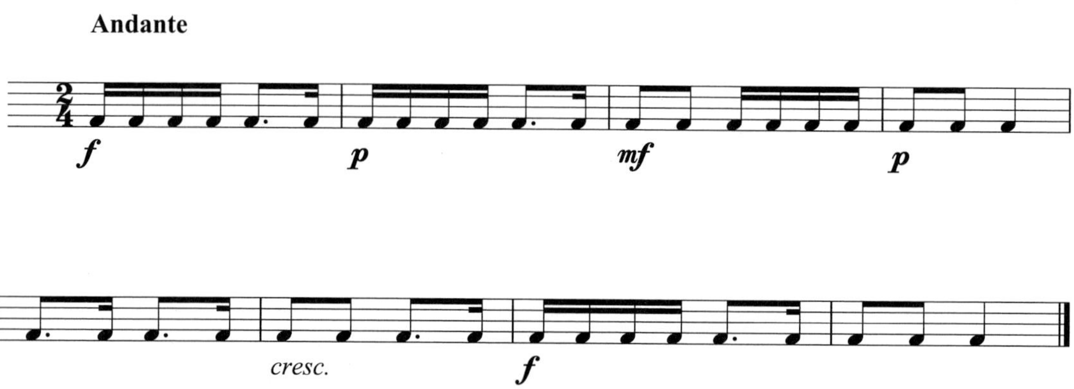


### RHYTHM 2.2.5

**RHYTHM 2.2.6**

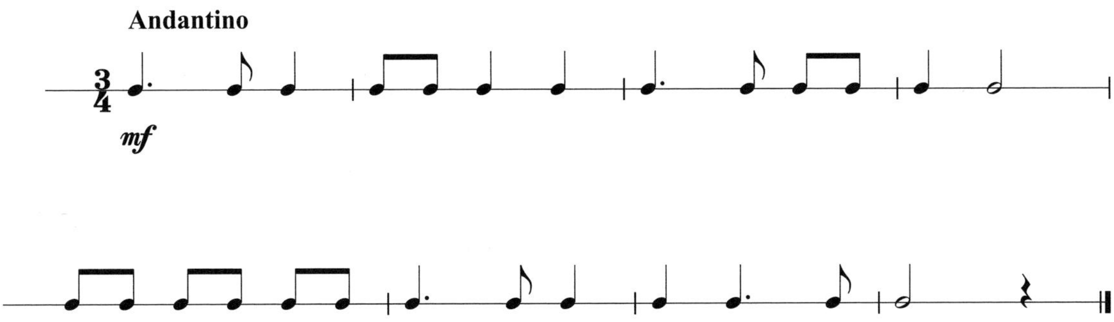


**RHYTHM 2.2.7**

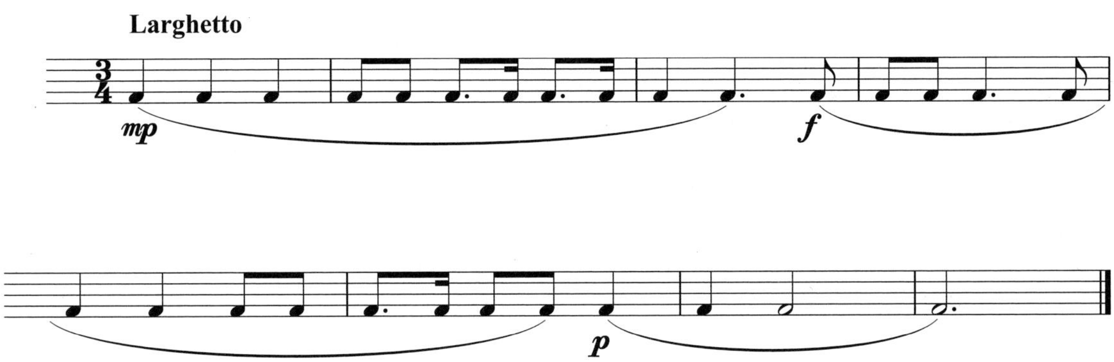


**RHYTHM 2.2.8**

**RHYTHM 2.2.9**

**RHYTHM 2.2.10**

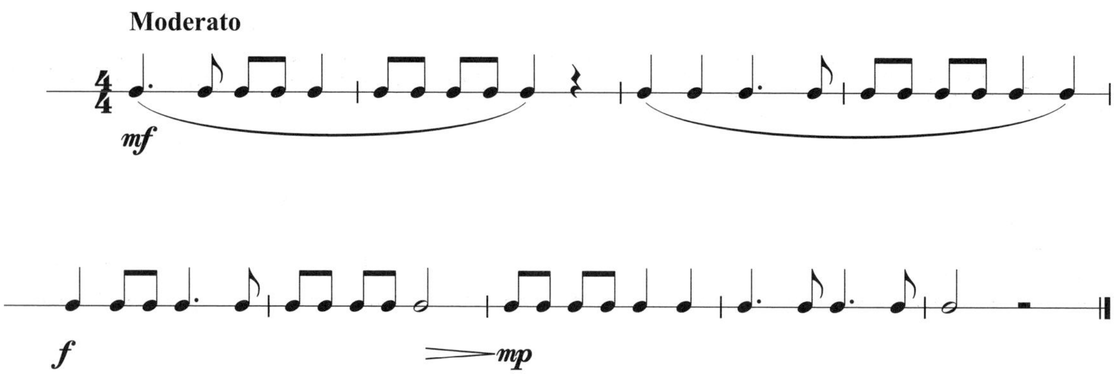


**RHYTHM 2.2.11**

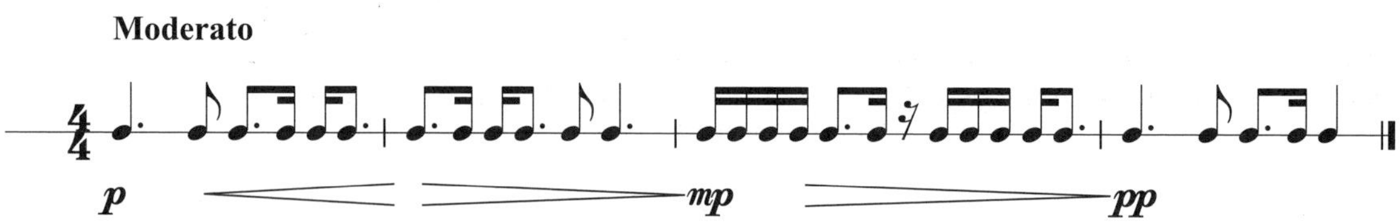


How do the rests and dynamics work together to create a musical story in the following rhythm? What challenges do the rests present?

**RHYTHM 2.2.12**

## Two-part Rhythms

**TWO-PART RHYTHM 2.2.1**

### TWO-PART RHYTHM 2.2.2

### TWO-PART RHYTHM 2.2.3

## Three-part Rhythm

### THREE-PART RHYTHM 2.2

## 2.3 Minor Scales and Minor Scale Degrees

### Facts You Need to Know

Minor scales differ from major scales in three important ways:

1. The minor seconds occur in different places:

   Between scale degrees 2 and 3
   Between scale degrees 5 and ♭6
   Between scale degrees ♯7 and 1

2. Scale degree 3 is a semitone lower than its position in the major scale.
3. Scale degrees 6 and 7 each have two possible positions: lowered and raised.

These differences often lead musicians to describe three forms of the minor scale. Each of these forms has the same lower five notes. They differ in the placement and usage of the variable scale degrees, 6 and 7.

1. The natural minor scale has lowered sixth and seventh scale degree.

**EXAMPLE 2.3.1**

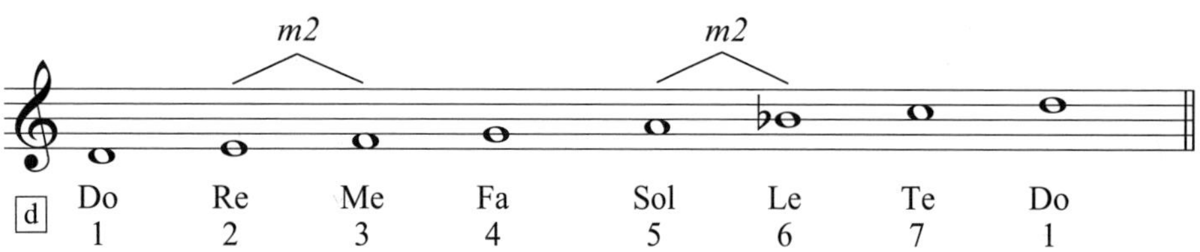


2. The harmonic minor scale has a lowered sixth and a raised seventh scale degree.

**EXAMPLE 2.3.2**

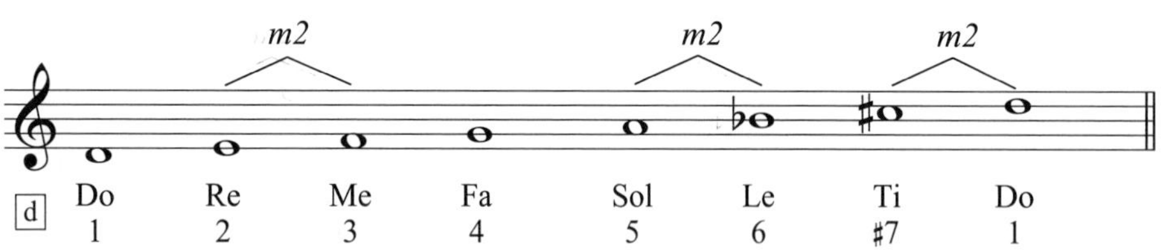


3. The melodic minor scale, which has raised sixth and seventh scale degrees.

**EXAMPLE 2.3.3**

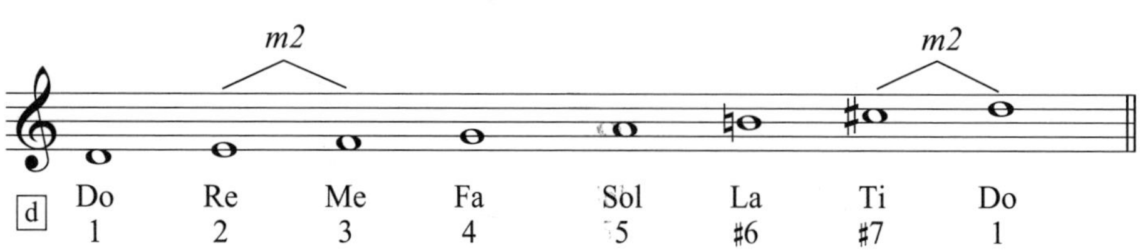

The placement of the sixth and seventh scale degrees follows some basic principles:

1. Scale degree 7 is raised when supported by dominant function harmony (V or vii°), regardless of the direction the melodic line is following.
2. Scale degree 7 is lowered when supported by tonic or predominant function harmony.
3. Scale degree 6 is also raised when supported by dominant function harmony and it is a non-chord tone that connects scale degree 5 to scale degree 7.
4. Scale degree 6 is lowered at all other times.
5. When scale degrees 6 and 7 are raised, they have a strong desire to resolve to the next higher scale degree. When lowered, they have a strong desire to resolve to the next lower scale degree.

The lowered sixth scale degree is one of the strongest tendency tones in tonal music. It has a very strong desire to resolve down to scale degree 5.

Just like the major mode, each scale degree in the minor mode has a unique sound and desire toward resolution. Memorize the following scale degree patterns to be able to identify each scale degree's unique sound:

**EXAMPLE 2.3.4**

## Hearing

The minor scale is often described as having a "sad," "dark," or "intense" sound when contrasted with its opposite, the major scale. Listen specifically for the darkness of scale degrees 3 and ♭6. Listen for the relative closeness between scale degrees 2 to 3, 5 to ♭6, and ♯7 to 1.

## Singing

As with the major mode, practice singing scales, chords, and melodies not as a succession of intervals but instead as a succession of scale degrees.

1. Give yourself a pitch and treat it as tonic. Sing each scale degree pattern in order.

**EXAMPLE 2.3.5**

2. Sing each scale degree in order, hearing the pattern that returns it to tonic in your head but not singing it.

## Assignments for Practice

1. Sing the scale degree patterns in a random order, always returning to the same tonic pitch.
2. With a practice partner, have one person establish a key at the piano and then play or sing random scale degrees within that key. The other person should try to identify each scale degree by singing its pattern.
3. If practicing alone, put yourself in the key of A minor at the piano. Close your eyes and play random "white key" pitches. See if you can correctly identify the scale degree of each by singing its scale degree pattern.
4. Given a tonic pitch, be able to identify how each pitch in that key wants to return to tonic using one of the patterns above.
5. Given a pitch, be able to sing any of the scale degree patterns below to establish a tonic pitch.
6. Practice all of the minor scales beginning at the top, descending to the bottom, and then returning to the top.
7. Leave out one or more scale degrees in the scale, and then check the accuracy of the following pitch. For example, here is the B-flat minor scale with scale degrees 4 and 6 removed.

**EXAMPLE 2.3.6**

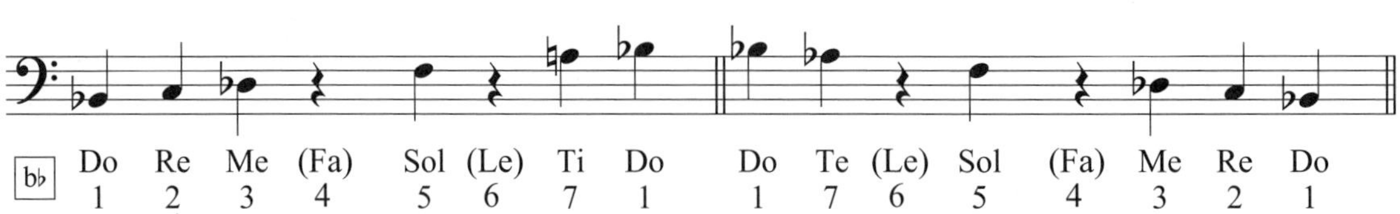

8. Practice singing minor scales beginning on any scale degree. For example, sing a minor scale from scale degree 2 up to scale degree 2 and back down.
9. Practice the minor scale in thirds, notated below. Notice the positions of the variable scale degrees. Try to figure out why each is in its raised or lowered position. Try singing the scale again, moving the variable scale degrees.

#### EXAMPLE 2.3.7

### Pitch Patterns

#### PITCH PATTERN 2.3.1

#### PITCH PATTERN 2.3.2

### Melodies

As always, focus on singing scale degrees instead of intervals in the melodies. Pay particular attention to the placement of the sixth and seventh scale degrees.

#### MELODY 2.3.1

**MELODY 2.3.2**

**MELODY 2.3.3**

**MELODY 2.3.4**

**MELODY 2.3.5**

**MELODY 2.3.6**

**MELODY 2.3.7**

**MELODY 2.3.8**

**MELODY 2.3.9**

**MELODY 2.3.10**

Notice that the second last measure uses the raised sixth and seventh scale degrees on a descending line. If you have trouble singing this, try playing scale degree 5 on a piano while you sing this measure.

MELODY 2.3.11

MELODY 2.3.12

MELODY 2.3.13

MELODY 2.3.14

### MELODY 2.3.15

## Duets

### DUET 2.3.1

### DUET 2.3.2

**DUET 2.3.3**

## Chorale

**CHORALE 2.3**

## Self-Accompanied Melody

**SELF-ACCOMPANIED MELODY 2.3**

## 2.4 Perfect Fourths

### Facts You Need to Know

Perfect fourths are one of the most defining intervals in tonal music, especially when they occur melodically in the bass.

Perfect fourths are perfect consonances, possessing the characteristic hollow, open, and ringing sound.

Perfect fourths occur in six places in the major scale:

1. Between scale degrees 5 and 1
2. Between scale degrees 1 and 4
3. Between scale degrees 2 and 5
4. Between scale degrees 3 and 6
5. Between scale degrees 6 and 2
6. Between scale degrees 7 and 3

Perfect fourths occur in seven places in the minor scale:

1. Between scale degrees 5 and 1
2. Between scale degrees 1 and 4
3. Between scale degrees 2 and 5
4. Between scale degrees 3 and ♭6
5. Between scale degrees 4 and ♭7
6. Between scale degrees ♯6 and 2
7. Between scale degrees ♭7 and 3

### Hearing

1. Listen for the hollow, open, and ringing sound of a perfect consonance.
2. Listen for the upper pitch having the more stable sound of tonic.
3. Listen for the lower pitch sounding like scale degree 5 and wanting to resolve up to the more stable, higher pitch.

### Singing

1. Use scale degrees 5 up to 1 in either the major or minor mode as your point of reference.
2. If singing an ascending interval, sing either an alternate pattern for scale degree 5 or sing an ascending scale to find tonic.

**EXAMPLE 2.4.1**

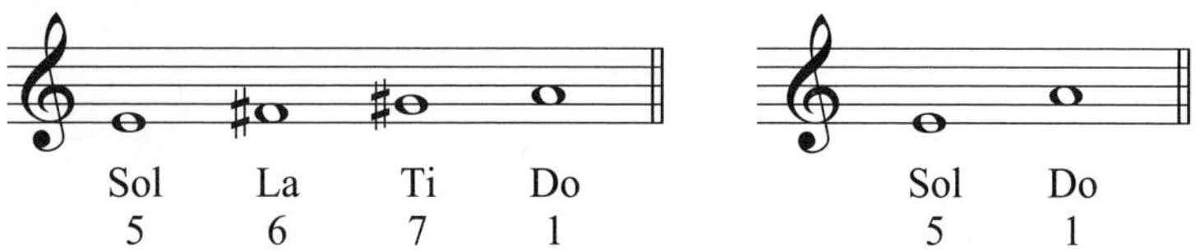


3. If singing a descending interval, hear the given pitch as tonic. If necessary, orient yourself around this tonic by singing all of the scale degree patterns.
4. Sing scale degrees 5 and 1 in the correct order, followed by the interval quality and size.

**EXAMPLE 2.4.2**

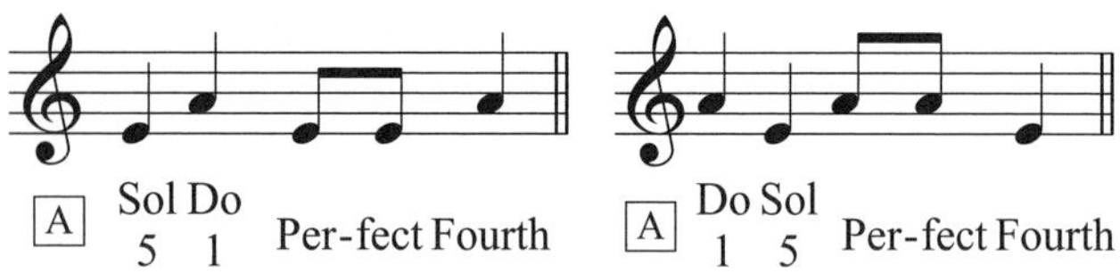


## Assignments for Practice

1. Practice giving yourself a pitch and singing a perfect fourth above it and then below it.
2. Learn the major and minor scales in fourths that appear below. Be aware that one dyad (pair of notes) ascending and one dyad descending (those from scale degrees 7 to 4) create an augmented fourth or tritone.

**EXAMPLE 2.4.3**

*Major Mode*

*Minor Mode*

3. Listen for and identify perfect fourths in music that you hear, sing, or practice.

### Pitch Patterns

**PITCH PATTERN 2.4.1**

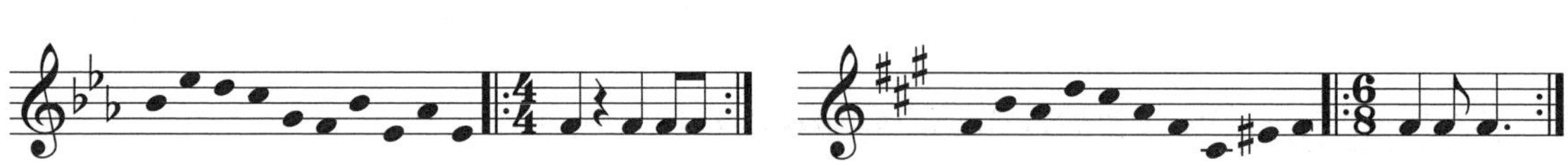

### PITCH PATTERN 2.4.2

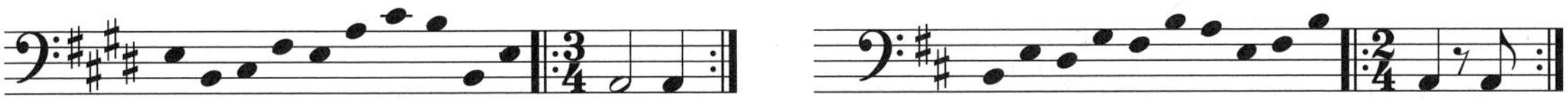

## Melodies

### MELODY 2.4.1

### MELODY 2.4.2

### MELODY 2.4.3

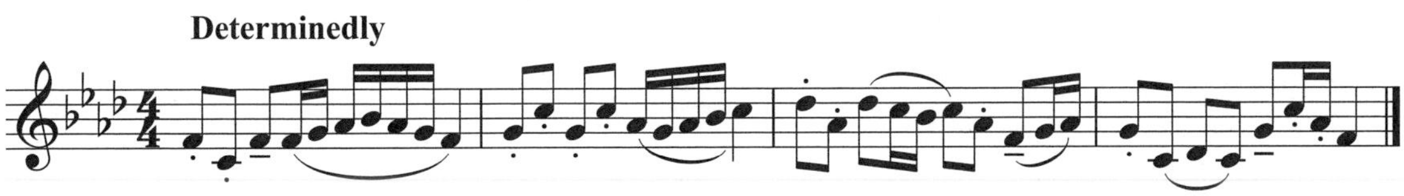


### MELODY 2.4.4

**MELODY 2.4.5**

**MELODY 2.4.6**

**MELODY 2.4.7**

**MELODY 2.4.8**

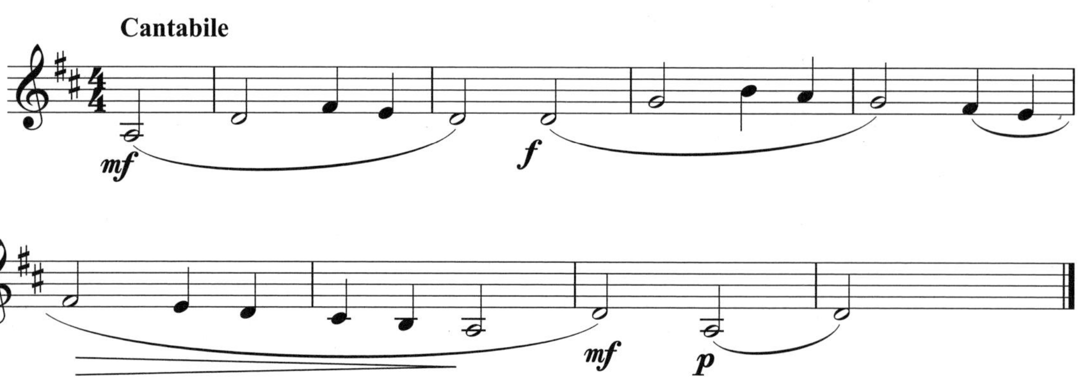

MELODY 2.4.9

MELODY 2.4.10

MELODY 2.4.11

Improvise tonic harmony in the blank measure below:

MELODY 2.4.12

### MELODY 2.4.13

Sing the perfect fourths between scale degrees 5 and 1 and 2 and 5 before attempting this melody.

### MELODY 2.4.14

### MELODY 2.4.15

## Duets

### DUET 2.4.1

### DUET 2.4.2

### DUET 2.4.3

## Chorale

### CHORALE 2.4

## Self-Accompanied Melody

### SELF-ACCOMPANIED MELODY 2.4

## 2.5 Major and Minor Sixths

### Major Sixths

#### Facts You Need to Know

Major sixths are imperfect consonances. They occur in four places in the major scale:

1. From scale degree 5 up to 3
2. From scale degree 1 up to 6
3. From scale degree 2 up to 7
4. From scale degree 4 up to 2

Major sixths occur in four places in the minor scale:

1. From scale degree 3 up to 1
2. From scale degree 4 up to 2
3. From scale degree ♭6 up to 4
4. From scale degree ♭7 up to 5

### Hearing

When identifying major sixths, listen for:

1. Scale degree 5 as the lowest note, wanting to resolve up by a perfect fourth to tonic.
2. Scale degree 3 as the higher note, wanting to resolve down through scale degree 2 to tonic.
3. The complex sound of an imperfect consonance, with the pitches spread farther apart than a third.

### Singing

Use the major sixth that occurs in the major mode between scale degrees 5 and 3 as your point of reference.

1. When singing an ascending major sixth, hear your given pitch as scale degree 5. Sing the pattern for scale degree 5 to find tonic. (One of the alternate patterns may be more useful because it finds the tonic pitch in the middle of the interval.)
2. When singing a descending major sixth, hear your given pitch as scale degree 3. Sing the pattern for scale degree 3 to find tonic.
3. Orient yourself around tonic by singing a major scale or scale degree patterns.

4. Find the other scale degree, either scale degree 3 above tonic or 5 below tonic.

5. Sing the scale degrees and interval quality and size.

**EXAMPLE 2.5.1**

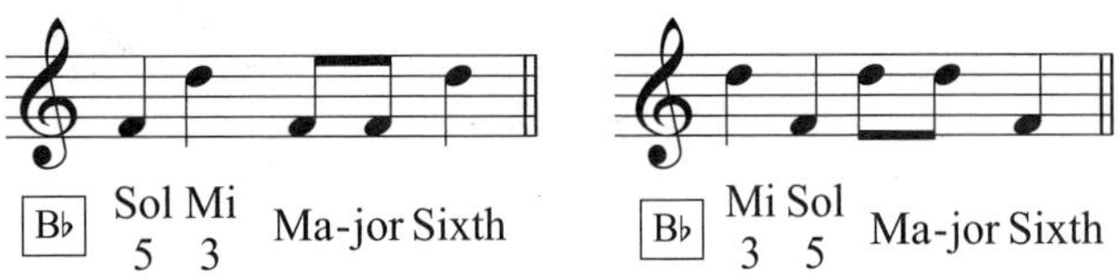


### Minor Sixths

#### Facts You Need to Know

Minor sixths are imperfect consonances.

Minor sixths occur in three places in the major scale:

1. From scale degree 7 up to 5
2. From scale degree 3 up to 1
3. From scale degree 6 up to 4

Minor sixths occur in three places in the minor scale:

1. From scale degree ♯7 up to 5
2. From scale degree 5 up to 3
3. From scale degree 1 up to ♭6

## Hearing

Minor sixths are commonly heard in two ways:

1. As scale degrees 7 up to 5 in the major mode.
2. As scale degrees 5 up to 3 in the minor mode (mirroring the way we hear major sixths).

## Singing Minor Sixths

1. Select which version of the minor sixth you want to use.
2. If ascending, hear the given pitch as scale degree 7 (or 5 in the minor mode) and sing its pattern to find tonic. If descending, hear the given pitch as scale degree 5 (or 3 in the minor mode) and sing its pattern to find tonic. If necessary, orient yourself around tonic by singing scale degrees.
3. Find the remaining note by hearing its scale degree pattern.

4. Sing the scale degrees followed by the interval quality and size.

EXAMPLE 2.5.2a

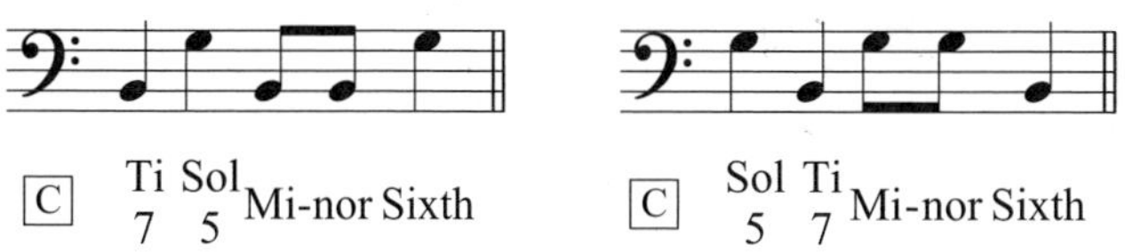


or

EXAMPLE 2.5.2b

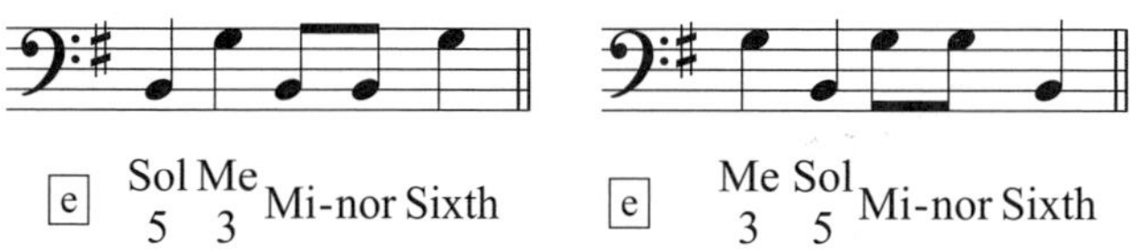


## Assignments for Practice

1. Practice giving yourself a pitch and singing major and minor sixths above and below it.
2. Practice giving yourself a pitch and singing all of the intervals you have studied above and below it.
3. Listen for and identify major and minor sixths in music that you hear, sing, or practice.

### Pitch Patterns

PITCH PATTERN 2.5.1

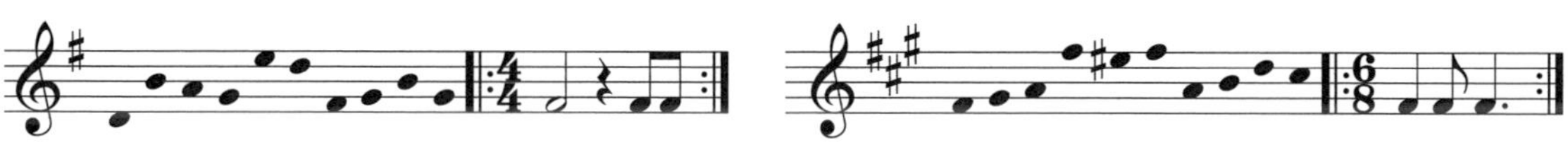

PITCH PATTERN 2.5.2

### Melodies

MELODY 2.5.1

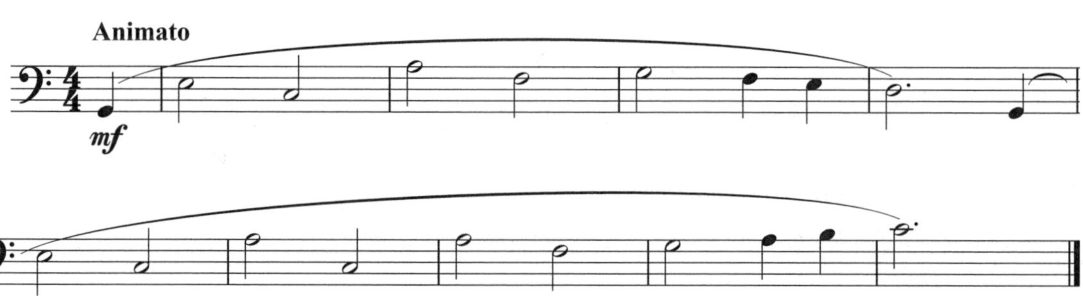

MELODY 2.5.2

Lebhaft

MELODY 2.5.3

Allegretto

MELODY 2.5.4

Waltz tempo

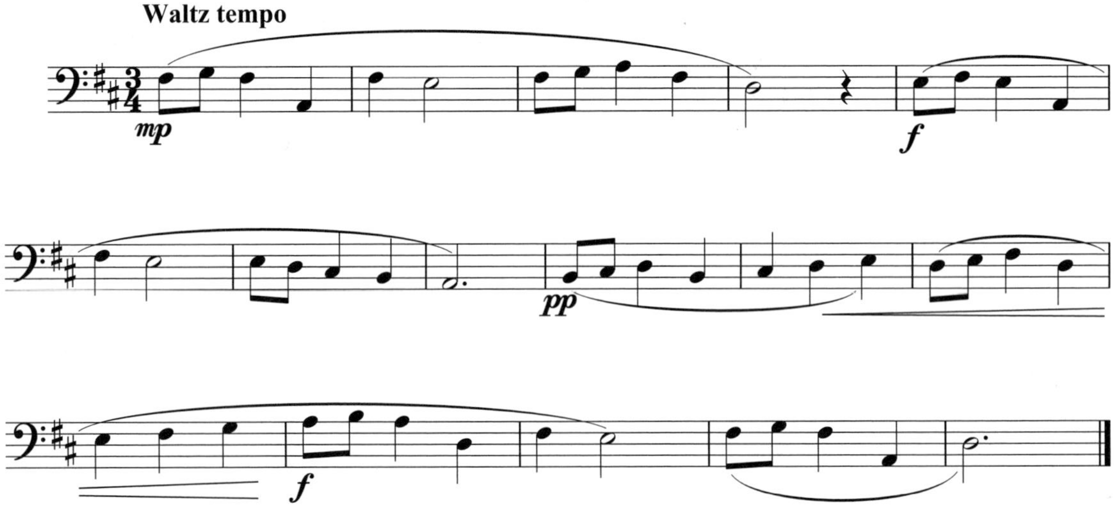

MELODY 2.5.5

Smoothly

MELODY 2.5.6

MELODY 2.5.7

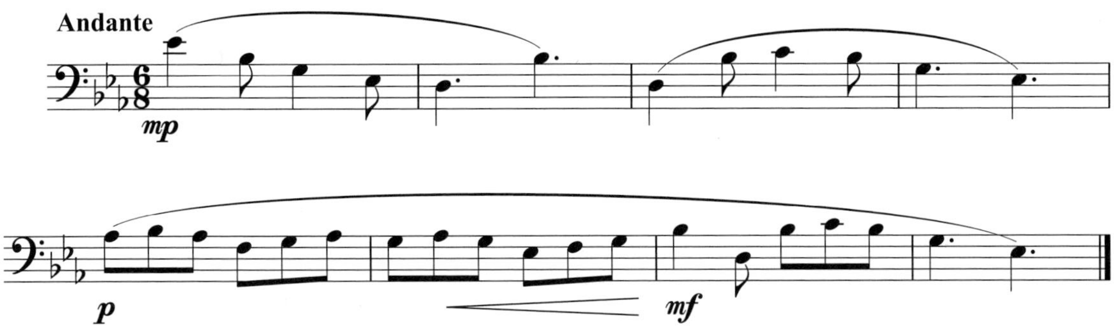


MELODY 2.5.8

MELODY 2.5.9

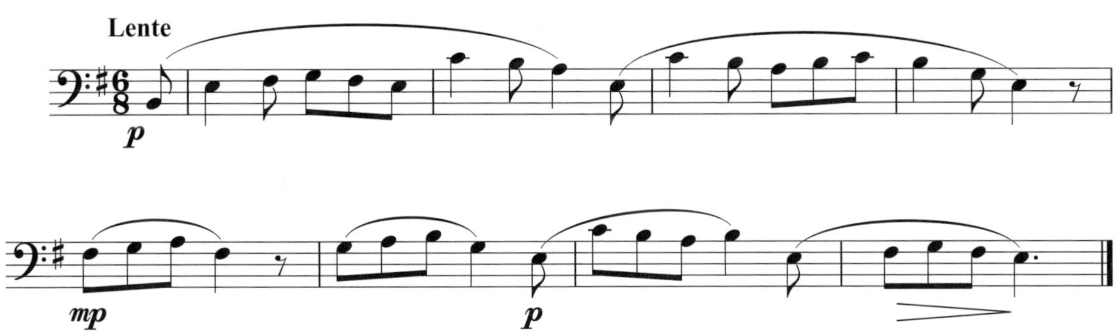

**MELODY 2.5.10**

**MELODY 2.5.11**

**MELODY 2.5.12**

**MELODY 2.5.13**

Improvise tonic harmony in the blank measure below:

**MELODY 2.5.14**

**MELODY 2.5.15**

## Duets

### DUET 2.5.1

### DUET 2.5.2

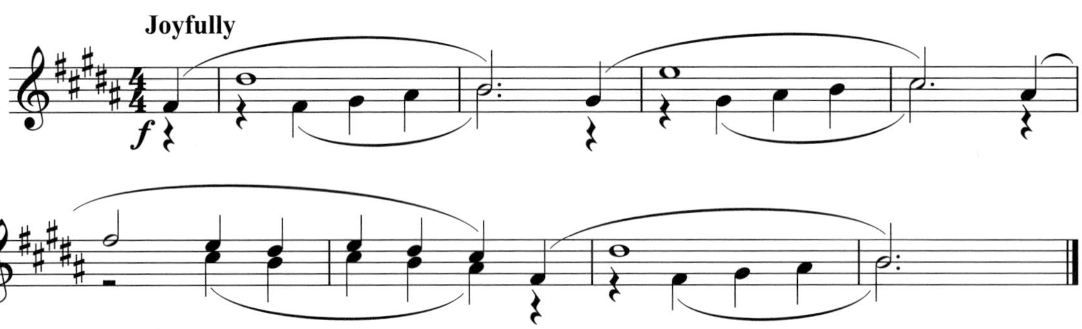


### DUET 2.5.3

## Chorale

### CHORALE 2.5

## Self-Accompanied Melody

### SELF-ACCOMPANIED MELODY 2.5

## 2.6 Minor Triads in Root Position

### Facts You Need to Know

Minor triads are often described as having a "dark," "sad," and stable sound.

Consist of a minor third between the root and third, a major third between the third and fifth, and perfect fifth between the root and fifth.

**EXAMPLE 2.6.1**

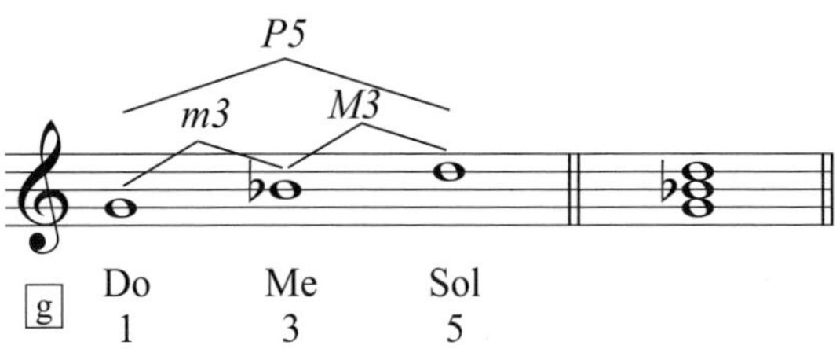


Minor triads occur in three places in the major scale:

1. As the supertonic (ii) triad, consisting of scale degrees 2, 4, and 6.
2. As the mediant (iii) triad, consisting of scale degrees 3, 5, and 7.
3. As the submediant (vi) triad, consisting of scale degrees 6, 1, and 3.

Minor triads occur in two places in the minor scale:

1. As the tonic (i) triad, consisting of scale degrees 1, 3, and 5.
2. As the subdominant (iv) triad, consisting of scale degrees 4, ♭6, and 1.

Orderings for root position minor triads are the same as orderings for major triads.

### Hearing

1. Listen for the dark, sad, and stable sound of the chord.
2. Listen for the component scale degrees. These will usually be 1, 3, and 5 in the minor mode, but be prepared that you could hear one of the other possibilities above.

### Singing

1. Use the tonic (i) triad in the minor mode consisting of scale degrees 1, 3, and 5 as your point of reference.
2. Based on the ordering of the triad you are asked to sing, determine the scale degree of the pitch that was given to you. It should be either scale degree 1, 3, or 5.

**EXAMPLE 2.6.2**

*Sing this pattern to find tonic if your given pitch is the...*

3. If necessary, sing the scale degree pattern for this pitch to find tonic.
4. Orient yourself in this key by singing its scale degree patterns.
5. Sing the component scale degrees in the correct order.

**EXAMPLE 2.6.3**

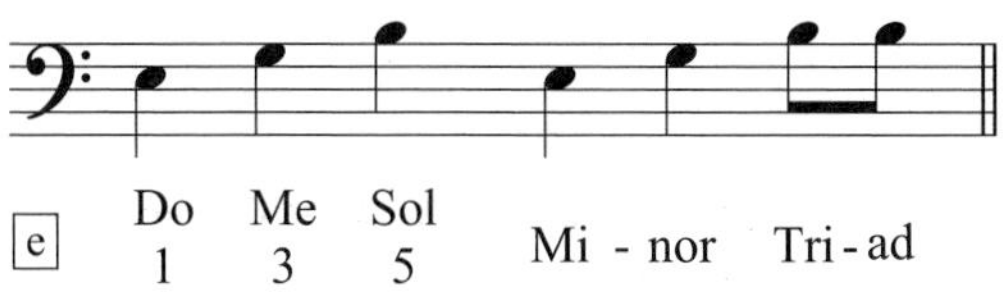


## Assignments for Practice

1. Sing through all six orderings of a minor triad beginning on the same pitch. Notice how the character, sound, and energy of your given pitch changes as you move through the orderings.
2. Listen for minor triads in the music you hear and perform.

**EXAMPLE 2.6.4**

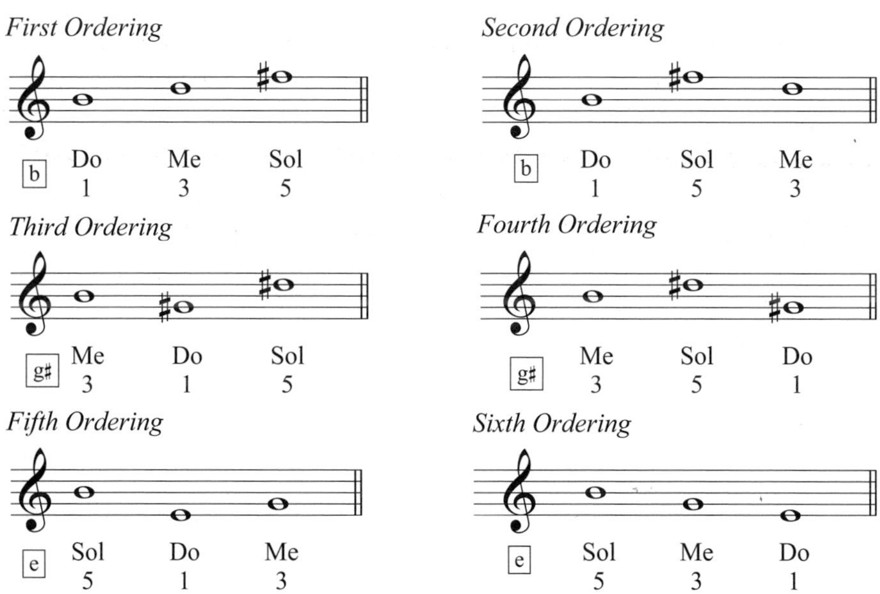

## Pitch Patterns

### PITCH PATTERN 2.6.1

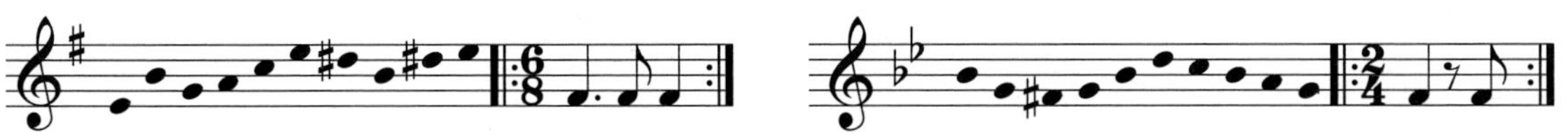

### PITCH PATTERN 2.6.2

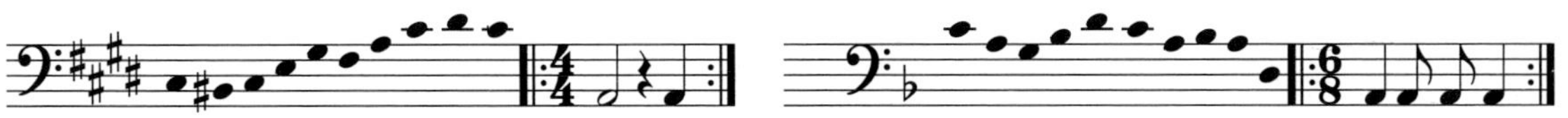

## Melodies

Look closely to determine the modality of each melody. In addition to key signature, look at the first and last pitch and accidentals. Most (but not all) music in a minor key will use accidentals to raise the leading tone. Be aware that some of these melodies may be in the major mode.

### MELODY 2.6.1

### MELODY 2.6.2

Improvise tonic harmony in the blank measures opposite:

**MELODY 2.6.3**

**MELODY 2.6.4**

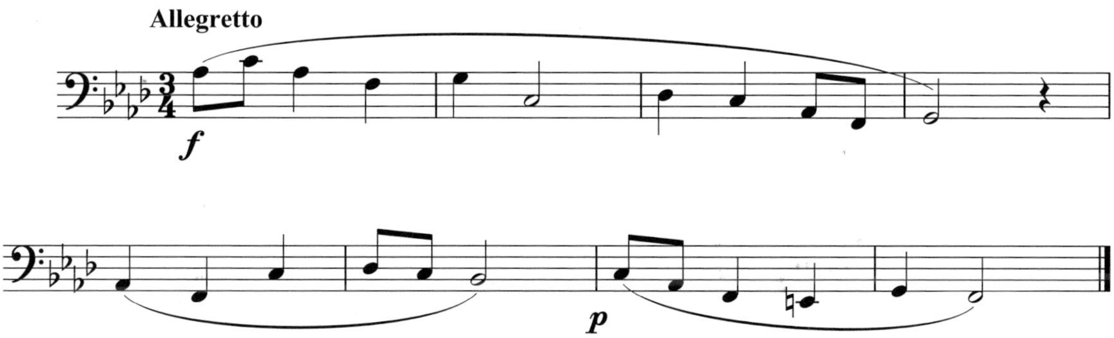


Improvise tonic harmony in the blank measures below:

**MELODY 2.6.5**

**MELODY 2.6.6**

**MELODY 2.6.7**

**MELODY 2.6.8**

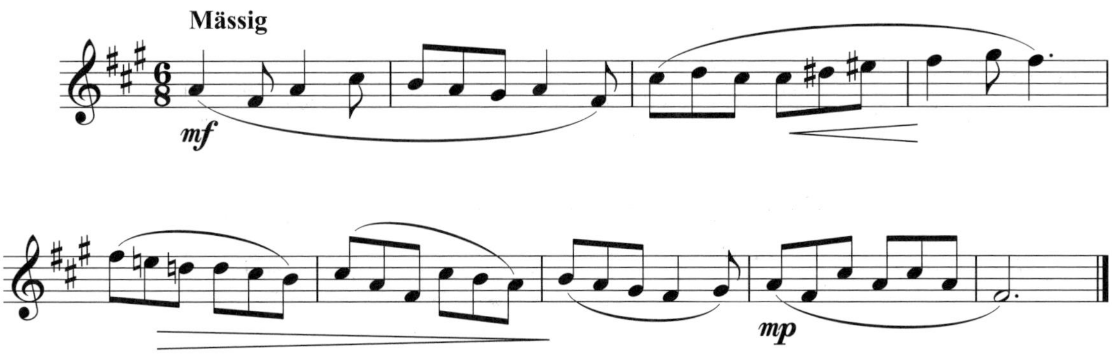


**MELODY 2.6.9**

**MELODY 2.6.10**

Improvise tonic harmony in the first two measures of the following melody. What do the combined articulation markings in measures 5 and 6 mean?

**MELODY 2.6.11**

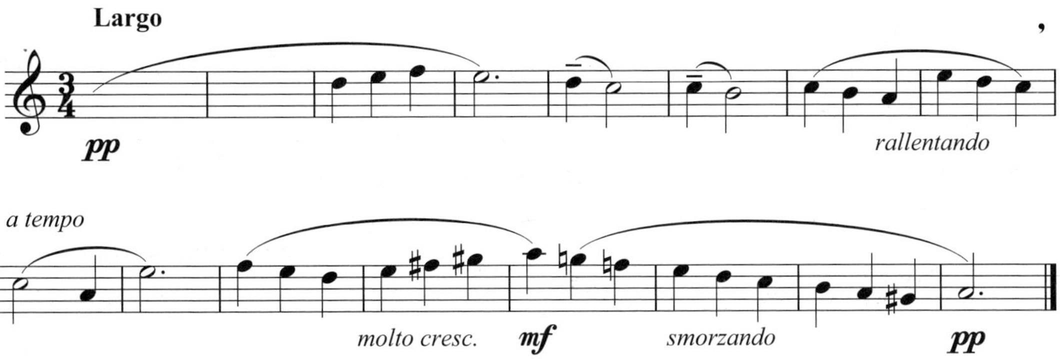


**MELODY 2.6.12**

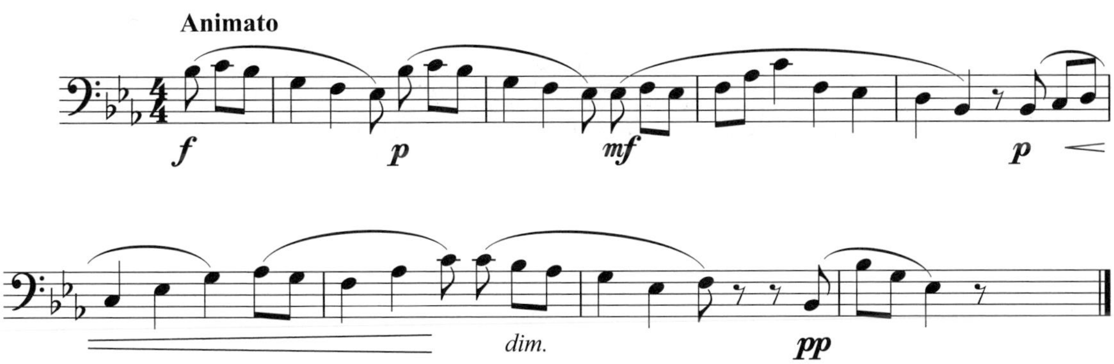


**MELODY 2.6.13**

## MELODY 2.6.14

## MELODY 2.6.15

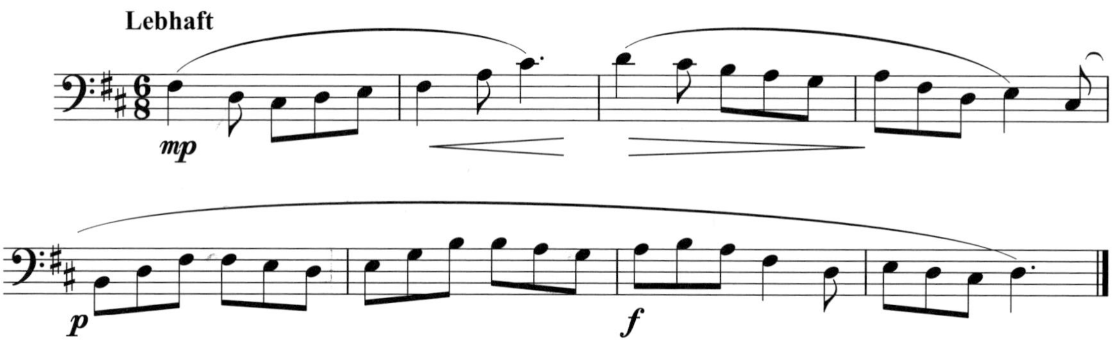


## Duets

## DUET 2.6.1

DUET 2.6.2

DUET 2.6.3

## Chorale

CHORALE 2.6

## Self-Accompanied Melody

### SELF-ACCOMPANIED MELODY 2.6

## 2.7 Major and Minor Triads in Inversion

### Facts You Need to Know

Triads possess three identifiers: root, quality, and inversion. We have already examined root position major and minor triads in this text.

Triads contain three chord members: the root, the third, and the fifth.

The inversion of a triad is determined by which of the three chord members occurs as the lowest pitch.

When the root of the chord is the lowest pitch, it is in root position.

When the third of the chord is the lowest pitch, it is in first inversion.

When the fifth of the chord is the lowest pitch, it is in second inversion.

The placement of the pitches above the bass note has no impact on the inversion of the triad. The following chords are all in first inversion:

**EXAMPLE 2.7.1**

## Hearing Inverted Triads

When listening to triads, begin by listening for quality. At present, we have studied only major and minor triads. Inverted triads generally retain the same general sound that identifies them as major or minor—bright and cheery for major or dark and sad for minor.

Next, listen for the scale degree of the bass or lowest pitch (triads can be in six orderings, so the lowest pitch might not always be the first pitch you hear). Taken out of context, root position triads will sound like scale degree 1 in the bass, first inversion will sound like scale degree 3 in the bass, and second inversion will sound like scale degree 5 in the bass.

Verify your answer by listening for the amount of stability in the triad—root position are most stable, first inversion have some instability, and second inversion have a lot of instability and sound like the upper pitches want to fall over into a more stable triad. Play the chords below to compare the sounds of the triadic inversions:

**EXAMPLE 2.7.2**

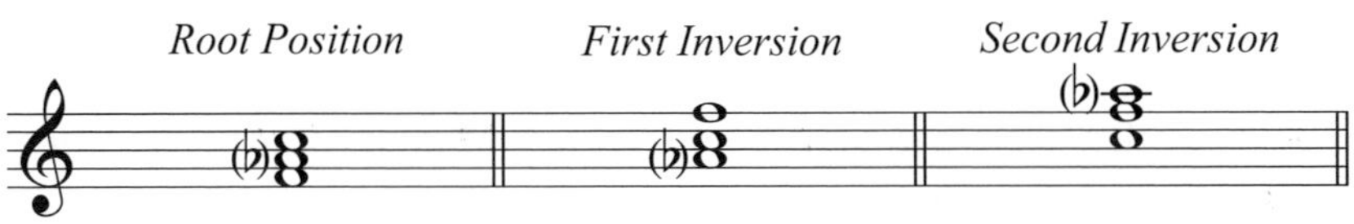


Indicate your answer by providing the quality (M or m) and inversion (using inversional symbol—nothing for root position, "6" for first inversion, and "$^6_4$" for second inversion.

## Singing

1. Determine the given pitch based on the information given to you. If you are asked to sing a root position triad, hear the given pitch as tonic; with first inversion it is scale degree 3, and with second inversion it is scale degree 5.
2. If necessary, find tonic and sing through the scale degree patterns in the correct mode to set up the key.
3. Sing the component scale degrees in the correct order.

**EXAMPLE 2.7.3**

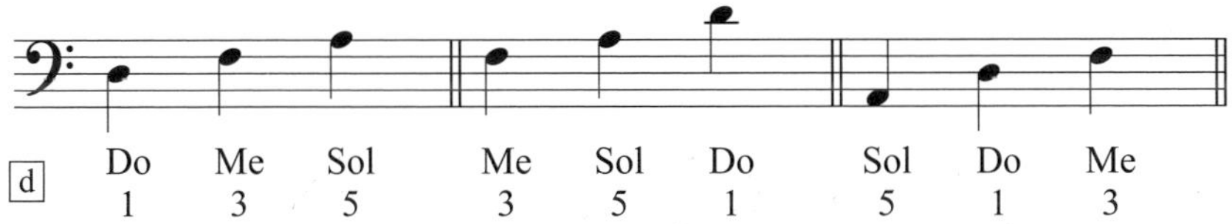


## Assignments for Practice

1. Practice singing root position, first inversion, and second inversion major and minor triads using the same starting pitch.

2. Sing through all six orderings of an inverted triad. Remember that ordering deals only with the placement of the high, middle, and low pitches in a triad.

## Pitch Patterns

### PITCH PATTERN 2.7.1

### PITCH PATTERN 2.7.2

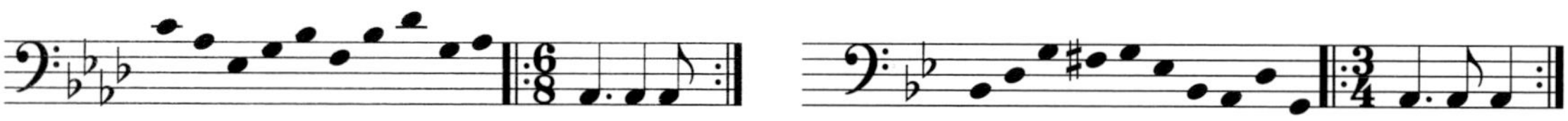

## Melodies

Find the triads in the following melodies. Identify their inversions and their component scale degrees. Remember to maintain their integrity by singing each pitch as a scale degree.

### MELODY 2.7.1

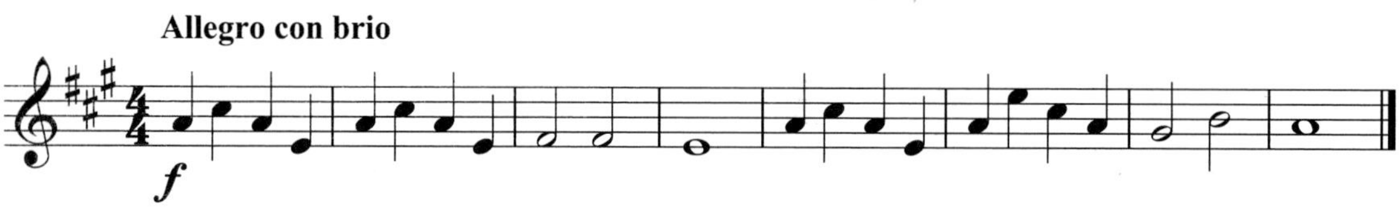


### MELODY 2.7.2

### MELODY 2.7.3

MELODY 2.7.4

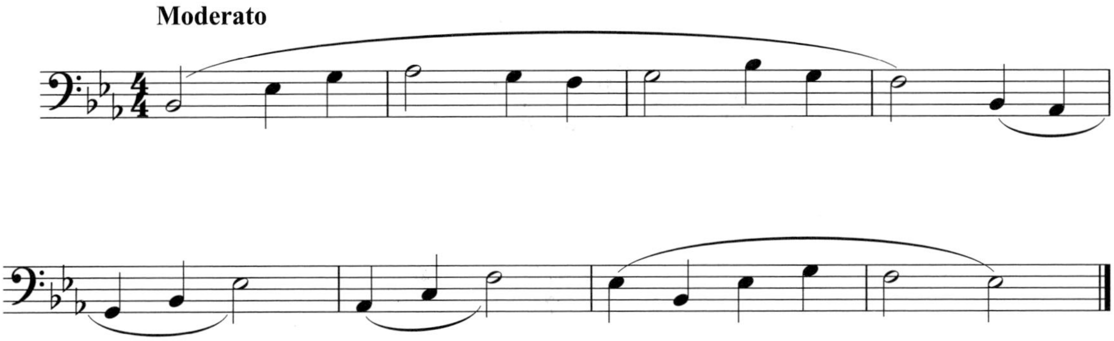


MELODY 2.7.5

MELODY 2.7.6

Describe the contour of the following melody and come up with two ways of bringing out that shape.

**MELODY 2.7.7**

**MELODY 2.7.8**

**MELODY 2.7.9**

**MELODY 2.7.10**

**MELODY 2.7.11**

**MELODY 2.7.12**

Improvise tonic harmony in the blank measure below:

**MELODY 2.7.13**

**MELODY 2.7.14**

What is a habanera? And what do you need to do to bring out this quality in the music?

**MELODY 2.7.15**

## Duets

**DUET 2.7.1**

**DUET 2.7.2**

## DUET 2.7.3

## Chorale

## CHORALE 2.7

## Self-Accompanied Melody

### SELF-ACCOMPANIED MELODY 2.7

## 2.8 Music from the Literature

### EXAMPLE 2.8.1

"The Doll's Burial," from *Album for the Young*, Op. 39, No. 7

**EXAMPLE 2.8.2**

**EXAMPLE 2.8.3**

**EXAMPLE 2.8.4**

**EXAMPLE 2.8.5**

**EXAMPLE 2.8.6**

*Violin Concerto in A Minor*,
Op. 3, No.6, Second movement

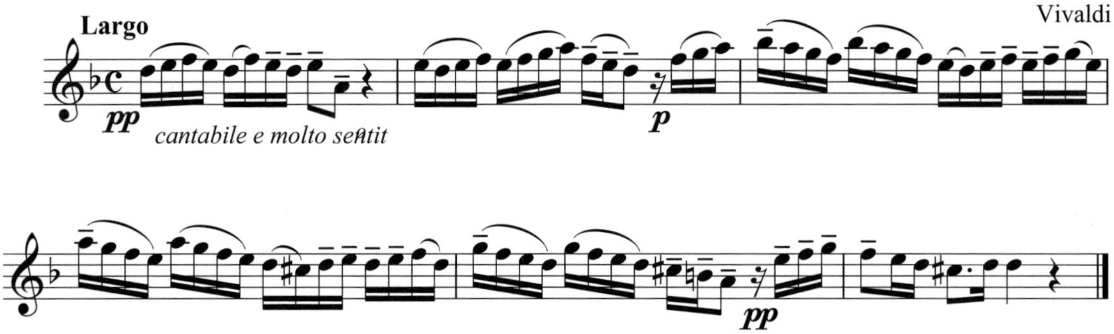


**EXAMPLE 2.8.7**

"Erstarrung," from *Winterreise*

**EXAMPLE 2.8.8**

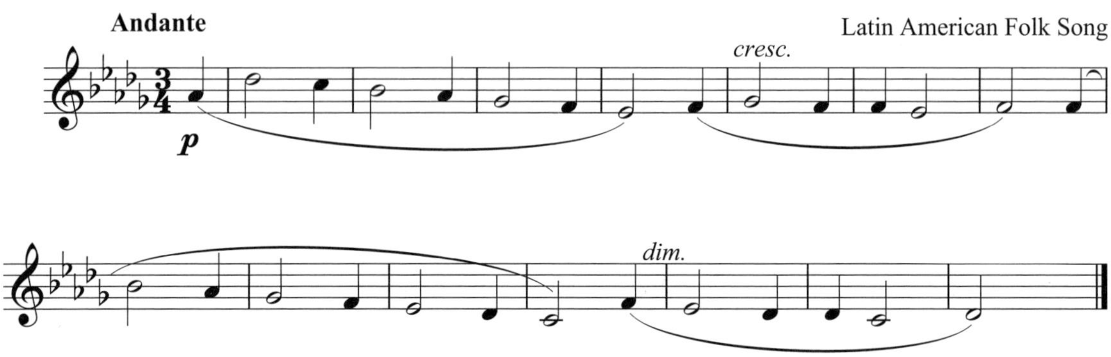


**EXAMPLE 2.8.9**

**EXAMPLE 2.8.10**

*Piano Sonata in E-flat Major*, K. 282,
Second movement, opening

**EXAMPLE 2.8.11**

*Aus den hebräischen Gesängen*,
Op. 25, No. 3

**EXAMPLE 2.8.12**

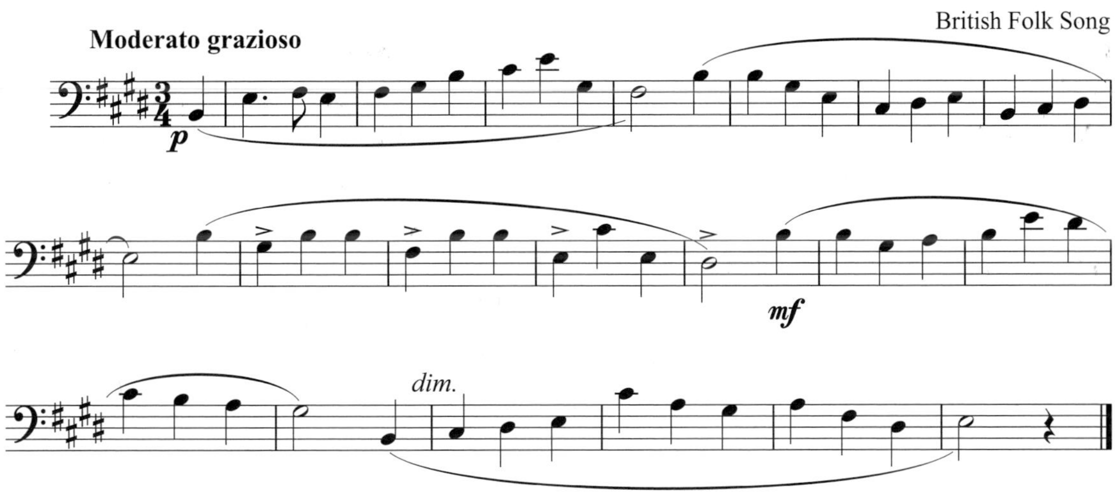


**EXAMPLE 2.8.13**

*Sonatina in C Major*,
Op. 36, No. 1, Second movement

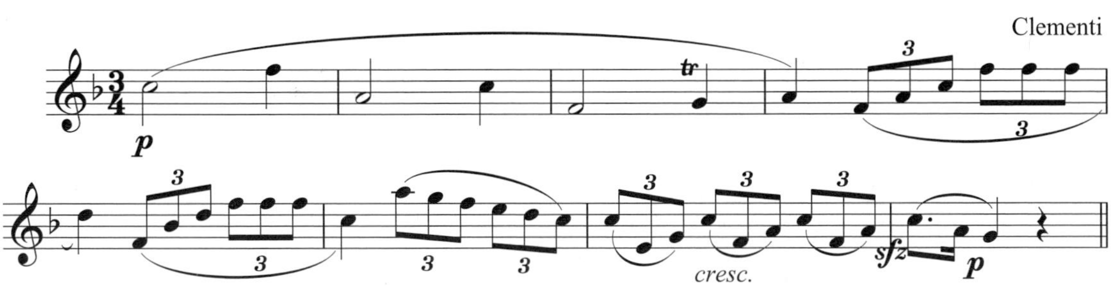

**EXAMPLE 2.8.14**

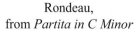

Rondeau,
from *Partita in C Minor*

J.S. Bach

**EXAMPLE 2.8.15**

"I Attempt from Love's Sickness,"
from *The Indian Queen*

Purcell

**EXAMPLE 2.8.16**

*Pietá, Signore!*

**Andantino**

Alessandro Stradella

**EXAMPLE 2.8.17**

*An den Sonnenschein*,
Op. 36, No. 4

**Im Volkston**

Schumann

**EXAMPLE 2.8.18**

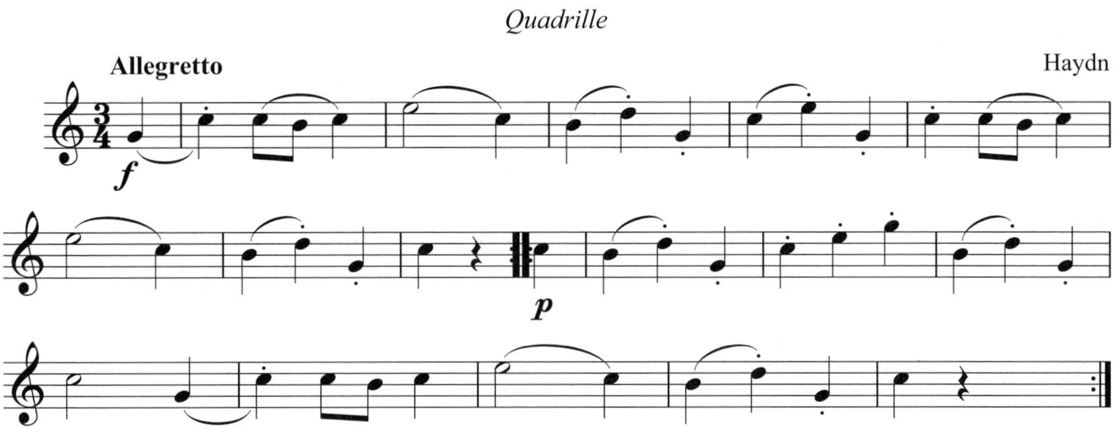


## Reflections: Professionalism

Professionalism is a set of attitudes and behaviors that are expected from practitioners of any field. This time of your life—your collegiate music study—is a time when you need to be learning and practicing the behaviors that are expected of musicians.

Musicians must be conversant in the multiple languages, styles, philosophies, structures, and idioms in which they are expected to perform. You must be able to understand musical systems well enough to enable you to transpose music to any key on the night of a performance, stylistically improvise a part within an ensemble, and musically realize a composer's or conductor's verbal instructions quickly and accurately.

Musicians must also understand how the music field works. Whether it involves networking with other musicians, understanding contracts, marketing yourself to contractors, or collaborating with other professionals, musicians must find and understand their place and obligations within the wider musical community.

Musicians are expected to demonstrate personal integrity, or a firm adherence to a set of values relating to ethical behavior and artistic excellence. Values such as honesty, forthrightness, and sincerity are essential for forming and maintaining relationships that will sustain your reputation and career. Professionals do not take ethical short cuts such as representing someone else's work or ideas as their own or presenting un- or under-prepared work. Artistic integrity is the adherence to a strict set of principles that govern how you will make artistic decisions. It also includes the principle that you will never let yourself make an unprepared or unmusical sound in any performance, whether for a teacher or an audience.

Musicians are also expected to perform acceptably well, even on their worst day. This characteristic is only developed one way—through diligent, regular, and efficiently directed practice.

A professional demonstrates self-respect through taking care of his or her mind and body. These characteristics are key for longevity in a career, and they ensure that you will be ready to perform artistically and effectively when the next professional opportunity comes along.

Confidence is an expression of self-respect and is only genuinely acquired through competence. It is the foundation on which all of your musical skills will rest, allowing you to develop a deeper and significant presence in the community of musicians. As musicians, we are constantly being told to find and correct our performance mistakes and to take extraordinary measures to make improvements to our performance. We are also constantly reminded of intense competition for jobs that we can only attain through demonstrating that we are "better" than other musicians in a competitive audition. In such an environment, it is very easy to lose sight of three important facts:

1. One's goal should be constant improvement, not perfection (which is unattainable anyway).
2. You wouldn't be where you are today if you weren't doing many things correctly—force yourself to focus on the positive and aim to transform the negatives into positives (instead of just identifying what is wrong).
3. Ultimately, we make music from and for ourselves, as a way of sharing what is most precious and unique within our souls.

Professional musicians manage their lives and obligations with responsibility and accountability. This includes being able to accomplish all of the multiple tasks you need to get done, including school work, practice, rehearsal, performance, personal tasks, and other jobs. No matter what the obligation, you need to make time to do it to the best of your ability. More importantly, you need to be able to prioritize and take inventory of your obligations and be able to say no to those that are less significant, or fulfilling others when you can. Accountability deals with establishing and maintaining the confidence that others can depend on you. It involves the ability to make and keep commitments (like showing up for rehearsals and performances) and the establishment of a standard of excellence.

Music is fundamentally about communication. As important as communicating in one's artistic medium is the ability to communicate about one's artistic medium through speaking and writing. In practice and rehearsal, you must be able to articulate where problems are occurring and offer concrete suggestions for correction. Most musicians make a substantial part of their living through teaching, which in essence is a highly refined form of directed communication. You are also an ambassador for the styles of music that you perform. You must be able to effectively communicate the relevance, necessity, and joy of what you do.

Professionals have a strong interest in making sure that their art and craft continue to develop. Most people begin their musical study with the belief that music is the vehicle through which they will fulfill their career aspirations. Professionals soon come to realize that just as music serves them, they have a responsibility to serve the art. This involves being an advocate for high-quality musical experiences, providing opportunities for the continued development and growth of your art, and adherence to the highest standards of performance and ethical behavior.

## 2.9 Dictation Materials

@

### I. Identification of Minor Scale Degrees

Your teacher will establish a key and then play its scale degrees in random order or as a specific pitch in a melody (by number—first, second, last, or by position—high or low). Identify each by writing its number in the appropriate space. Place an up arrow in front of scale degree 6 or 7 if you hear either of them in their raised position.

*Date:* . . . . . . . . . . . . . .

1. ____ 2. ____ 3. ____ 4. ____ 5. ____ 6. ____ 7. ____ 8. ____

*Date:* . . . . . . . . . . . . . .

1. ____ 2. ____ 3. ____ 4. ____ 5. ____ 6. ____ 7. ____ 8. ____

*Date:* . . . . . . . . . . . . . .

1. ____ 2. ____ 3. ____ 4. ____ 5. ____ 6. ____ 7. ____ 8. ____

*Date:* . . . . . . . . . . . . . .

1. ____ 2. ____ 3. ____ 4. ____ 5. ____ 6. ____ 7. ____ 8. ____

*Date:* . . . . . . . . . . . . . .

1. ____ 2. ____ 3. ____ 4. ____ 5. ____ 6. ____ 7. ____ 8. ____

## II. Identification of Major Scale Degrees

Your teacher will establish a key and then play its scale degrees in random order or as a specific pitch in a melody (by number—first, second, last, or by position—high or low). Identify each by writing its number in the appropriate space.

*Date:* . . . . . . . . . . . . . .

1. ____ 2. ____ 3. ____ 4. ____ 5. ____ 6. ____ 7. ____ 8. ____

*Date:* . . . . . . . . . . . . . .

1. ____ 2. ____ 3. ____ 4. ____ 5. ____ 6. ____ 7. ____ 8. ____

*Date:* . . . . . . . . . . . . . .

1. ____ 2. ____ 3. ____ 4. ____ 5. ____ 6. ____ 7. ____ 8. ____

*Date:* . . . . . . . . . . . . . .

1. ____ 2. ____ 3. ____ 4. ____ 5. ____ 6. ____ 7. ____ 8. ____

*Date:* . . . . . . . . . . . . . .

1. ____ 2. ____ 3. ____ 4. ____ 5. ____ 6. ____ 7. ____ 8. ____

## III. Interval Identification

Your teacher will play several intervals. Identify their quality and size as one of the following:

M2 = Major second
m2 = Minor second
M3 = Major third
m3 = Minor third

P4 = Perfect fourth
P5 = Perfect fifth
M6 = Major sixth
m6 = Minor sixth

P8 = Perfect octave
X = Other

Be sure to make a clear difference between your capital and lower-case Ms.

*Date:* . . . . . . . . . . . . . .

1. ____ 2. ____ 3. ____ 4. ____ 5. ____ 6. ____ 7. ____ 8. ____

*Date:* . . . . . . . . . . . . . .

1. ____ 2. ____ 3. ____ 4. ____ 5. ____ 6. ____ 7. ____ 8. ____

*Date:* . . . . . . . . . . . . . .

1. ____ 2. ____ 3. ____ 4. ____ 5. ____ 6. ____ 7. ____ 8. ____

*Date:* . . . . . . . . . . . . . .

1. ____ 2. ____ 3. ____ 4. ____ 5. ____ 6. ____ 7. ____ 8. ____

*Date:* . . . . . . . . . . . . . .

1. ____ 2. ____ 3. ____ 4. ____ 5. ____ 6. ____ 7. ____ 8. ____

## IV. Meter Identification

Your teacher will play several melodies. Listen for the metric division and number. Write a logical meter signature for each example. Possible answers are $\frac{2}{4}, \frac{3}{4}, \frac{4}{4}, \frac{2}{2}, \frac{6}{8}, \frac{9}{8}, \frac{12}{8}$ or “X” for other.

*Date:* . . . . . . . . . . . . . .

1. ____ 2. ____ 3. ____ 4. ____ 5. ____ 6. ____ 7. ____ 8. ____

*Date:* . . . . . . . . . . . . . .

1. ____ 2. ____ 3. ____ 4. ____ 5. ____ 6. ____ 7. ____ 8. ____

*Date:* . . . . . . . . . . . . . .

1. ____ 2. ____ 3. ____ 4. ____ 5. ____ 6. ____ 7. ____ 8. ____

*Date:* . . . . . . . . . . . . . .

1. ____ 2. ____ 3. ____ 4. ____ 5. ____ 6. ____ 7. ____ 8. ____

*Date:* . . . . . . . . . . . . . .

1. ____ 2. ____ 3. ____ 4. ____ 5. ____ 6. ____ 7. ____ 8. ____

## V. Melodic and Rhythmic Dictation

Your teacher will play a short melody or rhythm. Notate it on the staves below.

*Date:* . . . . . . . . . . . . . .

*Date:* . . . . . . . . . . . . . .

*Date:* . . . . . . . . . . . . . .

*Date:* . . . . . . . . . . . . . .

*Date:* . . . . . . . . . . . . . .

# Chapter 3

# Changing Meter; Second Division in Compound Meter; The Dominant Sound

## 3.1 Changing Meter I: Simple Changing Meter

### Facts You Need to Know

Simple changing meter refers to meter changes that occur between measures that have the same beat-note value, such as $\frac{3}{4}$ to $\frac{4}{4}$ or $\frac{6}{8}$ to $\frac{9}{8}$. The African American folk song "The Swallow" is an example of simple changing meter:

**EXAMPLE 3.1.1**

Lit-tle swal-low, fly to your nest, Who goes there, fly a fly a - way now.
Lit - tle swal - low, fly to your nest, fly a fly a - way.

Changing meter is essentially a study of metric integrity. When performing a piece that involves changing meter, it is essential to maintain the character of each individual meter, so that the listener can discern the metric stresses.

Hemiola (a rhythmic device where three groups of two are superimposed over two groups of three, or vice versa) is a common manifestation of changing meter. Unlike typical changing meter examples, the meter changes are shown through the phrasing or articulation, rather than written out. Measures 5–6 in the melody below, from the third movement of Ravel's *Valses Nobles et Sentimentales*, is an example of hemiola:

**EXAMPLE 3.1.2**

## Rhythms

Practice these rhythms first by just conducting; add the rhythm after you feel confident with the conducting pattern changes.

### RHYTHM 3.1.1

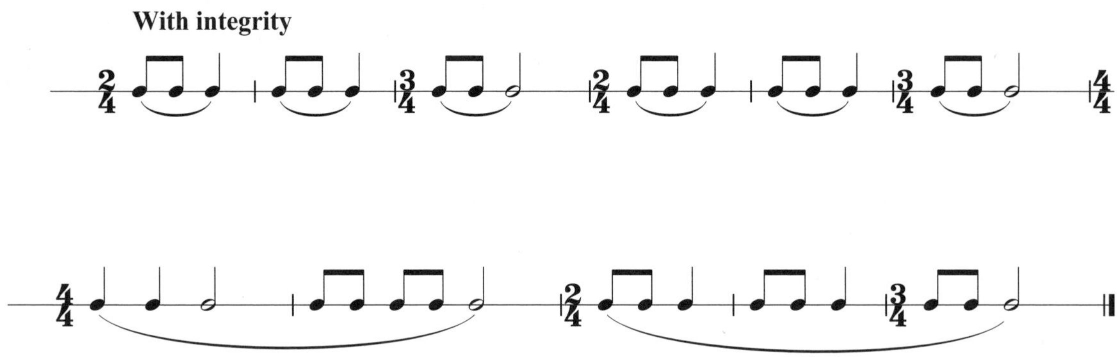


### RHYTHM 3.1.2

### RHYTHM 3.1.3

RHYTHM 3.1.4

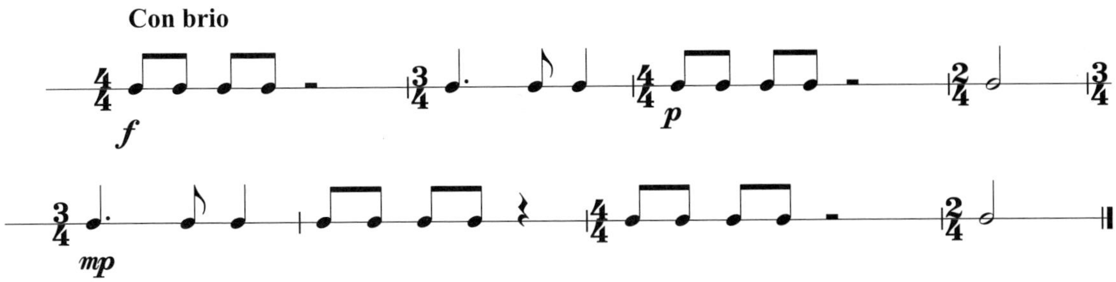


RHYTHM 3.1.5

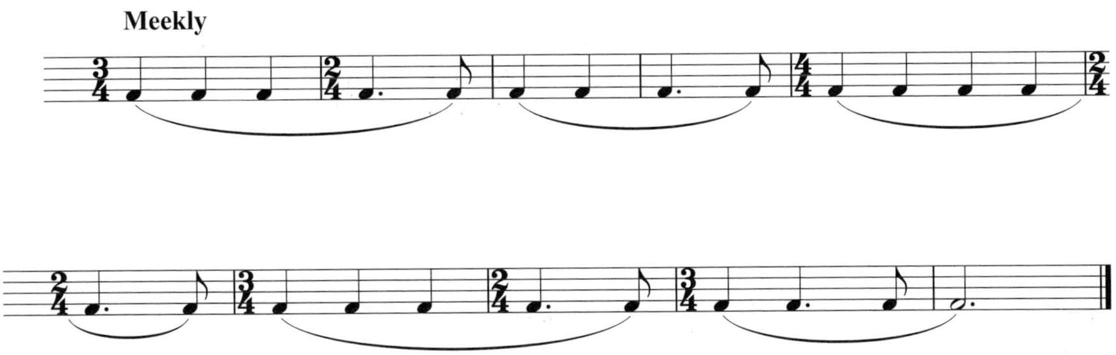


RHYTHM 3.1.6

RHYTHM 3.1.7

**RHYTHM 3.1.8**

**RHYTHM 3.1.9**

**RHYTHM 3.1.10**

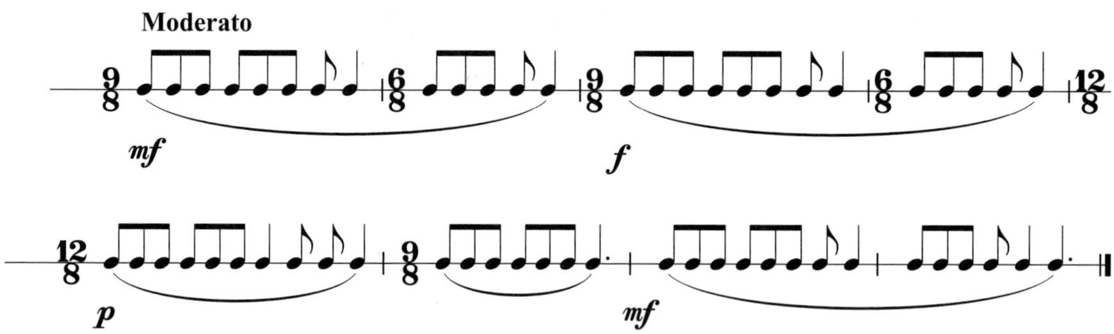


**RHYTHM 3.1.11**

Improvise a rhythm to fit with the metric structure opposite. Try to repeat rhythmic elements to unify your improvisation.

### RHYTHM 3.1.12

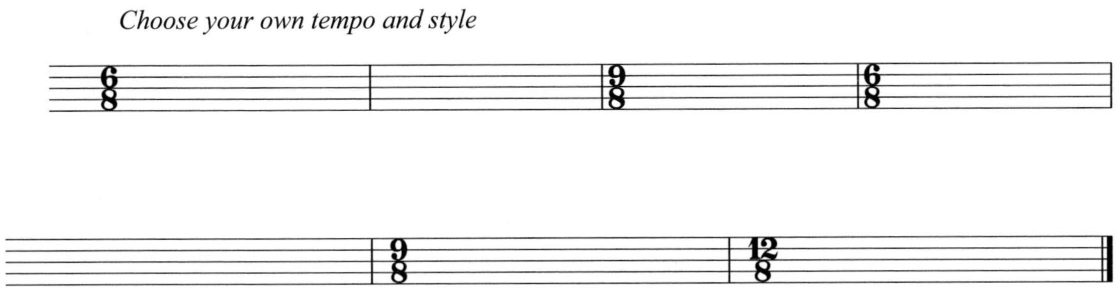


## Two-part Rhythms

### TWO-PART RHYTHM 3.1.1

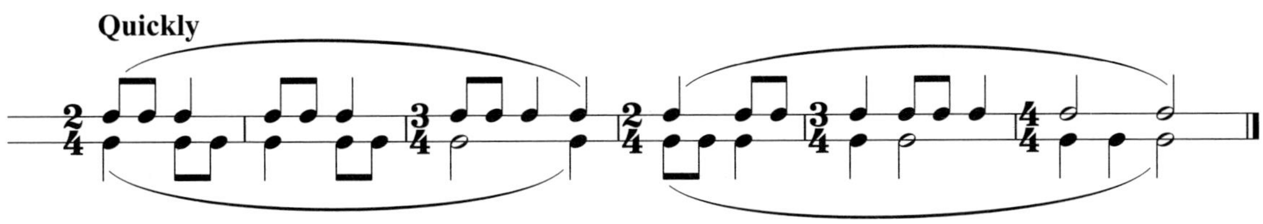


### TWO-PART RHYTHM 3.1.2

## Three-part Rhythm

### THREE-PART RHYTHM 3.1

## 3.2 Second Division of the Beat in Compound Meter

### Facts You Need to Know

Second division of the beat in compound meter occurs when the eighth-note division of the beat is doubled, as shown in the example below:

**EXAMPLE 3.2.1**

A phenomenon unique to second division in compound meter is that it combines both binary and ternary groupings. By definition, the beat in compound meter is divided into three parts (ternary structure), but each of those divisions is divided into only two parts (binary structure). Thus, there is a simple beat structure within compound meter.

The result of this phenomenon is that, depending on the articulation, melodic structure, and harmonic outline, the sixteenths can be perceived in a variety of ways. Below, the first beat in the measure shows a melodic arpeggiation of rhythmic figure, and the second, a primarily stepwise figure. The effect of the melodic structure gives a sense of line and sweep to the pattern. The listener hears a strong sense of the beat decorated by figuration, making the underlying (or outlining) rhythm figure the beat.

**EXAMPLE 3.2.2**

The next example results in a completely different perception of the same rhythm. The two-note slurs outline the sense of the eighth-note division; thus, the underlying rhythm becomes the division of the beat.

**EXAMPLE 3.2.3**

In the following example, the melodic structure divides the sixteenths into two groups of three, creating a hemiola effect between the divisions and melodic outline.

**EXAMPLE 3.2.4**

## Preparatory Exercises

Practice each of the following rhythms in preparation for reading more complex rhythms that use second division of the beat in compound meter. Always clap the divisions while you articulate the rhythm; they will provide a guidepost as you perform the rhythm.

You may find it helpful to count divisions or subdivisions while you clap; those numbers are provided underneath the rhythms.

**EXAMPLE 3.2.5**

1 2 3 4 5 6 1 2 3 4 5 6 1 2 3 4 5 6

Count with "a's" or without; in either case, line up the rhythms with the eighth-note divisions.

**EXAMPLE 3.2.6**

1 a 2 a 3 1 a 2 a 3 1 2 a 3 a 1 2 a 3 a

**EXAMPLE 3.2.7**

1 a 2 3 1 2 a 3 1 2 3 a

Look carefully at the rhythms below. Perform each by clapping the divisions and articulating the rhythm. Listen for accurate placement of the sixteenth note in the dotted-eighth-sixteenth figure below.

**EXAMPLE 3.2.8**

1 2 a 3

Notice that the sixteenth notes start on and not in between the divisions in the rhythm below.

**EXAMPLE 3.2.9**

1 2 3 a

**EXAMPLE 3.2.10**

1 2 a 3 a

**EXAMPLE 3.2.11**

## Rhythms

**RHYTHM 3.2.1**

**RHYTHM 3.2.2**

**RHYTHM 3.2.3**

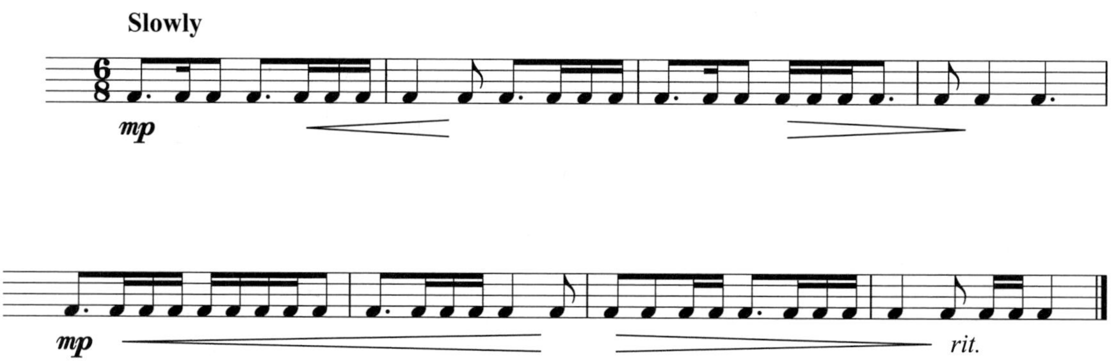

**RHYTHM 3.2.4**

**RHYTHM 3.2.5**

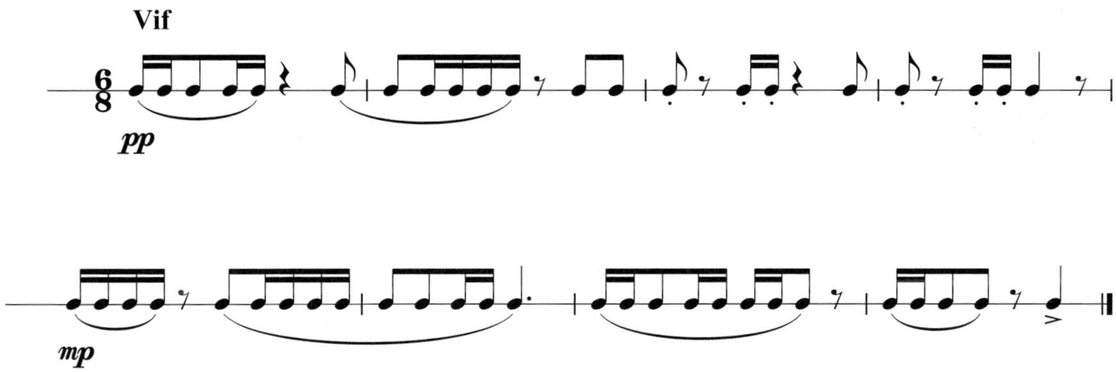


**RHYTHM 3.2.6**

**RHYTHM 3.2.7**

**RHYTHM 3.2.8**

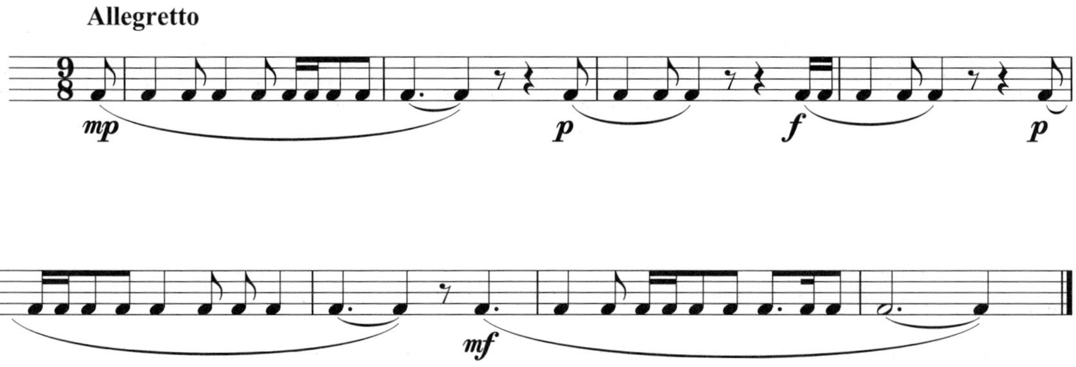


**RHYTHM 3.2.9**

**RHYTHM 3.2.10**

## Two-part Rhythms

**TWO-PART RHYTHM 3.2.1**

### TWO-PART RHYTHM 3.2.2

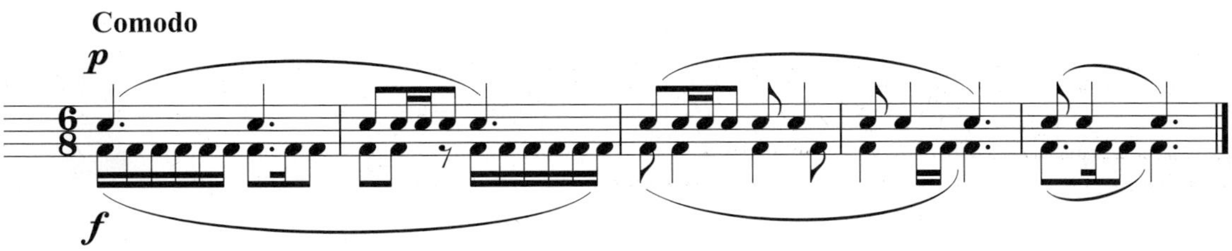


### TWO-PART RHYTHM 3.2.3

## Three-part Rhythm

### THREE-PART RHYTHM 3.2

## 3.3 Minor Sevenths and Tritones

### Minor Sevenths

**Facts You Need to Know**

Minor sevenths are wide and dissonant intervals.

Minor sevenths occur in five places in the major scale:

1. Between scale degrees 5 and 4
2. Between scale degrees 2 and 1
3. Between scale degrees 3 and 2
4. Between scale degrees 6 and 5
5. Between scale degrees 7 and 6

Minor sevenths occur in seven places in the minor scale:

1. Between scale degrees 1 and ♭7
2. Between scale degrees 2 and 1
3. Between scale degrees 4 and 3
4. Between scale degrees 5 and 4
5. Between scale degrees ♯6 and 5
6. Between scale degrees ♭7 and ♭6
7. Between scale degrees ♯7 and ♯6

Minor sevenths most commonly appear as scale degrees 5 and 4. These intervals strongly suggest a dominant sound because they are the root and seventh of the dominant seventh chord.

### Hearing

Begin by hearing the strong dominant sound of the interval. You will likely want to hear the top pitch resolving down by step to scale degree 3 and the bottom leaping up a perfect fourth to scale degree 1.

**EXAMPLE 3.3.1**

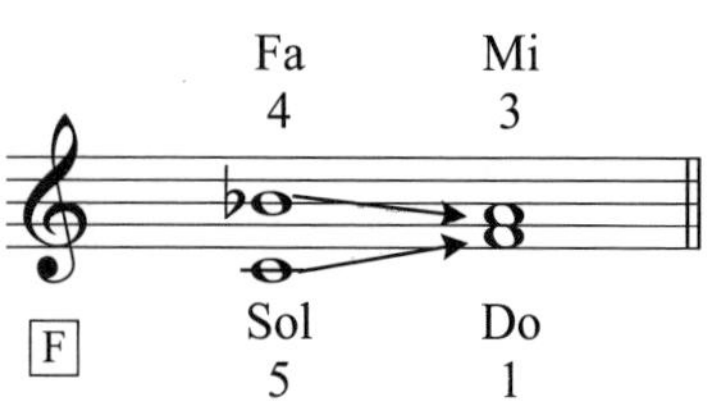


When played harmonically, listen for the interval's dissonant quality and wide spacing.

## Singing

Use scale degrees 5 to 4 in the major mode as your point of reference.

If ascending, hear the given pitch as scale degree 5. Sing an alternate pattern to find tonic. If necessary, orient yourself around this tonic pitch. Hear the higher pitch as scale degree 4. Sing the interval quality and size.

**EXAMPLE 3.3.2**

If descending, hear the given pitch as scale degree 4. Sing its scale degree pattern to find tonic. If necessary, orient yourself around this tonic pitch. Hear the lower pitch as scale degree 5. Sing the interval quality and size.

**EXAMPLE 3.3.3**

### Tritones

### Facts You Need to Know

Tritones are very strong intervals of medium width. Tritones occur in two places in the major mode:

1. Between scale degrees 4 and 7 (as an augmented fourth)
2. Between scale degrees 7 and 4 (as a diminished fifth)

Tritones occur in four places in the minor mode:

1. Between scale degrees 4 and ♯7 (as an augmented fourth)
2. Between scale degrees ♯7 and 4 (as a diminished fifth)
3. Between scale degrees 2 and ♭6 (as a diminished fifth)
4. Between scale degrees ♭6 and 2 (as an augmented fourth)

The tritone is one of the most defining elements of a dominant seventh chord.

## Hearing

Listen for a middle-sized, dissonant interval. Hear both pitches wanting to resolve by half step either in on each other or out away from each other.

**EXAMPLE 3.3.4**

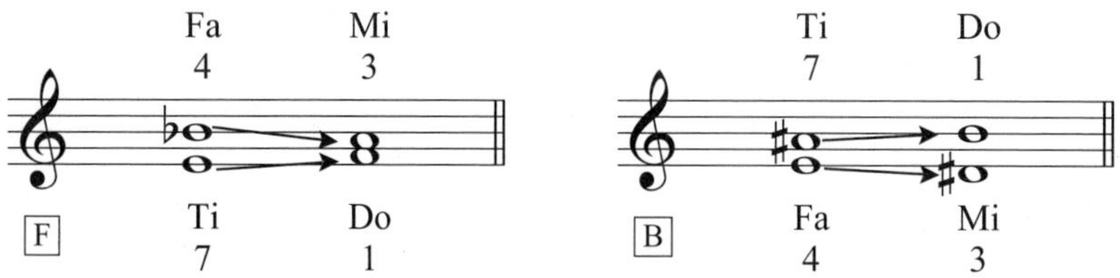


## Singing

Use scale degrees 7 and 4 in the major mode as your point of reference. Hear the given pitch as scale degree 7. Sing its pattern to find tonic, then orient yourself around this pitch. Find scale degree 4 above or below tonic, depending on the direction of the interval. Sing the interval quality and size.

**EXAMPLE 3.3.5**

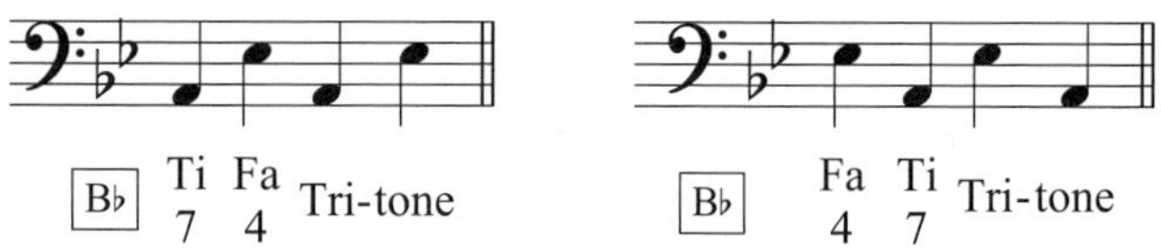


## Assignments for Practice

1. Practice giving yourself a pitch and singing minor sevenths and tritones above and below it.
2. Practice giving yourself a pitch and singing all of the intervals you have studied above and below it.
3. Listen for and identify minor sevenths and tritones in music that you hear, sing, or practice.

### Pitch Patterns

**PITCH PATTERN 3.3.1**

**PITCH PATTERN 3.3.2**

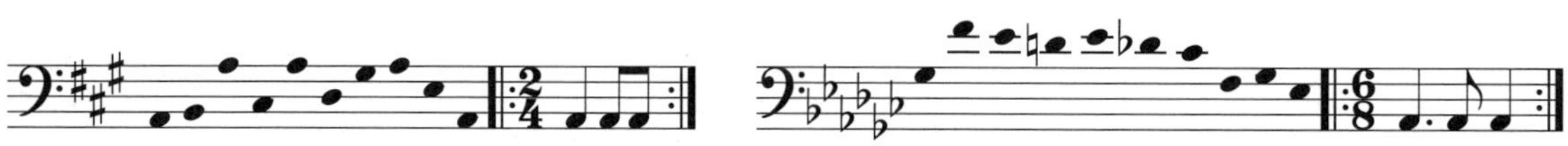

## Melodies

### MELODY 3.3.1

### MELODY 3.3.2

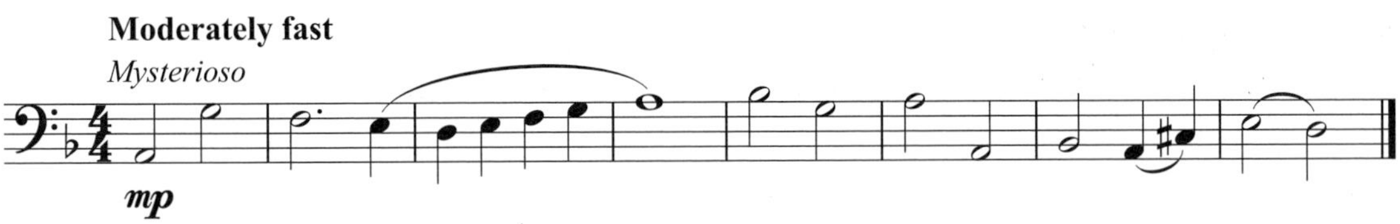


### MELODY 3.3.3

### MELODY 3.3.4

### MELODY 3.3.5

## MELODY 3.3.6

## MELODY 3.3.7

## MELODY 3.3.8

## MELODY 3.3.9

**MELODY 3.3.10**

**MELODY 3.3.11**

**MELODY 3.3.12**

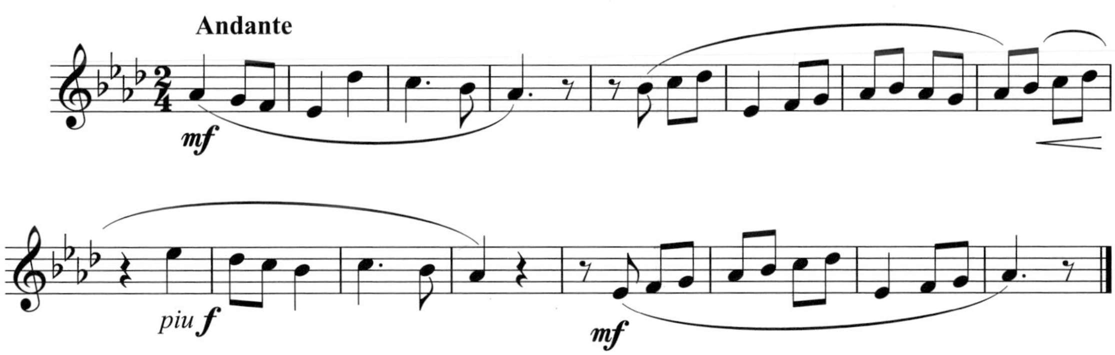


What structural characteristic of the second half of this melody makes it easier to sing, despite all of the wide leaps?

**MELODY 3.3.13**

Where is the focal point of the following melody? How do the minor sevenths that precede it heighten the sense of musical expectation?

### MELODY 3.3.14

### MELODY 3.3.15

## Duets

### DUET 3.3.1

## DUET 3.3.2

## DUET 3.3.3

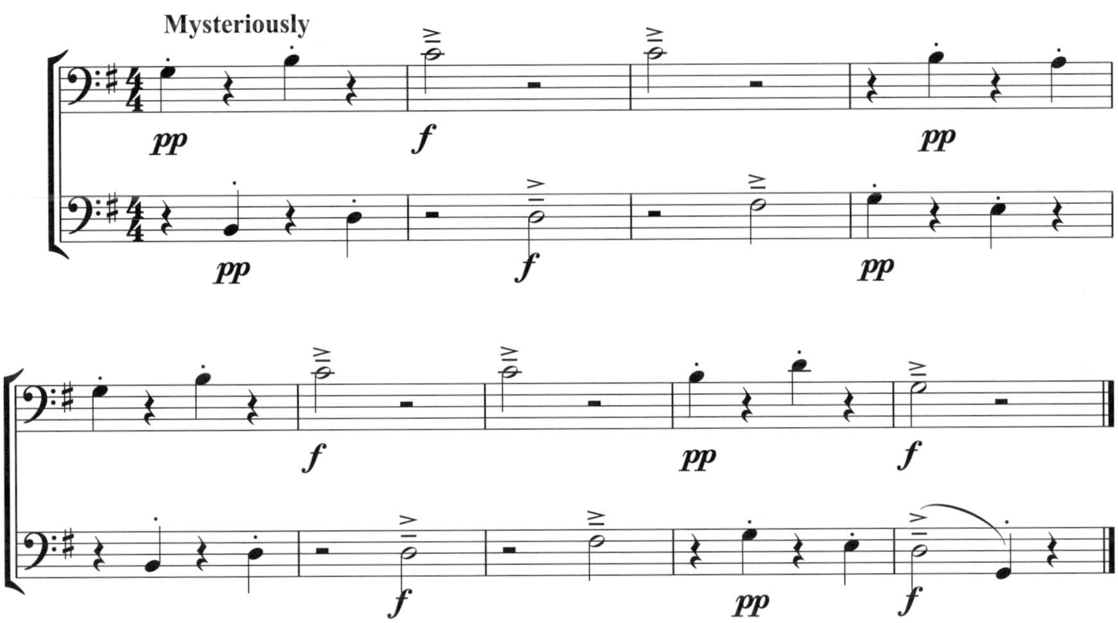

## Chorale

### CHORALE 3.3

## Self-Accompanied Melody

### SELF-ACCOMPANIED MELODY 3.3

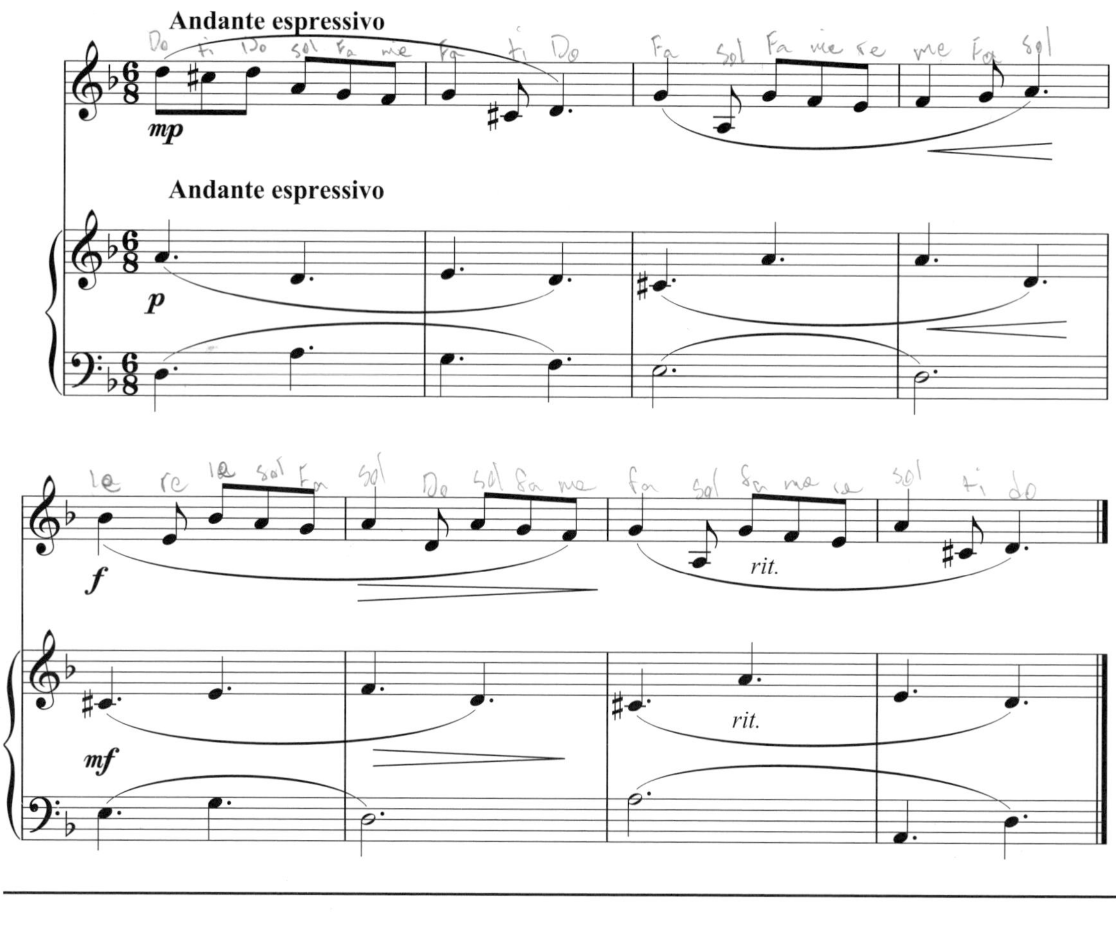

## 3.4 Dominant Seventh Chords

### Facts You Need to Know

Dominant seventh chords are one of the most tonally defining sounds in music. Most people know where tonic is after hearing only a dominant seventh chord. They occur on scale degree 5 in both the major and minor mode, and consist of scale degree 5, 7, 2, and 4. The interval structure of a dominant seventh chord appears below:

**EXAMPLE 3.4.1**

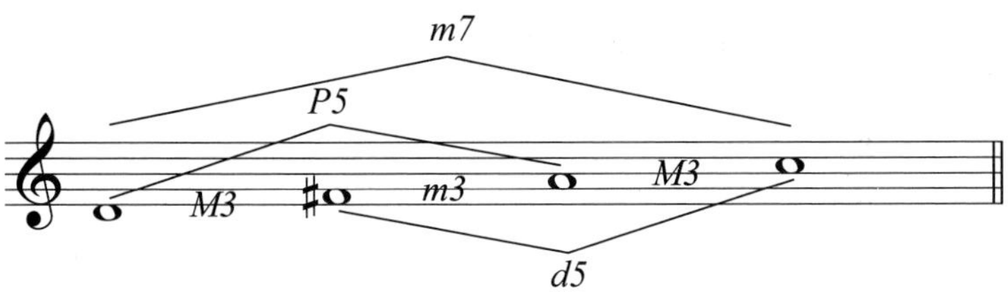


Each tone in a dominant seventh chord has a strong desire to resolve in a particular way:

**EXAMPLE 3.4.2**

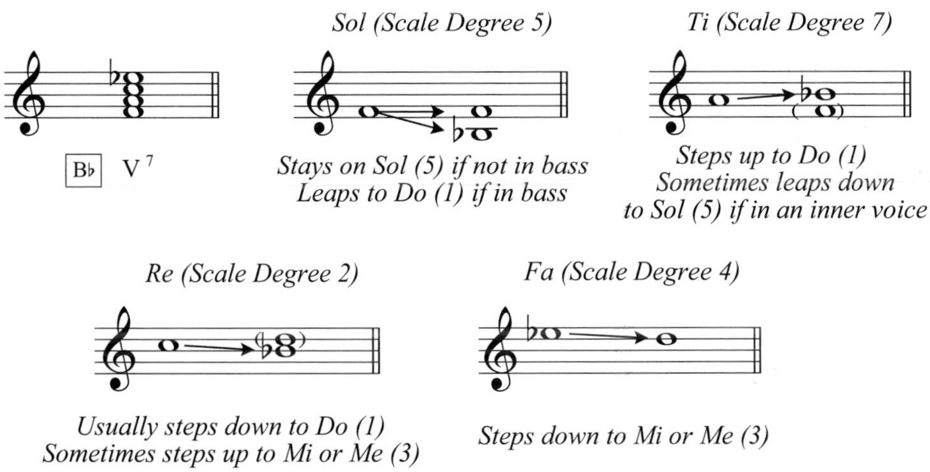


Like all seventh chords, dominant sevenths are invertible three times:

**EXAMPLE 3.4.3**

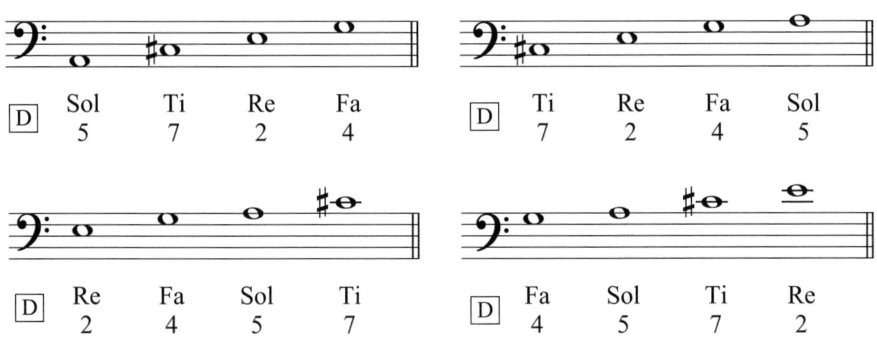

## Hearing

1. Dominant sevenths are very energetic chords with a strong desire toward resolution. Begin by hearing this desire toward motion.
2. To determine the chord inversion, listen for the scale degree that occurs in the bass. Hear where it wants to resolve.

If you hear the bass pitch wanting to leap up or down a fourth to tonic, then scale degree 5 is in the bass and the chord is in root position ($V^7$).

If you hear the bass pitch stepping up to tonic, then scale degree 7 is in the bass and the chord is in first inversion ($V^6_5$).

If you hear the bass pitch stepping down to tonic, then scale degree 2 is in the bass and the chord is in second inversion ($V^4_3$).

If you hear the bass pitch stepping down to scale degree 3, then scale degree 4 is in the bass and the chord is in third inversion ($V^4_2$).

Be careful! The desire of the bass pitch in second and third inversion dominant seventh chords can sound very similar. Pay particular attention to whether the bass pitch is stepping down to tonic or scale degree 3.

If you are asked to identify another pitch in the dominant seventh chord, the scale degrees behave the same way with the exception of scale degree 5. It will stay on the same pitch on the resolution if it is in an upper voice.

## Singing

Dominant seventh chords use scale degrees 5, 7, 2, and 4, whether in the major or minor mode. When given a bass pitch and a chord inversion:

1. Know which scale degree the given pitch represents based on the given inversion.

   $V^7$ (root position) means the given pitch is scale degree 5.
   $V^6_5$ means the given pitch is scale degree 7.
   $V^4_3$ means the given pitch is scale degree 2.
   $V^4_2$ means the given pitch is scale degree 4.

2. Find tonic by singing the pattern for the starting scale degree. If necessary, set yourself up in the key by singing all of the scale degree patterns (pay attention to whether you are in the major or minor mode).
3. Once you are comfortably in the key, sing the pattern below that corresponds to the chord inversion you have been asked to sing. If you have been asked to resolve to a tonic, sing the resolution that follows:

**EXAMPLE 3.4.4**

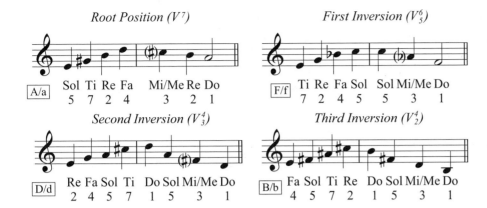

*Root Position* ($V^7$)

A/a Sol Ti Re Fa Mi/Me Re Do
5 7 2 4 3 2 1

*First Inversion* ($V^6_5$)

F/f Ti Re Fa Sol Sol Mi/Me Do
7 2 4 5 5 3 1

*Second Inversion* ($V^4_3$)

D/d Re Fa Sol Ti Do Sol Mi/Me Do
2 4 5 7 1 5 3 1

*Third Inversion* ($V^4_2$)

B/b Fa Sol Ti Re Do Sol Mi/Me Do
4 5 7 2 1 5 3 1

## Assignments for Practice

1. Sing all four inversions of the dominant seventh chord from the same pitch.
2. Sing the dominant seventh chords above and then reorder the pitches. Pay attention to the integrity of the dominant sound.

### Pitch Patterns

**PITCH PATTERN 3.4.1**

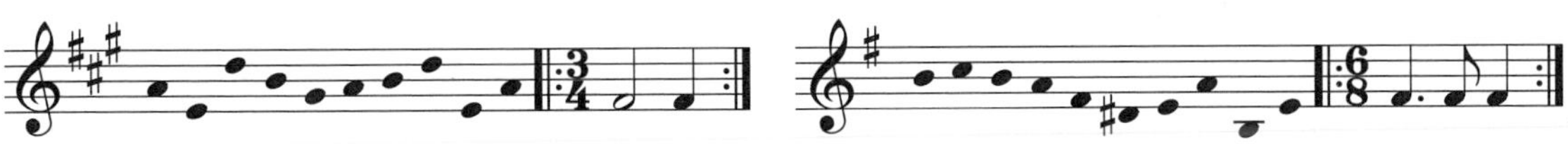

**PITCH PATTERN 3.4.2**

### Melodies

Find the dominant seventh chords in each melody before singing. After you learn the melody as written, sing it again but reorder the pitches of the dominant seventh chord.

**MELODY 3.4.1**

**Andante**

**MELODY 3.4.2**

**MELODY 3.4.3**

**MELODY 3.4.4**

**MELODY 3.4.5**

### MELODY 3.4.6

### MELODY 3.4.7

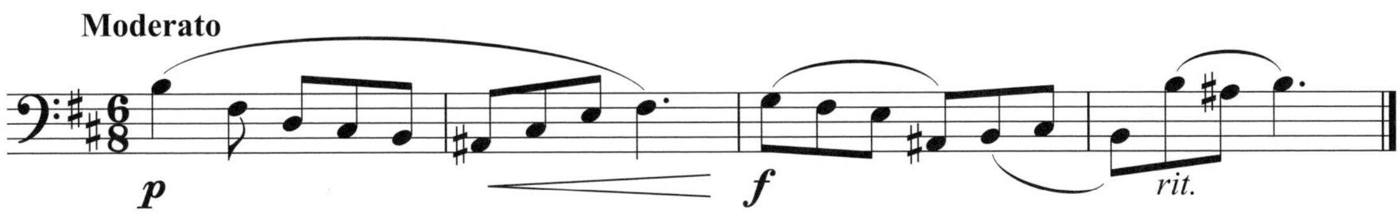


### MELODY 3.4.8

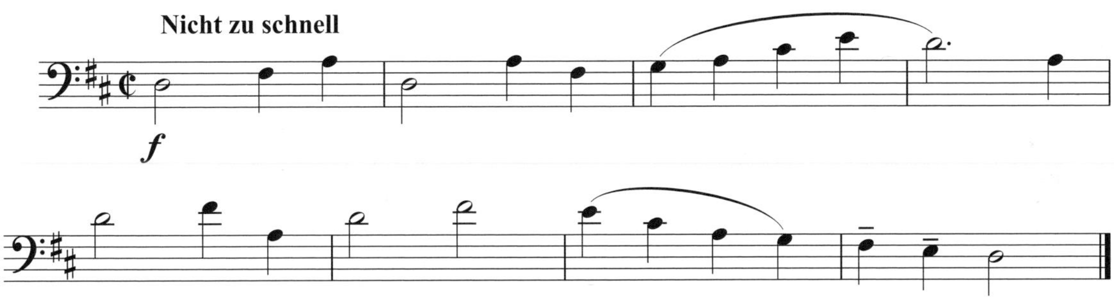


### MELODY 3.4.9

## MELODY 3.4.10

## MELODY 3.4.11

## MELODY 3.4.12

### MELODY 3.4.13

### MELODY 3.4.14

### MELODY 3.4.15

## Duets

### DUET 3.4.1

### DUET 3.4.2

DUET 3.4.3

Larghetto

## Chorale

CHORALE 3.4

Winsomely

## Self-Accompanied Melody

### SELF-ACCOMPANIED MELODY 3.4

## 3.5 Diminished Triads

### Facts You Need to Know

Diminished triads occur in one place in the major scale: as the leading tone (vii°) triad consisting of scale degrees 7, 2, and 4.

Diminished triads occur in two places in the minor scale:

1. As the leading tone (vii°) triad consisting of scale degrees ♮7, 2, and 4.
2. As the supertonic (ii°) triad consisting of scale degrees 2, 4, and ♭6.

Diminished triads consist of minor thirds between the root and third and between the third and fifth. The root and fifth form a diminished fifth (tritone).

**EXAMPLE 3.5.1**

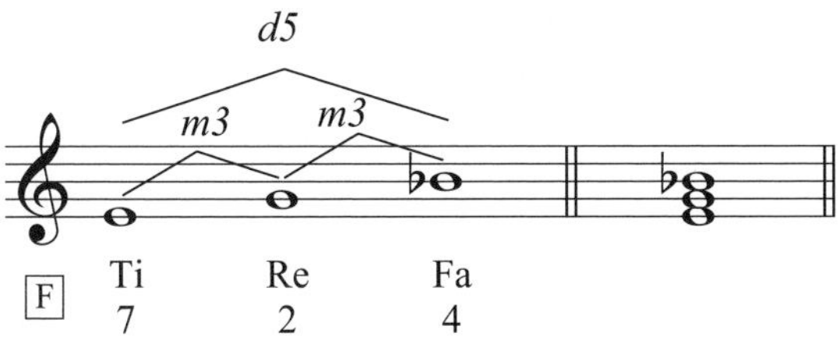


Leading tone triads carry dominant function. The supertonic triad in minor carries predominant function.

Leading tone triads behave like dominant seventh chords that are missing their root. As a result, the resolution of the chord tones is the same as for a dominant seventh chord:

Scale degree 7 moves up by step to scale degree 1.

Scale degree 2 moves down by step to scale degree 1 or up by step to scale degree 3. (This is the only tone in this chord that can be doubled. If more than one scale degree 2 is used, one will move up by step and the other will move down by step.)

Scale degree 4 moves down by step to scale degree 3.

**EXAMPLE 3.5.2**

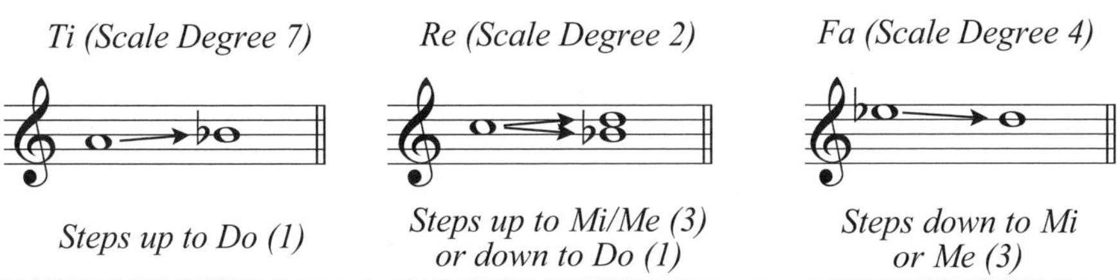


## Hearing

Most people hear diminished triads as dominant function chords. Listen for the strong desire of resolution to tonic and the individual tones' desires toward resolution to scale degrees 1 and 3. To determine inversion, listen for the scale degree in the bass by hearing its desire toward resolution.

## Singing

1. Use the leading tone triad (scale degrees 7, 2, and 4) in the major mode as your point of reference.
2. Determine the scale degree of your given pitch based on the requested inversion. Root position triads will begin on scale degree 7, first inversion on scale degree 2, and second inversion on scale degree 4.
3. Use scale degree patterns to find tonic; orient yourself around tonic.
4. Sing the component scale degrees. If you are asked to resolve the triad to tonic, use the following patterns:

**EXAMPLE 3.5.3**

G/g — Ti Re Fa Mi/Me Re Do — 7 2 4 3 2 1

E/e — Re Fa Ti Do Sol Mi/Me Do — 2 4 7 1 5 3 1

C♯/c♯ — Fa Ti Re Do Sol Mi/Me Do — 4 7 2 1 5 3 1

## Assignments for Practice

1. Give yourself a pitch and sing root position and first inversion diminished triads from it.
2. Resolve root position and first inversion diminished triads to both major and minor tonics.
3. Hear a diminished triad as supertonic in the minor key and resolve it through a dominant seventh chord to tonic.

**EXAMPLE 3.5.4**

a — ii° — $V^4_3$ — i

Re Fa Le Re Fa Sol Ti Do Sol Me Re Do

2 4 ♭6 2 4 5 ♯7 1 5 3 2 1

4. Sing through the three triadic qualities you have studied so far in rapid succession. Listen for the differences in sound and resolution as you sing the different triads.
5. Change the ordering of the pitches in your diminished triads and see if you can maintain the chord sound and integrity.

### Pitch Patterns

**PITCH PATTERN 3.5.1**

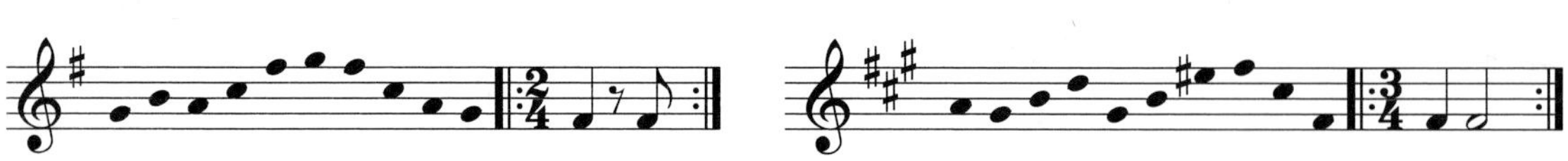

**PITCH PATTERN 3.5.2**

## Melodies

### MELODY 3.5.1

### MELODY 3.5.2

### MELODY 3.5.3

### MELODY 3.5.4

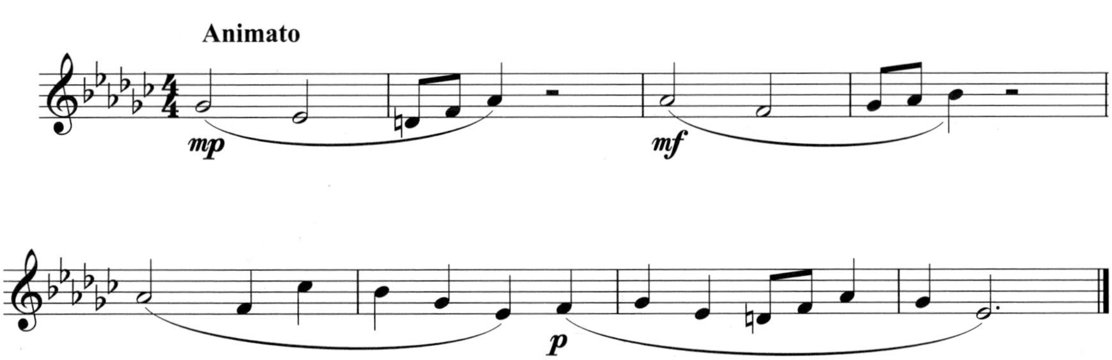

**MELODY 3.5.5**

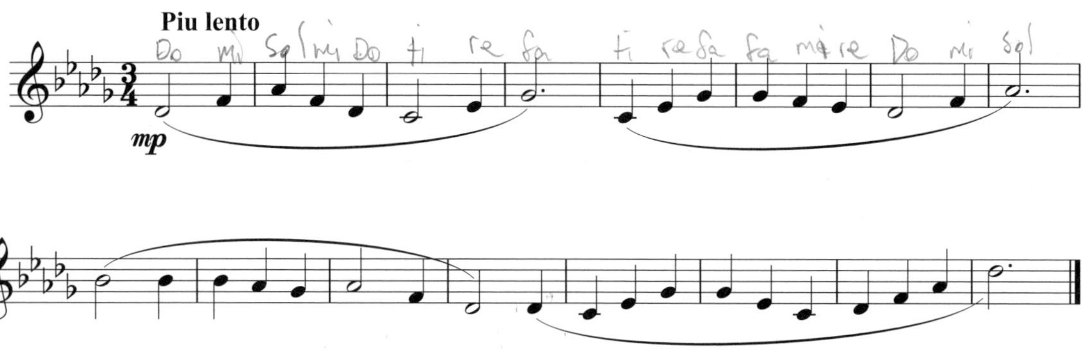


Provide your own tempo and style marking for the following melody.

**MELODY 3.5.6**

**MELODY 3.5.7**

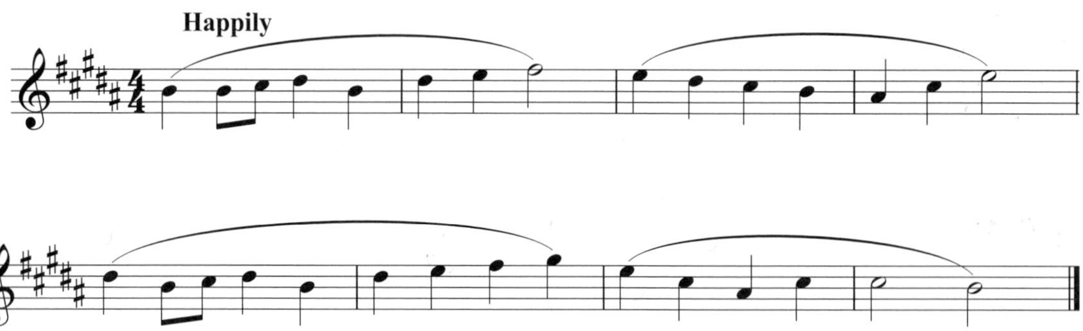


**MELODY 3.5.8**

MELODY 3.5.9

MELODY 3.5.10

MELODY 3.5.11

MELODY 3.5.12

MELODY 3.5.13

Pay attention to dynamics as you learn this melody.

MELODY 3.5.14

MELODY 3.5.15

## Duets

DUET 3.5.1

DUET 3.5.2

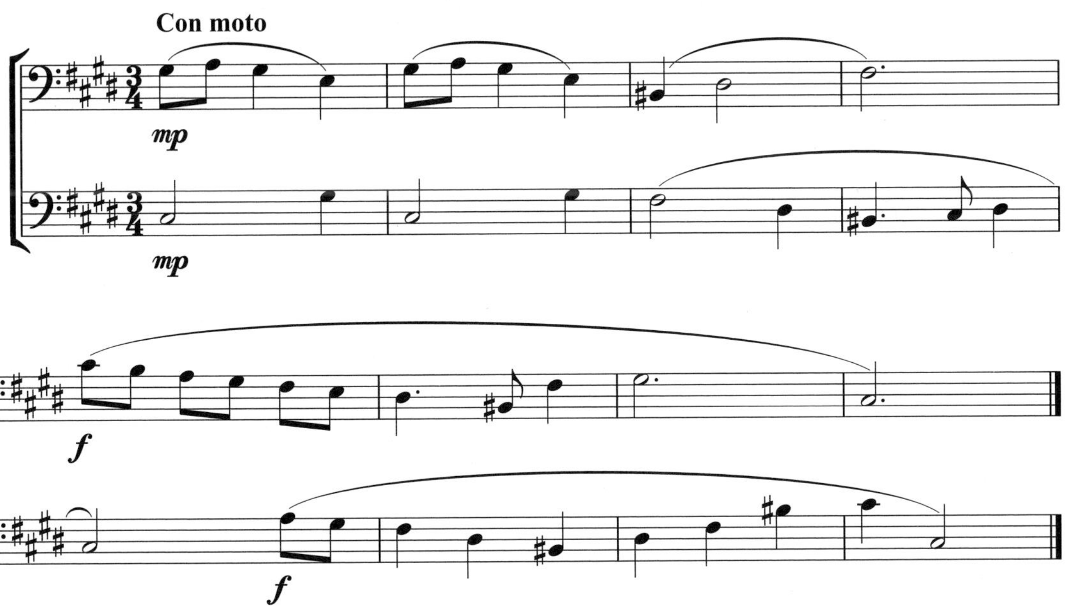

### DUET 3.5.3

## Chorale

### CHORALE 3.5

## Self-Accompanied Melody

### SELF-ACCOMPANIED MELODY 3.5

## 3.6 Improvisation II: Dominant Function

### Facts You Need to Know

Dominant function chords are the same in the major and minor modes:

1. Dominant triads (V) and seventh chords ($V^7$)
2. Leading tone triads (vii°) and seventh chords ($vii^{\circ 7}$ and $vii^{ø7}$)

Inverting chords does not change their function.

Dominant function chords all share scale degrees 7 and 2. Other important dominant sounding scale degrees are 5 and 4.

When singing dominant function, the movable scale degrees in the minor mode are usually placed in their raised position (♯6 and ♯7).

Dominant function chords must resolve to tonic function chords—usually tonic (I or i) and sometimes the submediant (vi or VI).

## Hearing

Dominant function chords possess a strong desire toward resolution. Listen for this energy that pulls the music to tonic. Listen also for the presence of scale degrees 7 and 2. To determine the specific dominant chord being used, listen for chord quality and inversion.

## Singing

When improvising dominant function, focus on singing scale degrees 5, 7, 2, and 4. On occasion scale degree 6 (♭6 in the minor mode) may be added.

Use the same three techniques for improvisation that you used for tonic function:

1. Repetition

**EXAMPLE 3.6.1**

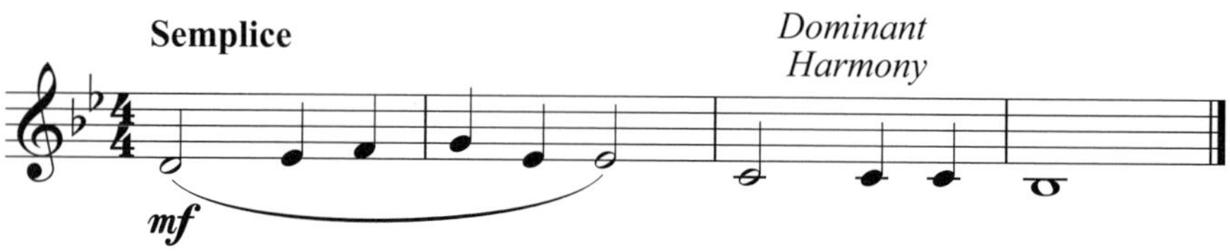


2. Arpeggiation

**EXAMPLE 3.6.2**

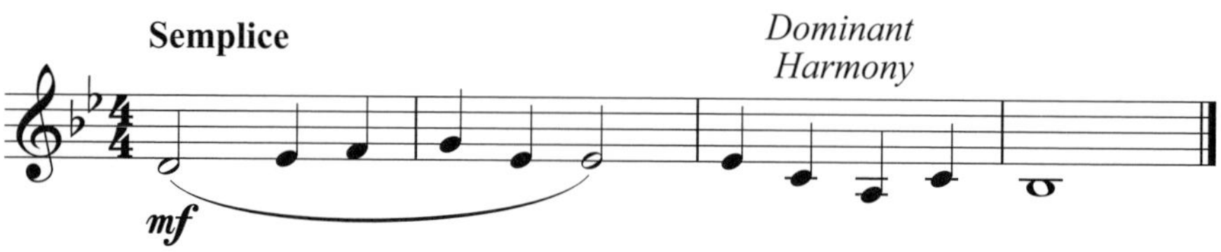


3. Connected arpeggiation

**EXAMPLE 3.6.3**

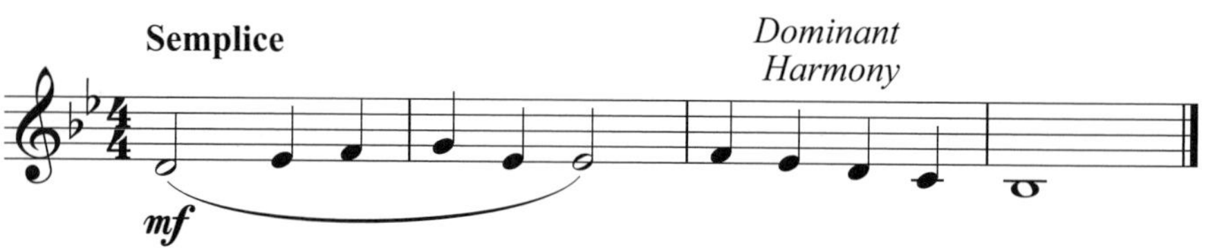


Be aware of the amount of time that you have to fill. Keep counting!

Notice that you are always on or next to a note that carries dominant function. Use this to smooth the transition into and out of your improvisation. For example, if the note before your improvisation is scale degree 3, begin on 2 or 4. If the note after your improvisation is scale degree 1, end on 7 or 2.

As always, use rhythmic and melodic components from elsewhere in the melody to help make your improvisation fit into the sound of the melody.

## Assignments for Practice

1. Give yourself a pitch and sing a major triad above it (you may vary the inversion). Hear it as a dominant triad, and find a logical way to resolve it to a tonic triad.
2. Repeat exercise #1, but resolve the dominant triad deceptively (to the submediant).

### Melodies

Improvise dominant harmony in the blank measures of the melodies.

**MELODY 3.6.1**

**MELODY 3.6.2**

**MELODY 3.6.3**

**MELODY 3.6.4**

**MELODY 3.6.5**

Improvise tonic or dominant harmony as indicated in the blank measures below.

**MELODY 3.6.6**

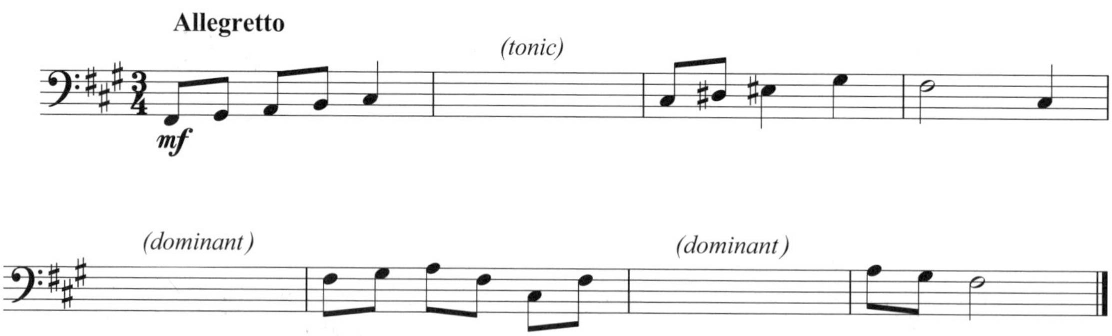


**MELODY 3.6.7**

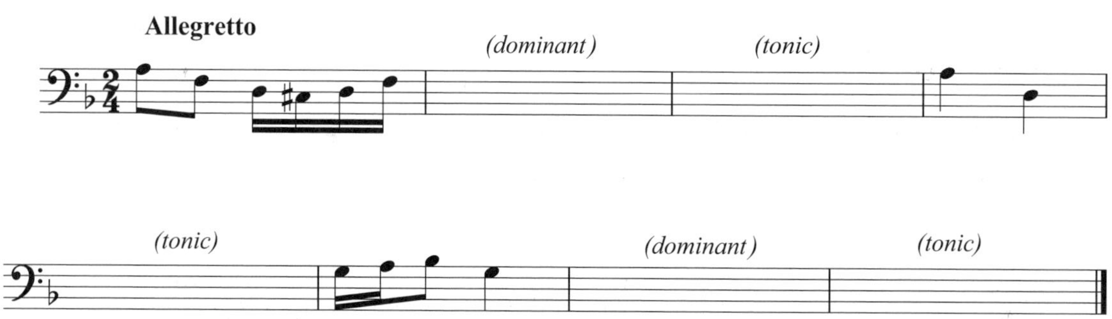


The following melodies present a phrase that uses only tonic and dominant harmony. Complete each by improvising a second phrase that relates to and completes the first.

**MELODY 3.6.8**

**Andante**

**MELODY 3.6.9**

**Allegro**

**MELODY 3.6.10**

**Geschwindt**

## Duets

**DUET 3.6.1**

**DUET 3.6.2**

## Self-Accompanied Melody

**SELF-ACCOMPANIED MELODY 3.6**

## 3.7 Music from the Literature

**EXAMPLE 3.7.1**

"Das Wandern,"
from *Die schöne Müllerin*

Schubert

**Allegro moderato**

**EXAMPLE 3.7.2**

"Mit dem grünen Lautenband,"
from *Die schöne Müllerin*

Schubert

**Moderato**

**EXAMPLE 3.7.3**

From *Song Without Words*,
Op. 30, No. 1

Mendelssohn

**Andante espressivo**

**EXAMPLE 3.7.4**

"Le Violette,"
from *Pierro et Demetrio*

**Allegretto** Alessandro Scarlatti

**EXAMPLE 3.7.5**

*Violin Concerto in A Minor*, Op. 3, No. 6, Third movement

**Presto** Vivaldi

**EXAMPLE 3.7.6**

**Maestoso** Russian Folk Song

**EXAMPLE 3.7.7**

"The Happy Farmer," from *Album for the Young*, Op. 68, No. 10

**Brisk and happy** Schumann

**EXAMPLE 3.7.8**

**Briskly** Tyrolian Folk Song

**EXAMPLE 3.7.9**

**Marcia pomposa**

Finnish Folk Song

**EXAMPLE 3.7.10**

"Sebben crudele," from *La constanza in amor vince l'inganno*

**Allegretto grazioso**

Antonio Caldera

**EXAMPLE 3.7.11**

**Moderato**

Swedish Folk Song

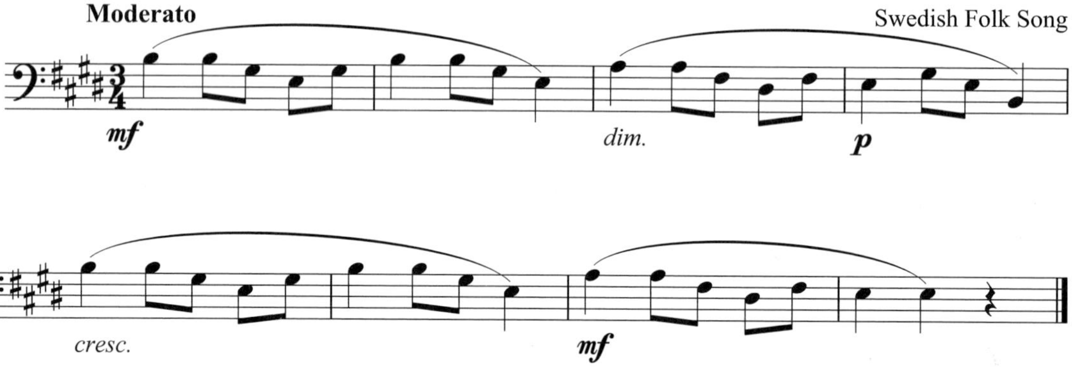


**EXAMPLE 3.7.12**

*Gavotte*

**Moderato**

Benjamin Carr

**EXAMPLE 3.7.13**

"I Attempt from Love's Sickness,"
from *The Indian Queen*

Purcell

**EXAMPLE 3.7.14**

*Piano Sonata in E-flat Major*, Third movement

**Presto**

Haydn

**EXAMPLE 3.7.15**

*Piano Sonata in F Major*, K. 547a,
First movement

m. 32–39

**Allegro**

Mozart

## Reflections: Musicality

"I can't believe you haven't heard about it yet!"

Which word did you emphasize when you read this sentence? Repeat it, consciously emphasizing a different word. How did the meaning change? Try it again. Be incredulous, angry, happy, sarcastic. What did you do to infuse the sentence with a different meaning? One inflection may make it seem as if you're talking to someone with a reputation for being "in the know"; with another, it might seem like you are delivering bad news.

But why does it matter, and what does any of this have to do with studying music? It matters because how you say something is as important as what you say; it is essential that you are able to communicate your intentions when you speak. The same is true in music. From our earliest training, we learn to play the notes on the page, but how we play them—how we communicate—is the essence of music making. It's what musicians call musicality, and it is one of the most alluring aspects of being a musician.

Think about the times, at a recital, when you think to yourself "Wow—her playing was so musical!" What makes us react that way? Somehow, we become aware of how the performer has connected to the music. The artist, wholly engrossed in the message, is compelled to communicate his emotions to the audience, and the audience is equally compelled to react: that's the power and magic of musicality. Musicality grows from passion, and passion feeds musicality. As artists, we have the need to express ourselves; we have the means to do so through music; we have the power to do so when we decide to take risks, challenge ourselves, and use our musical imaginations in new and inventive ways.

It is easy to understand and embrace the idea of musicality as it relates to performance on an instrument. Most musicians have spent a large part of their lives learning to express musical ideas and emotions on their instrument or their voice. But why does a chapter on musicality exist in an ear-training text? Can you, an aspiring musician, train your ear without regard to musicality? Probably, but do you want to? Devoid of musical intention, studying ear training will have little meaning to your musical life and development. Ear training is not a part of the curriculum in music schools across the country because administrators and professors want to find a way to torture students! It's there because it has an enormous impact on the development of musical skills, has the potential to strengthen your sensitivity to sound, and can cultivate your ability to communicate subtle shades of musical meaning. As you develop your sensitivity to sound, you will find yourself hearing music in a completely different way and responding to sound with newfound energy and knowledge. The more musical integrity you bring to your ear-training study, the greater the impact it can have on your growth as an artist.

So go for it—whether you find yourself in ear-training class, in the practice room, or on stage, make music happen. It's yours to own and share.

## 3.8 Dictation Materials

### I. Identification of Minor Scale Degrees

Your teacher will establish a key and then play its scale degrees in random order or as a specific pitch in a melody (by number—first, second, last, or by position—high or low). Identify each by writing its number in the appropriate space. Place an up arrow in front of scale degree 6 or 7 if you hear either of them in their raised position.

*Date:* . . . . . . . . . . . . . .

1. ____ 2. ____ 3. ____ 4. ____ 5. ____ 6. ____ 7. ____ 8. ____

*Date:* . . . . . . . . . . . . . .

1. ____ 2. ____ 3. ____ 4. ____ 5. ____ 6. ____ 7. ____ 8. ____

*Date:* . . . . . . . . . . . . . .

1. ____ 2. ____ 3. ____ 4. ____ 5. ____ 6. ____ 7. ____ 8. ____

*Date:* . . . . . . . . . . . . . .

1. ____ 2. ____ 3. ____ 4. ____ 5. ____ 6. ____ 7. ____ 8. ____

*Date:* . . . . . . . . . . . . . .

1. ____ 2. ____ 3. ____ 4. ____ 5. ____ 6. ____ 7. ____ 8. ____

## II. Identification of Major Scale Degrees

Your teacher will establish a key and then play its scale degrees in random order or as a specific pitch in a melody (by number—first, second, last, or by position—high or low). Identify each by writing its number in the appropriate space.

*Date:* . . . . . . . . . . . . . .

1. ____ 2. ____ 3. ____ 4. ____ 5. ____ 6. ____ 7. ____ 8. ____

*Date:* . . . . . . . . . . . . . .

1. ____ 2. ____ 3. ____ 4. ____ 5. ____ 6. ____ 7. ____ 8. ____

*Date:* . . . . . . . . . . . . . .

1. ____ 2. ____ 3. ____ 4. ____ 5. ____ 6. ____ 7. ____ 8. ____

*Date:* . . . . . . . . . . . . . .

1. ____ 2. ____ 3. ____ 4. ____ 5. ____ 6. ____ 7. ____ 8. ____

*Date:* . . . . . . . . . . . . . .

1. ____ 2. ____ 3. ____ 4. ____ 5. ____ 6. ____ 7. ____ 8. ____

## III. Interval Identification

Your teacher will play several intervals. Identify their quality and size as one of the following:

| | | |
|---|---|---|
| M2 = Major second | P4 = Perfect fourth | m6 = Minor sixth |
| m2 = Minor second | TT = Tritone | m7 = Minor seventh |

M3 = Major third P5 = Perfect fifth X = Other
m3 = Minor third M6 = Major sixth

Be sure to make a clear difference between your capital and lower-case Ms.

*Date:* . . . . . . . . . . . . . .

1. ____ 2. ____ 3. ____ 4. ____ 5. ____ 6. ____ 7. ____ 8. ____

*Date:* . . . . . . . . . . . . . .

1. ____ 2. ____ 3. ____ 4. ____ 5. ____ 6. ____ 7. ____ 8. ____

*Date:* . . . . . . . . . . . . . .

1. ____ 2. ____ 3. ____ 4. ____ 5. ____ 6. ____ 7. ____ 8. ____

*Date:* . . . . . . . . . . . . . .

1. ____ 2. ____ 3. ____ 4. ____ 5. ____ 6. ____ 7. ____ 8. ____

*Date:* . . . . . . . . . . . . . .

1. ____ 2. ____ 3. ____ 4. ____ 5. ____ 6. ____ 7. ____ 8. ____

### IV. Triad Quality Identification

Your teacher will play several triads. Indicate the quality and inversion. Possible answers are M for major, m for minor, and d for diminished.

*Date:* . . . . . . . . . . . . . .

1. ____ 2. ____ 3. ____ 4. ____ 5. ____ 6. ____ 7. ____ 8. ____

*Date:* . . . . . . . . . . . . . .

1. ____ 2. ____ 3. ____ 4. ____ 5. ____ 6. ____ 7. ____ 8. ____

*Date:* . . . . . . . . . . . . . .

1. ____ 2. ____ 3. ____ 4. ____ 5. ____ 6. ____ 7. ____ 8. ____

*Date:* . . . . . . . . . . . . . .

1. ____ 2. ____ 3. ____ 4. ____ 5. ____ 6. ____ 7. ____ 8. ____

*Date:* . . . . . . . . . . . . . .

1. ____ 2. ____ 3. ____ 4. ____ 5. ____ 6. ____ 7. ____ 8. ____

## V. Dominant Seventh Chord Identification

Your teacher will play several dominant seventh chords. Indicate the inversion for each by using the correct figured bass symbol.

*Date:* . . . . . . . . . . . . . .

1. ____ 2. ____ 3. ____ 4. ____ 5. ____ 6. ____ 7. ____ 8. ____

*Date:* . . . . . . . . . . . . . .

1. ____ 2. ____ 3. ____ 4. ____ 5. ____ 6. ____ 7. ____ 8. ____

*Date:* . . . . . . . . . . . . . .

1. ____ 2. ____ 3. ____ 4. ____ 5. ____ 6. ____ 7. ____ 8. ____

*Date:* . . . . . . . . . . . . . .

1. ____ 2. ____ 3. ____ 4. ____ 5. ____ 6. ____ 7. ____ 8. ____

*Date:* . . . . . . . . . . . . . .

1. ____ 2. ____ 3. ____ 4. ____ 5. ____ 6. ____ 7. ____ 8. ____

## VI. Melodic and Rhythmic Dictation

Your teacher will play a short melody or rhythm. Notate it on the staves below.

*Date:* . . . . . . . . . . . . . .

*Date:* . . . . . . . . . . . . . .

*Date:* . . . . . . . . . . . . . .

*Date:* . . . . . . . . . . . . . .

*Date:* . . . . . . . . . . . . . .

## VII. Harmonic Dictation

Write the soprano line, bass line, and provide a Roman numeral analysis (including inversional symbols) for the progression you hear on the grand staff below.

*Date:* . . . . . . . . . . . . . .

*Date:* . . . . . . . . . . . . . .

*Date:* . . . . . . . . . . . . . .

*Date:* . . . . . . . . . . . . . .

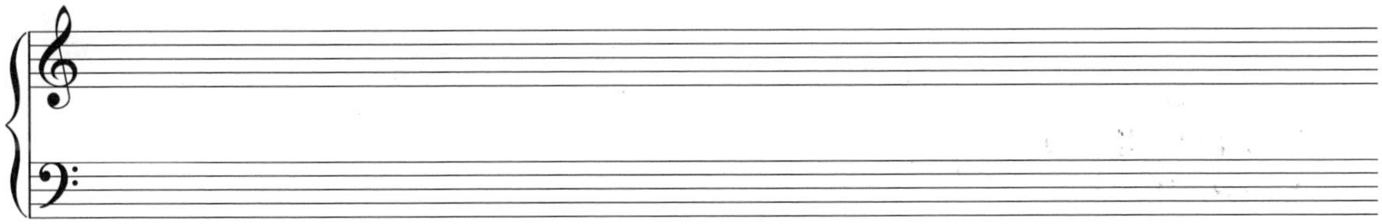

*Date:* . . . . . . . . . . . . . .

# Chapter 4

# Triplets and Duplets; Seventh Chords and Predominant Function

## 4.1 Irregular Divisions I: Triplets and Duplets

### Facts You Need to Know

A triplet is a group of three even notes performed in the same time as two notes of the same value.

Triplets are indicated with the number "3" and often have a slur or bracket above or below the notes.

The chart below shows the most common triplets in simple meter. Note that these one-beat triplets are always written using the same note value as the division of the beat.

**EXAMPLE 4.1.1**

Triplets look identical to compound meter divisions, but have a completely different function in music. They belong to a group of rhythms referred to as *irregular divisions of the beat* (including triplets, duplets, quintuplets, etc.). The most important use of triplets is one that emphasizes their "irregularity," creating a sense of resistance in music. Play the two melodies below:

**EXAMPLE 4.1.2**

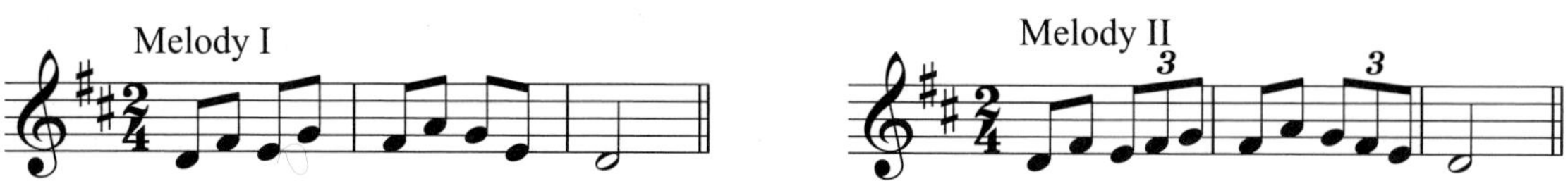


In Melody I, the melodic contour helps to shape the phrase, the rhythm plays a lesser role. Melody II uses the same basic melodic line, but is enhanced by triplets. Notice the sense of drive the triplets provide. In a case like this, performers will often give each note of the triplet the same amount of weight, which adds intensity and resistance.

Another common use of triplets is to employ them as a textural device, as shown in the example below.

**EXAMPLE 4.1.3**

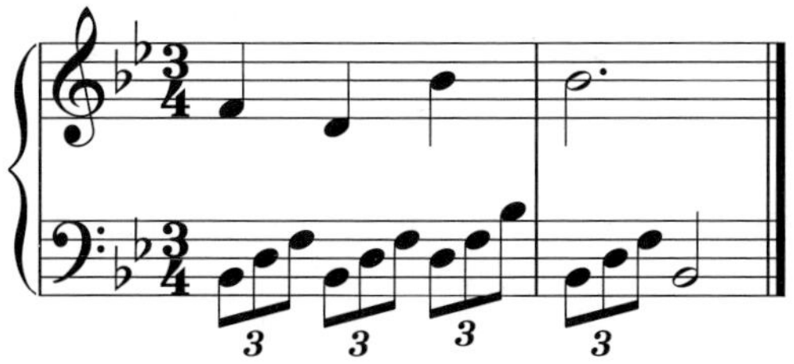


Here, the triplets act as an accompaniment figure below the melodic line, so the triplets begin to sound more like compound meter divisions—the sense of resistance is replaced by the undulating effect of the repeated three-note groupings. You hear this often in music; one of the most famous examples is Beethoven's "Moonlight" Sonata.

However, if a composer writes divisions in another voice over the undulating triplets, the sense of resistance returns because of the struggle of the two against three—each group of divisions fights to dominate the line, as evidenced in the example below.

**EXAMPLE 4.1.4**

### Two against Three

As you heard in the example above, placing triplets against the normal division creates rhythmic conflict and interest. The snarl of two against three creates tension and ambiguity in music. Many methods for learning to perform 2:3 exist. In order to achieve the best musical result, avoid relying on common "tricks" such as the saying "not diff-i-cult." Instead, use the following procedure:

1. Set the metronome to a moderate tempo; clap the beat and articulate the divisions.
2. Continue with the metronome, this time articulating triplets.
3. Repeat, switching between the two groupings. Be sure the triplets are even!
4. At the same tempo, clap eighth notes and articulate one group of triplets followed by a beat. Repeat this until you feel comfortable.
5. Clap divisions and articulate triplets, this time repeating the triplets continuously. You may also tap divisions with one hand, triplets with the other.
6. Once you master this, repeat the process clapping triplets and articulating divisions when you get to #4.

### Rhythm Reading

When performing triplets, listen carefully to ensure that the notes are even; it is easy to turn the triplet into another more common rhythm you've already studied, such as short-short long or the reverse. Performing triplets requires careful listening and adjustments. The preparatory exercises in this chapter will help you to develop this skill.

### Duplets

A duplet is a group of two equal notes performed in the same time as three notes of the same value. Duplets are indicated with the number "2" and often have a slur or bracket above or below the notes. The chart below shows the most common duplets in compound meter. Note that they are written using the same note value as the division of the beat.

**EXAMPLE 4.1.5**

Like their triplet counterparts, duplets are an irregular division of the beat that create a sense of resistance in music by seeming to slow down the momentum of the rhythm, as shown in the two melodic fragments below:

**EXAMPLE 4.1.6**

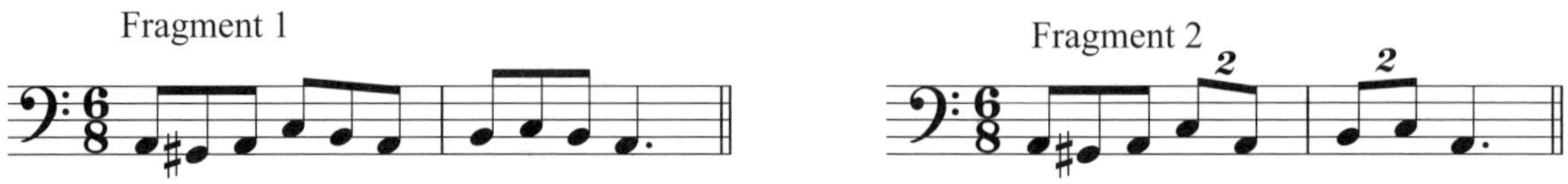


## Preliminary Exercises

Practice each exercise below with a metronome, clap the beat while articulating the rhythm (or clapping the rhythm); repeat until you are able to perform the rhythm with 100 percent accuracy. For an extra challenge, clap divisions while you articulate the rhythm.

## Triplets

### EXAMPLE 4.1.7

## Duplets

### EXAMPLE 4.1.8

## Rhythms

### RHYTHM 4.1.1

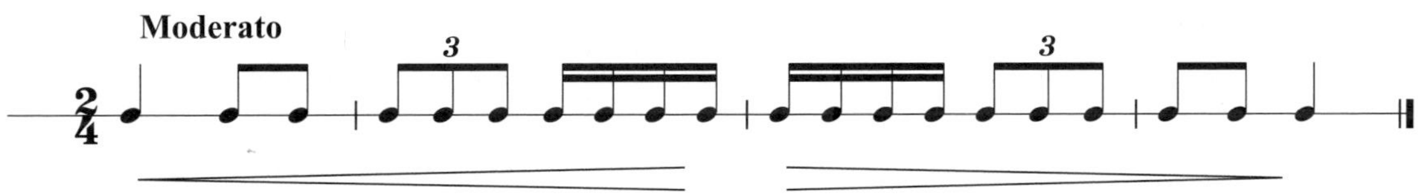

RHYTHM 4.1.2

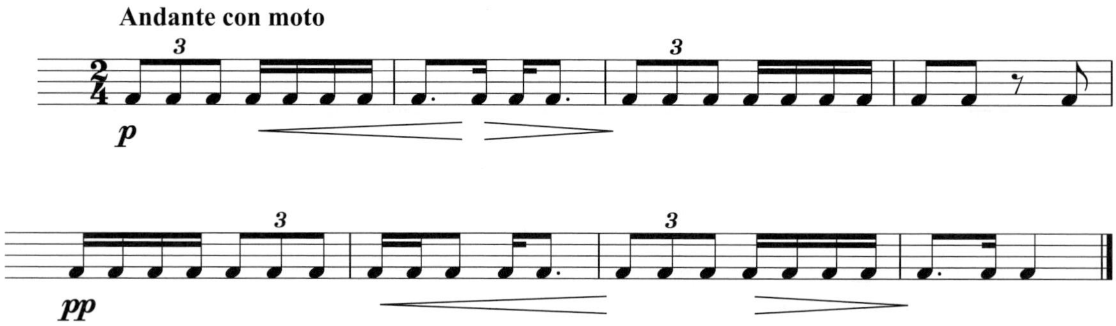


RHYTHM 4.1.3

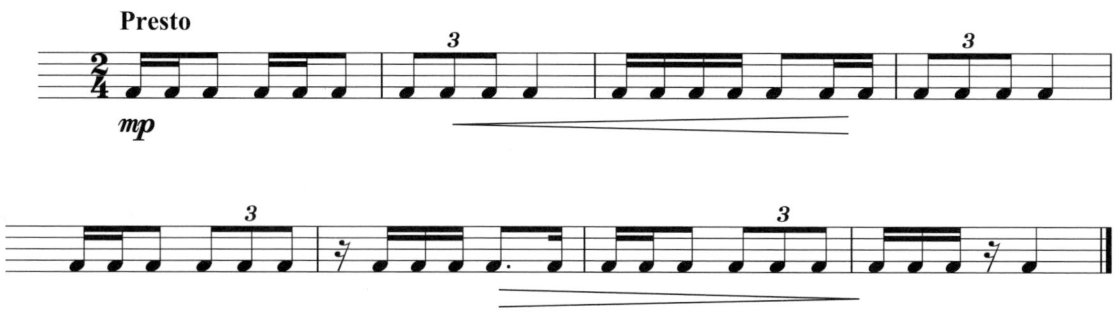


RHYTHM 4.1.4

RHYTHM 4.1.5

**RHYTHM 4.1.6**

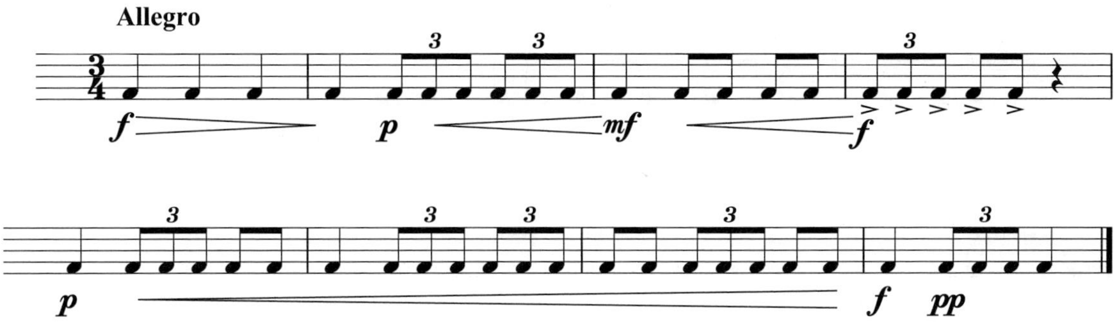


**RHYTHM 4.1.7**

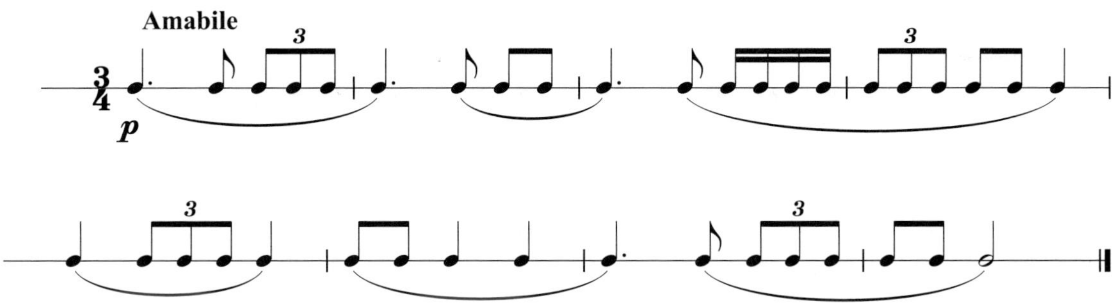


**RHYTHM 4.1.8**

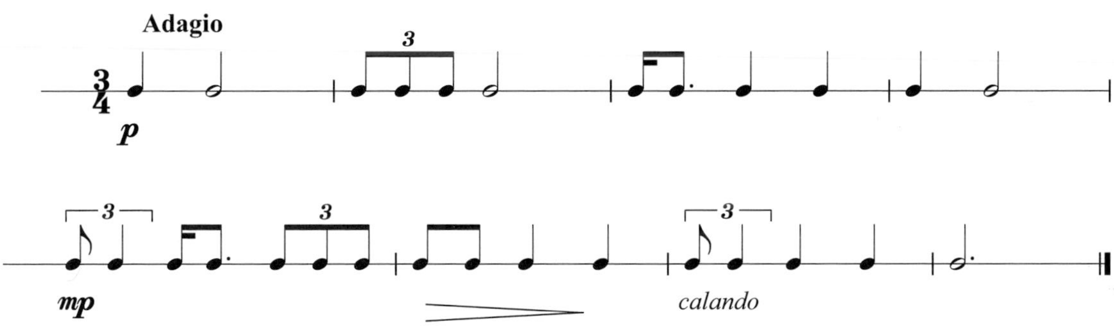


**RHYTHM 4.1.9**

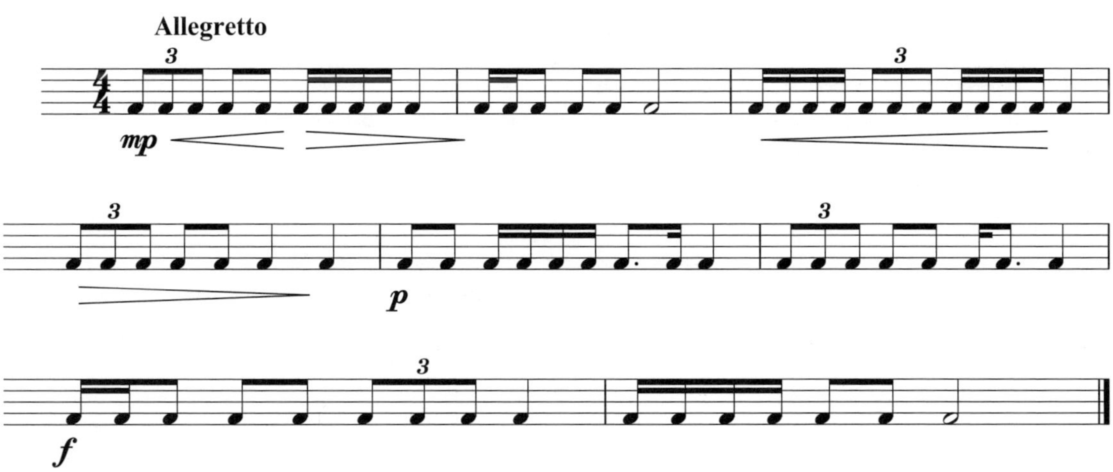

RHYTHM 4.1.10

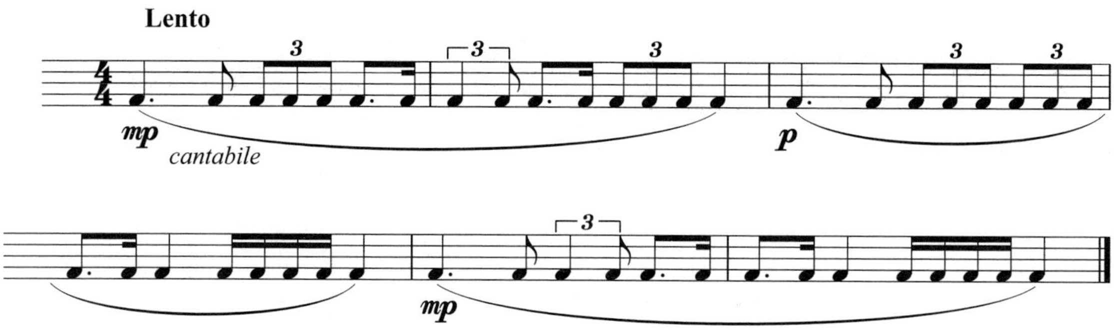


RHYTHM 4.1.11

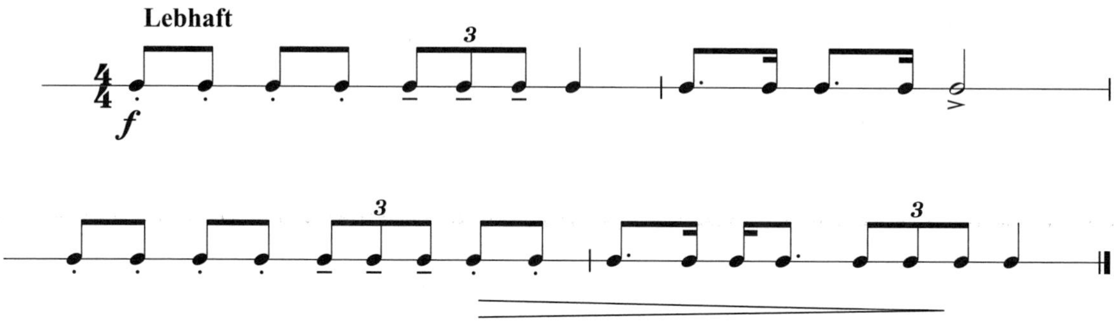


RHYTHM 4.1.12

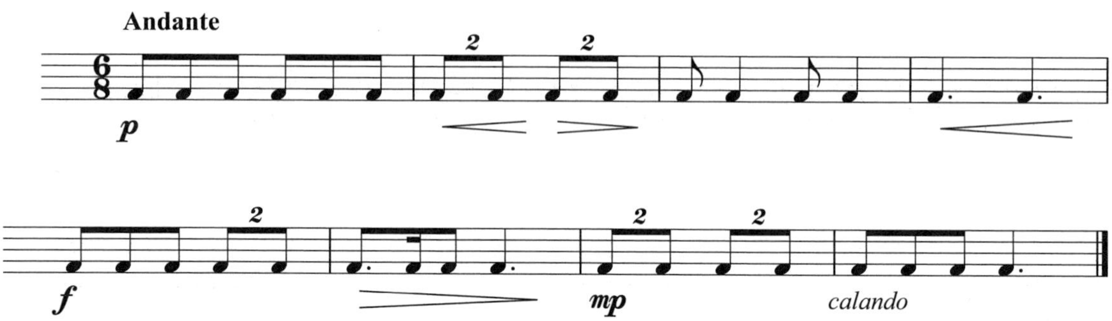


RHYTHM 4.1.13

RHYTHM 4.1.14

RHYTHM 4.1.15

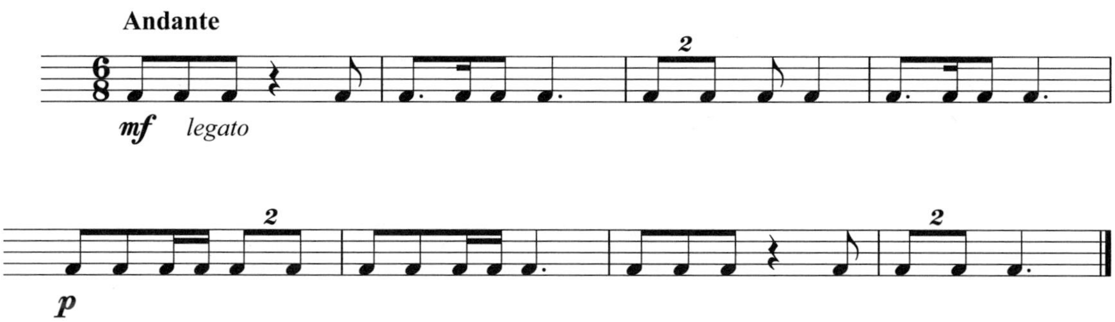


RHYTHM 4.1.16

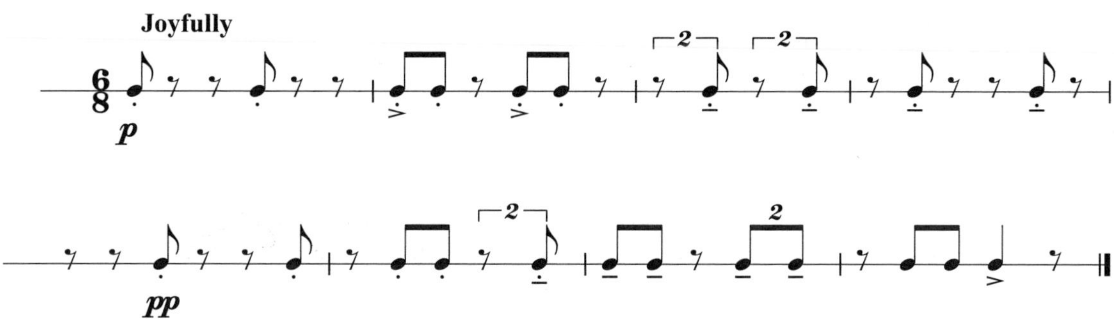


RHYTHM 4.1.17

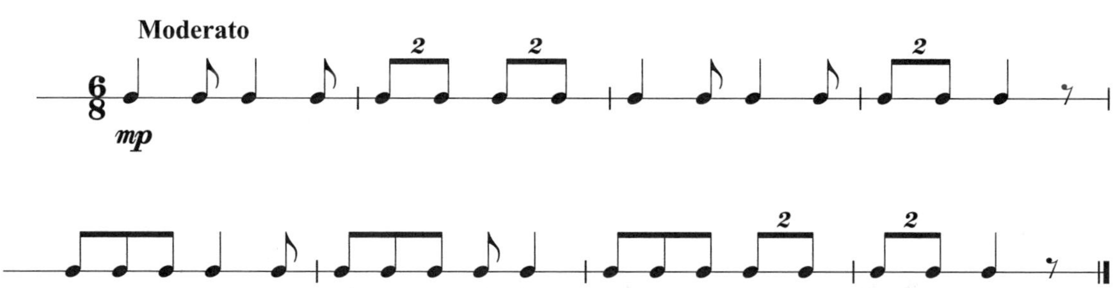

### RHYTHM 4.1.18

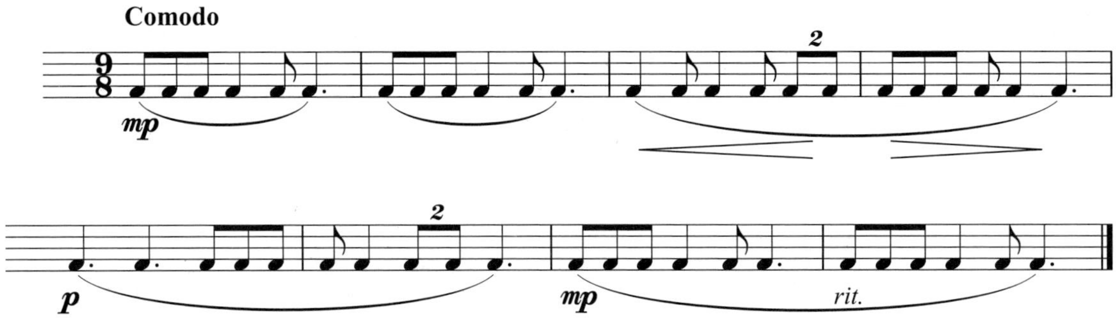


### RHYTHM 4.1.19

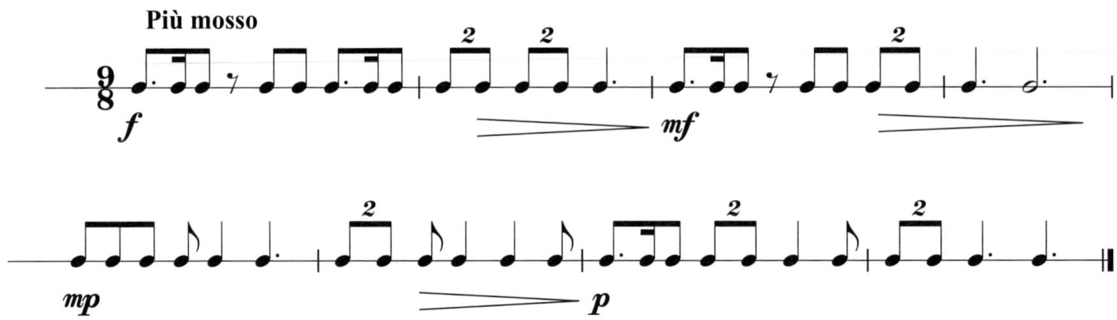


### RHYTHM 4.1.20

## Two-part Rhythms

### TWO-PART RHYTHM 4.1.1

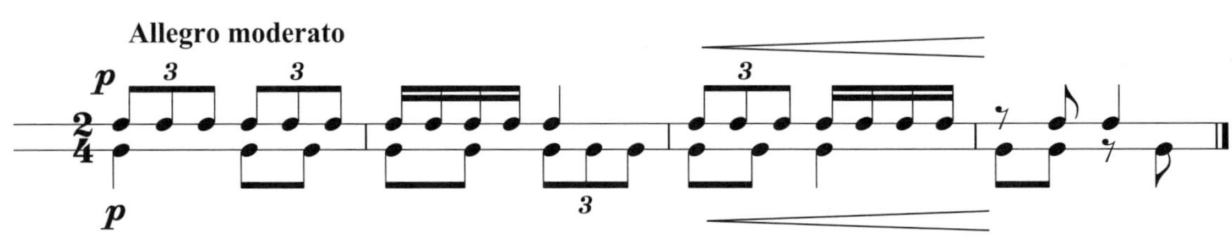

TWO-PART RHYTHM 4.1.2

TWO-PART RHYTHM 4.1.3

TWO-PART RHYTHM 4.1.4

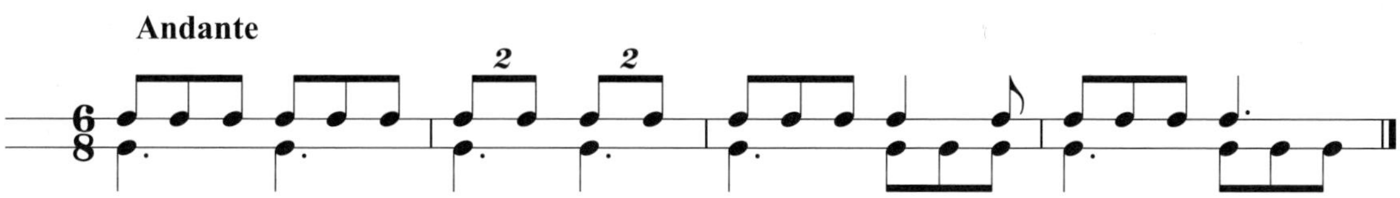


TWO-PART RHYTHM 4.1.5

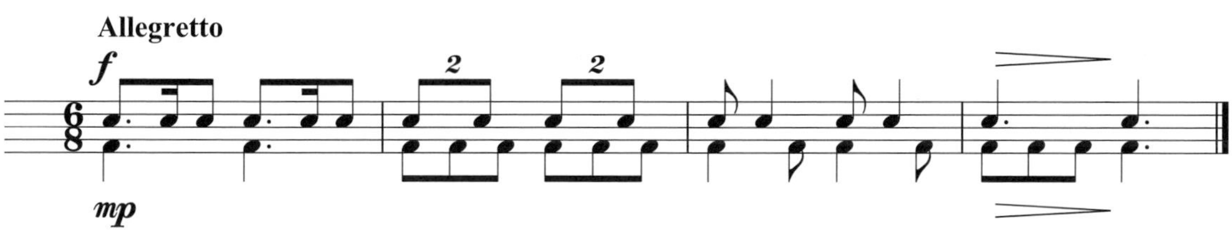

## Three-part Rhythm

### THREE-PART RHYTHM 4.1

## 4.2 Major Sevenths

### Facts You Need to Know

Major sevenths are wide dissonances.

Major sevenths occur in two places in the major scale:

1. Between scale degrees 1 and 7
2. Between scale degrees 4 and 3

Major sevenths occur in four places in the minor scale:

1. Between scale degrees 1 and ♯7
2. Between scale degrees 3 and 2
3. Between scale degrees ♭6 and 5
4. Between scale degrees ♭7 and ♯6, although this combination of scale degrees is extremely rare

## Hearing

1. Listen for a wide and biting dissonant sound.
2. Listen for the upper pitch having a strong desire to resolve up by minor second to tonic (creating a perfect octave).
3. Listen for the lower pitch having the stable and non-moving sound of tonic.

## Singing

1. Use scale degrees 1 up to 7 in the major mode as your point of reference.
2. If singing a descending interval, sing the pattern for scale degree 7 in both the higher and the lower octave to find tonic, or find the higher tonic and arpeggiate through the tonic triad to find the lower tonic.
3. If necessary, orient yourself around this tonic by singing all of the scale degree patterns.
4. Sing scale degrees 1 and 7 in the correct order, followed by the interval quality and size.

**EXAMPLE 4.2.1**

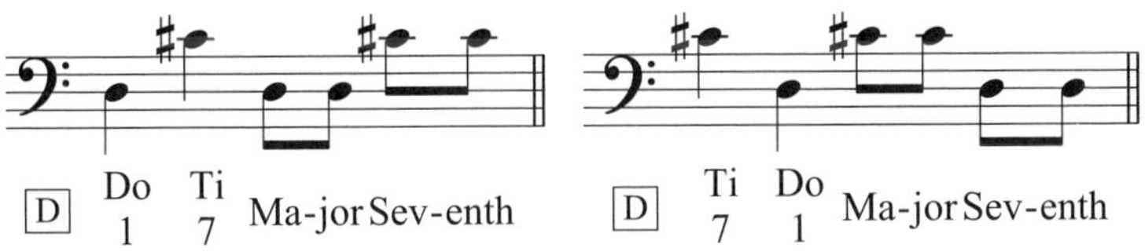


If you are singing a harmonic major seventh, don't back off from the dissonant sound. Enjoy it, and back off when the interval finally resolves.

## Assignments for Practice

Listen for and identify major sevenths in music that you hear, sing, or practice.

### Pitch Patterns

**PITCH PATTERN 4.2.1**

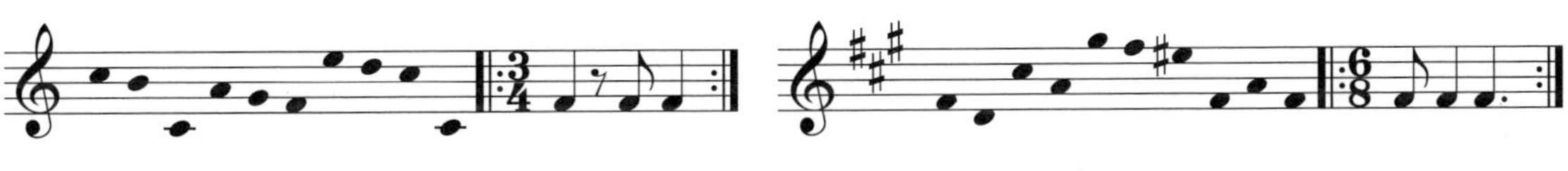

**PITCH PATTERN 4.2.2**

## Melodies

As you sing the following melodies, pay particular attention to the integrity of each pitch's scale degree. Notice also how each seventh you sing creates the expectation that the melody will need to fill in that musical space. How is that done?

**MELODY 4.2.1**

**MELODY 4.2.2**

**MELODY 4.2.3**

Does the following melody feel or sound different if you perform it in a simple duple meter ($^2_4$)?

**MELODY 4.2.4**

Provide your own tempo, style, and dynamic markings for the following two melodies.

MELODY 4.2.5

MELODY 4.2.6

MELODY 4.2.7

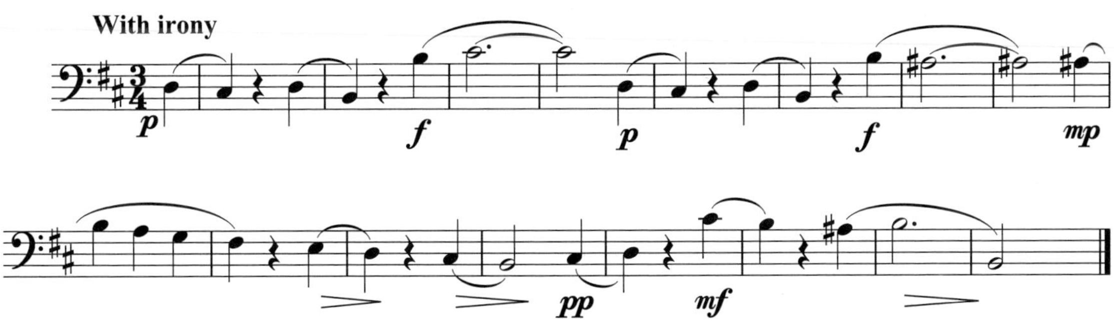


MELODY 4.2.8

## MELODY 4.2.9

## MELODY 4.2.10

## MELODY 4.2.11

## MELODY 4.2.12

## MELODY 4.2.13

## MELODY 4.2.14

## MELODY 4.2.15

## Duets

### DUET 4.2.1

### DUET 4.2.2

**DUET 4.2.3**

## Chorale

**CHORALE 4.2**

## Self-Accompanied Melody

### SELF-ACCOMPANIED MELODY 4.2

## 4.3 Compound Intervals

### Facts You Need to Know

Compound intervals are intervals that are wider than an octave. You can take any simple interval and move the pitches apart by an octave to create a compound interval:

Seconds become ninths
Thirds become tenths
Fourths become elevenths
Fifths become twelfths
Sixths become thirteenths
Sevenths become fourteenths

Compound intervals share the same scale degree content and other characteristics as their simple cousins.

## Hearing

As with all intervals, pay attention to what scale degrees make up the interval. Compound intervals will have a wider distance than one would expect from the scale degrees. For example, a major ninth (a compound major second) is typically heard as scale degree 1 to 2, but the distance of the ninth is far greater than one would expect between these scale degrees. To make sure you are hearing the interval correctly, try singing the lower pitch up an octave and making sure it is still below the upper pitch.

## Singing

1. As with all intervals, begin by knowing which scale degrees you are going to sing. Next, find tonic and orient yourself in this key. You may want to do part of the setup from both the lower and the upper tonic.
2. Find and sing the simple interval counterpart to the compound interval you are asked to sing. For example, if asked to sing an ascending major tenth, begin by singing an ascending major third:

**EXAMPLE 4.3.1**

3. Displace the appropriate pitch by an octave to create the compound interval:

**EXAMPLE 4.3.2**

## Exercises

Before singing the melodies below, find the wide leaps that form the compound intervals. Practice these in isolation before trying the entire melody. Because very few people have a vocal range that can accommodate very wide intervals, the following melodies generally limit leaps to a major tenth.

MELODY 4.3.1

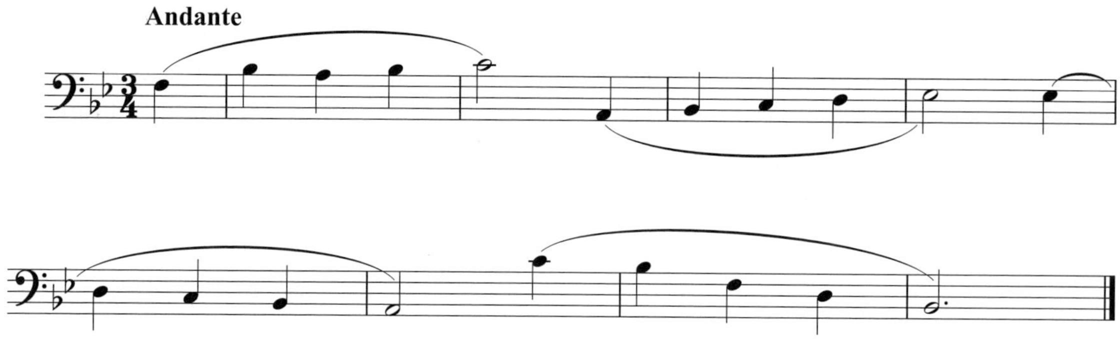


MELODY 4.3.2

MELODY 4.3.3

MELODY 4.3.4

**MELODY 4.3.5**

**MELODY 4.3.6**

**MELODY 4.3.7**

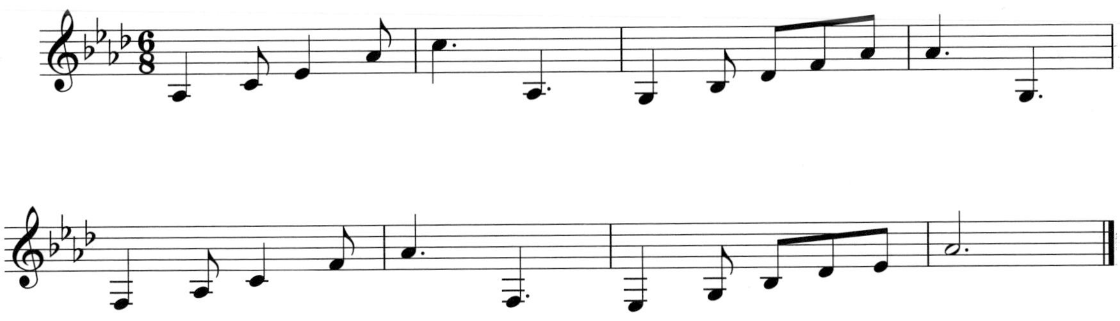

**MELODY 4.3.8**

**MELODY 4.3.9**

**MELODY 4.3.10**

**MELODY 4.3.11**

**MELODY 4.3.12**

MELODY 4.3.13

MELODY 4.3.14

MELODY 4.3.15

## MELODY 4.3.16

## Duets

### DUET 4.3.1

### DUET 4.3.2

## Self-Accompanied Melody

### SELF-ACCOMPANIED MELODY 4.3

## 4.4 Major-Major and Minor-Minor Seventh Chords

### Major-Major Seventh Chords

**Facts You Need to Know**

Major-major seventh chords are sometimes called "major seventh chords" by musicians. They consist of a major triad with a major third placed above it, forming a major seventh above the root. Major-major seventh chords appear in the major mode as:

$I^{M7}$, consisting of scale degrees 1, 3, 5, and 7
$IV^{M7}$, consisting of scale degrees 4, 6, 1, and 3

Major-major seventh chords appear in the minor mode as:

$III^{M7}$, consisting of scale degrees 3, 5, 7, and 1
$VI^{M7}$, consisting of scale degrees 6, 1, 3, and 5

As with all chords, adding a seventh does not change its function. As with all seventh chords, the chord seventh is a tendency tone that must resolve down by step.

## Hearing

When identifying root position MM7 chords, listen for these things:

1. Both scale degrees 7 (the leading tone) and 1 (tonic), in the texture.
2. A lack of desire to resolve—the chord as a whole is fairly stable. Scale degree 7, however, has both the leading tone's natural tendency to resolve up to tonic as well as a chord seventh's natural tendency to resolve down by step. This tension is one of the elements that makes this chord so beautiful and fun to sing.
3. A minor second (or minor ninth) will be in the texture if the chord is inverted—this is the only tonal seventh chord that contains a minor second.
4. To determine inversion, listen for the scale degree of the lowest pitch. If it is in root position, it will be scale degree 1; first inversion will be scale degree 3, second inversion will be scale degree 5, and third inversion will be scale degree 7.

## Singing MM7 Chords

1. Use the MM7 chord that appears as tonic in the major mode as your point of reference.
2. Know which scale degree your given pitch represents (1 if root position, 3 if first inversion, 5 if second inversion, and 7 if third inversion).
3. If necessary, sing the scale degree pattern for the given pitch to find tonic, and orient yourself in this key by singing all of the scale degree patterns in the major mode. You may want to focus on the patterns for scale degrees 1, 3, 5, and 7, as these will be the ones you use to sing the chord.
4. Sing scale degrees 1, 3, 5, and 7 in the order indicated by the inversion. Pay particular attention to the integrity of scale degree 7. Students often sing it too low, changing the chord into a much more "comfortable" dominant seventh chord.

**EXAMPLE 4.4.1**

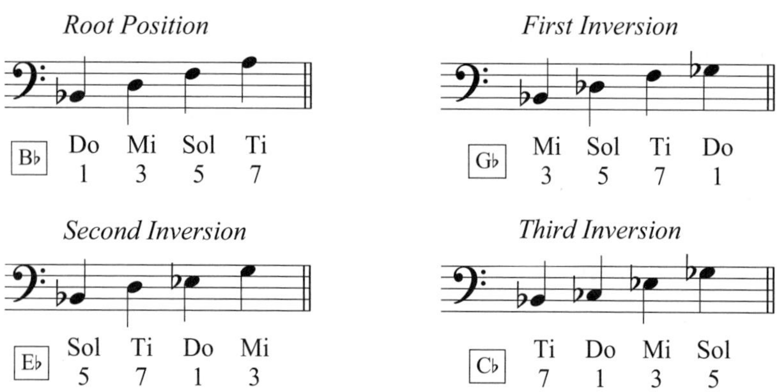

## Minor-Minor Seventh Chords

### Facts You Need to Know

Minor-minor seventh chords are often called "minor seventh" chords by musicians. They occur in three places in the major mode:

1. As $ii^7$, consisting of scale degrees 2, 4, 6, and 1
2. As $iii^7$, consisting of scale degrees 3, 5, 7, and 2
3. As $vi^7$, consisting of scale degrees 6, 1, 3, and 5

They occur in two places in the minor mode:

1. As $i^7$, consisting of scale degrees 1, 3, 5, and 7
2. As $iv^7$, consisting of scale degrees 4, 6, 1, and 3

## Hearing

Minor-minor seventh chords typically sound like predominant chords. Listen for the fifth and seventh wanting to resolve down by step to a dominant seventh chord and then to tonic in the major mode. This three-chord progression is characteristic of the $mm^7$ chord.

**EXAMPLE 4.4.2**

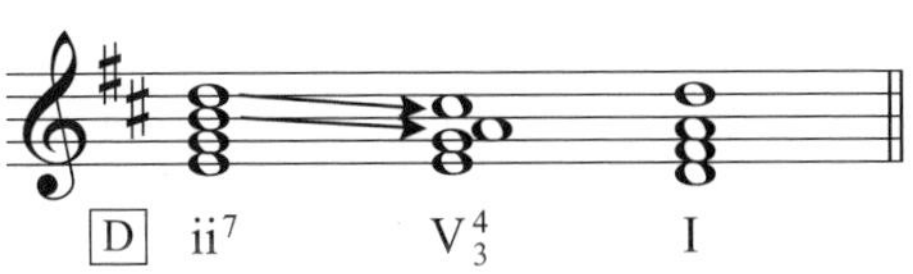


## Singing

1. Use the supertonic seventh chord ($ii^7$) in the major mode as your point of reference.
2. Determine the scale degree of the given pitch based on the requested inversion.
3. If necessary, sing that scale degree's pattern to find tonic, and orient yourself in that key. Focus on scale degrees 2, 4, 6, and 1.
4. Sing scale degrees 2, 4, 6, and 1 in the correct order.

**EXAMPLE 4.4.3**

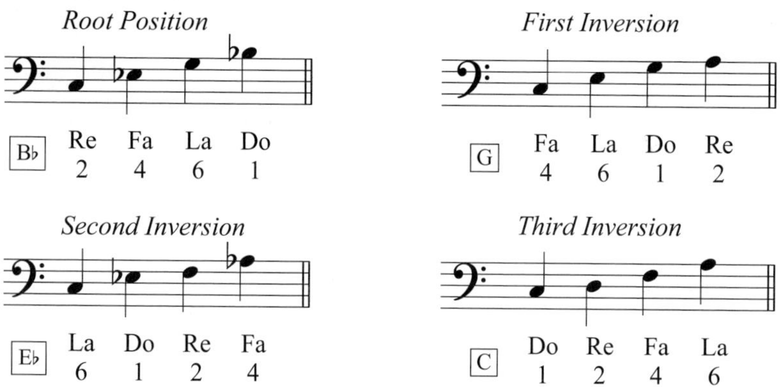


5. Pay attention to how these chords want to resolve through a dominant to tonic. Memorize the following progressions:

**EXAMPLE 4.4.4**

## Assignments for Practice

1. Practice singing MM$^7$ and mm$^7$ chords in all inversions and orderings from the same starting pitch.
2. Sing a MM7 followed rapidly by a Mm$^7$, then a mm$^7$ starting on the same pitch. Notice the similarities and differences between the sounds. Notice how each has a different desire to resolve. How many pitches need to move to change a MM$^7$ into a Mm$^7$ How many to change a Mm$^7$ into a mm$^7$?

## Pitch Patterns

### PITCH PATTERN 4.4.1

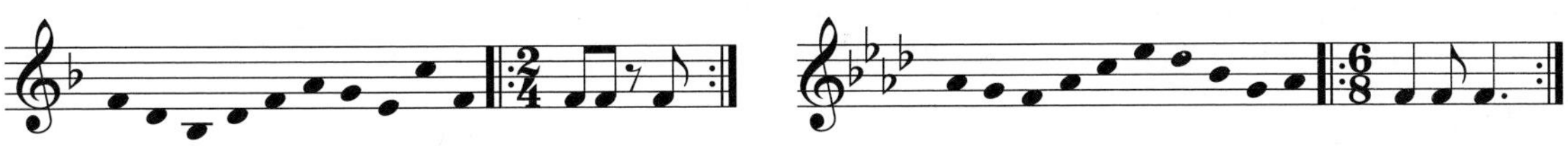

### PITCH PATTERN 4.4.2

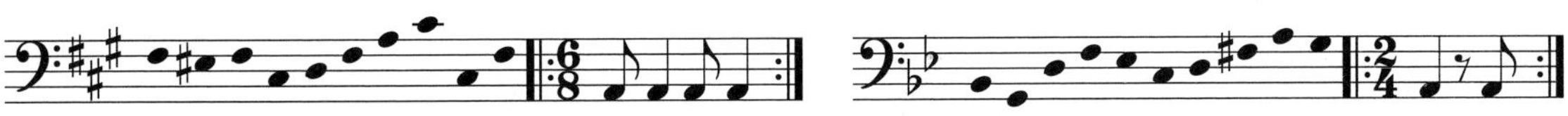

## Melodies

### MELODY 4.4.1

### MELODY 4.4.2

### MELODY 4.4.3

**MELODY 4.4.4**

**MELODY 4.4.5**

**MELODY 4.4.6**

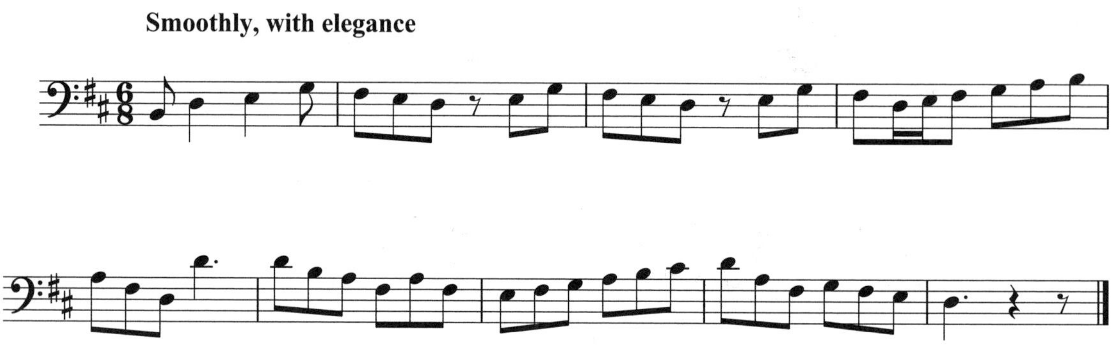


**MELODY 4.4.7**

**MELODY 4.4.8**

**MELODY 4.4.9**

**MELODY 4.4.10**

**MELODY 4.4.11**

### MELODY 4.4.12

### MELODY 4.4.13

### MELODY 4.4.14

### MELODY 4.4.15

## Duets

### DUET 4.4.1

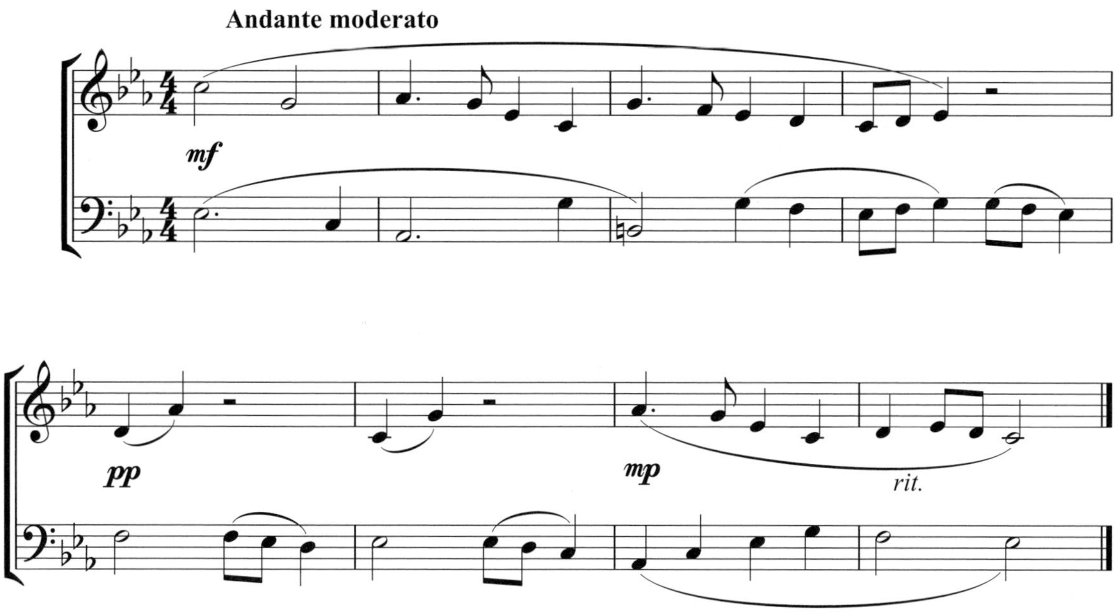


### DUET 4.4.2

**DUET 4.4.3**

## Chorale

**CHORALE 4.4**

## Self-Accompanied Melody

### SELF-ACCOMPANIED MELODY 4.4

## 4.5 Diminished Seventh Chords

### Half-Diminished (Diminished-Minor) Seventh Chords

#### Facts You Need to Know

Half-diminished seventh chords consist of a diminished triad with a major third placed above it, forming a minor seventh above the root.

They appear in the major mode in only one place:

As vii$^{ø7}$, consisting of scale degrees 7, 2, 4, and 6

They appear in the minor mode in only one place:

As ii$^{ø7}$, consisting of scale degrees 2, 4, 6, and 1

As with all chords, adding a seventh does not change its function. As with all seventh chords, the chord seventh is a tendency tone that must resolve down by step.

## Hearing

When identifying root position dm7 chords, listen for these things:

1. Both scale degrees 7 (the leading tone) and 6 (the submediant), in the texture.
2. A strong dominant sound and desire to resolve to a major tonic.
3. To determine inversion, listen for the scale degree of the lowest pitch. If it is in root position, it will be scale degree 7; first inversion will be scale degree 2, second inversion will be scale degree 4, and third inversion will be scale degree 6.

## Singing dm7 Chords

1. Use the dm7 chord that appears as the leading tone seventh chord in the major mode as your point of reference.
2. Know which scale degree your given pitch represents (7 if root position, 2 if first inversion, 4 if second inversion, and 6 if third inversion).
3. If necessary, sing the scale degree pattern for the given pitch to find tonic, and orient yourself in this key by singing all of the scale degree patterns in the major mode. You may want to focus on the patterns for scale degrees 7, 2, 4, and 6, as these will be the ones you use to sing the chord.
4. Sing scale degrees 7, 2, 4, and 6 in the order indicated by the inversion.

**EXAMPLE 4.5.1**

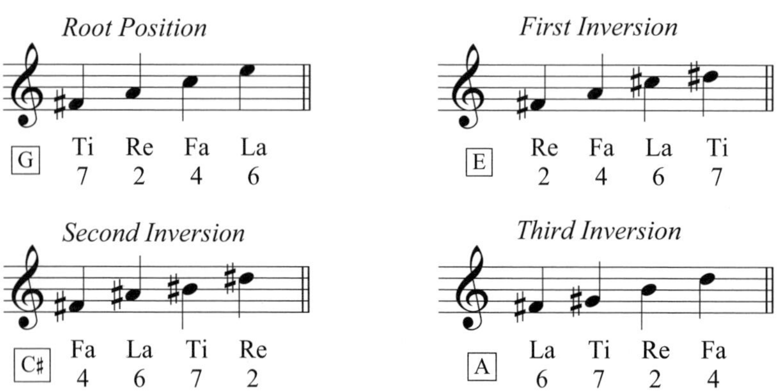


### Fully Diminished (Diminished-Diminished) Seventh Chords

#### Facts You Need to Know

Fully diminished seventh chords occur diatonically in only one place in the entire tonal system: as the leading tone seventh chord (vii°$^7$) in the minor mode.

## Hearing

Fully diminished seventh chords have a strong dominant sound that wants to resolve to the tonic triad in the minor mode. Listen specifically for the presence of scale degrees ♯7 and ♭6.

Fully diminished seventh chords are symmetrical—all of the intervals are the same (the second is an augmented second which is enharmonically the same as a minor third). As a result, it is not possible to determine the inversion when taken out of context.

## Singing

1. Use the leading tone seventh chord (vii°7) in the minor mode as your point of reference.
2. Hear the given pitch as the leading tone (♯7).
3. If necessary, sing that scale degree's pattern to find tonic, and orient yourself in that key. Focus on scale degrees ♯7, 2, 4, and 6.
4. Sing scale degrees ♯7, 2, 4, and 6 in the correct order.

**EXAMPLE 4.5.2**

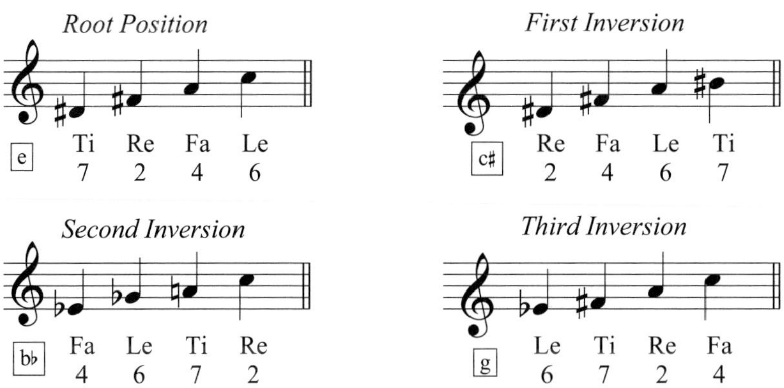


## Assignments for Practice

1. Practice singing half and fully diminished seventh chords in all inversions and orderings from the same starting pitch.
2. Sing a half-diminished seventh chord and treat it as a supertonic seventh chord in the minor mode. Sing through a dominant seventh to tonic, as illustrated below. See what happens if you invert the first chord.

**EXAMPLE 4.5.3**

3. Sing a MM7 followed rapidly by a $Mm^7$, a $mm^7$, a $dm^7$, and a $dd^7$ starting on the same pitch. Notice the similarities and differences between the sounds. Notice how each has a different desire to resolve. How many pitches need to move to change from one chord to the next?

## Pitch Patterns

### PITCH PATTERN 4.5.1

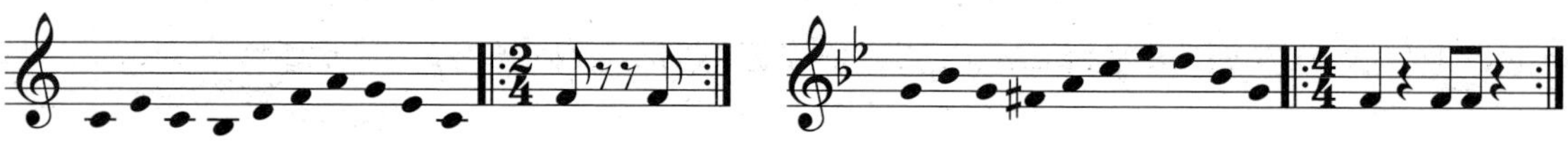

### PITCH PATTERN 4.5.2

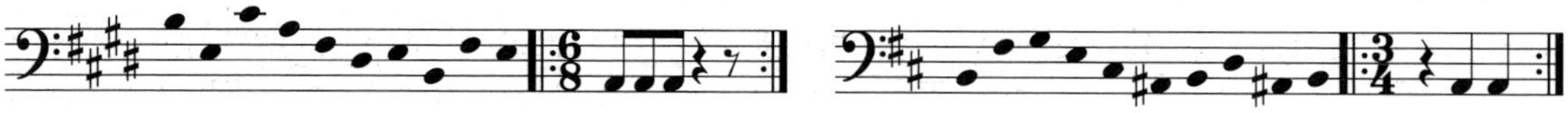

## Melodies

### MELODY 4.5.1

### MELODY 4.5.2

**MELODY 4.5.3**

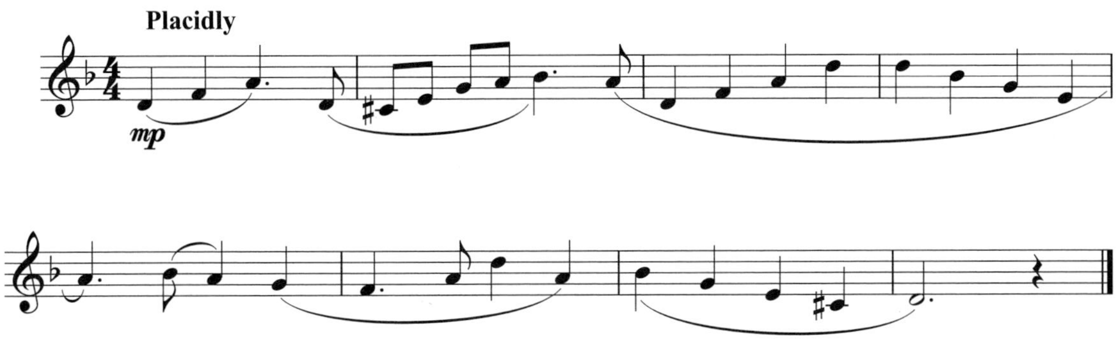


**MELODY 4.5.4**

**MELODY 4.5.5**

**MELODY 4.5.6**

**MELODY 4.5.7**

**MELODY 4.5.8**

**Allegro con brio**

**MELODY 4.5.9**

**Behaglich**

**MELODY 4.5.10**

**Lento**

**MELODY 4.5.11**

**Sadly**

MELODY 4.5.12

MELODY 4.5.13

MELODY 4.5.14

MELODY 4.5.15

## Duets

### DUET 4.5.1

### DUET 4.5.2

DUET 4.5.3

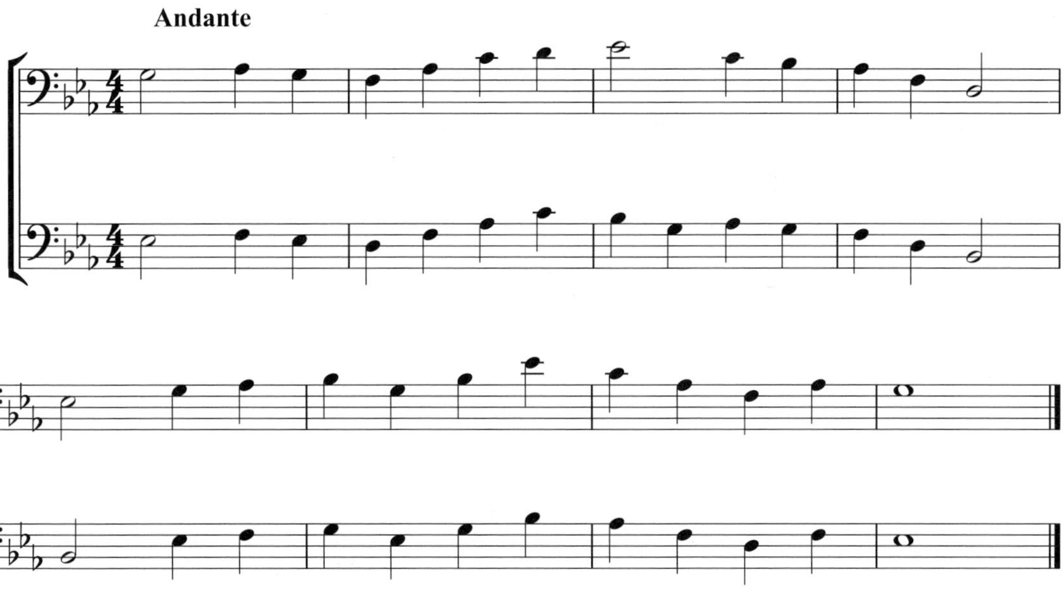


## Chorale

CHORALE 4.5

## Self-Accompanied Melody

### SELF-ACCOMPANIED MELODY 4.5

## 4.6 Improvisation III: Predominant Function

### Facts You Need to Know

Predominant function chords serve two musical roles:

1. To prepare and lead to the dominant.
2. To smoothly lead away from the tonic.

Predominant function chords are the same in the major and minor modes:

1. Subdominant chords (IV in major, iv in minor)
2. Supertonic chords (ii in major, ii° in minor)
3. Submediant chords (vi in major, VI in minor)

Inverting chords does not change their function, nor does adding sevenths.

Predominant function chords all share scale degree 6 (lowered form in minor). The scale degrees to focus on when improvising predominant function are 2, 4, 6, and 1. Scale degree 3 may also be used to a lesser extent.

## Hearing

Predominant chords often create the sensation of expansion and motion away from the tonic chord. They also lead to the very strong pull of the dominant chord. As such, they possess neither the stability of tonic function nor the desire toward resolution of dominant function. Listen for a lack of stability in the sound but not the direct pull toward tonic. To determine the specific predominant chord being used, listen for chord quality and inversion.

## Singing

When improvising predominant function, focus on singing scale degrees 2, 4, 6, and 1. Use the same three techniques for improvisation that you used for tonic function:

1. Repetition

**EXAMPLE 4.6.1**

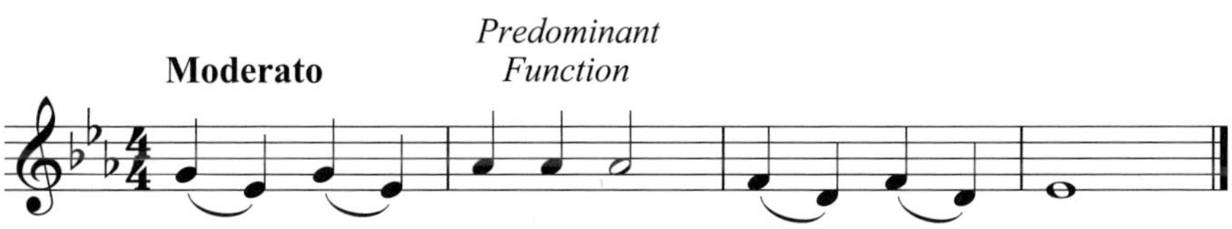


2. Arpeggiation

**EXAMPLE 4.6.2**

3. Connected arpeggiation

**EXAMPLE 4.6.3**

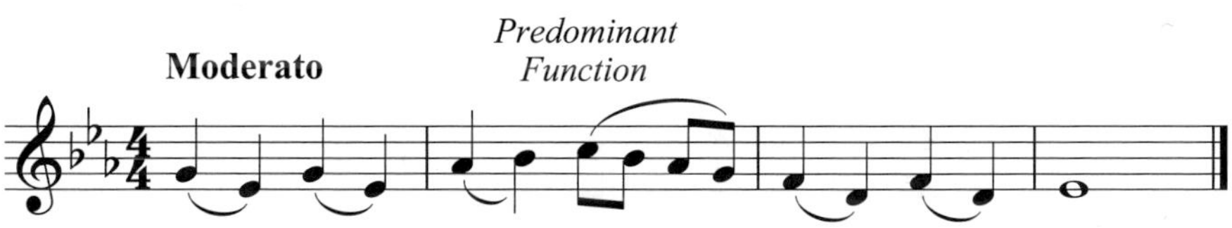


Be aware of the amount of time that you have to fill. Keep counting!

As always, use rhythmic and melodic components from elsewhere in the melody to help make your improvisation fit into the sound of the melody.

## Assignments for Practice

### Melodies

Improvise predominant harmony in the blank measures of the melodies.

**MELODY 4.6.1**

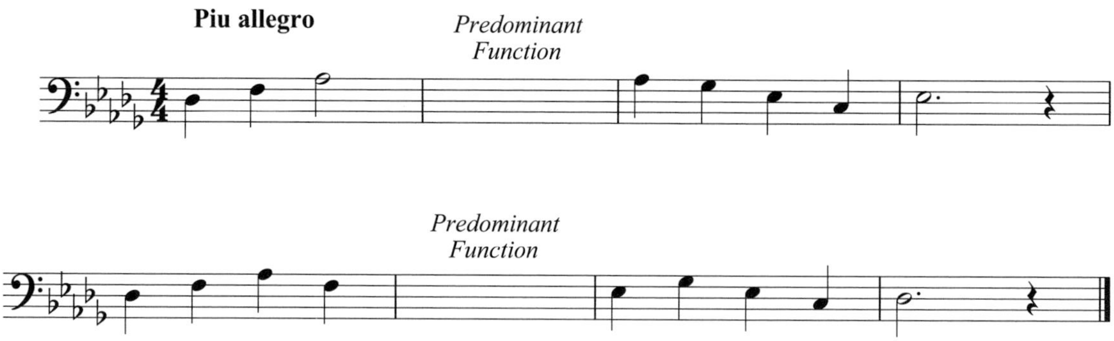


**MELODY 4.6.2**

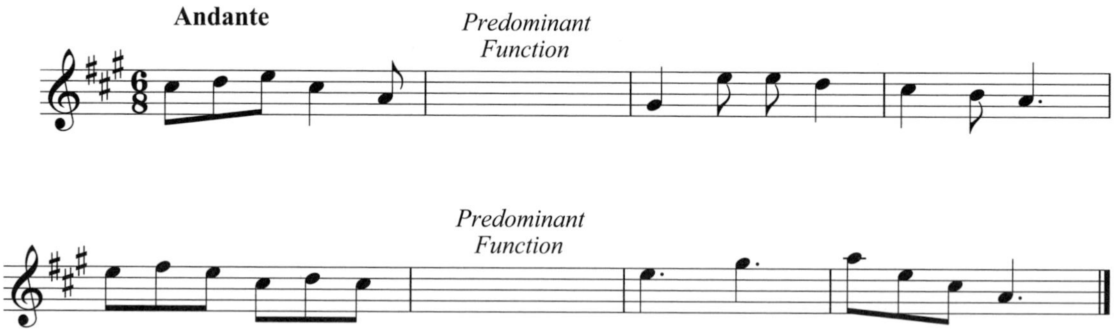


**MELODY 4.6.3**

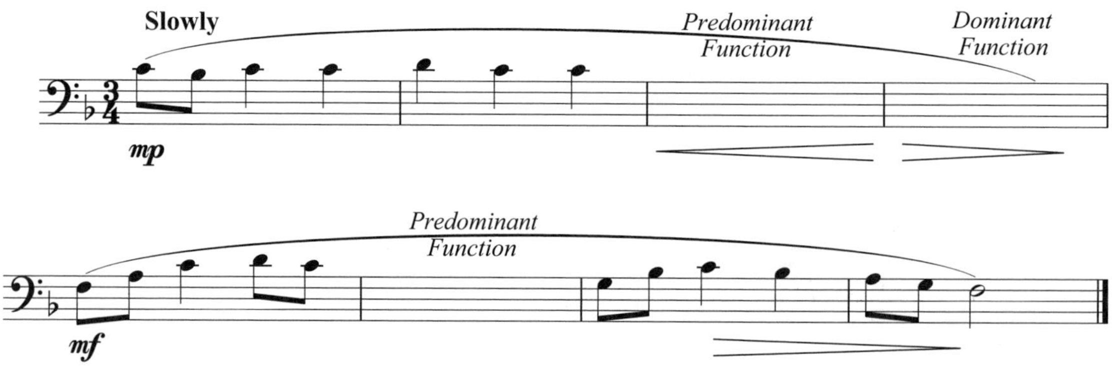

MELODY 4.6.4

MELODY 4.6.5

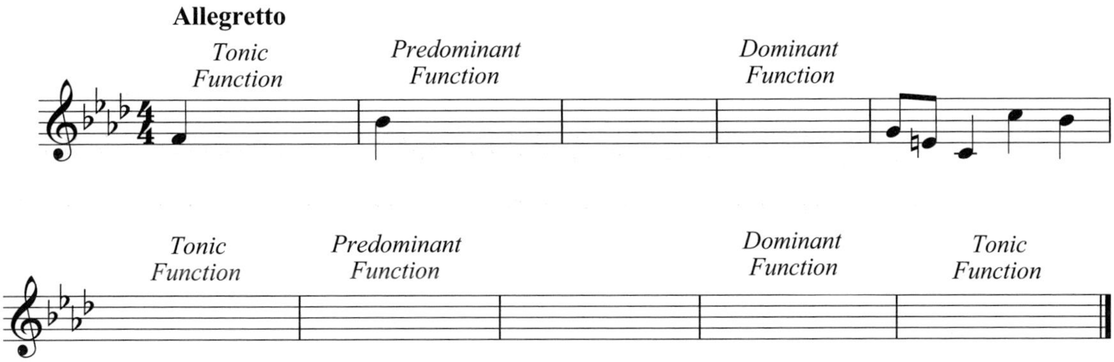


MELODY 4.6.6

MELODY 4.6.7

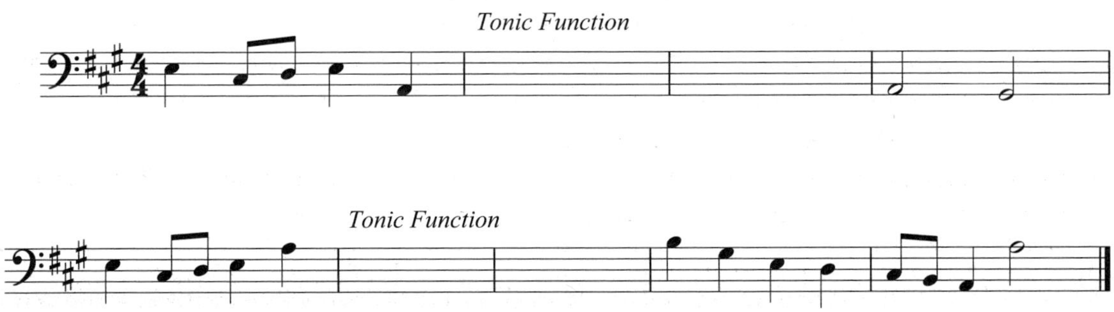

**MELODY 4.6.8**

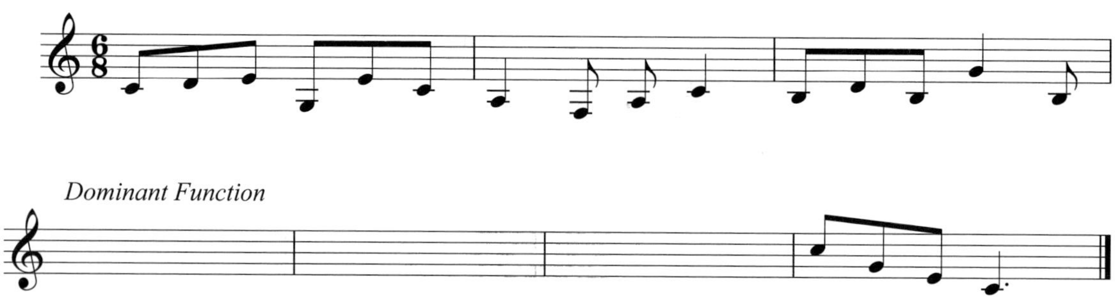


**MELODY 4.6.9**

**MELODY 4.6.10**

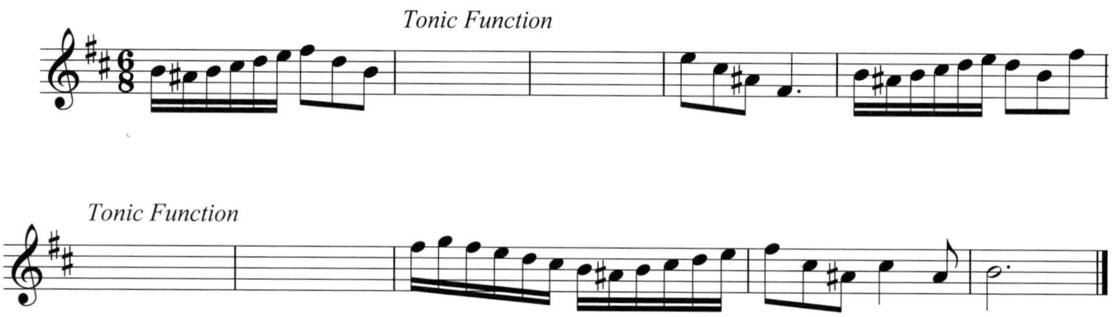


**MELODY 4.6.11**

**MELODY 4.6.12**

**MELODY 4.6.13**

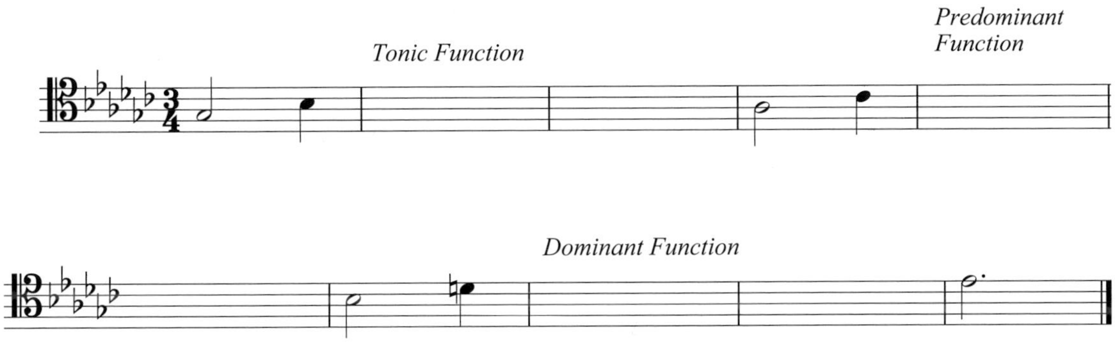


**MELODY 4.6.14**

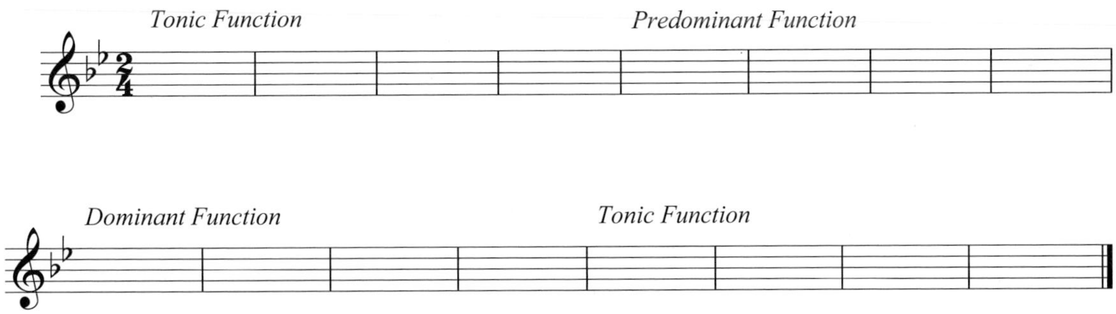


**MELODY 4.6.15**

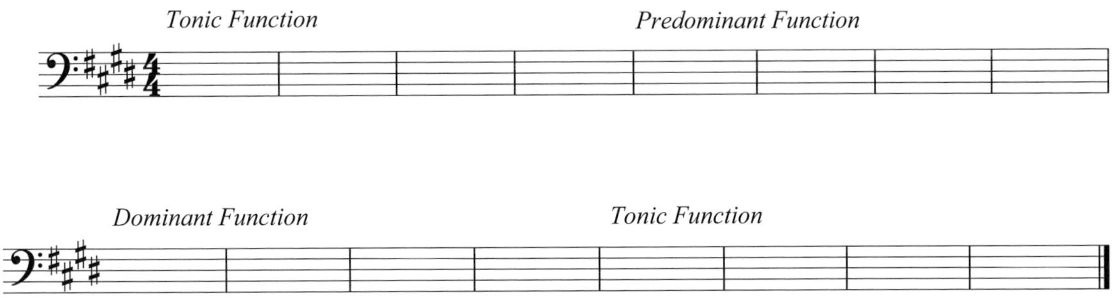

## Duets

### DUET 4.6.1

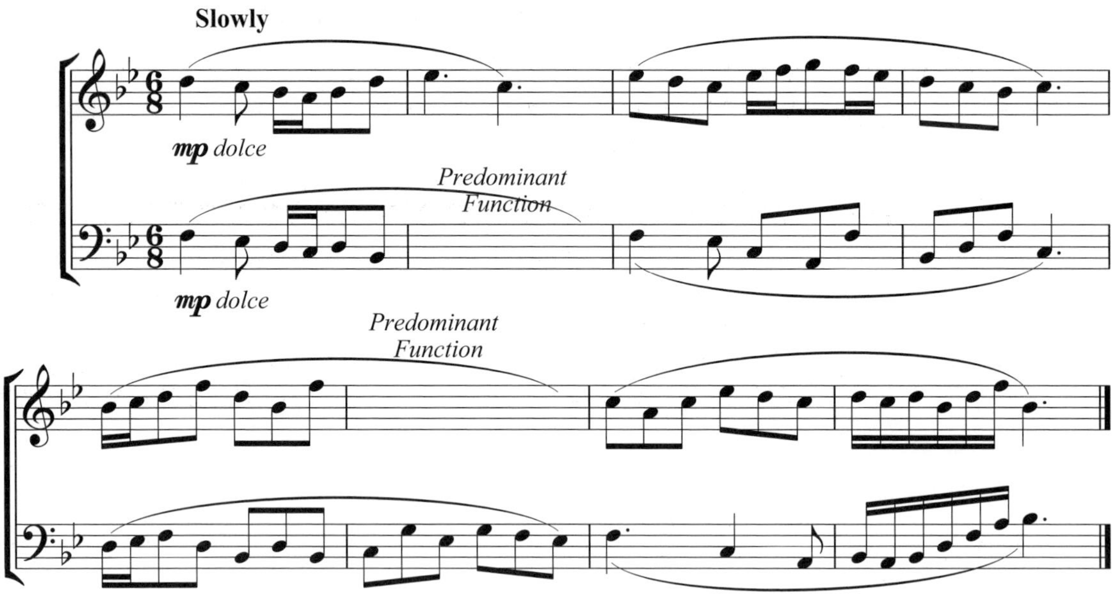


### DUET 4.6.2

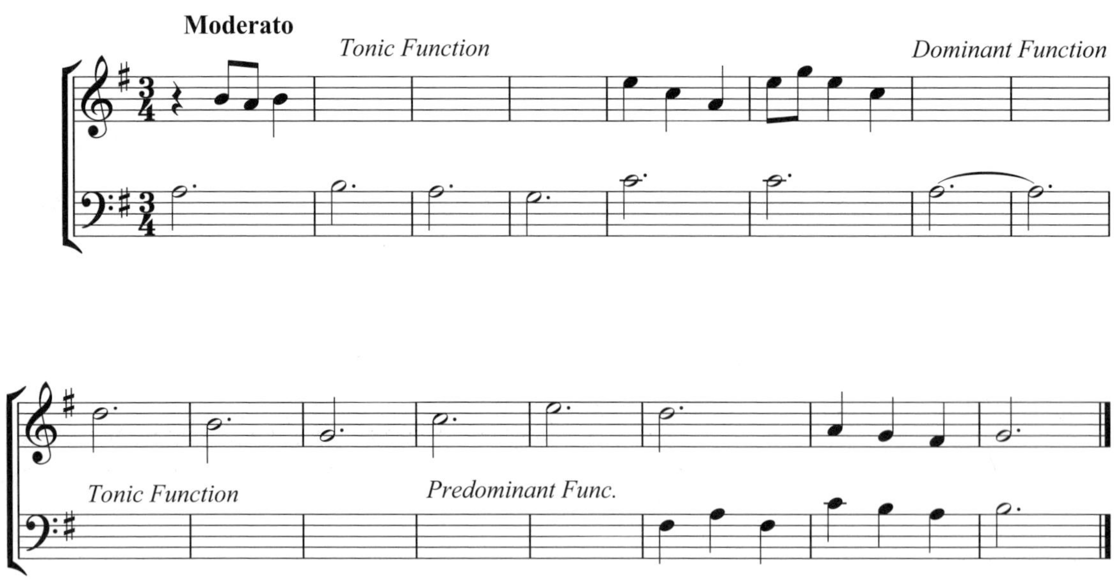

## Self-Accompanied Melody

### SELF-ACCOMPANIED MELODY 4.6

## 4.7 Music from the Literature

### EXAMPLE 4.7.1

Chorale, from *Cantata 140*

Violin I

J.S. Bach

### EXAMPLE 4.7.2

*Minuet*

Domenico Scarlatti

**EXAMPLE 4.7.3**

"Moravian Dance," from *Suite*, Op. 3

**Con moto**

Leoš Janáček

**EXAMPLE 4.7.4**

*To Spring*,
Op. 43, No. 6

**Allegro appassionato**

Edvard Grieg

**EXAMPLE 4.7.5**

"La fille aux cheveux de lin," from *Préludes pour Piano*, Book I

Claude Debussy

**EXAMPLE 4.7.6**

*Russian Folk Dance*

Beethoven

**EXAMPLE 4.7.7**

"Gute-nacht," from *Winterreise*

**Moderato**

Franz Schubert

**EXAMPLE 4.7.8**

*Se tu m'ami, se sospiri*

**Andantino**

Giovanni Pergolesi

**EXAMPLE 4.7.9**

*To a Wild Rose*, Op. 51, No. 1

**With simple tenderness**

Edward MacDowell

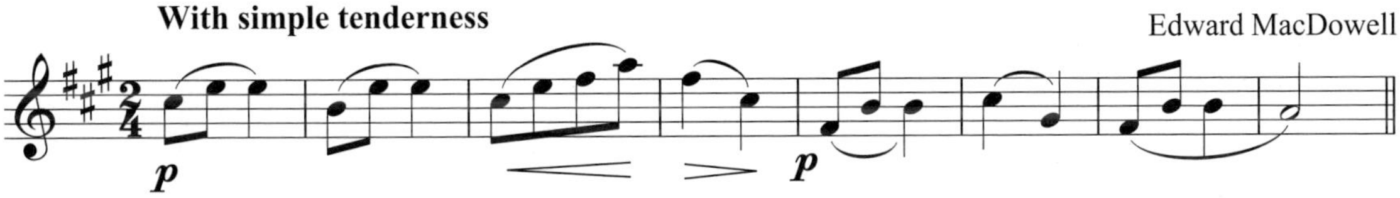


**EXAMPLE 4.7.10**

*Sonatina No. 34 in D Major*

**Presto**

Georg Anton Benda

**EXAMPLE 4.7.11**

## Reflections: Listening

Listening is the very foundation of our work as musicians. Though we tend to think of listening as something automatic (it's what we *do*, after all!) it is not; listening is a skill we need to cultivate throughout our careers.

Musicians use listening in a number of ways: as a means to becoming familiar with repertoire, to refine our aural sensitivity, and to be our own best critic. Being an effective listener is our pathway to learning and artistry. Developing critical listening skills helps us to practice more efficiently; be a better ensemble member and more knowledgeable audience member; become more sensitive to harmonic color; play or sing with better intonation; and become highly sensitive to what we hear. At its most fundamental, listening is a primary ingredient of communication, and communication is at the heart of our work. The artistic refinement we develop through well-honed listening skills allows us to achieve better communication with other musicians and our audience alike.

So what is listening, exactly? Listening is an active experience that requires focus and concentration. It is a multi-step process that involves first hearing something, then categorizing and incorporating it into a schema you understand, then interpreting it, personalizing it to use in your own way. Listening requires an open mind, so that we don't just hear what we want to hear, but instead are able to tune into what is really happening. For example, in a chamber group, listening well means recognizing that you are the person playing out of tune rather than assuming that those around you are wrong; it also means being open to what you hear. Your playing partner may decide to use rubato in a new way or deliberately toy with a tempo; listening with an open mind allows you to respond immediately to what you hear.

Listening is an experience that happens in time; once the moment is gone, we can't get it back—that's why focus and concentration is so important. The challenge is to develop the ability to hear, categorize, and interpret in rapid-fire fashion. Perhaps you experience the need for this rapid reaction when you take melodic dictation, for example. You hear a melody, and start to write, but if the melody continues, you need to still be listening while you write. Focus is essential!

Memory is also in important part of developing listening skills. In order to use and incorporate what you hear, you need the ability to retain it over the short and long term. Learning to recognize intervals is a matter of memory, for example. You listen to an interval and categorize its sound by reacting to the color and timbre of what you hear. That, in turn, helps you to memorize the individual characteristics of the interval. In this way, listening is turned into knowledge.

Developing your inner hearing—the ability to hear inside your head—is another essential part of listening. Inner hearing plays an important role in intonation. To play in tune, you need to hear a pitch before you play or sing it, then refine its center once you create sound and hear how what you're playing relates to the sound around you. Inner hearing helps fuel our musical imaginations and creativity. It helps us to imagine how we want a piece to sound as we work on our interpretation of it, helps us to see music we hear and to hear music we see. Perhaps there is no better example in all of music than the genius of Beethoven, who wrote some of his most deeply creative music after experiencing total hearing loss. His inner hearing was astounding.

Developing your listening skill happens through practicing a mindful approach. Take advantage of the opportunities you have every day, in classes, ensembles, and the practice room, to groom your skill.

## 4.8 Dictation Materials

### I. Identification of Minor Scale Degrees

Your teacher will establish a key and then play its scale degrees in random order or as a specific pitch in a melody (by number—first, second, last, or by position—high or low). Identify each by writing its number in the appropriate space. Place an up arrow in front of scale degree 6 or 7 if you hear either of them in their raised position.

*Date:* . . . . . . . . . . . . . .

1. ____ 2. ____ 3. ____ 4. ____ 5. ____ 6. ____ 7. ____ 8. ____

*Date:* . . . . . . . . . . . . . .

1. ____ 2. ____ 3. ____ 4. ____ 5. ____ 6. ____ 7. ____ 8. ____

*Date:* . . . . . . . . . . . . . .

1. ____ 2. ____ 3. ____ 4. ____ 5. ____ 6. ____ 7. ____ 8. ____

*Date:* . . . . . . . . . . . . . .

1. ____ 2. ____ 3. ____ 4. ____ 5. ____ 6. ____ 7. ____ 8. ____

*Date:* . . . . . . . . . . . . . .

1. ____ 2. ____ 3. ____ 4. ____ 5. ____ 6. ____ 7. ____ 8. ____

### II. Identification of Major Scale Degrees

Your teacher will establish a key and then play its scale degrees in random order or as a specific pitch in a melody (by number—first, second, last, or by position—high or low). Identify each by writing its number in the appropriate space.

*Date:* . . . . . . . . . . . . . .

1. ____ 2. ____ 3. ____ 4. ____ 5. ____ 6. ____ 7. ____ 8. ____

*Date:* . . . . . . . . . . . . . .

1. ____ 2. ____ 3. ____ 4. ____ 5. ____ 6. ____ 7. ____ 8. ____

*Date:* . . . . . . . . . . . . . .

1. ____ 2. ____ 3. ____ 4. ____ 5. ____ 6. ____ 7. ____ 8. ____

*Date:* . . . . . . . . . . . . . .

1. ____ 2. ____ 3. ____ 4. ____ 5. ____ 6. ____ 7. ____ 8. ____

*Date:* . . . . . . . . . . . . . .

1. ____ 2. ____ 3. ____ 4. ____ 5. ____ 6. ____ 7. ____ 8. ____

### III. Interval Identification

Your teacher will play several intervals. Identify their quality and size as one of the following:

M2 = Major second
m2 = Minor second
M3 = Major third
m3 = Minor third
P4 = Perfect fourth
TT = Tritone
P5 = Perfect fifth
M6 = Major sixth
m6 = Minor sixth
M7 = Major seventh
m7 = Minor seventh
P8 = Perfect octave
M9 = Major ninth
m9 = Minor ninth
M10 = Major tenth
m10 = Minor tenth

Be sure to make a clear difference between your capital and lower-case Ms.

*Date:* . . . . . . . . . . . . . .

1. ____ 2. ____ 3. ____ 4. ____ 5. ____ 6. ____ 7. ____ 8. ____

*Date:* . . . . . . . . . . . . . .

1. ____ 2. ____ 3. ____ 4. ____ 5. ____ 6. ____ 7. ____ 8. ____

*Date:* . . . . . . . . . . . . . .

1. ____ 2. ____ 3. ____ 4. ____ 5. ____ 6. ____ 7. ____ 8. ____

*Date:* . . . . . . . . . . . . . .

1. ____ 2. ____ 3. ____ 4. ____ 5. ____ 6. ____ 7. ____ 8. ____

*Date:* . . . . . . . . . . . . . .

1. ____ 2. ____ 3. ____ 4. ____ 5. ____ 6. ____ 7. ____ 8. ____

### IV. Triad Quality Identification

Your teacher will play several triads. Indicate the quality and inversion. Possible answers are M for major, m for minor, and d for diminished.

*Date:* ..............

1. ____ 2. ____ 3. ____ 4. ____ 5. ____ 6. ____ 7. ____ 8. ____

*Date:* ..............

1. ____ 2. ____ 3. ____ 4. ____ 5. ____ 6. ____ 7. ____ 8. ____

*Date:* ..............

1. ____ 2. ____ 3. ____ 4. ____ 5. ____ 6. ____ 7. ____ 8. ____

*Date:* ..............

1. ____ 2. ____ 3. ____ 4. ____ 5. ____ 6. ____ 7. ____ 8. ____

*Date:* ..............

1. ____ 2. ____ 3. ____ 4. ____ 5. ____ 6. ____ 7. ____ 8. ____

## V. Seventh Chord Identification

Your teacher will play several seventh chords. Indicate the quality (MM, Mm, mm, dm, or dd) and inversion for each by using the correct figured bass symbol.

*Date:* ..............

1. ____ 2. ____ 3. ____ 4. ____ 5. ____ 6. ____ 7. ____ 8. ____

*Date:* ..............

1. ____ 2. ____ 3. ____ 4. ____ 5. ____ 6. ____ 7. ____ 8. ____

*Date:* ..............

1. ____ 2. ____ 3. ____ 4. ____ 5. ____ 6. ____ 7. ____ 8. ____

*Date:* ..............

1. ____ 2. ____ 3. ____ 4. ____ 5. ____ 6. ____ 7. ____ 8. ____

*Date:* ..............

1. ____ 2. ____ 3. ____ 4. ____ 5. ____ 6. ____ 7. ____ 8. ____

## VI. Melodic and Rhythmic Dictation

Your teacher will play a short melody or rhythm. Notate it on the staves below.

*Date:* . . . . . . . . . . . . . .

*Date:* . . . . . . . . . . . . . .

*Date:* . . . . . . . . . . . . . .

*Date:* . . . . . . . . . . . . . .

*Date:* . . . . . . . . . . . . . .

## VII. Harmonic Dictation

Write the soprano line, bass line, and provide a Roman numeral analysis (including inversional symbols) for the progression you hear on the grand staff below.

*Date:* . . . . . . . . . . . . . .

*Date:* . . . . . . . . . . . . . .

*Date:* . . . . . . . . . . . . . .

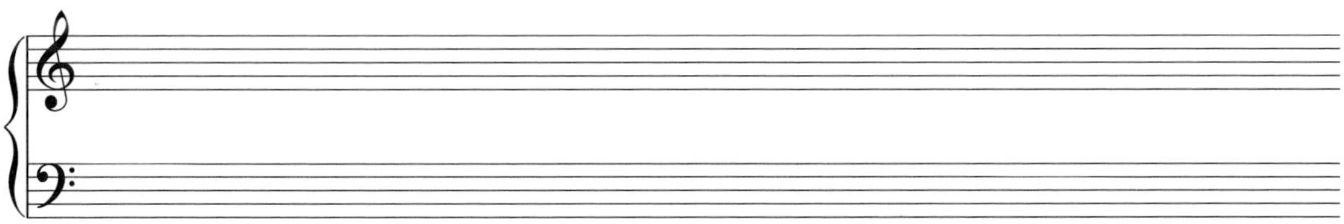

*Date:* . . . . . . . . . . . . . .

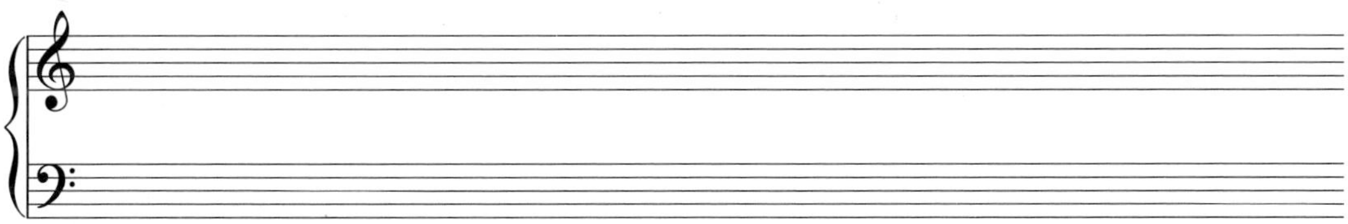

*Date:* . . . . . . . . . . . . . .

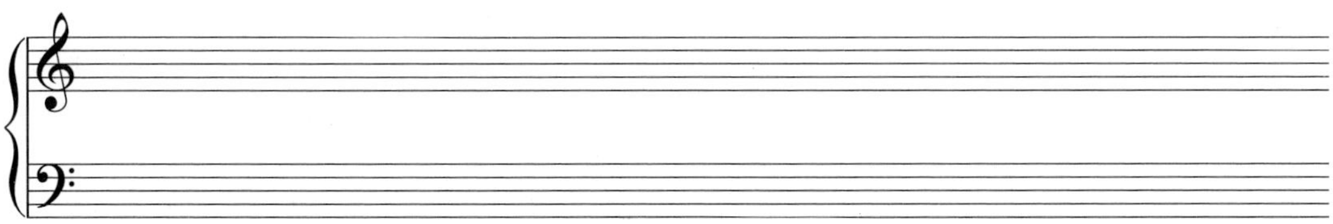

# Chapter 5

# Less Common Meters; C Clefs and Harmonic Progression

## 5.1 Less Common Simple and Compound Meters

### Facts You Need to Know

In this text, "Less Common Meters" are defined as simple meters that use a half note or eighth note as the beat-note value (except $\frac{2}{2}$), and compound meters that use the dotted-eighth or dotted-half note as the beat-note.

### Reading in Less Common Simple Meters

Reading music written in these meters may seem difficult because it looks so different from what you are most accustomed to seeing. You can minimize this perceived difficulty if you keep these basic principles in mind:

1. In simple meters, regardless of the beat-note value, each beat divides naturally into two parts, and each division further divides into two.
2. Regardless of the beat-note value, the 2:1 relationship between notes always remains the same: a half note has two quarter notes, a quarter has two eighths, etc.

Refer to the charts in Sections 1.1 and 1.2 for a visual representation of these note-value equivalents and how they relate to specific meters.

To read in less common meters:

1. Look at the time signature; determine the beat-note value and number of beats in a measure.
2. Once you know the beat-note value, remind yourself what the division and multiple of the beat will be.
3. Use *the same counting system* in these meters as you do in more frequently encountered meter. For example, if you typically count with "+'s" in $\frac{2}{4}$, do the same in $\frac{2}{8}$ (as in example A opposite).

**EXAMPLE 5.1.1**

Example A:

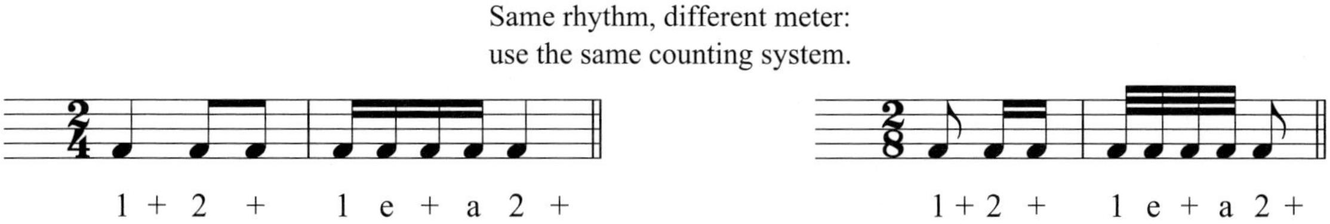
Same rhythm, different meter:
use the same counting system.
1 + 2 + 1 e + a 2 +
1 + 2 + 1 e + a 2 +

Many students try to relate a less common meter to one with a quarter note as the beat-note value (as in example B below). Avoid this technique—it makes rhythm reading more complicated and cumbersome! Doing so also eliminates one of the most important elements in performance: the integrity of the written meter.

**EXAMPLE 5.1.2**

Example B:

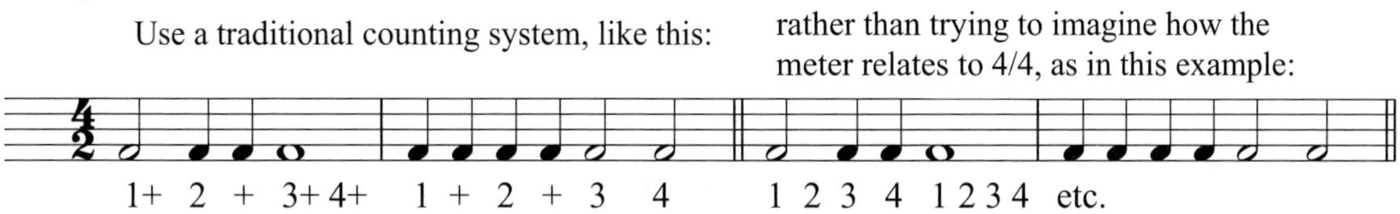
Use a traditional counting system, like this:
rather than trying to imagine how the
meter relates to 4/4, as in this example:
1+ 2 + 3+ 4+ 1 + 2 + 3 4
1 2 3 4 1 2 3 4 etc.

Use the same process to read in less common compound meters (such as $\frac{6}{16}$ and $\frac{6}{4}$): Determine the value of the beat-note and divisions and remember that in compound meter, the beat is always divided into three parts. Refer to the charts in Chapter 2, Section 2.1, Compound Meters, to see examples of these infrequently used compound meters. As in simple meter, use the same counting method for these meters as you do in $\frac{6}{8}$—it is the easiest and most direct way to ensure accuracy.

## Rhythms

**RHYTHM 5.1.1**

Adagio

**RHYTHM 5.1.2**

Adagio
p

**RHYTHM 5.1.3**

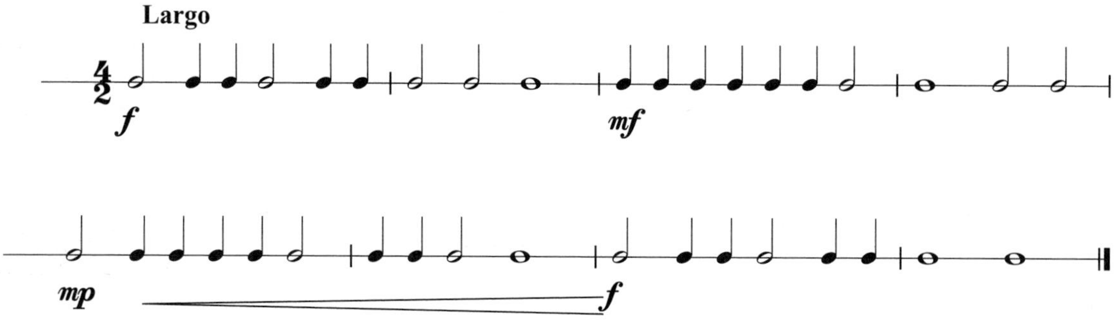


**RHYTHM 5.1.4**

**RHYTHM 5.1.5**

**RHYTHM 5.1.6**

**RHYTHM 5.1.7**

**RHYTHM 5.1.8**

**RHYTHM 5.1.9**

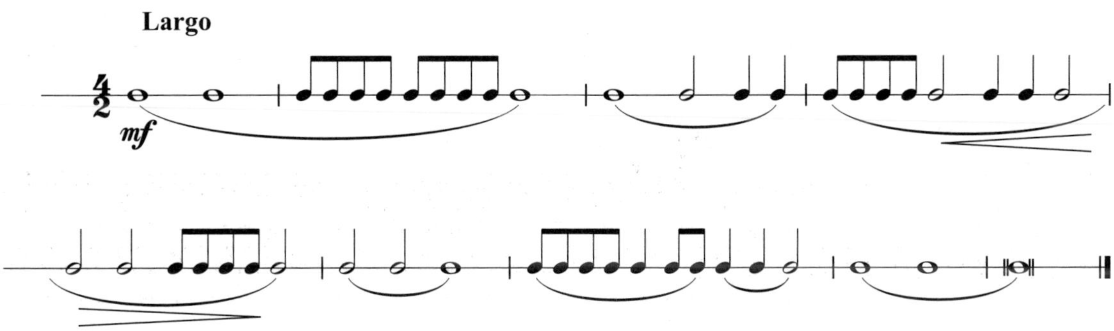


**RHYTHM 5.1.10**

**RHYTHM 5.1.11**

**RHYTHM 5.1.12**

**RHYTHM 5.1.13**

**RHYTHM 5.1.14**

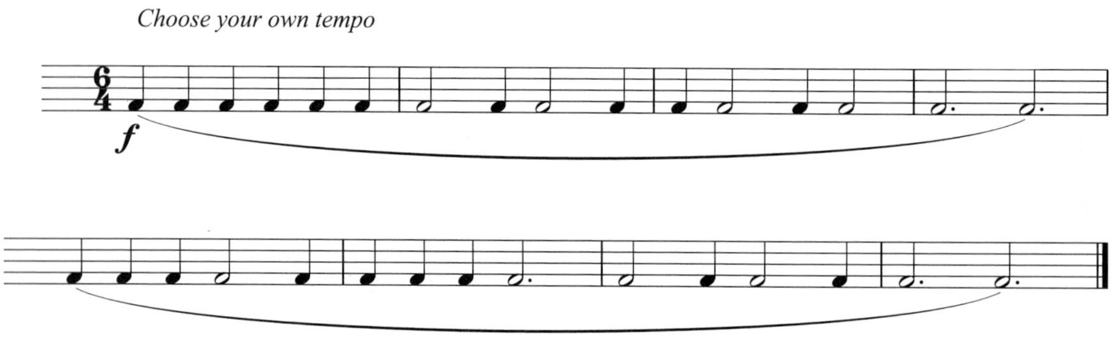

**RHYTHM 5.1.15**

---

## 5.2 Reading the Alto and Tenor Clefs

### Facts You Need to Know

The location of pitches on the staff is determined by the placement of a clef at the beginning of each line of music. This clef shows the location of one pitch, from which we can figure out where all of the remaining pitches are.

We have already worked with the G clef, which is used for the treble clef, and the F clef, which is used for the bass clef. The remaining clef is the C clef, which shows the location of the pitch C4 (or middle C). When the C clef is placed on the third or middle line, the music is in alto clef. When it is placed on the fourth line, it is in tenor clef. The placement of notes on the alto and tenor staves appears below:

**EXAMPLE 5.2.1**

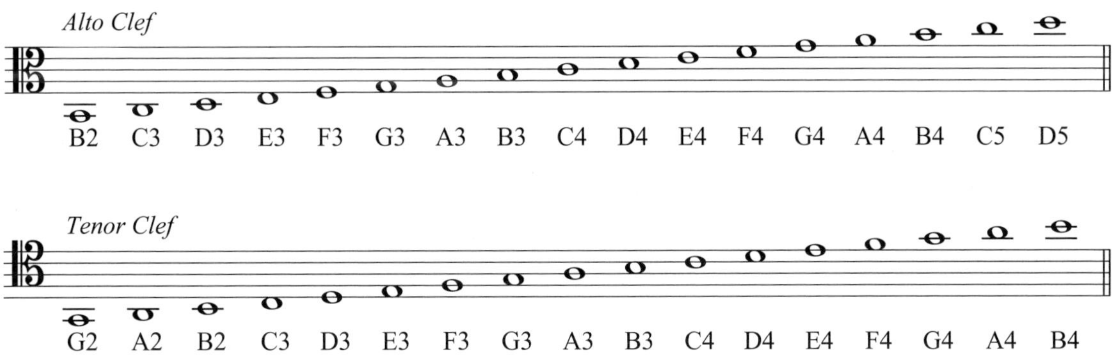


Alto clef is the primary clef used by violists, so anybody who might read a string score some day needs to become proficient with it. It is also used for trombones and some older vocal parts. Tenor clef is used frequently by cellos, bassoons, and trombones, and again it appears in some older vocal parts.

## Reading in the Alto and Tenor Clefs

Just as with the treble and bass clefs, begin to develop reading fluency by selecting two or three lines to use as "reference points" on the staff: first line F, third line C and fifth line G are good choices for the alto staff, and the second line F and fourth line C are good choices for the tenor staff. Scan the notes in each exercise before you begin, looking for large leaps, relating them to your established points of reference.

**EXAMPLE 5.2.2**

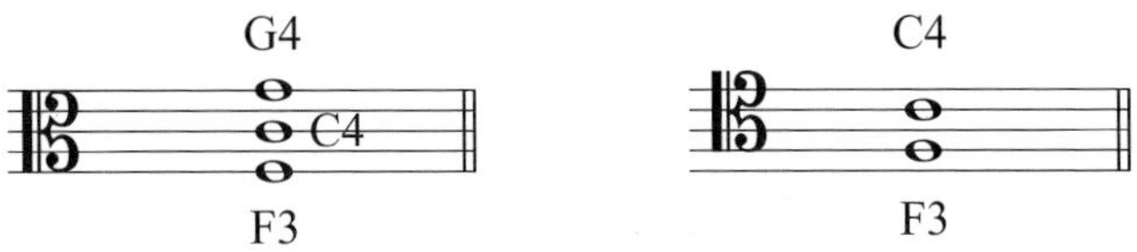


Once again, the only way to effectively master this skill is to do it. Devote some time each day to reading clefs until you are fluent with all of them.

## Assignments for Practice

### Pitch Patterns

**PITCH PATTERN 5.2.1**

**PITCH PATTERN 5.2.2**

**PITCH PATTERN 5.2.3**

**PITCH PATTERN 5.2.4**

**PITCH PATTERN 5.2.5**

## Melodies

### MELODY 5.2.1

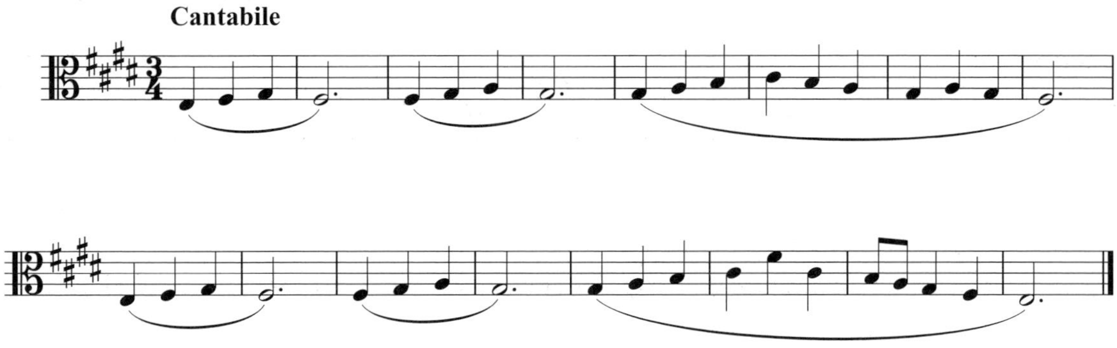


### MELODY 5.2.2

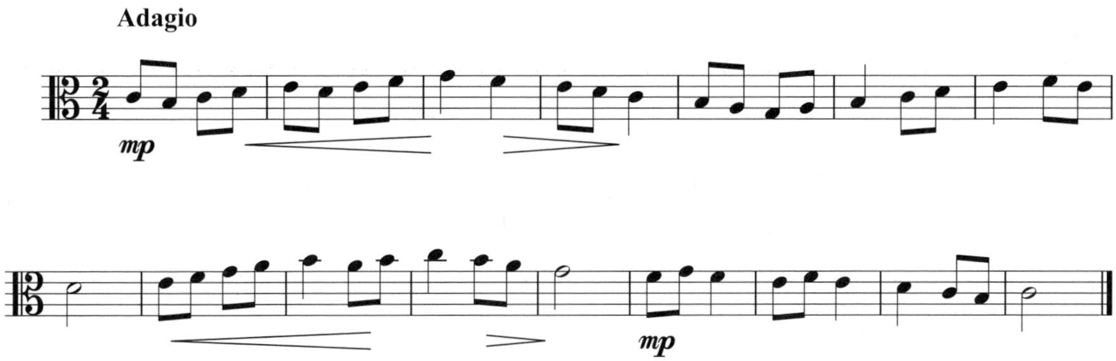


### MELODY 5.2.3

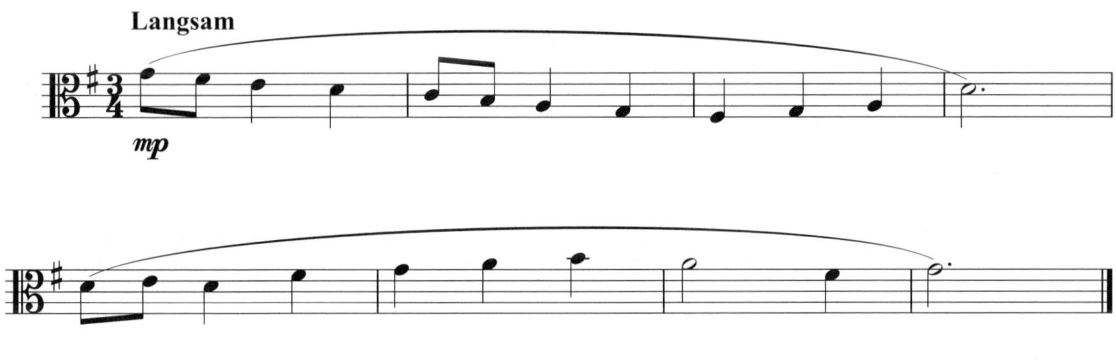


### MELODY 5.2.4

MELODY 5.2.5

MELODY 5.2.6

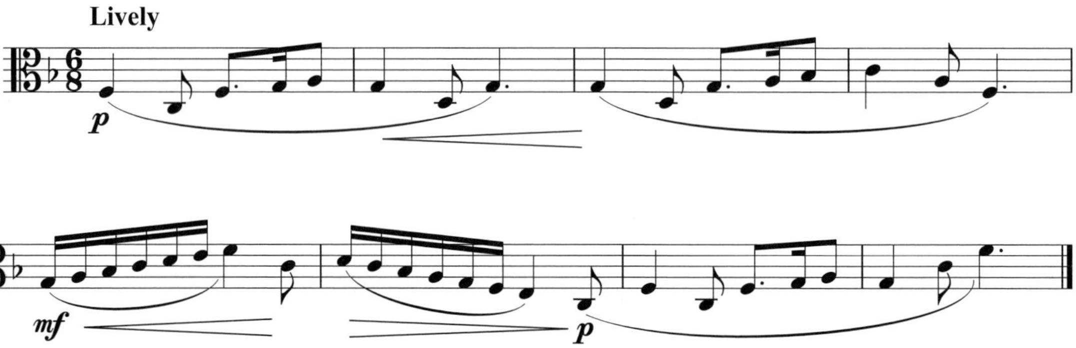


MELODY 5.2.7

MELODY 5.2.8

MELODY 5.2.9

MELODY 5.2.10

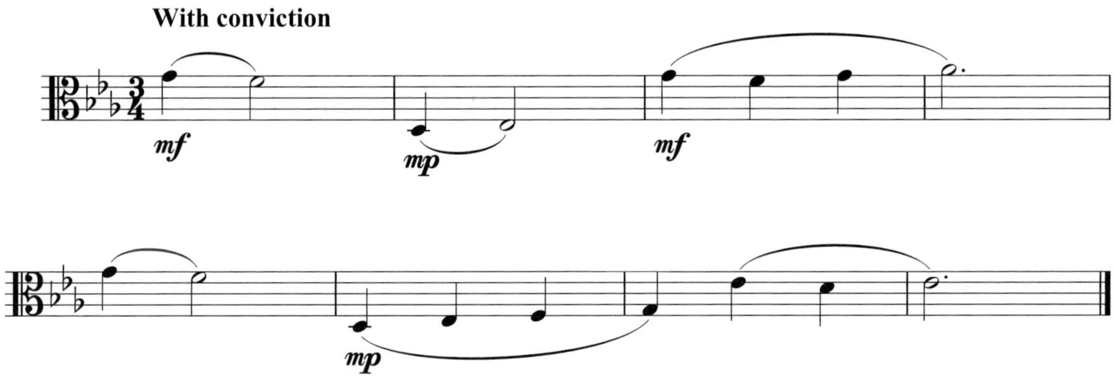


MELODY 5.2.11

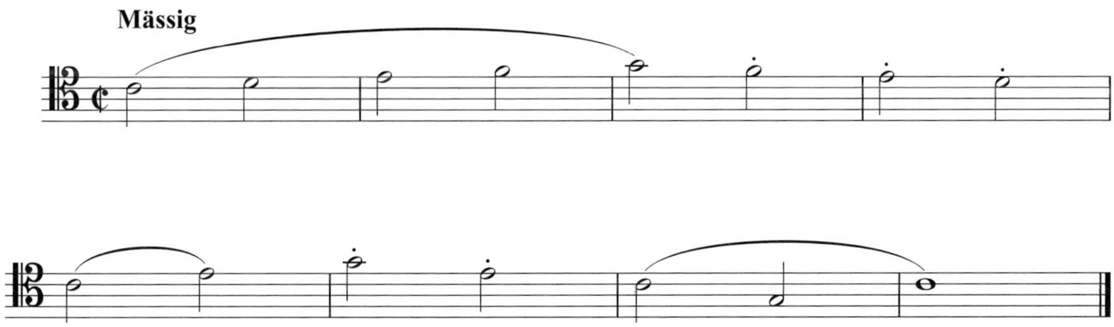


MELODY 5.2.12

### MELODY 5.2.13

### MELODY 5.2.14

### MELODY 5.2.15

### MELODY 5.2.16

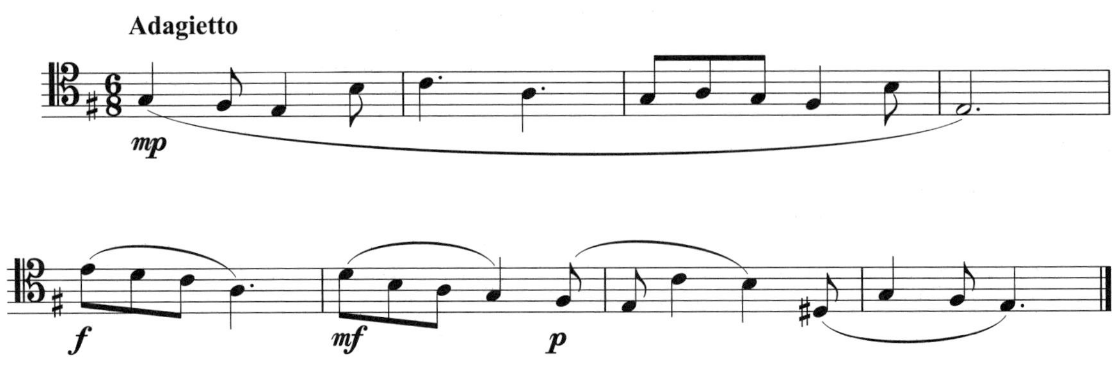

**MELODY 5.2.17**

**MELODY 5.2.18**

**MELODY 5.2.19**

**MELODY 5.2.20**

## 5.3 Harmonic Progressions

### Arpeggiating Harmonic Progressions

#### Facts You Need to Know

Up to now, this text's approach toward harmony has been how to express one of the three harmonic functions through improvisation. This chapter focuses on realizing harmonic progressions over which a melody may be improvised.

Harmonic progressions may be realized melodically through arpeggiating chords. Listen for how the melody you sing suggests the progression of chords. In other words, sing melodically, but hear harmonically.

When arpeggiating progressions, be aware of:

1. The Roman numeral of the chord you are singing and its component scale degrees.
2. The root motion (direction and distance) between chords. There are only six possibilities:

    Up or down by second
    Up or down by third
    Up or down by fourth

All other root motions are inversions of one of the above (motion down by fifth is the same as up by fourth).

The root motion governs how the voices typically move. By knowing the root motion and the location of each chord member, you can figure out each pitch's most common motion.

Here are some other factors to listen for:

1. If you are singing a tendency tone (a note with a strong desire to resolve to a particular place), do what the note tells you it wants to do.
2. If the bass is moving by step, move in the opposite direction.
3. Move the smallest possible distance to a note in the next chord—usually a second or a third.
4. If you are singing a chord seventh, step down by second.

Note that these aren't the only options. After you become comfortable using these, experiment with other possibilities.

### Singing

1. Begin by figuring out the scale degrees that make up each chord.
2. Arpeggiate the first chord.
3. Use the information in the list above to figure out how the voices should move. In general, keep common tones between chords, and have moving tones make the smoothest connection between chords by moving the smallest possible distance.

4. Above all, listen for the underlying harmonic progression.

This is one way that you might realize the following progression:

I – IV – ii – $V^7$ – I

**EXAMPLE 5.3.1**

## 5.4 Frequently Used Progressions

### Common Progressions

Some sequential harmonic progressions appear regularly enough that it is worthwhile to simply memorize them. Sequences create musical tension by creating the expectation of eventual departure from the given pattern. As you memorize these patterns, see if you can come up with other musical ways to express the same progressions.

### The Circle of Fifths Progression

**EXAMPLE 5.4.1**

## The Circle of Fifths Using Seventh Chords Progression

**EXAMPLE 5.4.2**

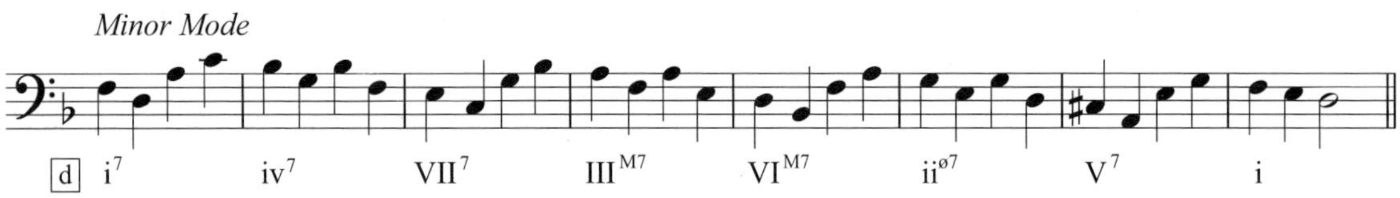


## The Descending Thirds Progression

Note that you will likely need to shift octaves at least once during this progression in order to keep it in your vocal range. Shifts below are marked with a "*". Make the shifts where they make the most sense to your voice by stepping up from the fifth of the previous chord.

**EXAMPLE 5.4.3**

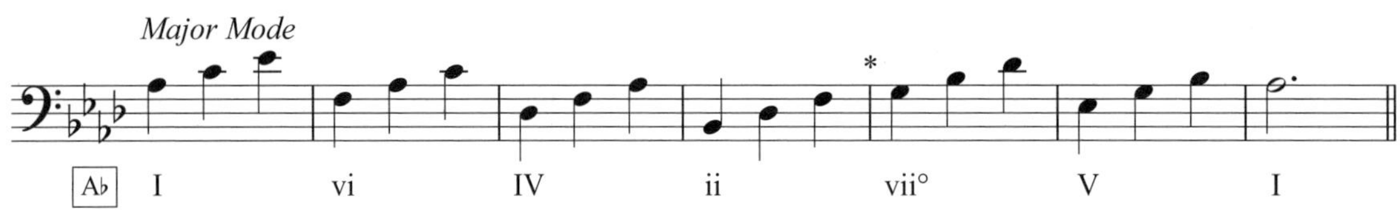


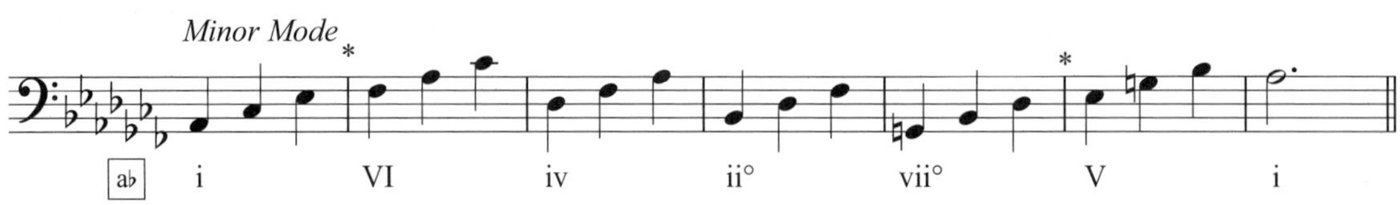


## The Filled-in Descending Thirds Progression

This progression commonly appears in two ways: with the "filling-in" chords in either root position or first inversion. Both appear below. What structure does the bass line create when these chords are in first inversion? Why does the second chord become a minor dominant in this case?

**EXAMPLE 5.4.4**

## The Ascending Seconds Progression

**EXAMPLE 5.4.5**

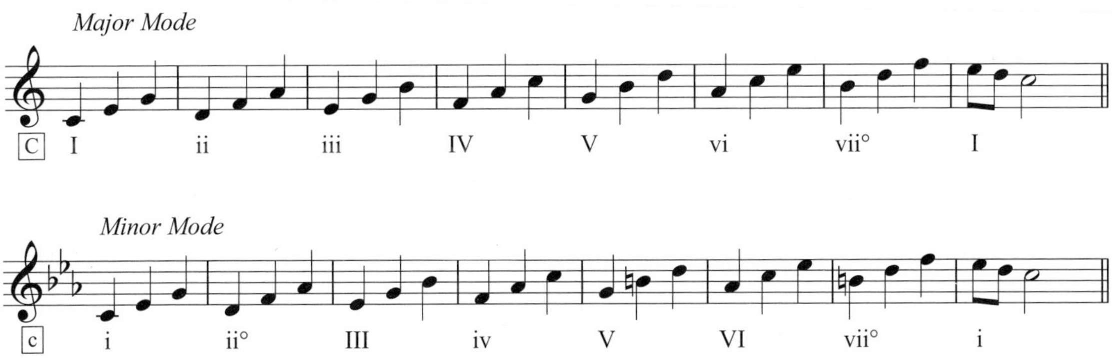

### The Filled-in Ascending Seconds Progression

**EXAMPLE 5.4.6**

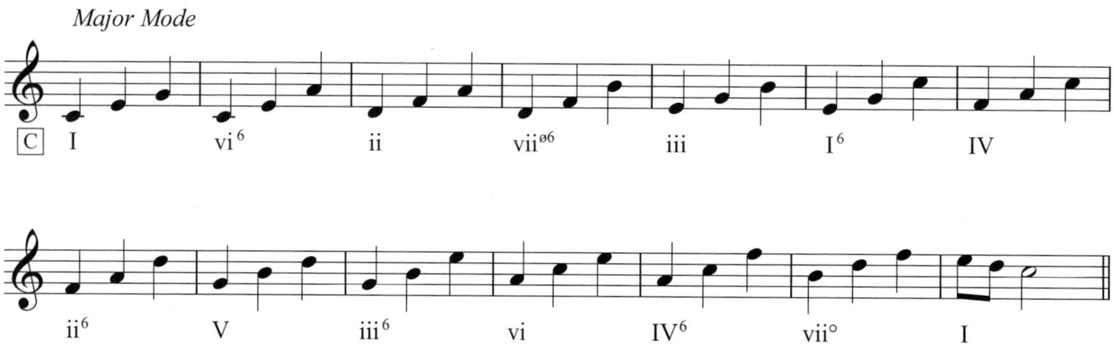


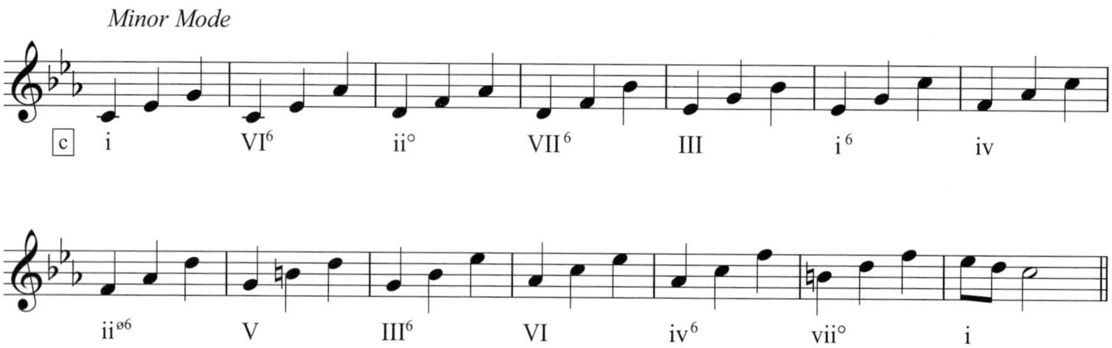


Once you have learned these patterns, practice starting one and then shifting to another where they share a common chord (e.g., begin with the circle of fifths and switch to descending thirds on the supertonic chord).

---

## 5.5 Improvising Melodies Over Harmonic Progressions

### Facts You Need to Know

Melody and harmony are linked together. A melody makes sense when it conforms to a functional harmonic progression. When we sing melodically, we are also hearing harmonically.

We can identify the prevailing harmony by a Roman numeral at any moment in music based on the scale degrees that seem to be the most prominent in the measure along with the chord class that we are hearing (tonic, predominant, or dominant). We have already practiced expressing each of these chord classes individually; now it is time to practice moving between chord classes.

## Singing

1. Establish a meter. In most tonal music, chords usually change every measure. This rate of change (called harmonic rhythm) sometimes speeds up as the music approaches a cadence.
2. Most melodies begin on the third or fifth of the initial tonic chord. Most melodies end on scale degree 1 on the final tonic chord. Plan a melodic shape that takes you to a climactic point about two-thirds of the way through the progression.
3. When singing, keep track of the harmonic function of the Roman numeral you are singing. Use your knowledge of which scale degrees communicate each harmonic function to emphasize the progression. Use your three improvisatory techniques (repetition, arpeggiation, and connected arpeggiation) to move through each harmonic function.
4. Look for changes in harmonic function (tonic, predominant, dominant) rather than chord changes. At the end of each functional group (chords that share the same function, like a string of predominants), consider the smoothest transition to scale degrees that communicate the next function. In most cases, you need only move by step from one harmonic function to the next.
5. Always keep track of the meter! Know where you are in each measure and change harmonies at the ends of measures.
6. As you become more comfortable improvising, take some chances. Introduce leaps to chord tones, then leaps to non-chord tones.
7. Always let your musical instincts be your guide. If a note sounds like it wants to resolve down, let it resolve down.

# 5.6 Progressions for Apreggiation and Improvisation

## Harmonic Progressions

First, arpeggiate through the harmonic progressions below. You may make any chord into a seventh chord if it makes musical sense to you. Next, improvise a melody over the progressions. Establish a meter and maintain a harmonic rhythm of one chord per measure.

1. I – IV – V – I
2. I – V$^{(7)}$ – I
3. I – vii° – I
4. I – vii° – V – I
5. I – ii – V – I
6. I – ii – vii° – I
7. I – IV – ii – V – I
8. I – IV – ii – vii° – I
9. I – vi – ii – V – I
10. I – vi – IV – ii – vii° – V – I
11. I – IV – I – V – I
12. I – IV – ii – V – I

13. I – IV – vii° – iii – vi – ii – V – I
14. I – ii – V – I – V – I
15. I – ii – vii° – V – I
16. I – iii – vi – ii – V – I
17. I – V – vi – iii – IV – I – IV – V – I
18. I – IV – ii – V – vi – IV – ii – V – I
19. I – vii° – I – IV – I – V – I
20. I – vi – IV – ii – V – I

Minor Mode

1. i – V – i
2. i – iv – V – i
3. i – VI – V – i
4. i – ii° – V – i
5. i – VI – ii° – V – I
6. i – VI – iv – ii° – vii° – V – i
7. i – iv – VII – III – VI – ii° – V – i
8. i – VII – III – iv – ii° – V – i
9. i – ii° – V – i
10. i – iv – ii° – vii° – i
11. i – vii° – i
12. i – vii° – V – i
13. i – iv – i – vii° – i
14. i – iv – vii° – i
15. i – iv – V – i
16. i – iv – VII – III – VI – ii° – V – i
17. i – VI – iv – V – i – V – i
18. i – v – VI – III – iv – i – V – i
19. i – iv – V – i
20. i – III – iv – V – i – V – i

## Reflections: Perseverance

Most students choose to major in music because they cannot imagine doing anything else—it's a choice born out of passion for the art and fueled by a desire to perform, create, or teach. It's likely a mentor counseled you about what it's like to study music—warning you that the road to becoming a musician is a difficult one, fraught with challenges that require self-determination and commitment. Undeterred, you chose to persevere; music is what you do, who you are.

Now that your study of music has begun in earnest, perhaps you are beginning to understand the warning you received. The demands on your time seem to come from every direction. You're expected to practice three to five hours a day, spend hours in rehearsal, attend classes, and complete assignments on time. You feel like you have no life.

Wait—isn't college supposed to be fun?

It is. And it really is possible to manage the demands and pressure you may be feeling. It requires perseverance. The key is to remind yourself of your long-term goals, develop the discipline to know when to work and when to play, and learn to use your time well.

Long before you registered for classes, you closed your eyes and imagined yourself in front of an audience, a school choir or other group actually earning a living doing something that you love, and doing it joyfully. Let that image continue to be inspiration for you throughout your education. Though the picture may change, having a long-term goal is still an important motivator that can help you through during difficult periods.

See yourself as being successful. Professionals agree that we all have the ability to create our future, but that to do so, we need to believe in our ability to grow, change, and persevere. Making a change or learning something new is a long process, and it's normal to experience ups and downs during growth. It took Thomas Edison over one hundred attempts to create the light bulb—and rather than think he did it wrong ninety-nine times, he recognized that he learned something new with every attempt.

Discipline and determination are attributes that contribute to success in any field. A struggling baseball player will come to the park early to take extra batting practice; a swimmer may stay after practice to do extra laps, and professional musicians often recount their own days as students, when they woke up an hour early to do that extra bit of practicing. The determination to succeed motivates the people in each of these examples; self-discipline permits them to carry out the action that leads toward success.

Learning to manage your time will help you to persevere through the challenges you face. Time management seems so blasé, so unartistic, so . . . boring. Counterintuitive though it may seem, better management of your time will actually result in more freedom and less stress.

Set priorities. Create a daily schedule, with slots for practicing, studying, and rehearsing—think of it as an "action plan" to help you to stay on track. Mark upcoming performances, academic obligations, etc. on a calendar, then work backwards from those dates to set intermediary, attainable goals. Remember, studying music requires the development of skills. Skill development, by its very nature, happens best over an extended period. Cramming doesn't work; your mind, body, and ear need time for new skills to "settle."

Small steps are essential to your success. Trust that your passion will fuel your ability to persevere through the trials of becoming an artist, and that through the personal insights gained by experiencing success, defeat, joy, and pain, you will have a wider range of emotions to call upon in all your artistic pursuits. Your ability to make art happen is the ultimate reward.

## 5.7 Dictation Materials

@

### I. Triad Quality Identification

Your teacher will play several triads. Indicate the quality and inversion. Possible answers are M for major, m for minor, and d for diminished.

*Date:* . . . . . . . . . . . . . .

1. ____ 2. ____ 3. ____ 4. ____ 5. ____ 6. ____ 7. ____ 8. ____

*Date:* . . . . . . . . . . . . . .

1. ____ 2. ____ 3. ____ 4. ____ 5. ____ 6. ____ 7. ____ 8. ____

*Date:* . . . . . . . . . . . . . .

1. ____ 2. ____ 3. ____ 4. ____ 5. ____ 6. ____ 7. ____ 8. ____

*Date:* . . . . . . . . . . . . . .

1. ____ 2. ____ 3. ____ 4. ____ 5. ____ 6. ____ 7. ____ 8. ____

*Date:* . . . . . . . . . . . . . .

1. ____ 2. ____ 3. ____ 4. ____ 5. ____ 6. ____ 7. ____ 8. ____

## II. Seventh Chord Identification

Your teacher will play several seventh chords. Indicate the quality (MM, Mm, mm, dm, or dd) and inversion for each by using the correct figured bass symbol.

*Date:* . . . . . . . . . . . . . .

1. ____ 2. ____ 3. ____ 4. ____ 5. ____ 6. ____ 7. ____ 8. ____

*Date:* . . . . . . . . . . . . . .

1. ____ 2. ____ 3. ____ 4. ____ 5. ____ 6. ____ 7. ____ 8. ____

*Date:* . . . . . . . . . . . . . .

1. ____ 2. ____ 3. ____ 4. ____ 5. ____ 6. ____ 7. ____ 8. ____

*Date:* . . . . . . . . . . . . . .

1. ____ 2. ____ 3. ____ 4. ____ 5. ____ 6. ____ 7. ____ 8. ____

*Date:* . . . . . . . . . . . . . .

1. ____ 2. ____ 3. ____ 4. ____ 5. ____ 6. ____ 7. ____ 8. ____

## III. Melodic and Rhythmic Dictation

Your teacher will play a short melody or rhythm. Notate it on the staves below.

*Date:* . . . . . . . . . . . . . .

*Date:* ..............

*Date:* ..............

*Date:* ..............

*Date:* ..............

## IV. Harmonic Dictation

Write the soprano line, bass line, and provide a Roman numeral analysis (including inversional symbols) for the progression you hear on the grand staff below.

*Date:* . . . . . . . . . . . . . .

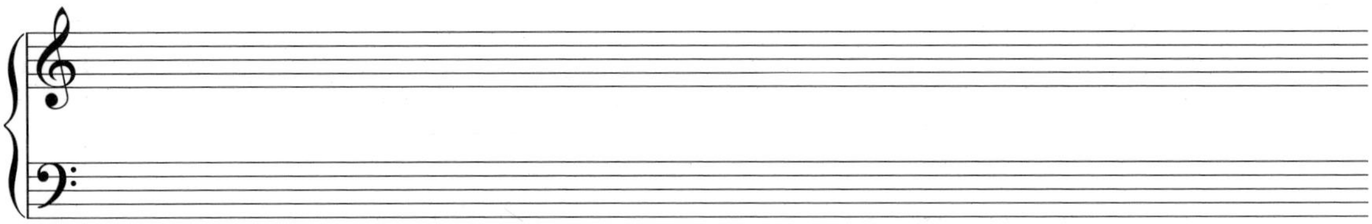

*Date:* . . . . . . . . . . . . . .

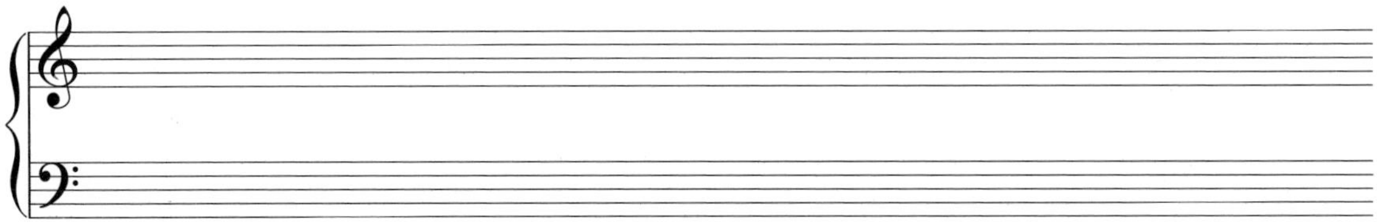

*Date:* . . . . . . . . . . . . . .

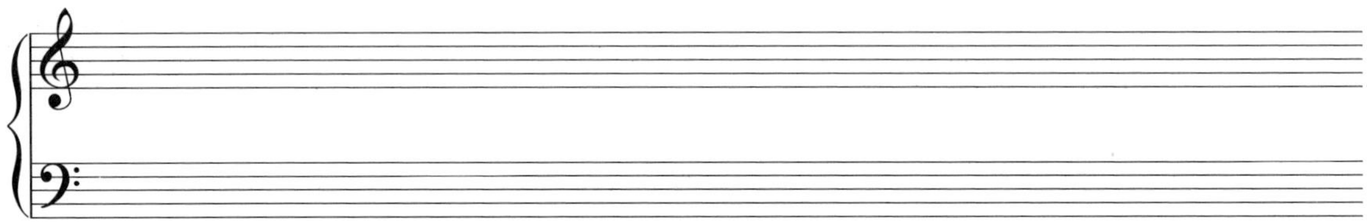

*Date:* . . . . . . . . . . . . . .

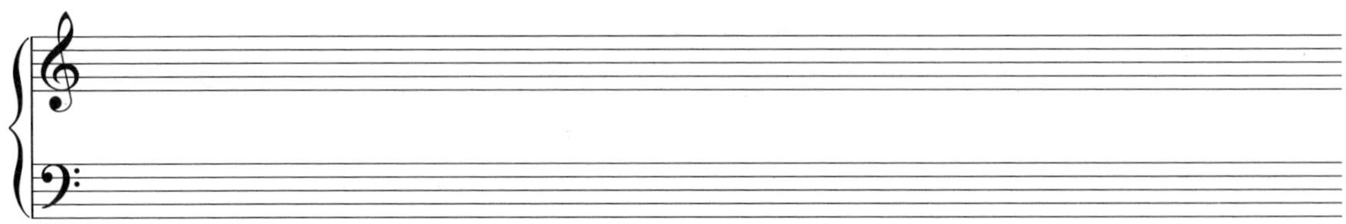

*Date:* . . . . . . . . . . . . . .

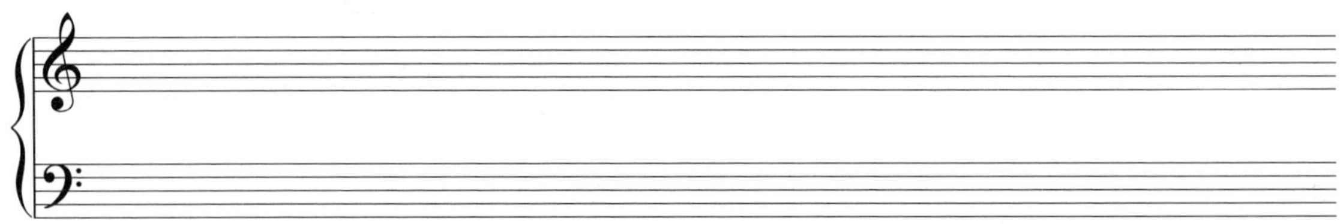

## Chapter 6

# Syncopation; Beginning Non-Modulating Chromaticism

## 6.1 Syncopation

### Facts You Need to Know

Syncopation occurs when a weak beat or weak part of a beat—any that is not normally emphasized—is stressed.

Listeners and performers alike become accustomed to certain regularities in music—the resolution of V–I, the leading tone resolving up to tonic, and the structural power of metric stress. Syncopation disrupts our perception of the beat or meter, creating ambiguity and tension in music. It helps to give music a sense of forward motion because of our innate need for the syncopation to resolve itself.

Syncopation occurs most frequently in three ways: by stressing normally weak beats or divisions; by placing rests on strong beats of a measure or on divisions of the beat (resulting in "off-beats"); and by using a tie across a barline, so that the first beat of the measure is obscured.

In the example below, Mozart shifts the emphasis from beats 1 and 3 to the "and" or divisions of those beats, creating a syncopation.

**EXAMPLE 6.1.1**

*Sonata in G Major*, K. 301, First movement, m. 48–51

**Allegro con spirito** **Mozart**

In the development section of the same sonata, Mozart first uses eighth notes on the beat, then on off-beats, in the same passage. Play the example below and listen to how the energy changes in the syncopated measure (m.4).

**EXAMPLE 6.1.2**

*Sonata in G Major*, K. 301, First movement, m. 107–111

**Allegro con spirito** **Mozart**

In this example, Beethoven makes the crusis of the measure intentionally indistinct through the use of syncopation.

**EXAMPLE 6.1.3**

*Sonata in A Minor*, Op. 23, Third movement, m. 33–40

**Allegro molto** **Beethoven**

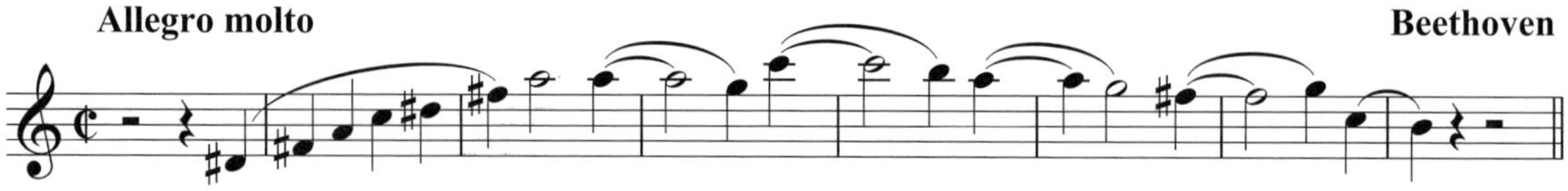

## Performing Syncopation

Syncopated rhythms are notated in two ways: either using ties to show the syncopation (measure 1, below), or using a single note (measure 2).

**EXAMPLE 6.1.4**

One of the challenges of performing a syncopated passage is keeping the tempo steady. Western music is heavily dependent on the beat, so when it is missing or obscured, we tend to compensate by rushing. It can be helpful to practice syncopated rhythms first without ties, then repeat it with ties, hearing the tied note in your head as you articulate.

## Rhythms

### RHYTHM 6.1.1

### RHYTHM 6.1.2

### RHYTHM 6.1.3

### RHYTHM 6.1.4

### RHYTHM 6.1.5

Easy

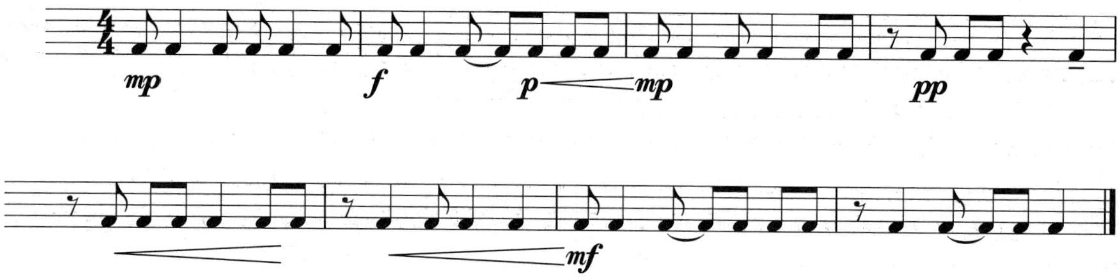


### RHYTHM 6.1.6

Vif

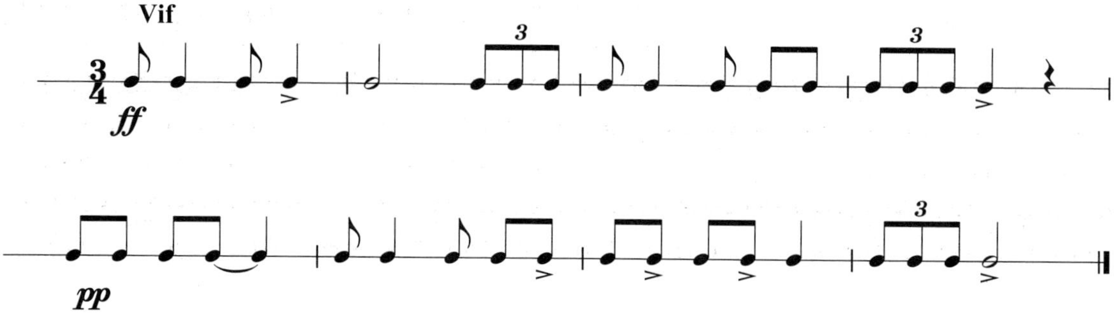


### RHYTHM 6.1.7

Con fuoco

### RHYTHM 6.1.8

Risoluto

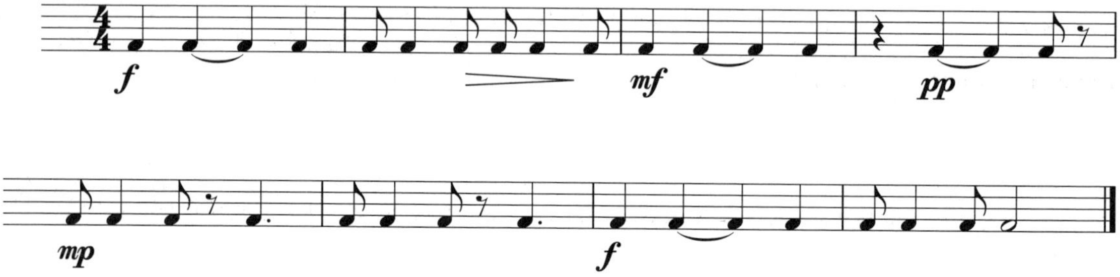

**RHYTHM 6.1.9**

**RHYTHM 6.1.10**

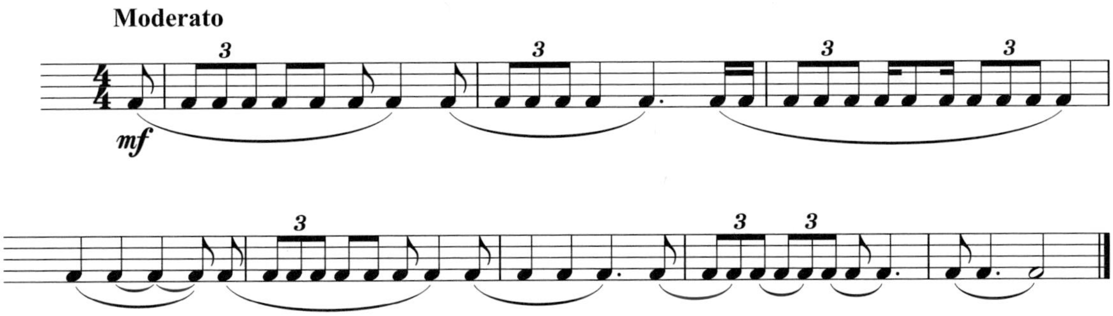


**RHYTHM 6.1.11**

**RHYTHM 6.1.12**

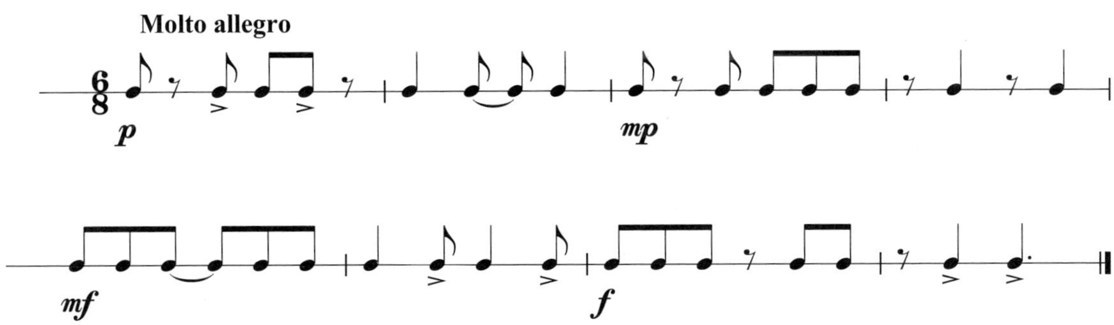

### RHYTHM 6.1.13

**Presto**

### RHYTHM 6.1.14

**Moderato**

### RHYTHM 6.1.15

**Con moto**

### RHYTHM 6.1.16

**Andantino**

**RHYTHM 6.1.17**

**RHYTHM 6.1.18**

**RHYTHM 6.1.19**

## Two-part Rhythms

### TWO-PART RHYTHM 6.1.1

### TWO-PART RHYTHM 6.1.2

## Three-part Rhythm

### THREE-PART RHYTHM 6.1

## 6.2 The Chromatic Scale and Surface Chromaticism

### Facts You Need to Know

The term "chromatic" is derived from the Greek word for "color."

Chromaticism "fills in" the spaces between diatonic scale degrees. It adds musical color to melodies and serves as the foundation for altered chords, tonicization, and modulation.

The chromatic scale consists of twelve pitches, each roughly the same distance from the pitches around them (depending on the tuning system in use).

Chromatic pitches are named based on their direction of resolution. Pitches that resolve up are named like a leading tone to the resolution pitch (e.g., a pitch resolving up to E would be a D-sharp, not an E-flat). Pitches that resolve down are named like the seventh of a dominant seventh to the resolution pitch (e.g., a pitch resolving down to F would be a G-flat, not an F-sharp).

Chromatic pitches are dissonant and have a strong desire toward resolution. They sound "outside" of the key, generally drawing attention to themselves.

Surface chromaticism, or chromaticism that is not a part of the underlying chord, usually takes the form of passing tones that fill in the space between diatonic notes, neighboring tones that reinforce the importance of the tone to which they resolve, and appoggiaturas which create strong desire toward resolution, usually to a tone supported by the underlying harmony.

### Hearing

1. When listening for chromaticism, notice pitches that sound like they do not belong in the key and that draw attention to themselves through their desire to resolve to a more stable diatonic pitch.
2. Next, hear the direction of resolution. If it resolves up, write the chromatic pitch as a leading tone to the resolution pitch. If it resolves down, write the chromatic pitch as a minor second above the resolution pitch.

### Singing

To sing a chromatic scale, begin by hearing a diatonic major or minor scale:

**EXAMPLE 6.2.1**

Wherever a major second occurs, insert a leading tone to the upper pitch. If descending, insert a dominant chord seventh to the lower pitch.

#### EXAMPLE 6.2.2

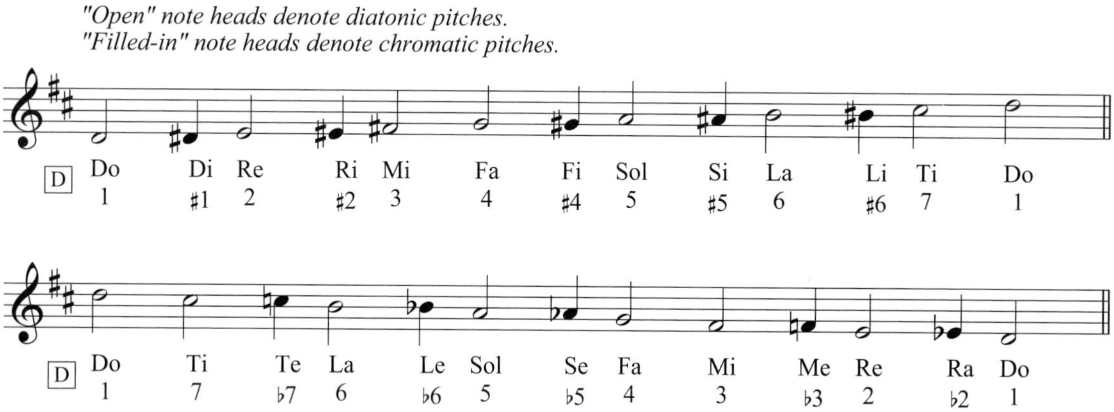


Pay particular attention to the integrity of the underlying diatonic scale. There is a tendency to spread the minor seconds, leading to going out of the key. If you need to, stop on every diatonic pitch and check its scale degree pattern back to tonic.

## Assignments for Practice

1. Sing a diatonic major or minor scale with upper or lower chromatic neighbors to each pitch.

#### EXAMPLE 6.2.3

2. Arpeggiate through a I–IV–V–I progression, adding upper or lower chromatic neighbors to each pitch.

### Pitch Patterns

#### PITCH PATTERN 6.2.1

**PITCH PATTERN 6.2.2**

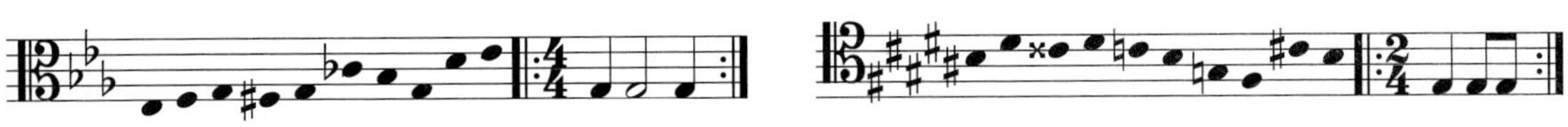

**PITCH PATTERN 6.2.3**

## Melodies

**MELODY 6.2.1**

**MELODY 6.2.2**

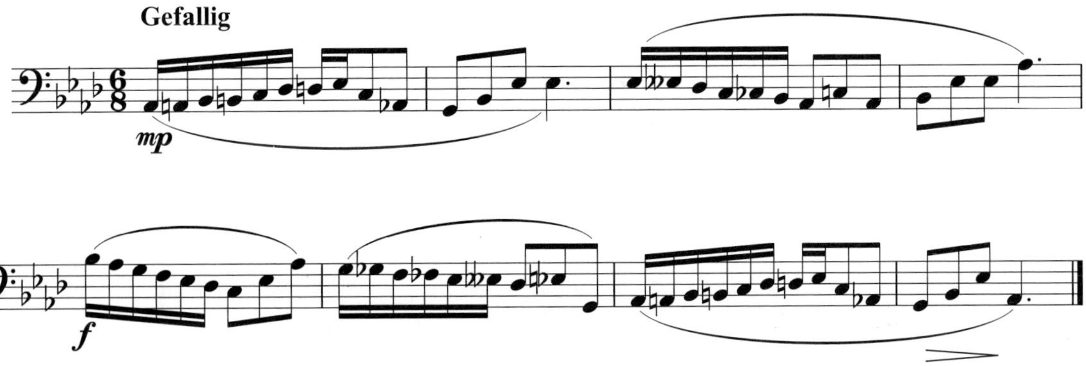


**MELODY 6.2.3**

**MELODY 6.2.4**

**MELODY 6.2.5**

**MELODY 6.2.6**

**MELODY 6.2.7**

**MELODY 6.2.8**

**MELODY 6.2.9**

**MELODY 6.2.10**

**MELODY 6.2.11**

### MELODY 6.2.12

### MELODY 6.2.13

### MELODY 6.2.14

### MELODY 6.2.15

## Duets

### DUET 6.2.1

### DUET 6.2.2

### DUET 6.2.3

## Chorale

### CHORALE 6.2

## Self-Accompanied Melody

### SELF-ACCOMPANIED MELODY 6.2

## 6.3 Modal Mixture

### Facts You Need to Know

Modal mixture is the use of scale degrees from a key's parallel major or minor mode.

Major and minor scales have three scale degrees that differ from each other: the third, sixth, and seventh.

When composers "borrow" scale degrees (and the chords they create) into the opposite mode, new possibilities for chord colors result that do not fundamentally change the harmonic structure of the music.

Most mixture arises from the borrowing of scale degree 6 from the minor mode into the major mode. This is often used in predominant function to increase a chord's desire to resolve to the dominant, as when a major subdominant is turned into a minor subdominant or a minor supertonic is made into a diminished supertonic.

**EXAMPLE 6.3.1**

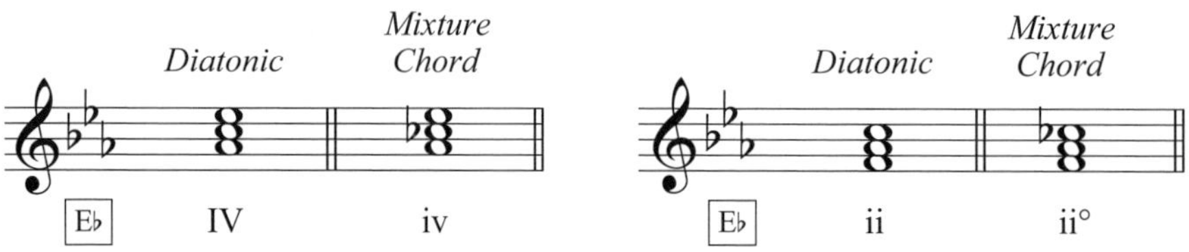


Borrowing scale degree 6 from the minor mode into the diminished seventh chord increases that chord's desire toward resolution to tonic.

**EXAMPLE 6.3.2**

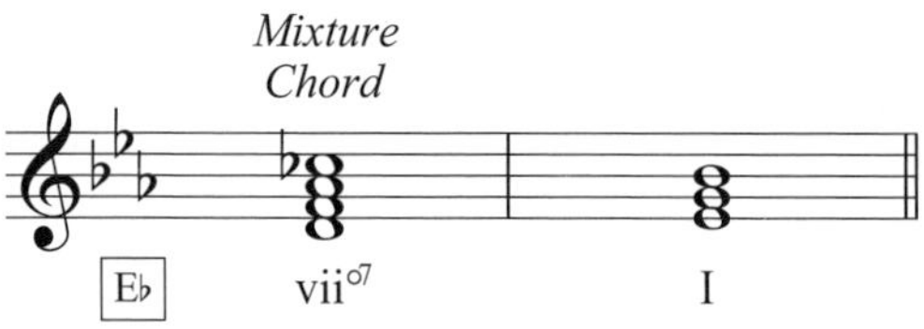


Scale degree 3 is borrowed from the minor to the major in two circumstances:

1. To create a minor tonic.
2. Along with scale degree 6 to create the correct quality of the borrowed submediant triad.

Scale degree 3 is frequently borrowed from the major mode into the minor on a final tonic chord, creating what is commonly called a Picardy third.

**EXAMPLE 6.3.3**

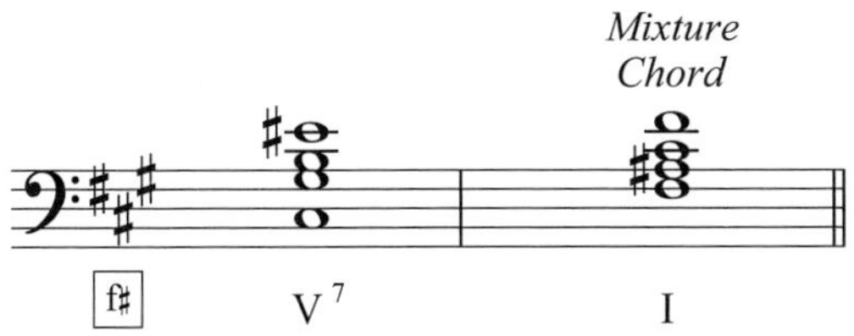


The lowered scale degree 7 is rarely borrowed in tonal music. Some musicians think of the raising of the leading tone in minor as a form of modal mixture.

## Hearing

Listen for a chord, usually with predominant function, that has an unusual color.

Listen for an intensified desire toward resolution created by adding the lowered sixth scale degree.

Listen for the chord quality of the altered chord. If it matches the quality that you would expect in the parallel mode, then it is most likely a borrowed chord.

## Singing

1. Begin by singing the requested melody or progression diatonically, without borrowing any tones.
2. You may want to sing through the scale degree patterns, replacing the pattern for the borrowed scale degree with the similar pattern from the parallel mode. Get used to this sound.
3. Sing the melody or progression, inserting the borrowed scale degree. Pay attention to how it changes the musical color and desire toward resolution.

## Assignments for Practice

### Pitch Patterns

**PITCH PATTERN 6.3.1**

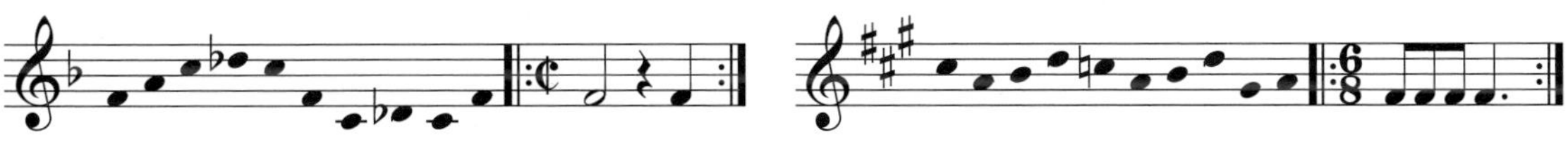

**PITCH PATTERN 6.3.2**

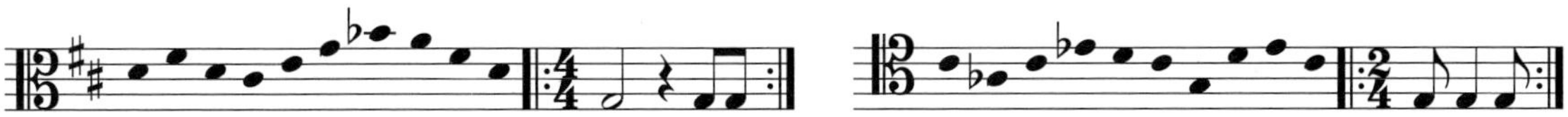

### PITCH PATTERN 6.3.3

## Harmonic Progressions

1. I – IV – iv – V – I
2. i – ii° – V – I
3. I – VI – V – I
4. I – ii – ii° – V – I
5. I – IV – vii°7 – I – V – I

## Melodies

### MELODY 6.3.1

### MELODY 6.3.2

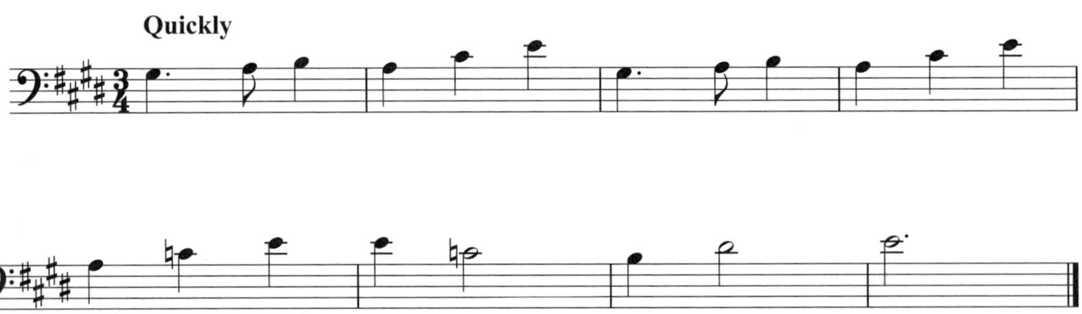


### MELODY 6.3.3

MELODY 6.3.4

MELODY 6.3.5

MELODY 6.3.6

MELODY 6.3.7

**MELODY 6.3.8**

**MELODY 6.3.9**

**MELODY 6.3.10**

**MELODY 6.3.11**

MELODY 6.3.12

MELODY 6.3.13

MELODY 6.3.14

MELODY 6.3.15

## Duets

### DUETS 6.3.1

### DUETS 6.3.2

**DUETS 6.3.3**

## Chorale

**CHORALE 6.3**

## Self-Accompanied Melody

### SELF-ACCOMPANIED MELODY 6.3

## 6.4 Music from the Literature

### EXAMPLE 6.4.1

*Studies of Caprices of Paganini*, Op. 3, No. 4

Schumann

**EXAMPLE 6.4.2**

*Waltz*, Op. 39, No. 4

m. 17-32

**Leicht beschwingt** Reinhold

**EXAMPLE 6.4.3**

*Piano Sonata in A Major*, K. 331
First movement, Var. 1

**Andante grazioso** Mozart

**EXAMPLE 6.4.4**

*Sonata in F Major for Violin and Piano*, Op. 24, No. 1
Fourth movement

**Allegro ma non troppo** Beethoven

Violin

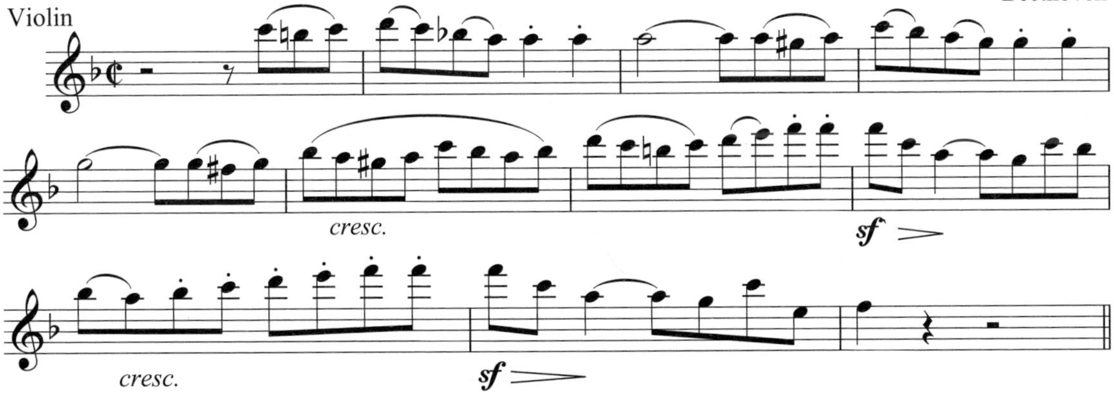

**EXAMPLE 6.4.5**

*Variations on a Theme of Handel*, Op. 24,
Var. II

Brahms

**EXAMPLE 6.4.6**

*15 Variationen mit Fuge*, "Eroica," Op. 35
A dur

Beethoven

**EXAMPLE 6.4.7**

*Piano Sonata in G Major*, Op. 31, No. 1,
Second movement

Beethoven

**EXAMPLE 6.4.8**

*Melody for Left Hand*, Op. 108, No. 12

Ludwig Schytte

## Reflections: Creativity

Making music is an inherently creative activity. Composers think up music; performers interpret the composer's intentions; and even the audience gets into the act by trying to understand what the composer and performer are trying to say through music.

The types of creativity used by composers and audiences are different. Composers create something new from nothingness. Performers and audiences derive meaning from something presented to them. The creativity of the performer and the audience is the comprehension of another person's creation or discovery. This form of creativity requires a vocabulary—knowledge of the "rules" that constitute musical style. As we learn more about how music works, about how the common structures that appear in music typically behave, we increase our ability to comprehend music and to recognize instances when we are hearing something new. We become literate in music. Eventually we develop the ability to have original musical thoughts of our own.

These original thoughts then lead to the creativity of the composer. This often involves rethinking how traditional musical materials are used. A composer might create sound in a non-traditional way, such as when a percussionist uses a double bass bow on a vibraphone. He or she might rethink the use of pitch, relying on quarter or eighth tones. Or they may rethink the "rules" of harmony, such as when some composers of the early twentieth century started to write atonal music. Each of these requires asking the simple question: "What if?"

Creativity is a skill that works best when practiced. As a musician, you are asked to develop both forms of creativity. If you compose or improvise, you are undoubtedly being asked to develop your ability to ask "What if?" The result of this type of activity is often not nearly as important as the process of asking the question. Performers need to develop this form of creativity because our traditional notation system cannot possibly communicate every characteristic of the composer's intention. One must always bring a part of him or her to the process of realizing somebody else's music.

Likewise, musicians must be good listeners, able to understand what they hear. The ability to follow someone else's creative path is essential to becoming an effective musician. After all, as performers, ultimately our job is to facilitate communication between the composer (or his composition) and the audience.

How then to practice this skill? Creativity requires some freedom to ask "What if?" without fear of failure. That is what your time as a student musician is all about. You are in a safe environment where experimental failures are not only expected—they are encouraged. Development of creativity also requires you to learn and assemble a toolbox of structures and techniques that you have learned and can recognize. Remember that you are building a vocabulary of musical images, and you are learning to speak in the language of music!

## 6.5 Dictation Materials

@

### I. Identification of Minor Scale Degrees

Your teacher will establish a key and then play its scale degrees in random order or as a specific pitch in a melody (by number—first, second, last, or by position—high or low). Identify each by writing its number in the appropriate space. Place an up arrow in front of scale degree 6 or 7 if you hear either of them in their raised position.

*Date:* ..............

1. ____ 2. ____ 3. ____ 4. ____ 5. ____ 6. ____ 7. ____ 8. ____

*Date:* ..............

1. ____ 2. ____ 3. ____ 4. ____ 5. ____ 6. ____ 7. ____ 8. ____

*Date:* ..............

1. ____ 2. ____ 3. ____ 4. ____ 5. ____ 6. ____ 7. ____ 8. ____

*Date:* ..............

1. ____ 2. ____ 3. ____ 4. ____ 5. ____ 6. ____ 7. ____ 8. ____

*Date:* ..............

1. ____ 2. ____ 3. ____ 4. ____ 5. ____ 6. ____ 7. ____ 8. ____

### II. Identification of Major Scale Degrees

Your teacher will establish a key and then play its scale degrees in random order or as a specific pitch in a melody (by number—first, second, last, or by position—high or low). Identify each by writing its number in the appropriate space.

*Date:* ..............

1. ____ 2. ____ 3. ____ 4. ____ 5. ____ 6. ____ 7. ____ 8. ____

*Date:* ..............

1. ____ 2. ____ 3. ____ 4. ____ 5. ____ 6. ____ 7. ____ 8. ____

*Date:* ..............

1. ____ 2. ____ 3. ____ 4. ____ 5. ____ 6. ____ 7. ____ 8. ____

*Date:* ..............

1. ____ 2. ____ 3. ____ 4. ____ 5. ____ 6. ____ 7. ____ 8. ____

*Date:* . . . . . . . . . . . . . .

1. ____ 2. ____ 3. ____ 4. ____ 5. ____ 6. ____ 7. ____ 8. ____

## III. Interval Identification

Your teacher will play several intervals. Identify their quality and size as one of the following:

M2 = Major second
m2 = Minor second
M3 = Major third
m3 = Minor third
P4 = Perfect fourth
TT = Tritone
P5 = Perfect fifth
M6 = Major sixth
m6 = Minor sixth
M7 = Major seventh
m7 = Minor seventh
P8 = Perfect octave
M9 = Major ninth
m9 = Minor ninth
M10 = Major tenth
m10 = Minor tenth

Be sure to make a clear difference between your capital and lower-case Ms.

*Date:* . . . . . . . . . . . . . .

1. ____ 2. ____ 3. ____ 4. ____ 5. ____ 6. ____ 7. ____ 8. ____

*Date:* . . . . . . . . . . . . . .

1. ____ 2. ____ 3. ____ 4. ____ 5. ____ 6. ____ 7. ____ 8. ____

*Date:* . . . . . . . . . . . . . .

1. ____ 2. ____ 3. ____ 4. ____ 5. ____ 6. ____ 7. ____ 8. ____

*Date:* . . . . . . . . . . . . . .

1. ____ 2. ____ 3. ____ 4. ____ 5. ____ 6. ____ 7. ____ 8. ____

*Date:* . . . . . . . . . . . . . .

1. ____ 2. ____ 3. ____ 4. ____ 5. ____ 6. ____ 7. ____ 8. ____

## IV. Triad Quality Identification

Your teacher will play several triads. Indicate the quality and inversion. Possible answers are M for major, m for minor, and d for diminished.

*Date:* . . . . . . . . . . . . . .

1. ____ 2. ____ 3. ____ 4. ____ 5. ____ 6. ____ 7. ____ 8. ____

*Date:* . . . . . . . . . . . . . .

1. ____ 2. ____ 3. ____ 4. ____ 5. ____ 6. ____ 7. ____ 8. ____

*Date:* . . . . . . . . . . . . . .

1. ____ 2. ____ 3. ____ 4. ____ 5. ____ 6. ____ 7. ____ 8. ____

*Date:* . . . . . . . . . . . . . .

1. ____ 2. ____ 3. ____ 4. ____ 5. ____ 6. ____ 7. ____ 8. ____

*Date:* . . . . . . . . . . . . . .

1. ____ 2. ____ 3. ____ 4. ____ 5. ____ 6. ____ 7. ____ 8. ____

## V. Seventh Chord Identification

Your teacher will play several seventh chords. Indicate the quality (MM, Mm, mm, dm, or dd) and inversion for each by using the correct figured bass symbol.

*Date:* . . . . . . . . . . . . . .

1. ____ 2. ____ 3. ____ 4. ____ 5. ____ 6. ____ 7. ____ 8. ____

*Date:* . . . . . . . . . . . . . .

1. ____ 2. ____ 3. ____ 4. ____ 5. ____ 6. ____ 7. ____ 8. ____

*Date:* . . . . . . . . . . . . . .

1. ____ 2. ____ 3. ____ 4. ____ 5. ____ 6. ____ 7. ____ 8. ____

*Date:* . . . . . . . . . . . . . .

1. ____ 2. ____ 3. ____ 4. ____ 5. ____ 6. ____ 7. ____ 8. ____

*Date:* . . . . . . . . . . . . . .

1. ____ 2. ____ 3. ____ 4. ____ 5. ____ 6. ____ 7. ____ 8. ____

## VI. Melodic and Rhythmic Dictation

Your teacher will play a short melody or rhythm. Notate it on the staves below.

*Date:* . . . . . . . . . . . . . .

*Date:* ..............

*Date:* ..............

*Date:* ..............

*Date:* ..............

## VII. Harmonic Dictation

Write the soprano line, bass line, and provide a Roman numeral analysis (including inversional symbols) for the progression you hear on the grand staff below.

*Date:* . . . . . . . . . . . . . .

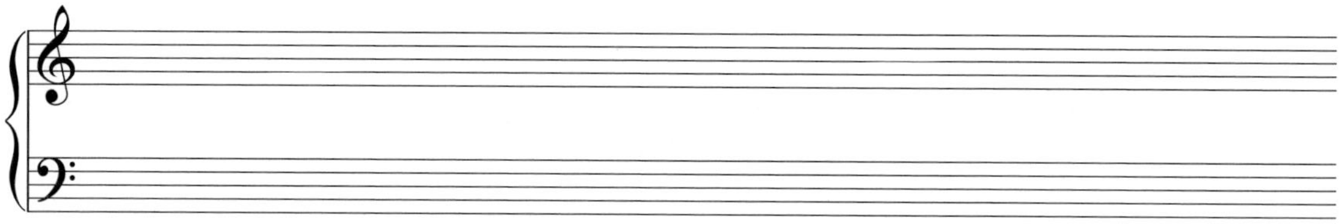

*Date:* . . . . . . . . . . . . . .

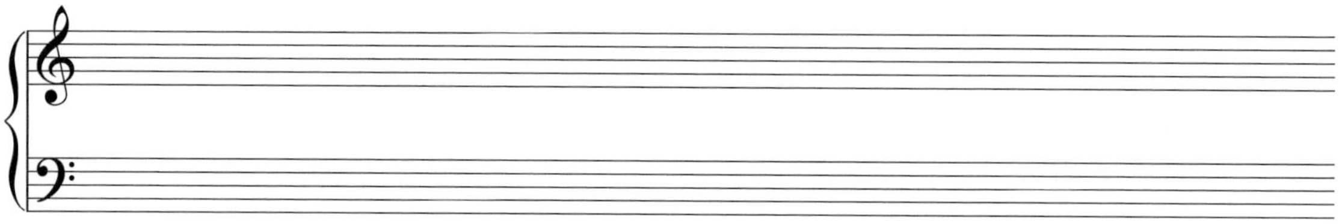

*Date:* . . . . . . . . . . . . . .

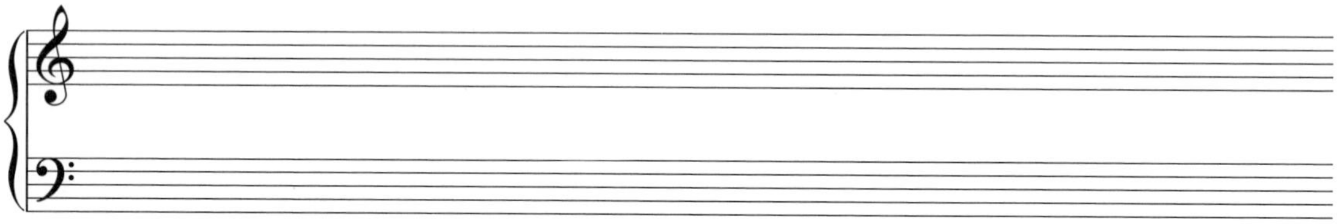

*Date:* . . . . . . . . . . . . . .

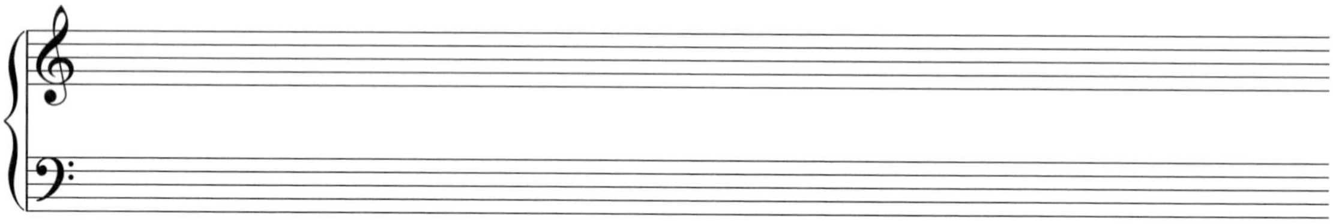

*Date:* . . . . . . . . . . . . . .

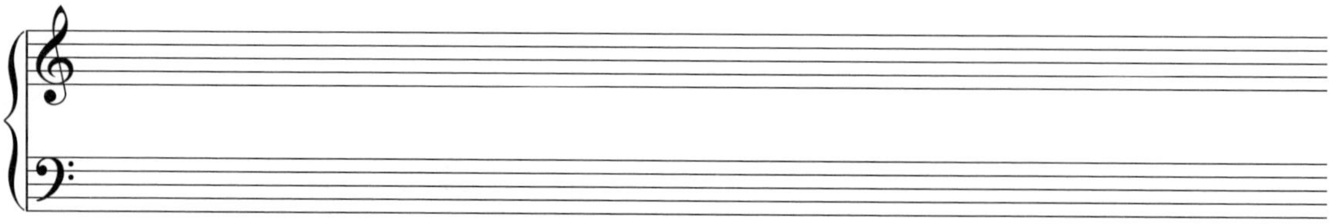

# Chapter 7

# Triplets and Duplets; More Non-Modulating Chromaticism

## 7.1 Irregular Divisions II: Triplets and Duplets in Augmentation and Diminution

### Facts You Need to Know

Diminuted Triplets

A triplet in diminution is equal to one division of the beat, as shown in the figure below.

Diminuted triplets are notated using the same note value as the subdivision of the beat.

EXAMPLE 7.1.1

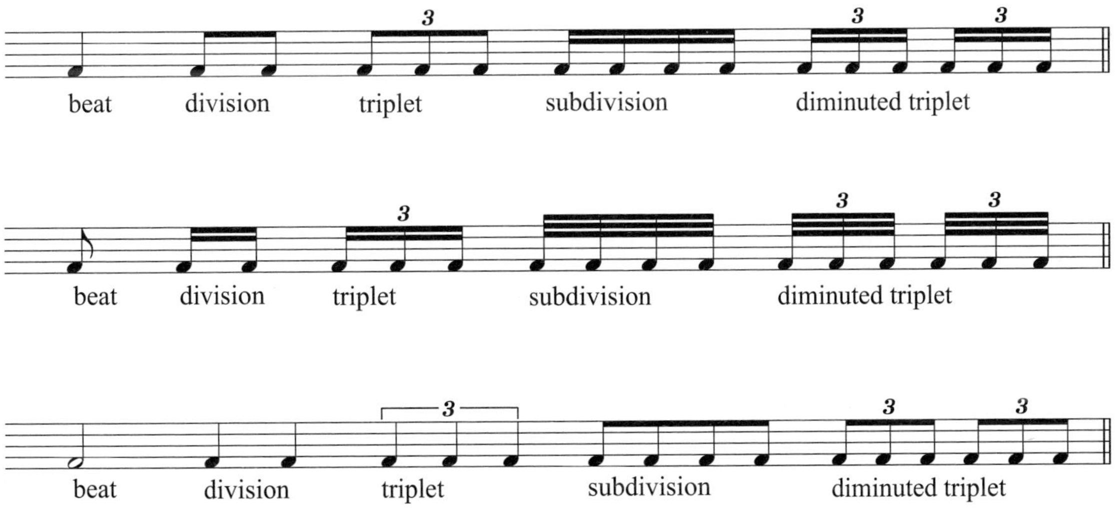


Diminuted triplets add rhythmic energy to music. When employed over several beats or measures, diminuted triplets act as a textural device, becoming an accompanimental figure that ornaments a melodic line. Play the example below to hear this usage of diminuted triplets:

**EXAMPLE 7.1.2**

## Performing Diminuted Triplets

Counting diminuted triplets as suggested below allows you to reinforce the beat and division while you get the sound of the triplet in your ear. If you have difficulty, begin by clapping divisions while articulating the rhythm, then change to clapping the beat while articulating.

**EXAMPLE 7.1.3**

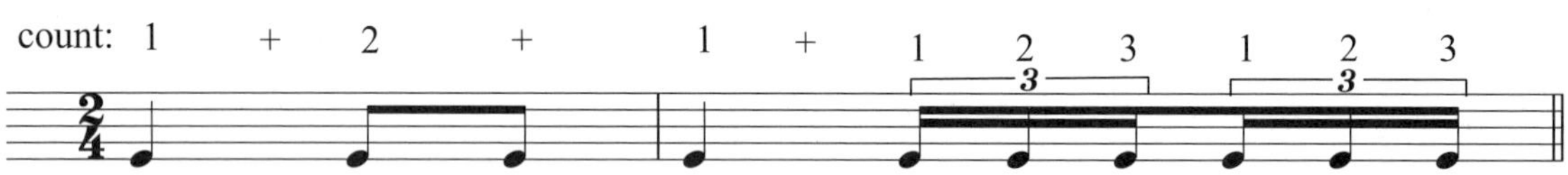


## Augmented Triplets

Augmented triplets occur over two beats, as indicated in the figure below. They are notated using the same note value as the beat.

**EXAMPLE 7.1.4**

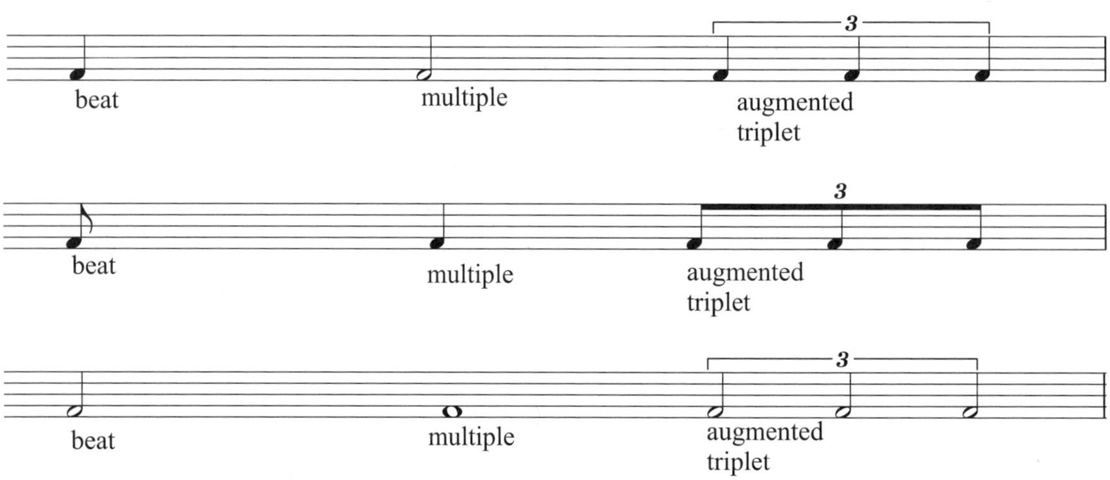

Augmented triplets have a dramatic musical effect. Because they exist over two beats, the second beat is obscured, creating metric ambiguity. The sense of resistance and pull that results makes these triplets emphatic and bold.

### Performing Augmented Triplets

In order to perform augmented triplets, it is necessary to be able to feel the "missing" (or obscured) beat; in essence, you need to be able to feel 2:3.

Practice this skill by clapping one-beat triplets while articulating augmented triplets, as shown in the example below. (This exercise creates a 2:1 ratio, which will help you to be able to hear exactly how the augmented triplet fits in the meter.) After performing this exercise with triplets, repeat immediately, this time practicing by clapping just beats, as shown.

**EXAMPLE 7.1.5**

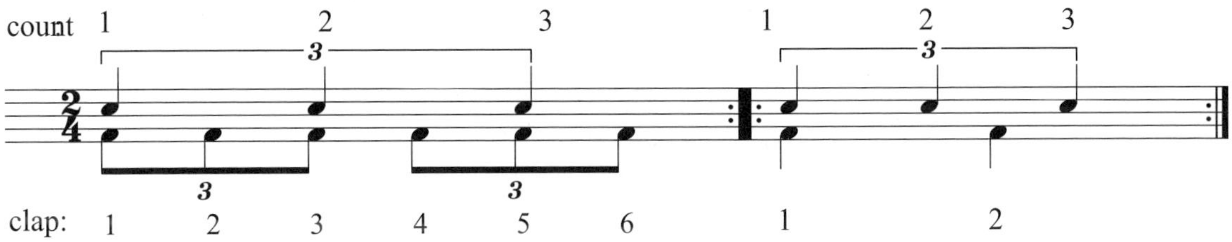


## Rhythms

**RHYTHM 7.1.1**

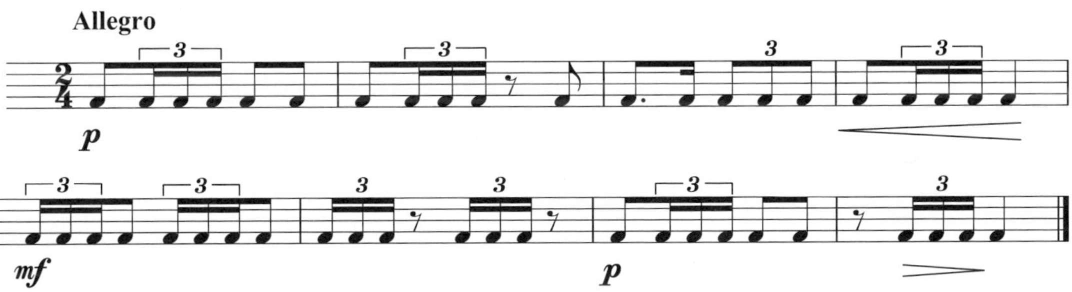


**RHYTHM 7.1.2**

RHYTHM 7.1.3

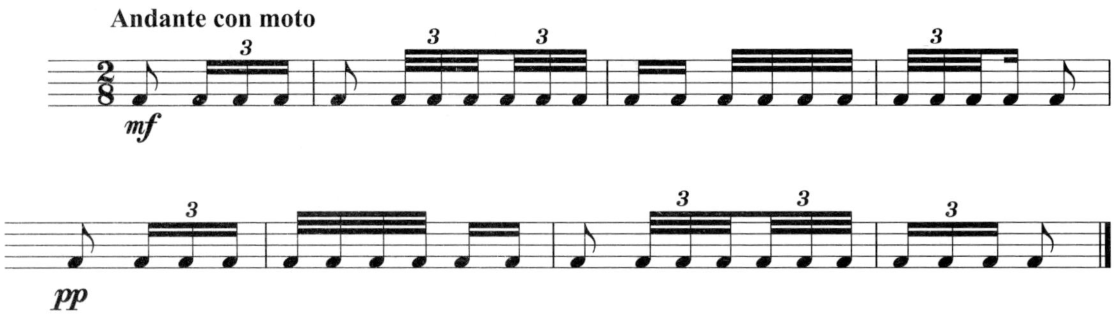


RHYTHM 7.1.4

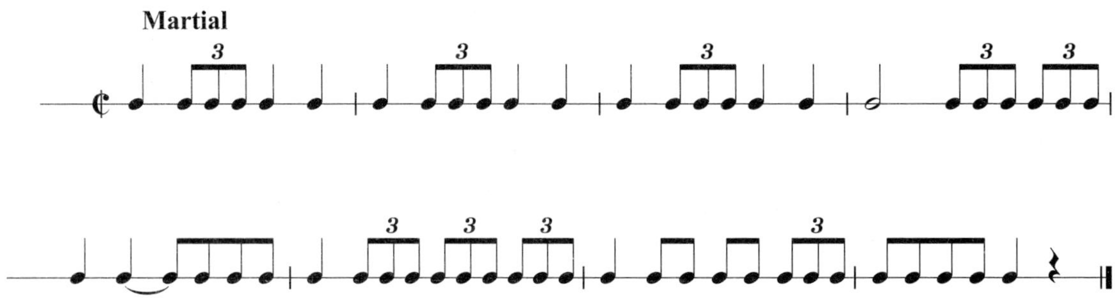


RHYTHM 7.1.5

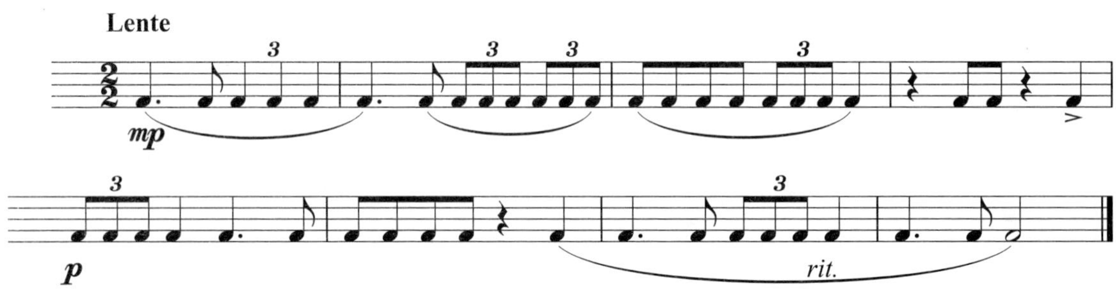


RHYTHM 7.1.6

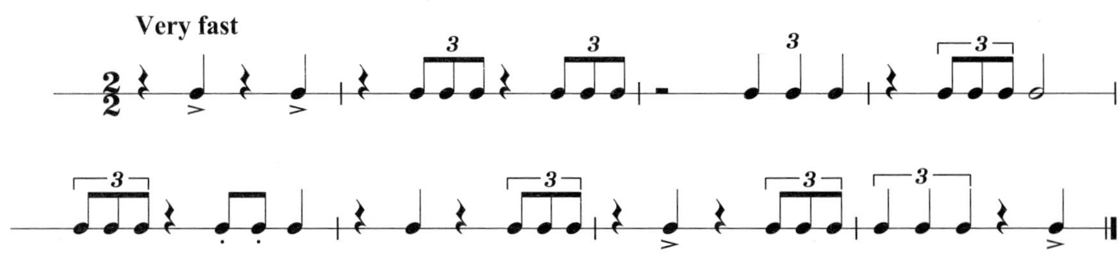

RHYTHM 7.1.7

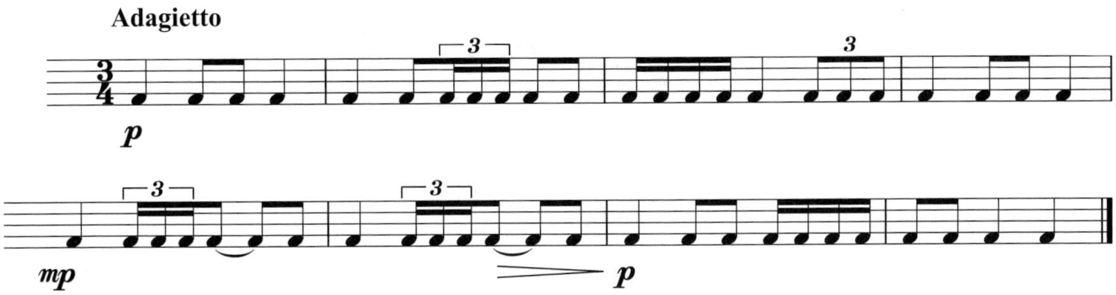


RHYTHM 7.1.8

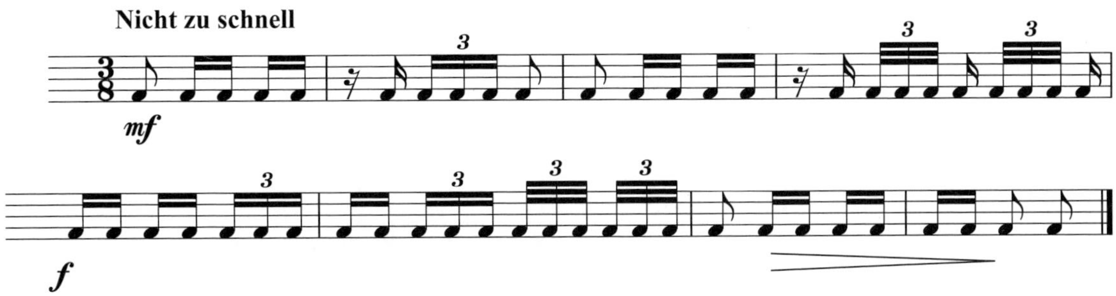


RHYTHM 7.1.9

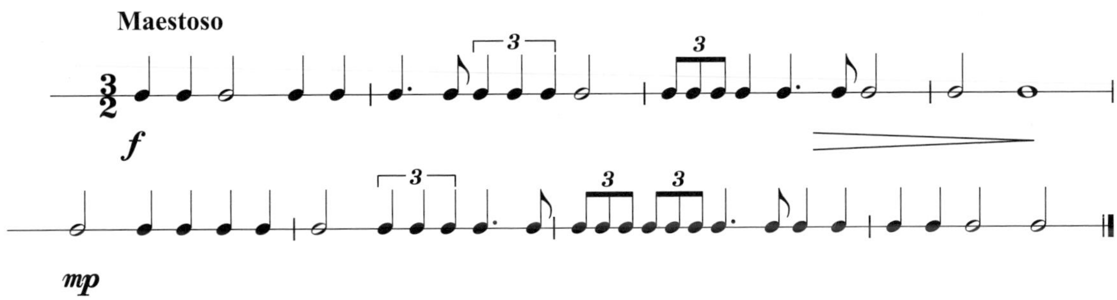


RHYTHM 7.1.10

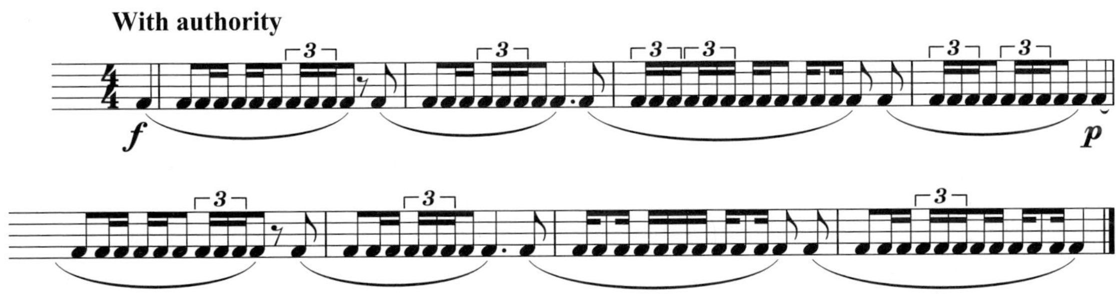

### RHYTHM 7.1.11

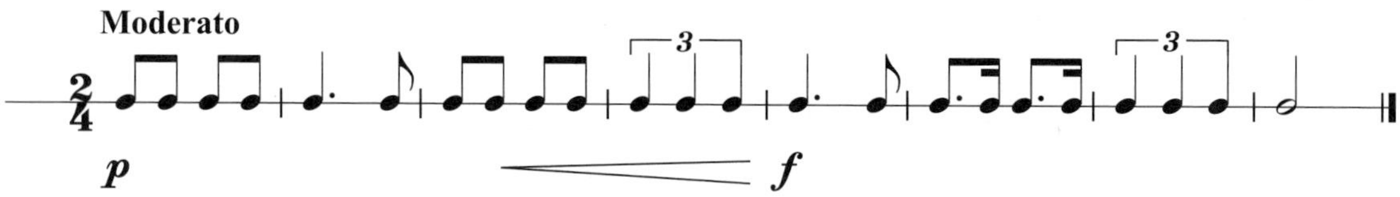


### RHYTHM 7.1.12

### RHYTHM 7.1.13

### RHYTHM 7.1.14

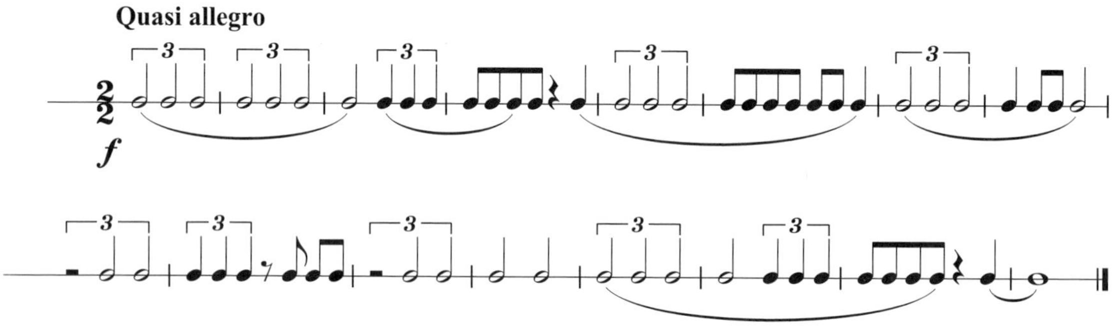


### RHYTHM 7.1.15

### RHYTHM 7.1.16

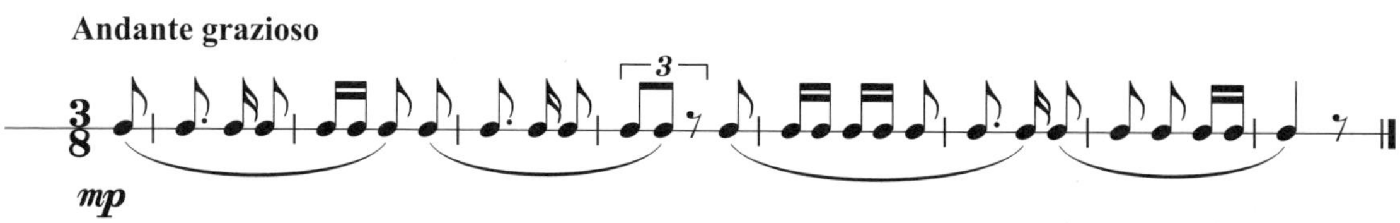

## RHYTHM 7.1.17

## RHYTHM 7.1.18

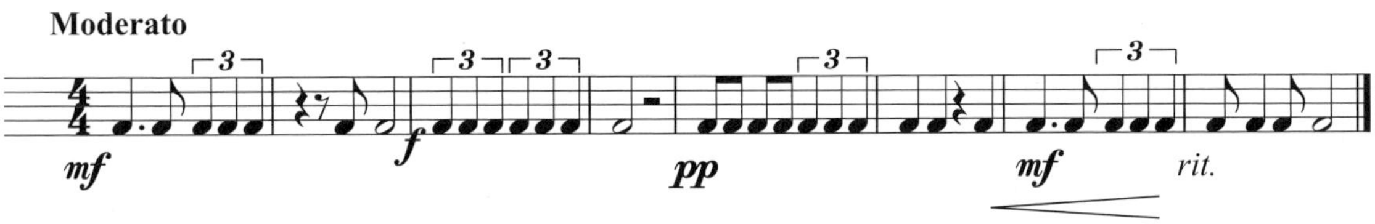


## RHYTHM 7.1.19

## RHYTHM 7.1.20

## Two-part Rhythms

### TWO-PART RHYTHM 7.1.1

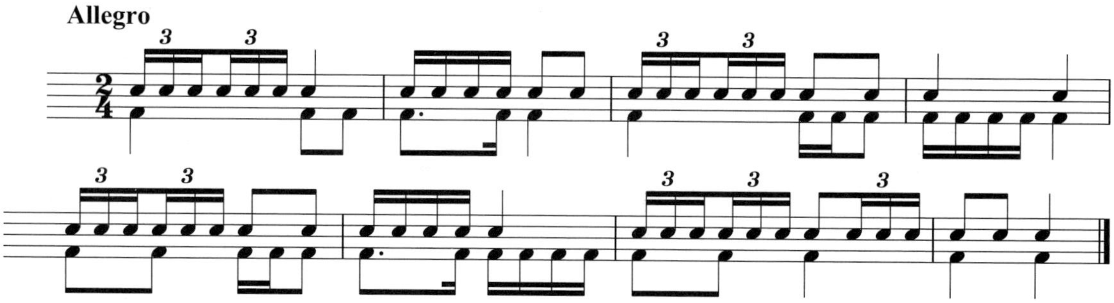


### TWO-PART RHYTHM 7.1.2

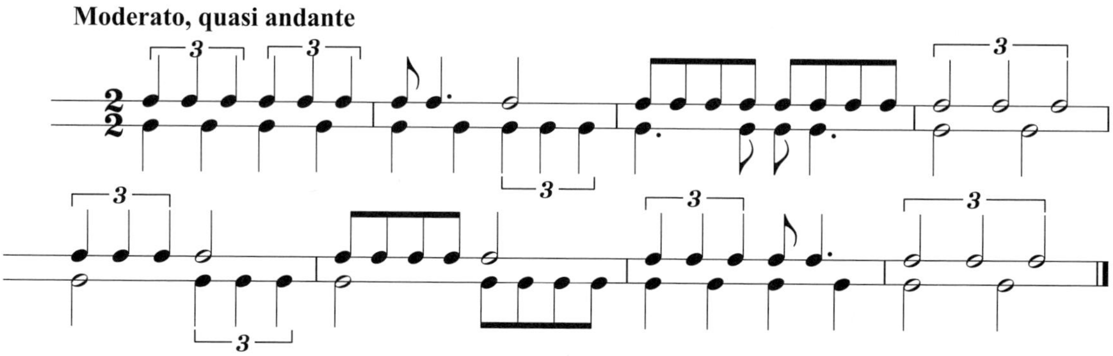


## Three-part Rhythms

### THREE-PART RHYTHM 7.1.1

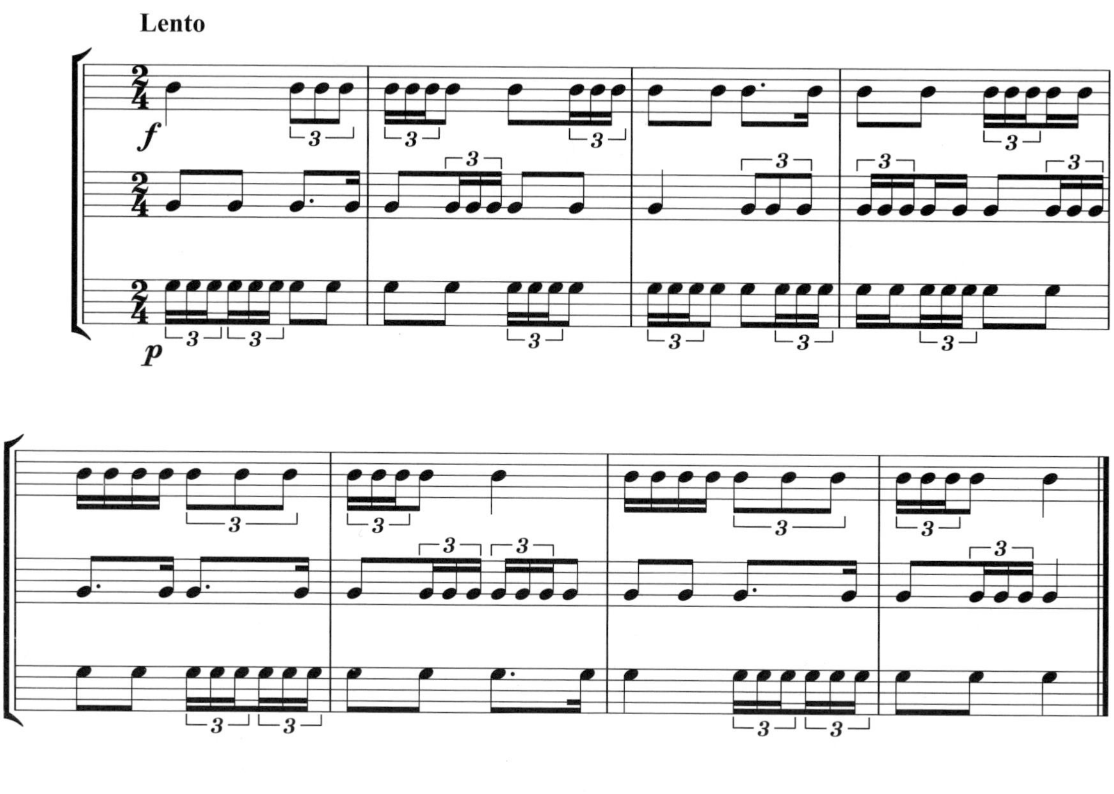

**THREE-PART RHYTHM 7.1.2**

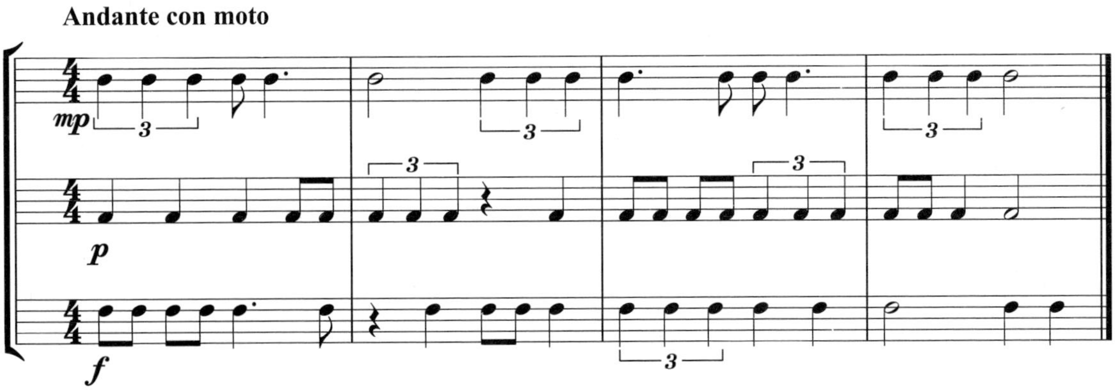


## 7.2 Secondary Dominants and Leading Tone Chords

### Facts You Need to Know

Secondary function is a form of tonicization, or temporary creation of the feeling of tonic in a non-tonic scale degree. The most common secondary functions are secondary (sometimes called applied) dominants.

Secondary dominants are created by changing a diatonic triad to one of the dominant chord qualities:

1. Major triads that function like V to the tonicized scale degree.
2. Diminished triads that function like vii°.
3. Major-minor (dominant) seventh chords that function like V$^7$.
4. Diminished seventh chords (half or fully) that function like vii$^{ø7}$ or vii$^{o7}$.

In general, this means that you are either creating a leading tone to the tonicized scale degree by raising a pitch, or you are creating a fourth scale degree to the tonicized scale degree (the seventh of a dominant seventh chord) by lowering a pitch.

Secondary dominants can be used in the same places as the diatonic chords they replace (a V/V acts like the predominant ii it replaces), but they aren't used to tonicize scale degrees over which diminished chords are built (vii° in major, ii° in minor). They can resolve in any way that a normal dominant can (normally, deceptively, etc.).

You can extend a tonicization by using chromatically altered predominants and dominants before arriving at the tonicized scale degree.

**EXAMPLE 7.2.1**

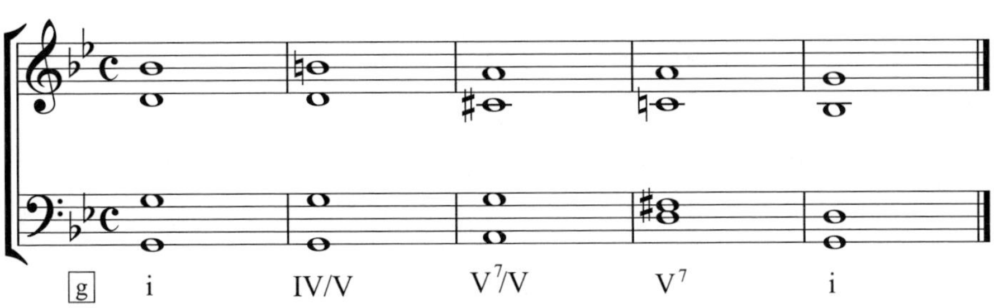

## Hearing

Listen for a chromatic tone or chord. If the chromatic tone acts like a leading tone to a diatonic scale degree, then it will be a secondary dominant to the chord built on that scale degree. If the chromatic tone acts like a dominant chord seventh, then it will be a secondary dominant to the chord whose root is a third below the resolution tone.

## Singing

1. Begin by singing the diatonic triad for which the secondary dominant chord will substitute.
2. Alter the chord to make it a secondary dominant by either:

   a. Raising the third of a minor triad to create a major triad (you are creating a new leading tone to the tonicized chord).
   b. Raising the third and the fifth of a diminished triad to create a major triad.
   c. Adding a minor seventh to either of the alterations above or to any major triad to create a major-minor seventh chord.

Major Mode

**EXAMPLE 7.2.2**

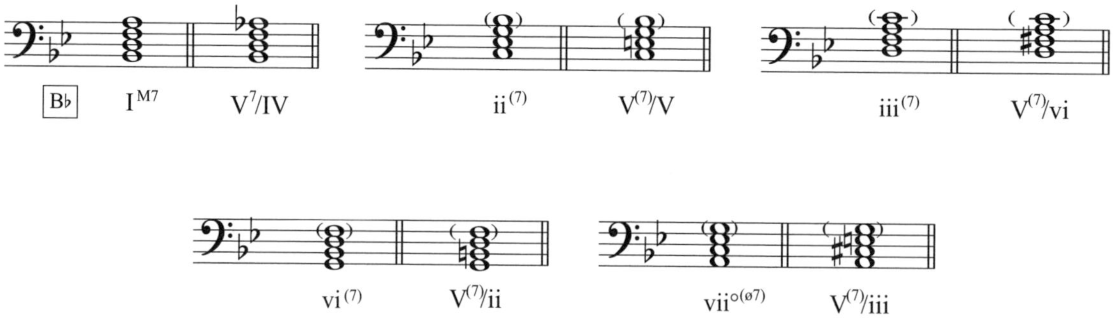


Minor Mode

**EXAMPLE 7.2.3**

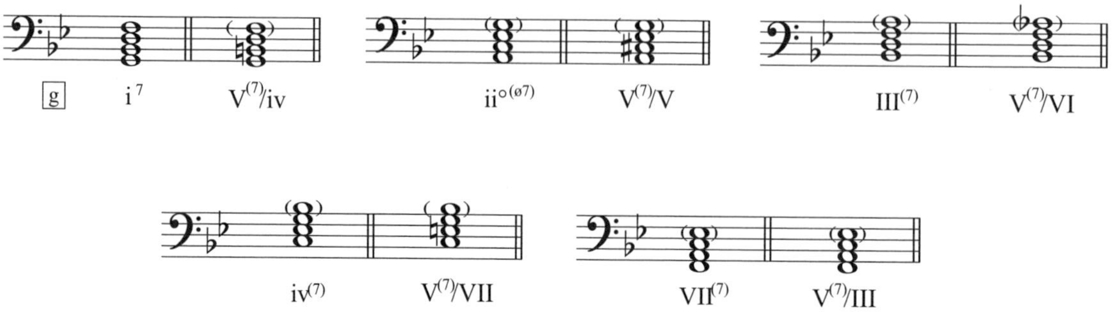


   d. Removing the root from the dominant chord created using the options above to create a diminished triad or seventh chord.

Major Mode

**EXAMPLE 7.2.4**

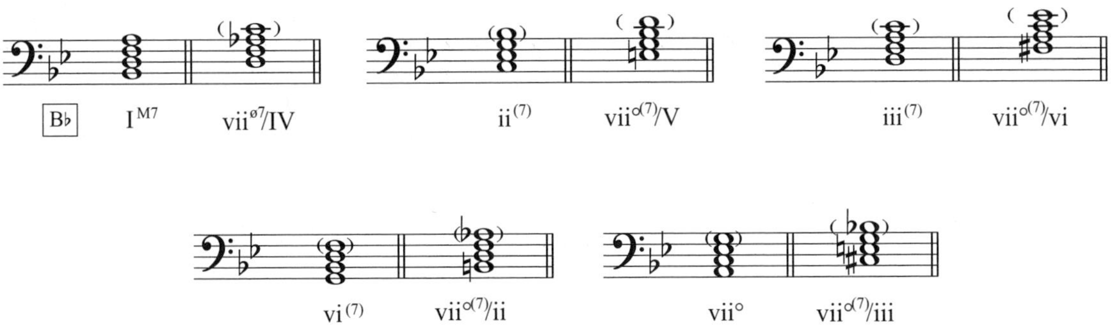


Minor Mode

**EXAMPLE 7.2.5**

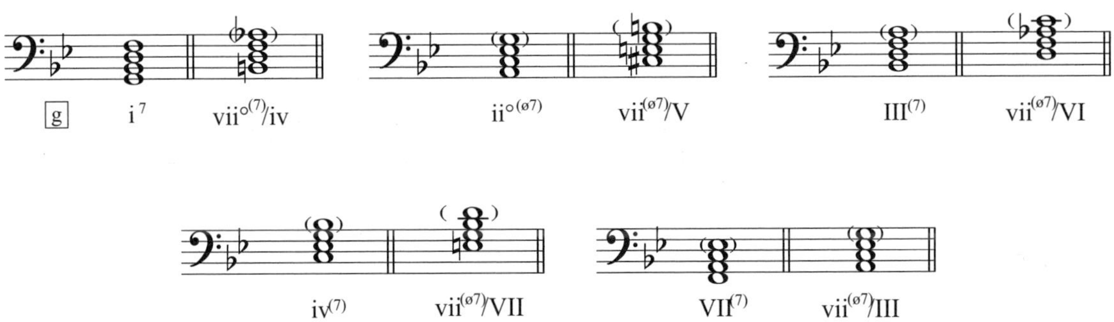


3. Resolve the secondary dominant chord like you would any dominant or leading tone triad or seventh chord.

## Assignments for Practice

1. Sing the circle of fifths progression using seventh chords found below (this is the same progression you learned in Chapter 5).

**EXAMPLE 7.2.6**

Change each chord that can be a secondary function chord into one. For example, inserting a V$^{(7)}$/V would make the progression sound like:

**EXAMPLE 7.2.7**

Do this for all chords that can be changed into secondary dominants.
Try this in both the major and the minor modes.

2. Do the above exercise, but add in multiple secondary dominants. What happens if every chord that can be made into a secondary dominant is?

## Pitch Patterns

**PITCH PATTERN 7.2.1**

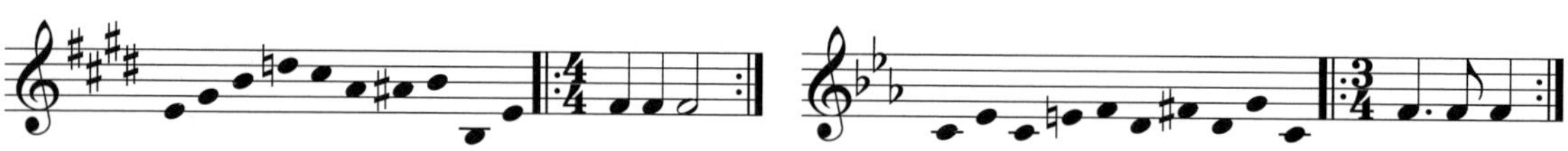

**PITCH PATTERN 7.2.2**

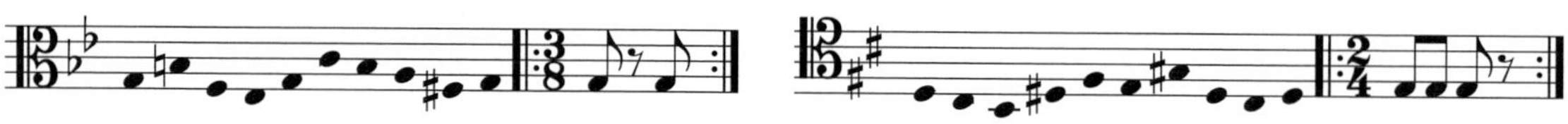

**PITCH PATTERN 7.2.3**

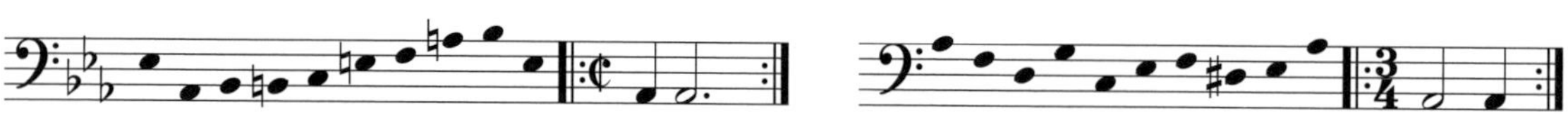

## Harmonic Progressions

1. I – V$^7$/IV – ii – V$^7$/V – V — I
2. i – V$^7$/iv – iv – V$^7$/VII – VII – III – V$^7$/VI – VI – ii° – V – I
3. I – V$^7$/vi – vi – V$^7$/ii – ii – V – vii°/vi – vi – V$^7$/V – V – I
4. I – vii°/ii – ii – vii$^{ø7}$/V – V – I
5. i – V$^7$/iv – V$^7$/VII – V$^7$/III – V$^7$/VI – VI – V$^7$/V – V – i

## Melodies

### MELODY 7.2.1

### MELODY 7.2.2

### MELODY 7.2.3

### MELODY 7.2.4

MELODY 7.2.5

MELODY 7.2.6

MELODY 7.2.7

MELODY 7.2.8

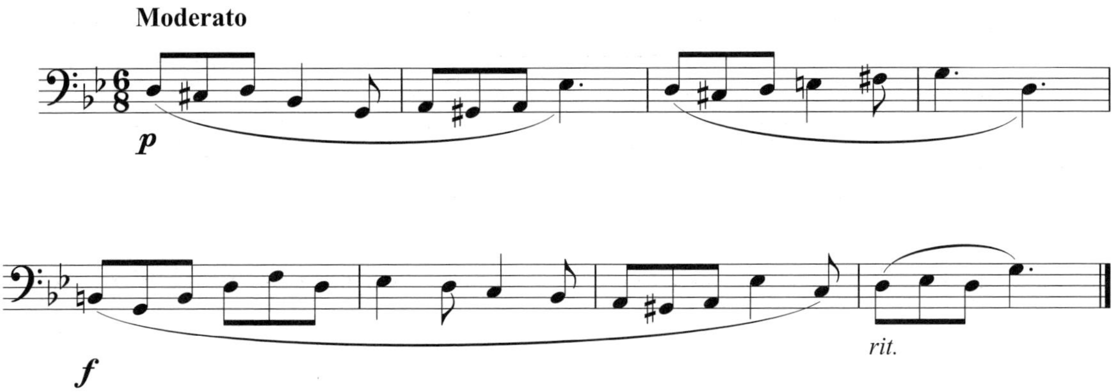


MELODY 7.2.9

MELODY 7.2.10

MELODY 7.2.11

MELODY 7.2.12

MELODY 7.2.13

MELODY 7.2.14

MELODY 7.2.15

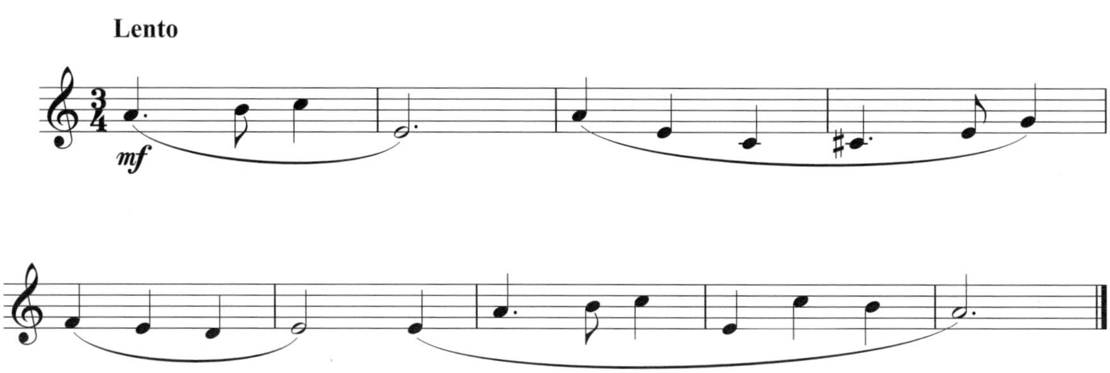

MELODY 7.2.16

MELODY 7.2.17

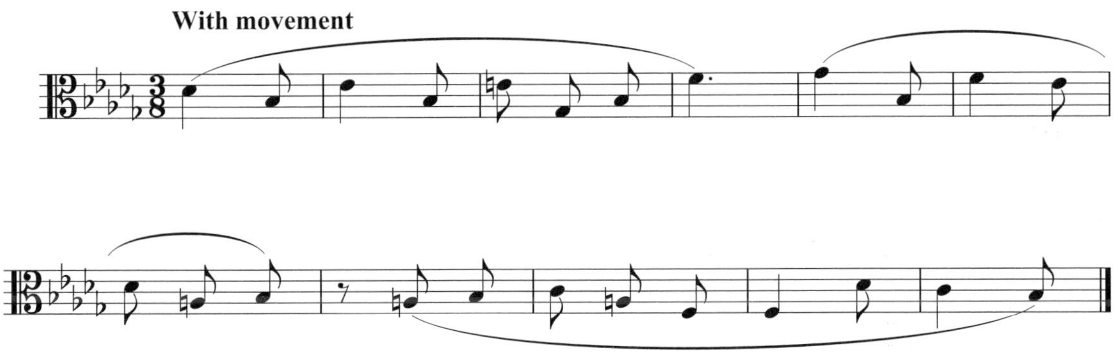


MELODY 7.2.18

MELODY 7.2.19

**MELODY 7.2.20**

## Duets

**DUET 7.2.1**

**DUET 7.2.2**

DUET 7.2.3

## Chorale

CHORALE 7.2

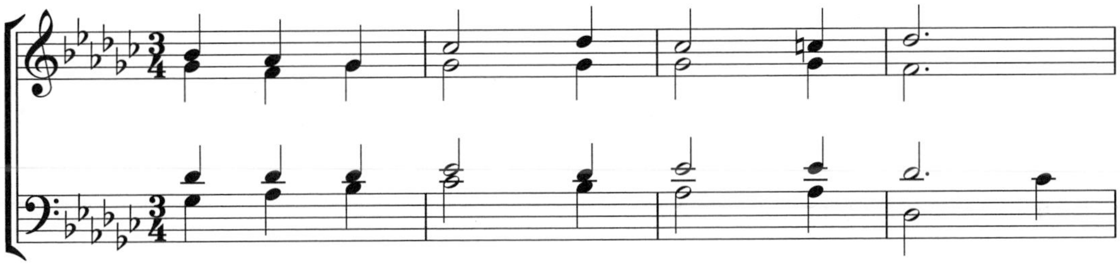

## Self-Accompanied Melody

### SELF-ACCOMPANIED MELODY 7.2

## 7.3 The Neapolitan Chord

### Facts You Need to Know

Neapolitan chords are major triads built on the lowered second scale degree. They most commonly appear in the minor mode and in first inversion, although root position Neapolitans are not uncommon.

When appearing in the major mode, scale degree 6 is found in its lowered, minor position.

Neapolitan chords are predominant chords consisting of scale degrees ♭2, 4, and ♭6.

They are distinguishable by their strikingly dark sound, major quality, and they are usually found in first inversion. When resolving to the dominant, the lowered second scale degree moves down to the leading tone.

**EXAMPLE 7.3.1**

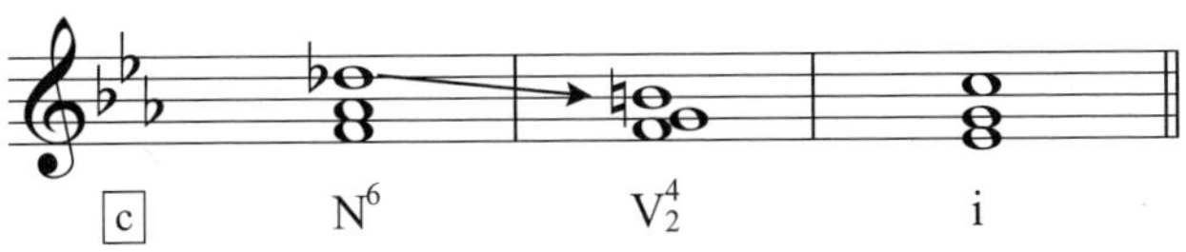


This resolution is sometimes embellished by moving through a cadential six-four chord or a vii°7/V.

### Hearing

Listen for a chromatic chord that precedes the dominant. Neapolitans will have a very strong and dark sound and will often have scale degree 4 (and sometimes scale degree ♭2) in the bass.

### Singing

Know the scale degree your given pitch represents. If necessary, use the scale degree pattern to find tonic, and orient yourself in that key by singing scale degree patterns. Sing the component scale degrees in the correct order. Memorize the resolutions that appear below and be able to sing them from any pitch.

**EXAMPLE 7.3.2**

*Resolving Directly to Dominant*

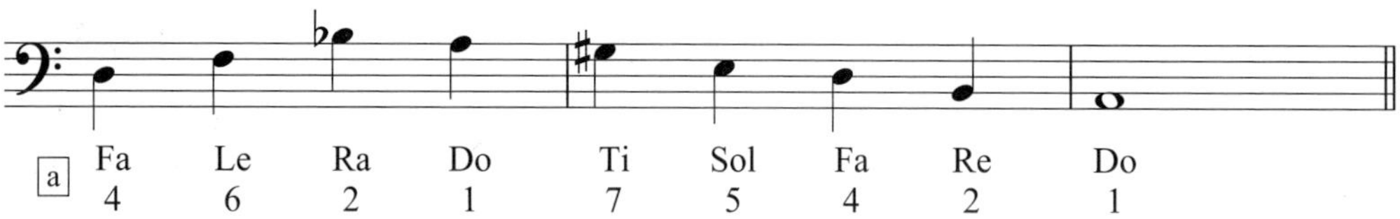


*Resolving through a Cadential $^6_4$*

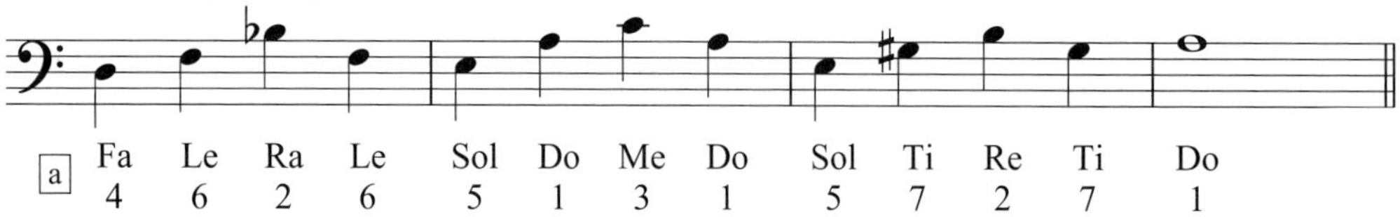


*Resolving through a vii°⁷/V*

## Assignments for Practice

### Pitch Patterns

**PITCH PATTERN 7.3.1**

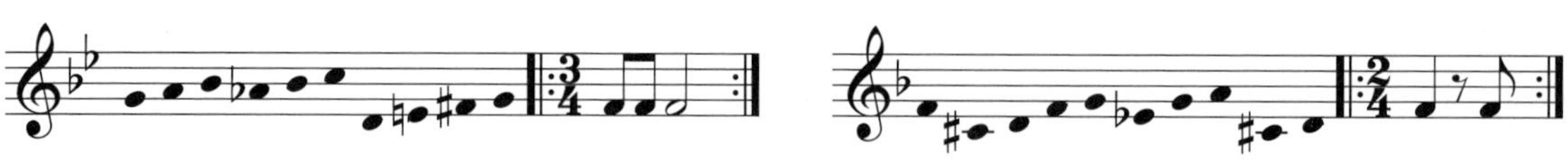

**PITCH PATTERN 7.3.2**

**PITCH PATTERN 7.3.3**

### Harmonic Progressions

1. i – $N^6$ – $V^7$ – i
2. i – N – $V^7$ – i
3. i – VI – $N^6$ – $i^6_4$ – $V^7$ – i
4. i – VI – $N^6$ – $vii^{ø7}/V$ – $V^7$ – i
5. I – $I^4_2$ – $V^4_2/IV$ – $IV^6$ – $N^6$ – V – I

## Melodies

### MELODY 7.3.1

**With purpose**

### MELODY 7.3.2

**Slowly, with regret**

### MELODY 7.3.3

**Quickly and sneakily**

MELODY 7.3.4

MELODY 7.3.5

MELODY 7.3.6

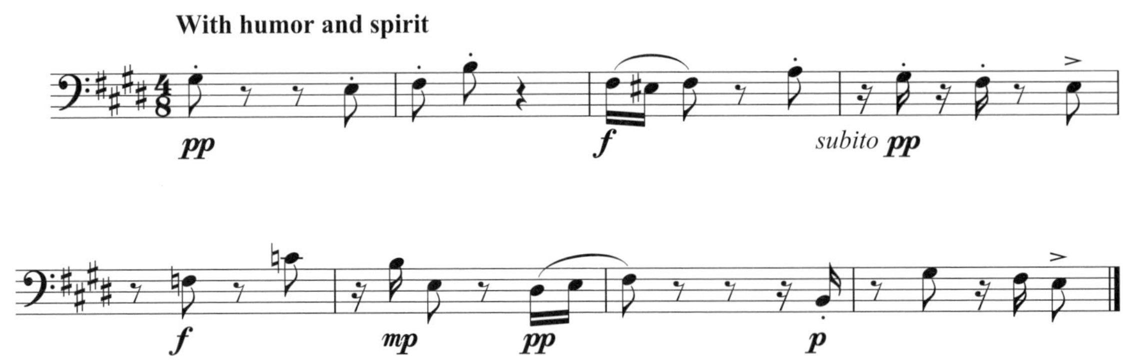


MELODY 7.3.7

MELODY 7.3.8

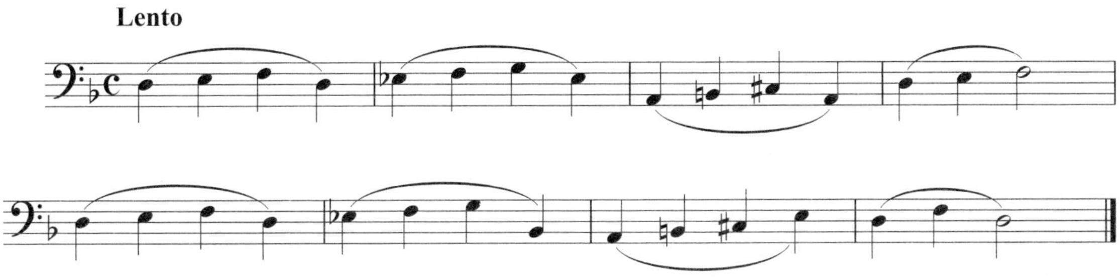


MELODY 7.3.9

MELODY 7.3.10

MELODY 7.3.11

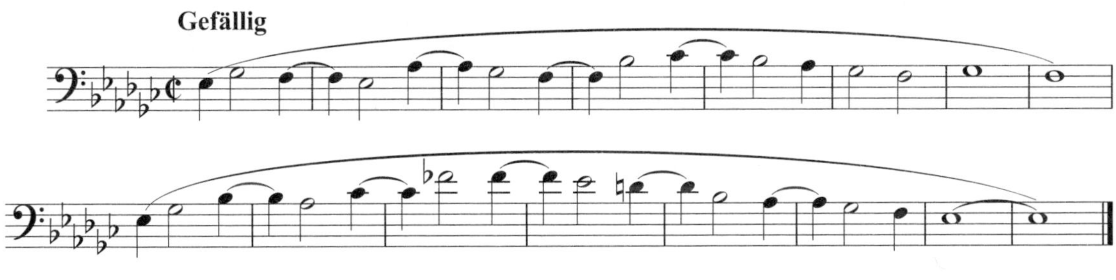

**MELODY 7.3.12**

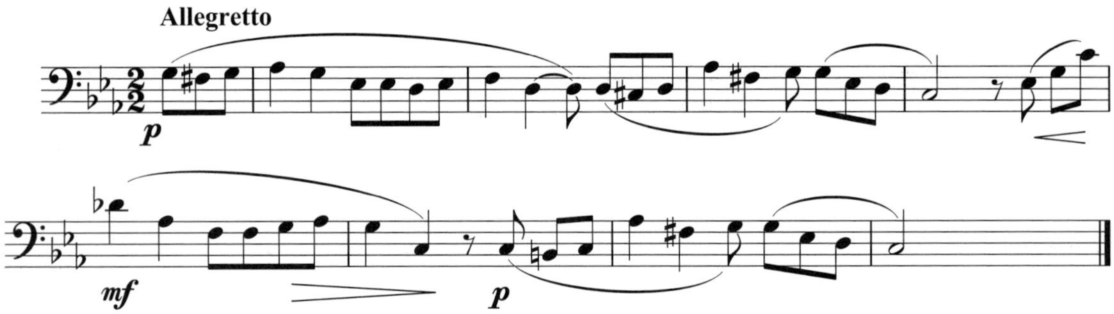


**MELODY 7.3.13**

**MELODY 7.3.14**

**MELODY 7.3.15**

## Duets

### DUET 7.3.1

Pensieroso

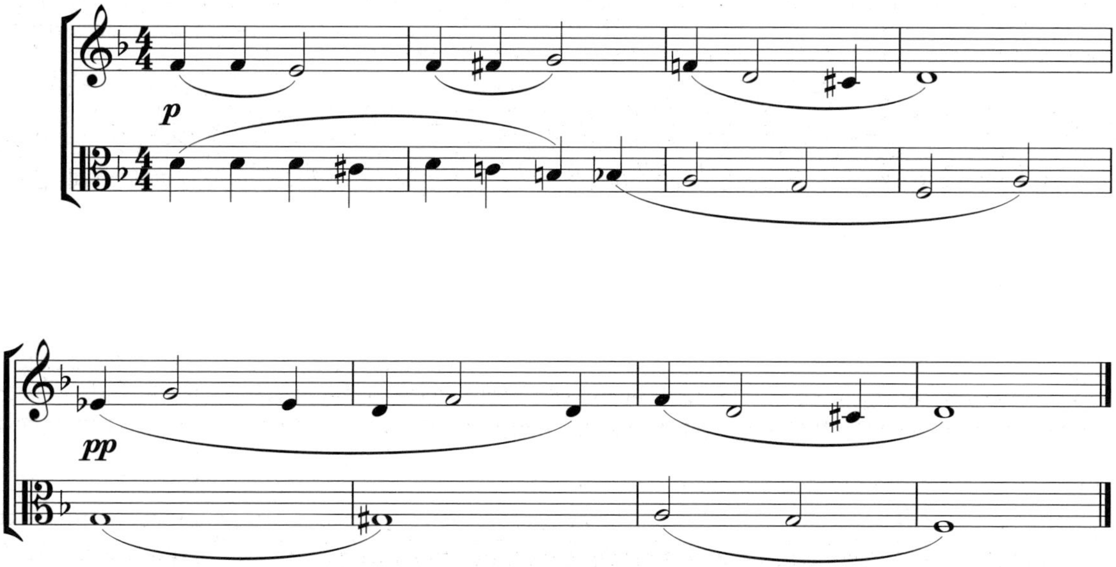


### DUET 7.3.2

Pensieroso

## Chorale

### CHORALE 7.3

## Self-Accompanied Melody

### SELF-ACCOMPANIED MELODY 7.3

## 7.4 Augmented Sixth Chords

### Facts You Need to Know

Augmented sixth chords are predominant chords that consist of the minor sixth scale degree (typically in the bass), scale degree 1, and scale degree ♯4. They get their name from the interval formed between the sixth scale degree and the raised fourth scale degree.

An additional tone is often present, giving the chord a unique sound and name. Those names are:

| | |
|---|---|
| *Italian* | No additional tone or doubled scale degree 1 |
| *French* | Additional scale degree 2 |
| *German* | Additional scale degree 3 |

**EXAMPLE 7.4.1**

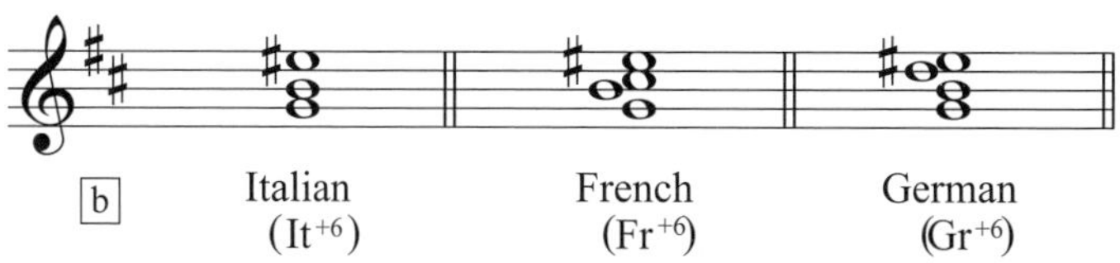


These chords arise out of the minor mode, so scale degrees 6 and 3 will appear in their lowered position.

These chords lead to the dominant by having scale degrees 6 and ♯4 move away from each other by half a step to form an octave. The remaining tones usually resolve down by step or stay on the common tone. The remaining tones in the German augmented sixth almost always delay their resolution by one chord, creating a cadential six-four chord. This helps to avoid problems with parallel voice leading.

**EXAMPLE 7.4.2**

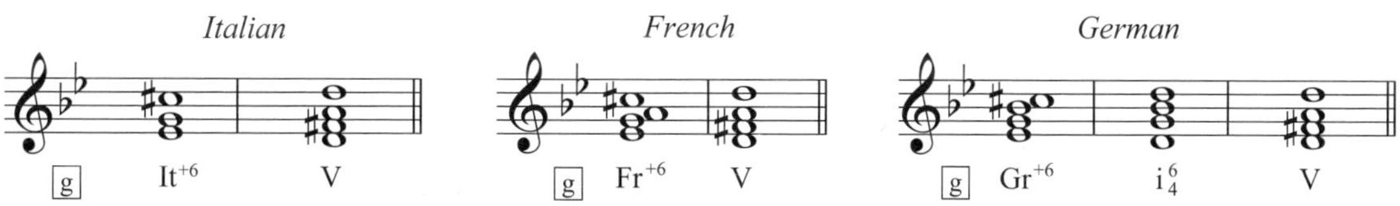


When appearing in the major mode, scale degree 6 will be borrowed from the minor mode. In German augmented sixth chords appearing in the major mode, scale degree 3 will often be enharmonically spelled as ♯2, reflecting its tendency to resolve up to scale degree 3 in the cadential six-four chord.

**EXAMPLE 7.4.3**

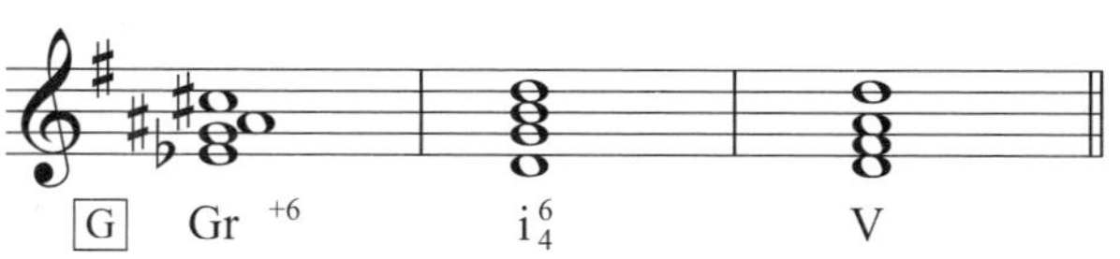

## Hearing

Listen for a chromatic chord that precedes the dominant. Augmented sixth chords will have scale degree ♭6 in the bass, and the chromatically altered ♯4 will slide away from the bass to form an octave.

## Singing

Your given pitch will generally be the lowered sixth scale degree. If necessary, use the scale degree pattern to find tonic, and orient yourself in that key by singing scale degree patterns. Sing the component scale degrees in the correct order.

Typical augmented sixth chords and their resolutions appear in the example below. Memorize and be able to sing these progressions from any note.

**EXAMPLE 7.4.4**

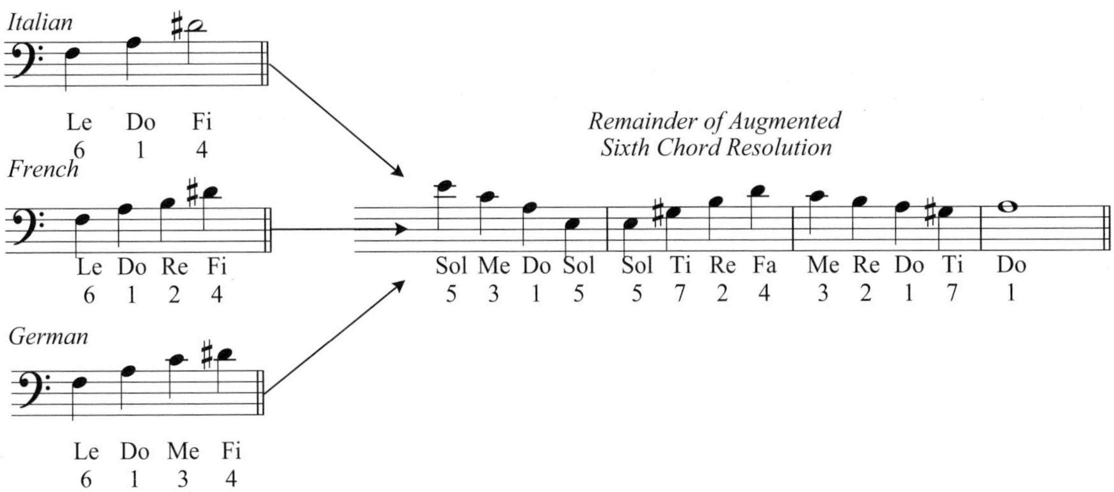


## Assignments for Practice

### Pitch Patterns

**PITCH PATTERN 7.4.1**

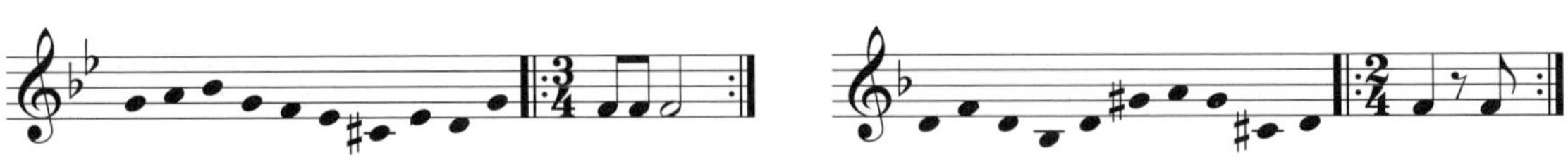

**PITCH PATTERN 7.4.2**

### PITCH PATTERN 7.4.3

## Harmonic Progressions

1. i – $It^{+6}$ – $V^7$ – i
2. i – $ii^{o6}$ – $Fr^{+6}$ – $V^7$ – i
3. i – iv – $Gr^{+6}$ – $i^6_4$ – $V^7$ – i
4. i – $v^6$ – $iv^6$ – $It^{+6}$ – $V^7$ – i
5. I – $V^4_2$/IV – $IV^6$ – $Gr^{+6}$ – $I^6_4$ – $V^7$ – I

## Melodies

### MELODY 7.4.1

### MELODY 7.4.2

**MELODY 7.4.3**

**MELODY 7.4.4**

**MELODY 7.4.5**

**MELODY 7.4.6**

MELODY 7.4.7

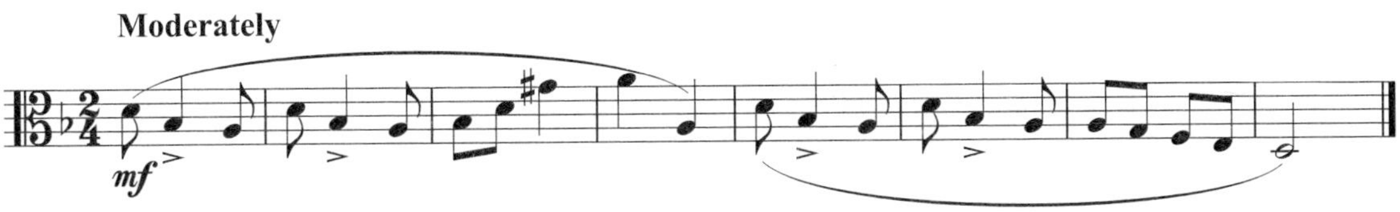


MELODY 7.4.8

MELODY 7.4.9

MELODY 7.4.10

MELODY 7.4.11

MELODY 7.4.12

MELODY 7.4.13

MELODY 7.4.14

**MELODY 7.4.15**

## Duets

**DUET 7.4.1**

**DUET 7.4.2**

## Chorale

### CHORALE 7.4

## Self-Accompanied Melody

### SELF-ACCOMPANIED MELODY 7.4

## 7.5 Extended and Altered Dominant Chords

### Facts You Need to Know

Different colorings of the dominant sound can be achieved by stacking additional diatonic thirds on top of the dominant seventh chord. The staff below shows the most common "tall" dominant chords and their resolutions. Notes in parentheses are commonly left out of extended dominant chords.

**EXAMPLE 7.5.1**

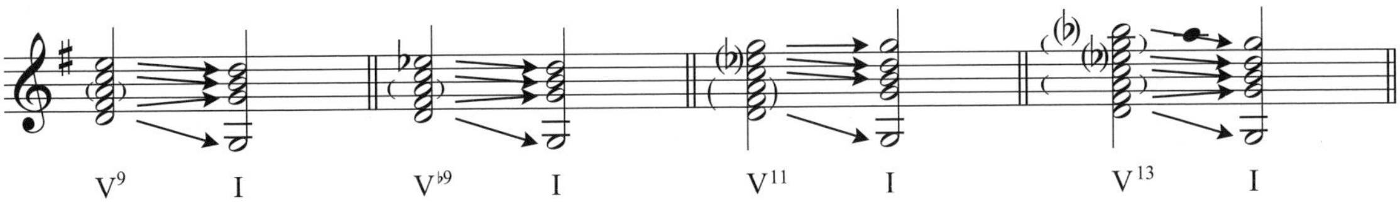


As dominant chords are made taller, they are less likely to appear in inversion. Most dominant ninth, eleventh, and thirteenth chords appear in root position. Dominant chords can also be altered by raising or lowering the chord fifth (scale degree two) by a half step.

**EXAMPLE 7.5.2**

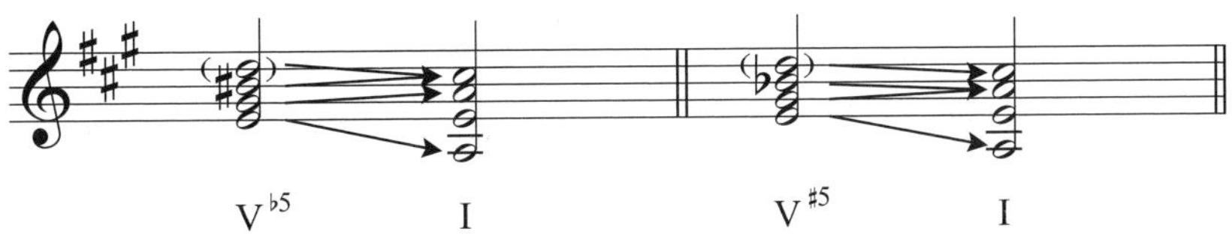


Neither altering the fifth chord nor adding diatonic notes on top of a dominant chord change its function.

### Hearing

Listen for the dominant quality of the sound and its desire to resolve to tonic. Notice that in most cases, the bass pitch will be scale degree five. Listen for these specific features:

Dominant ninths: Listen for scale degree six, often as the highest note of the texture.

Dominant elevenths: Listen for the sound of a subdominant triad with scale degree five in the bass.

Dominant thirteenths: Listen for scale degree three in the soprano resolving down (sometimes by step through scale degree two) to tonic.

Altered dominants: Listen for how the altered scale degree wants to continue to move in the direction of its alteration.

## Singing

Know the scale degree content of the chord you are asked to sing. Sing scale degree five in the bass with the other required scale degrees above it.

## Assignments for Practice

### Pitch Patterns

#### PITCH PATTERN 7.5.1

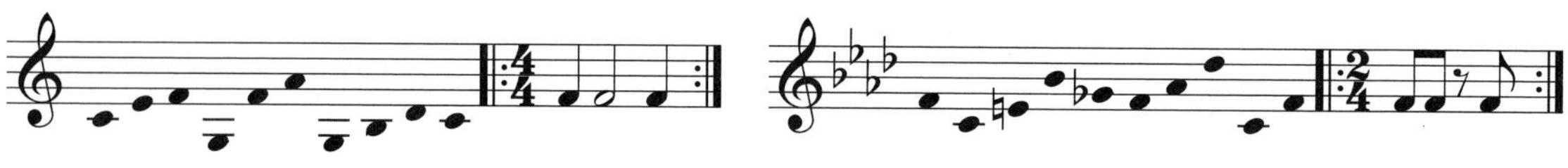

#### PITCH PATTERN 7.5.2

#### PITCH PATTERN 7.5.3

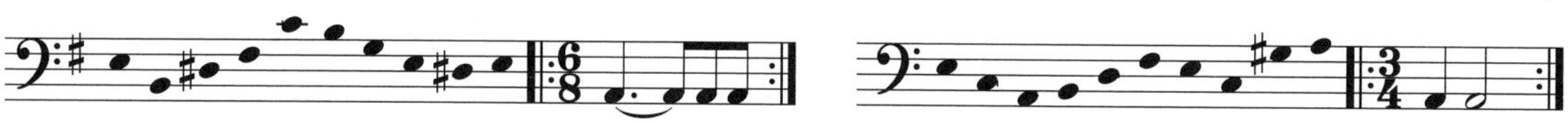

### Melodies

#### MELODY 7.5.1

**MELODY 7.5.2**

**MELODY 7.5.3**

**MELODY 7.5.4**

**MELODY 7.5.5**

**MELODY 7.5.6**

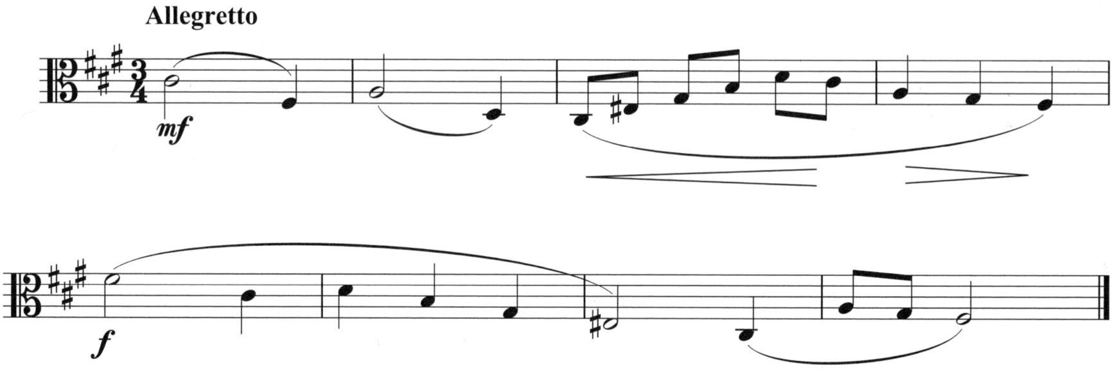


**MELODY 7.5.7**

**MELODY 7.5.8**

MELODY 7.5.9

MELODY 7.5.10

MELODY 7.5.11

## MELODY 7.5.12

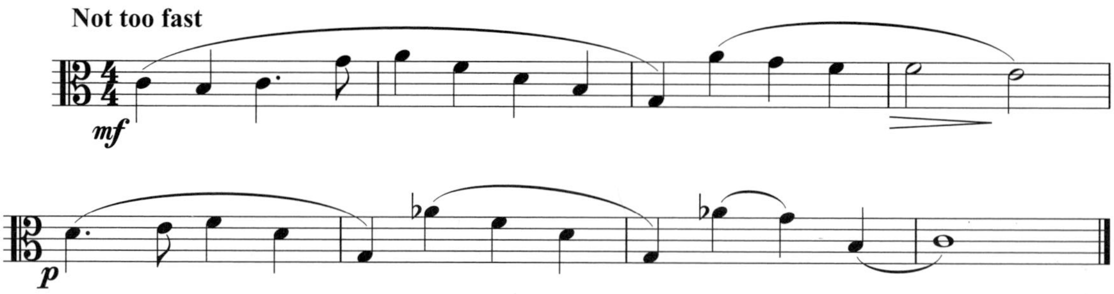


## MELODY 7.5.13

## MELODY 7.5.14

### MELODY 7.5.15

## Duets

### DUET 7.5.1

### DUET 7.5.2

**DUET 7.5.3**

## Chorale

**CHORALE 7.5**

## Self-Accompanied Melody

### SELF-ACCOMPANIED MELODY 7.5

## 7.6 Music from the Literature

### EXAMPLE 7.6.1

*Piano Sonata in C Major*, Op. 53, III

m. 313–333

Beethoven

**EXAMPLE 7.6.2**

*Sonata in G Major for Violin and Piano*, Op. 100, III

m. 295–318

Dvorak

**EXAMPLE 7.6.3**

*Polka*, Op. 39, No. 14

m. 23–30

Tchaikovsky

**EXAMPLE 7.6.4**

"Fugue in E-flat Major," from *The Well-Tempered Clavier*, Book 1

m. 6–11

J.S. Bach

**EXAMPLE 7.6.5**

*Sonata for Piano and Violin*, K. 302, I

m. 85–91

Mozart

**EXAMPLE 7.6.6**

*Sonata for Piano and Violin*, K. 377,
II

Mozart

**EXAMPLE 7.6.7**

*Piano Sonata in F Minor*, Op. 5, No. 3,
II

Brahms

**EXAMPLE 7.6.8**

*Little Flower*, Op. 205, No. 7

Cornelius Gurlitt

**EXAMPLE 7.6.9**

**EXAMPLE 7.6.10**

**EXAMPLE 7.6.11**

*Piano Sonata in G Major*, Op. 31, No. 1, III

Beethoven

**Rondo**
**Allegretto**

**EXAMPLE 7.6.12**

m. 19–27

"Der Müller und der Bach," from *Die schöne Müllerin*

Schubert

**Moderato**

## Reflections: Confidence

Think about the most skilled performers you know. Are there any characteristics that they seem to share? If you're like most people, one characteristic on your list is likely to be confidence. Skilled performers put their audience at ease by making everything sound easy. The moment they take the stage, they communicate to their audience that they are in charge, and that the listener need not worry that the performance will turn out all right. Even when the performer wants the audience to believe that the music is incredibly difficult, their demeanor suggests a certain false concern—that they are merely acting to get the desired dramatic effect.

Now think back on a performance you attended (not your own) that did not go so well. Did the performer exude confidence as he or she took the stage? Did he or she maintain this level of control throughout the performance? Most likely, the performer communicated his or her uncertainty about the performance that the audience innately read and understood. The end result: a less than satisfying performance. Audiences seem to be very attuned to the confidence level of the performer, and it directly affects their enjoyment of the music. When the performer demonstrates confidence, the audience is at ease and able to enjoy the music. When the performer seems uncertain, then the audience experiences the discomfort of the performer and is less able to enjoy the music.

Confidence occurs when preparation, experience, vision, passion, and communication come together. Preparation is perhaps the key element of confidence. Preparation suggests that during practice you have worked out all of the difficult elements so that you know how you will execute them during the performance.

It suggests that you have achieved a level of comfort with your decisions regarding technical and musical presentation, so that you know exactly what you will do and when you will do it to execute as good a performance as you can. Surprises are a certainty when it comes to performance. Preparation involves dealing with unexpected mistakes as they arise during practice and figuring out ways to work through them. Preparation means that, when you take the stage, you know that you have done all you could do to present the performance that you want.

Experience is a second element of confidence. The more you do something, the more comfortable you will be doing it again. In terms of musical performance, the only way to gain experience is through performing. The key element of gaining experience, however, is getting used to presenting well-prepared and successful performances. Simply getting on stage and playing does no good if your performances are not thoughtful, well prepared, and musically and emotionally satisfying to you.

Vision is the ability to see how the audience should experience the performance and to make that image reality. Successful performers understand what makes a performance work and how to make their vision a reality. This skill can be developed by thoughtfully and critically watching others' performances and modeling your stage presence after what you see and like (this is one reason most colleges have a performance attendance requirement!).

Successful performers love to perform. They couldn't imagine doing anything else with their life. Even though they may play the same piece in public for years, their exploration of the music and their passion for performing it never wanes—their performances still sound fresh and new.

Performance is a medium of communication. One must have something to say in order to have a successful performance, and then he or she must say it so that the audience understands.

Can confidence be learned? Mostly yes. Preparation, experience, and vision are matters that are in your control. Communication comes from studying music through performance, analysis, and thoughtful listening. The only element that seems innate (either you have it or you don't) is passion. If you've made it this far in your musical career, chances are you have it (otherwise you would have studied something else in college!). Notice how most elements are in your control. That means it is *your* responsibility to cultivate and practice these skills and attributes to become a seasoned and confident performer.

## 7.7 Dictation Materials

@

### I. Identification of Minor Scale Degrees

Your teacher will establish a key and then play its scale degrees in random order or as a specific pitch in a melody (by number—first, second, last, or by position—high or low). Identify each by writing its number in the appropriate space. Place an up arrow in front of scale degree 6 or 7 if you hear either of them in their raised position.

*Date:* . . . . . . . . . . . . . .

1. ____ 2. ____ 3. ____ 4. ____ 5. ____ 6. ____ 7. ____ 8. ____

*Date:* . . . . . . . . . . . . . .

1. ____ 2. ____ 3. ____ 4. ____ 5. ____ 6. ____ 7. ____ 8. ____

*Date:* . . . . . . . . . . . . . .

1. ____ 2. ____ 3. ____ 4. ____ 5. ____ 6. ____ 7. ____ 8. ____

*Date:* . . . . . . . . . . . . . .

1. ____ 2. ____ 3. ____ 4. ____ 5. ____ 6. ____ 7. ____ 8. ____

*Date:* . . . . . . . . . . . . . .

1. ____ 2. ____ 3. ____ 4. ____ 5. ____ 6. ____ 7. ____ 8. ____

## II. Identification of Major Scale Degrees

Your teacher will establish a key and then play its scale degrees in random order or as a specific pitch in a melody (by number—first, second, last, or by position—high or low). Identify each by writing its number in the appropriate space.

*Date:* . . . . . . . . . . . . . .

1. ____ 2. ____ 3. ____ 4. ____ 5. ____ 6. ____ 7. ____ 8. ____

*Date:* . . . . . . . . . . . . . .

1. ____ 2. ____ 3. ____ 4. ____ 5. ____ 6. ____ 7. ____ 8. ____

*Date:* . . . . . . . . . . . . . .

1. ____ 2. ____ 3. ____ 4. ____ 5. ____ 6. ____ 7. ____ 8. ____

*Date:* . . . . . . . . . . . . . .

1. ____ 2. ____ 3. ____ 4. ____ 5. ____ 6. ____ 7. ____ 8. ____

*Date:* . . . . . . . . . . . . . .

1. ____ 2. ____ 3. ____ 4. ____ 5. ____ 6. ____ 7. ____ 8. ____

## III. Interval Identification

Your teacher will play several intervals. Identify their quality and size as one of the following:

| | | |
|---|---|---|
| M2 = Major second | TT = Tritone | m7 = Minor seventh |
| m2 = Minor second | P5 = Perfect fifth | P8 = Perfect octave |
| M3 = Major third | M6 = Major sixth | M9 = Major ninth |
| m3 = Minor third | m6 = Minor sixth | m9 = Minor ninth |
| P4 = Perfect fourth | M7 = Major seventh | M10 = Major tenth |
| | | m10 = Minor tenth |

Be sure to make a clear difference between your capital and lower-case Ms.

*Date:* . . . . . . . . . . . . . .

1. ____ 2. ____ 3. ____ 4. ____ 5. ____ 6. ____ 7. ____ 8. ____

*Date:* . . . . . . . . . . . . . .

1. ____ 2. ____ 3. ____ 4. ____ 5. ____ 6. ____ 7. ____ 8. ____

*Date:* . . . . . . . . . . . . . .

1. ____ 2. ____ 3. ____ 4. ____ 5. ____ 6. ____ 7. ____ 8. ____

*Date:* . . . . . . . . . . . . . .

1. ____ 2. ____ 3. ____ 4. ____ 5. ____ 6. ____ 7. ____ 8. ____

*Date:* . . . . . . . . . . . . . .

1. ____ 2. ____ 3. ____ 4. ____ 5. ____ 6. ____ 7. ____ 8. ____

## IV. Triad Quality Identification

Your teacher will play several triads. Indicate the quality and inversion. Possible answers are M for major, m for minor, and d for diminished.

*Date:* . . . . . . . . . . . . . .

1. ____ 2. ____ 3. ____ 4. ____ 5. ____ 6. ____ 7. ____ 8. ____

*Date:* . . . . . . . . . . . . . .

1. ____ 2. ____ 3. ____ 4. ____ 5. ____ 6. ____ 7. ____ 8. ____

*Date:* . . . . . . . . . . . . . .

1. ____ 2. ____ 3. ____ 4. ____ 5. ____ 6. ____ 7. ____ 8. ____

*Date:* . . . . . . . . . . . . . .

1. ____ 2. ____ 3. ____ 4. ____ 5. ____ 6. ____ 7. ____ 8. ____

*Date:* . . . . . . . . . . . . . .

1. ____ 2. ____ 3. ____ 4. ____ 5. ____ 6. ____ 7. ____ 8. ____

## V. Seventh Chord Identification

Your teacher will play several seventh chords. Indicate the quality (MM, Mm, mm, dm, or dd) and inversion for each by using the correct figured bass symbol.

*Date:* . . . . . . . . . . . . . .

1. ____ 2. ____ 3. ____ 4. ____ 5. ____ 6. ____ 7. ____ 8. ____

*Date:* . . . . . . . . . . . . . .

1. ____ 2. ____ 3. ____ 4. ____ 5. ____ 6. ____ 7. ____ 8. ____

*Date:* . . . . . . . . . . . . . .

1. ____ 2. ____ 3. ____ 4. ____ 5. ____ 6. ____ 7. ____ 8. ____

*Date:* . . . . . . . . . . . . . .

1. ____ 2. ____ 3. ____ 4. ____ 5. ____ 6. ____ 7. ____ 8. ____

*Date:* . . . . . . . . . . . . . .

1. ____ 2. ____ 3. ____ 4. ____ 5. ____ 6. ____ 7. ____ 8. ____

## VI. Melodic and Rhythmic Dictation

Your teacher will play a short melody or rhythm. Notate it on the staves below.

*Date:* . . . . . . . . . . . . . .

*Date:* . . . . . . . . . . . . . .

*Date:* . . . . . . . . . . . . . .

*Date:* . . . . . . . . . . . . . .

*Date:* . . . . . . . . . . . . . .

## VII. Harmonic Dictation

Write the soprano line, bass line, and provide a Roman numeral analysis (including inversional symbols) for the progression you hear on the grand staff below.

*Date:* . . . . . . . . . . . . . .

*Date:* . . . . . . . . . . . . . .

*Date:* . . . . . . . . . . . . . .

*Date:* . . . . . . . . . . . . . .

*Date:* . . . . . . . . . . . . . .

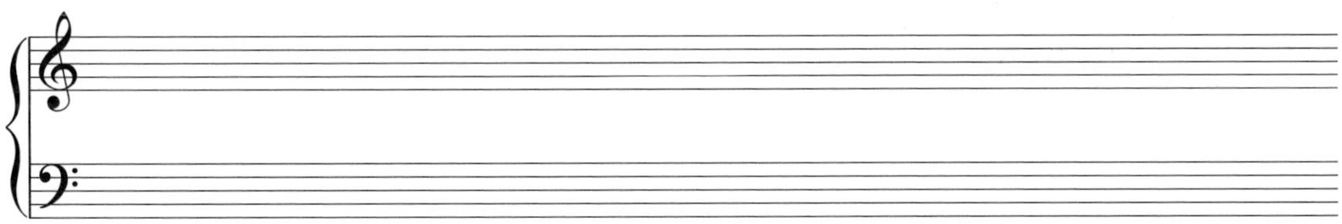

# Chapter 8

# Triplets; Other Clefs; Beginning Modulation

## 8.1 Divisions of the Beat into Numbers Greater than Four

**Facts You Need to Know**

The groupings in this class of irregular divisions include those that occur in groups of four or more; they are found in simple or compound meter. Each of these groupings is equal to one beat.

The examples below show the irregular divisions in this class.

### Simple Meter

**EXAMPLE 8.1.1**

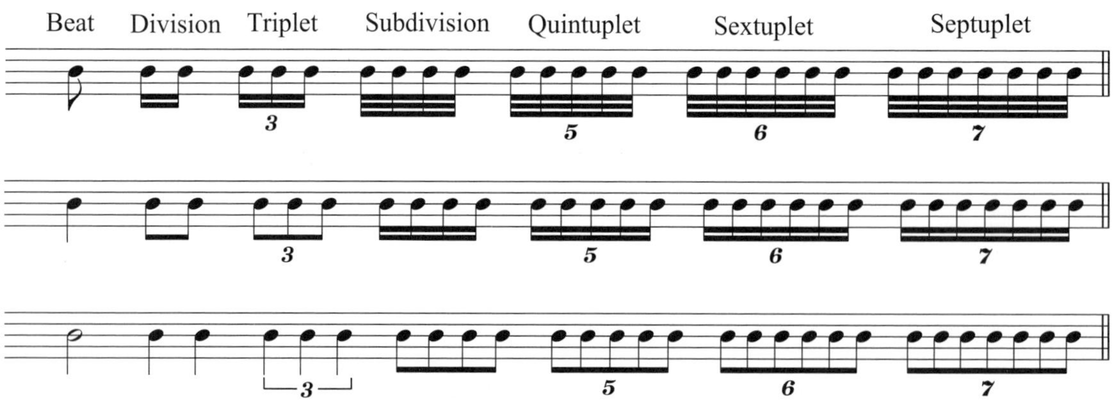

## Compound Meter

**EXAMPLE 8.1.2**

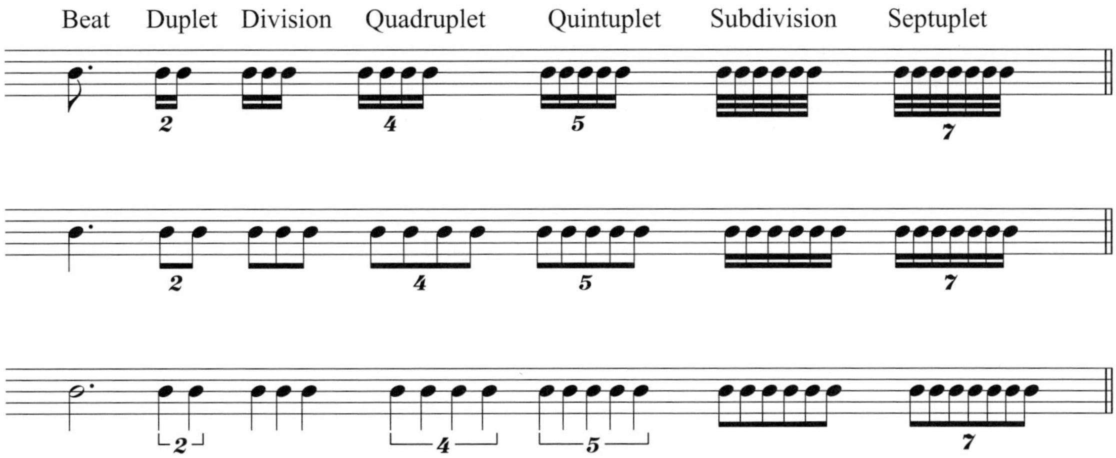


In simple meter, the groupings of 5 (*quintuplet*), 6 (*sextuplet*), and 7 (*septuplet*) serve primarily as a rhythmic flourish or melodic embellishment.

In compound meter, the groupings of 4 (*quadruplet*) and 5 (also a *quintuplet*) are faster than the regular division of the beat, and therefore have a stronger sense of resistance; these groups "fight" the natural metric divisions. The septuplet, on the other hand, is more akin to its simple meter counterpart, acting as a flourish or embellishment in a passage.

### Performing Large Groupings of Irregular Division

When performing these large groups of divisions:

1. Listen for evenness: each note should be the same length.
2. Avoid reorganizing the group: make sure a quintuplet is exactly that, not a group of 2+3.
3. Keep the tempo steady. (It's easy to make an accelerando or ritardando toward the end of a group as you realize you've started too slow or too fast; know the tempo in advance and keep to it!)

Practice technique:

1. Set a metronome to a slow beat (quarter=60 or slower); clap and articulate the beat.
2. At the same tempo, clap the beat, articulate divisions.
3. Repeat, clapping a triplet, then groups of 4, 5, 6, and 7.
4. Repeat each individual group until you are able to perform it accurately at least four times in a row.
5. Write down a group of numbers between 1 and 7. (For example, 3–1–4–7–5.) Set a metronome, then clap the beat and perform the grouping you wrote. Repeat at a variety of tempi.

## Rhythms

### RHYTHM 8.1.1

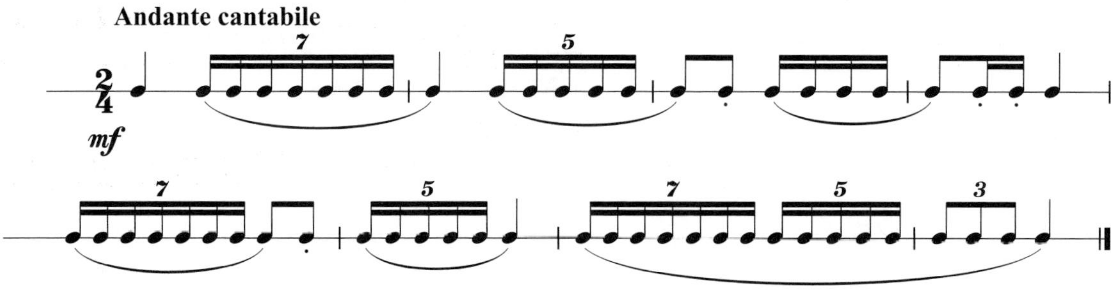


### RHYTHM 8.1.2

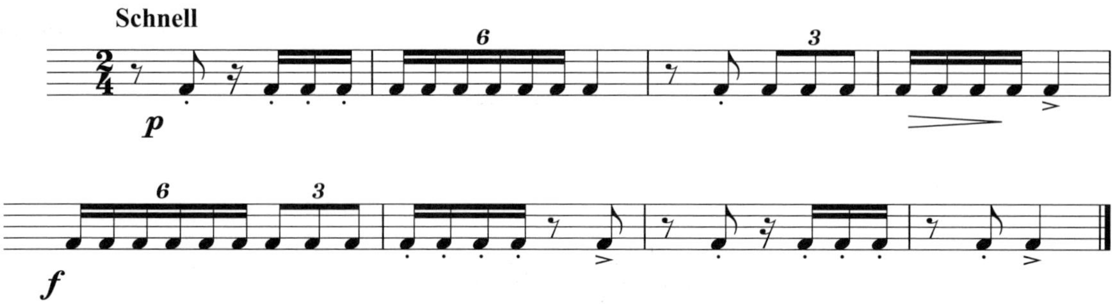


### RHYTHM 8.1.3

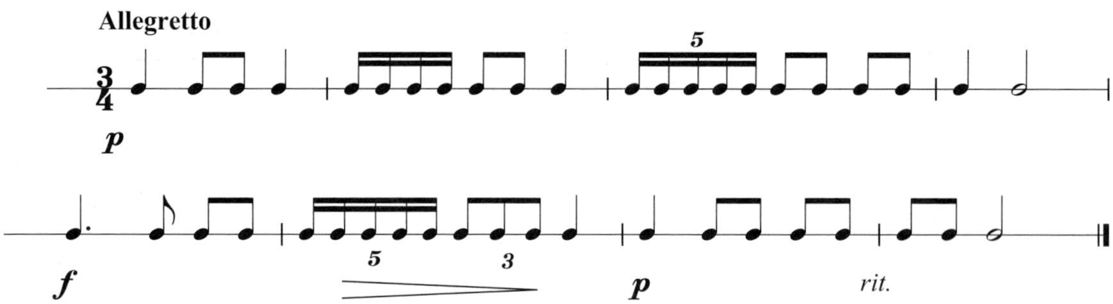


### RHYTHM 8.1.4

RHYTHM 8.1.5

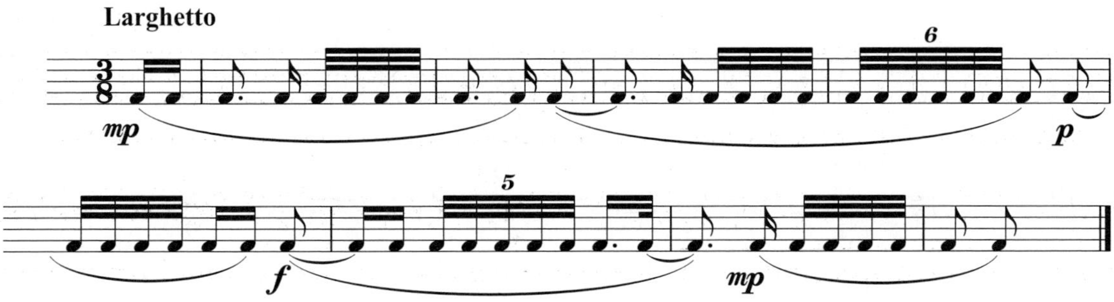


RHYTHM 8.1.6

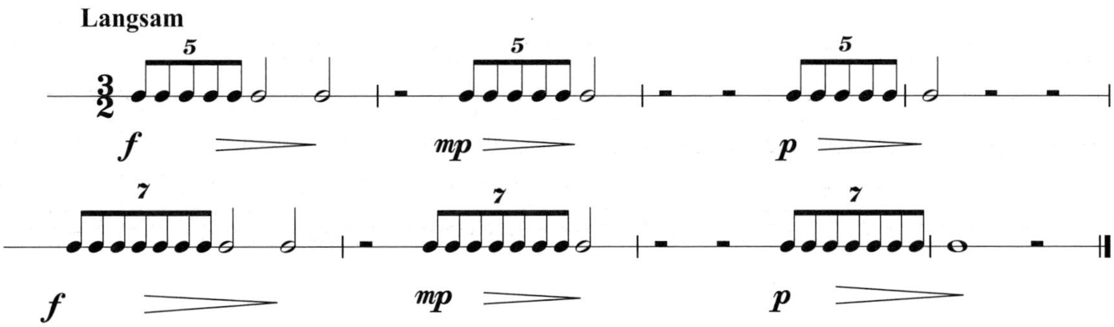


RHYTHM 8.1.7

RHYTHM 8.1.8

**RHYTHM 8.1.9**

Evenly

**RHYTHM 8.1.10**

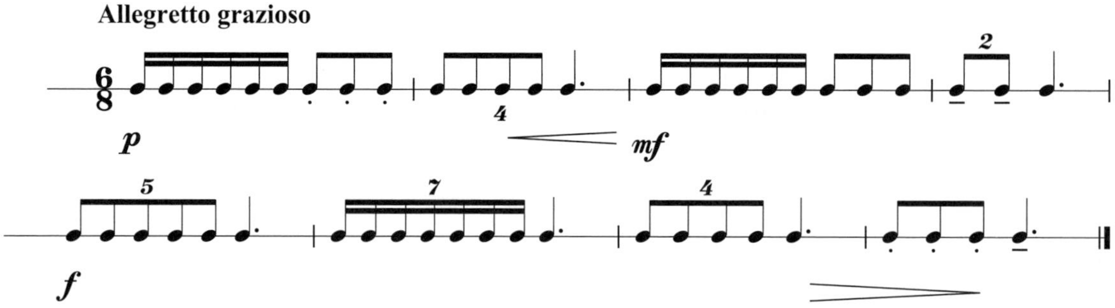
Allegretto grazioso
p
mf
f

**RHYTHM 8.1.11**

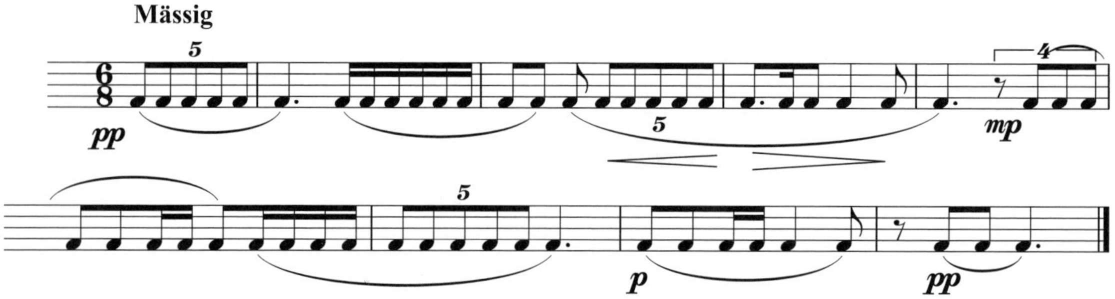
Mässig
pp
mp
p
pp

**RHYTHM 8.1.12**

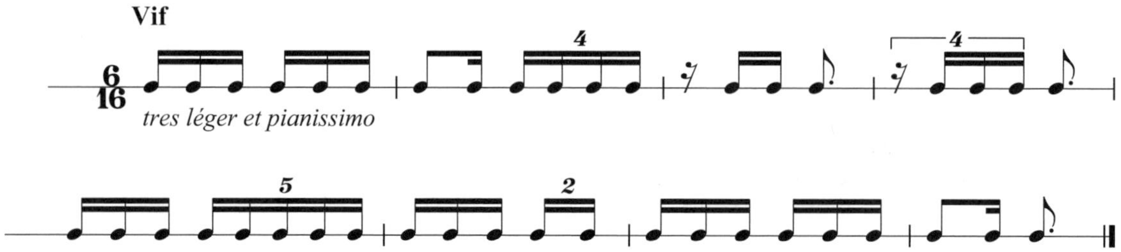
Vif
tres léger et pianissimo

RHYTHM 8.1.13

RHYTHM 8.1.14

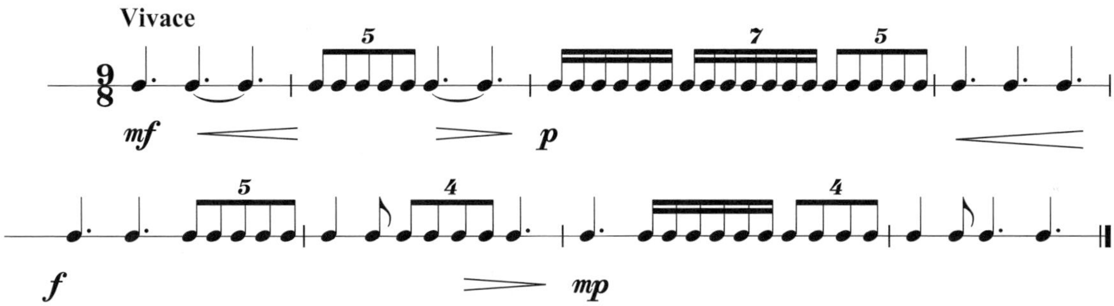


RHYTHM 8.1.15

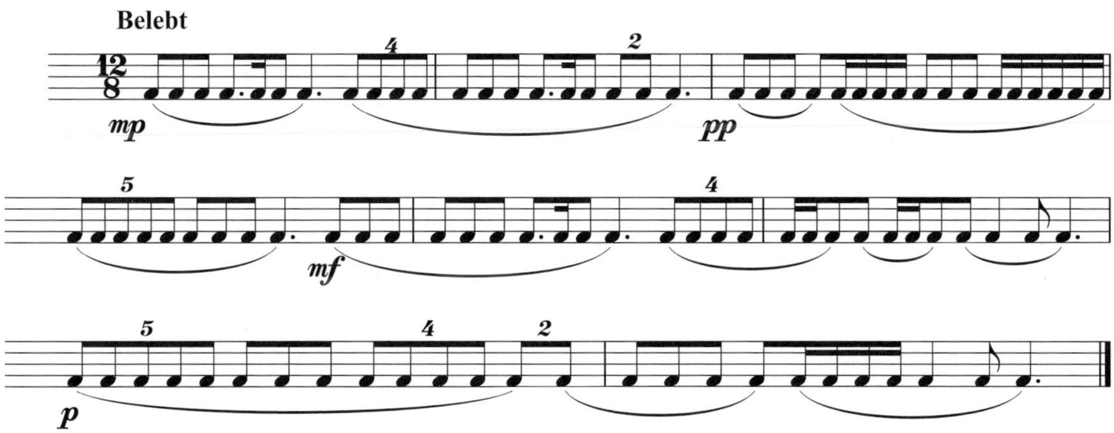


## Two-part Rhythms

### TWO-PART RHYTHM 8.1.1

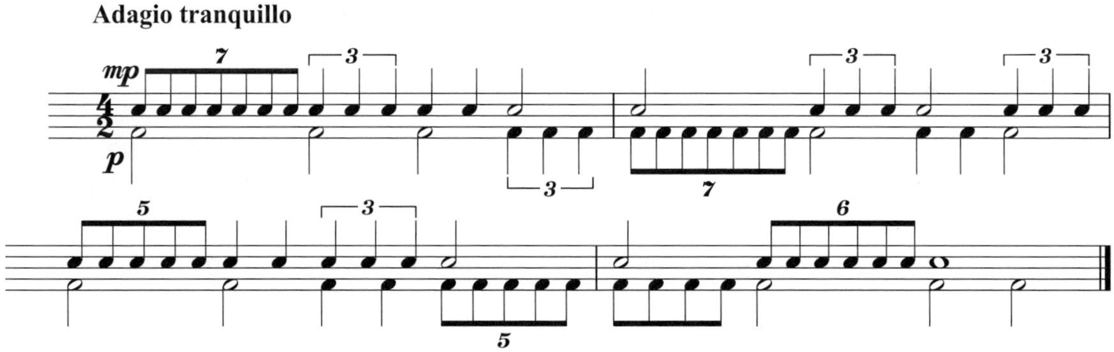

**TWO-PART RHYTHM 8.1.2**

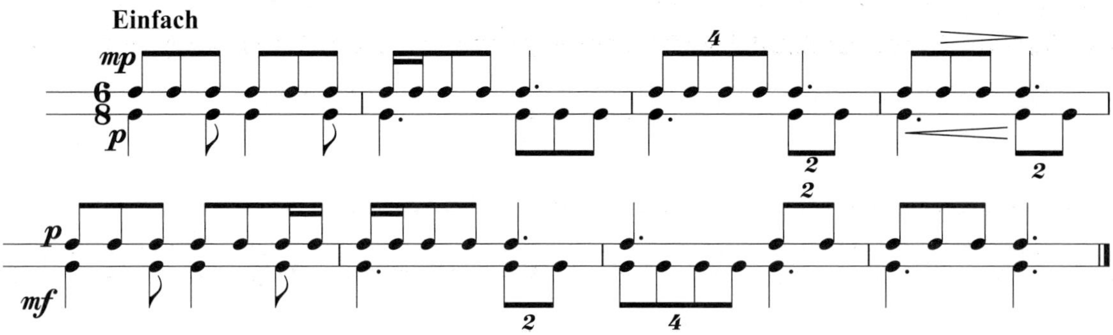


## Three-part Rhythm

**THREE-PART RHYTHM 8.1**

---

## 8.2 Reading in Other Clefs

### Facts You Need to Know

Our notational system has evolved so that any line or space can represent any note name, depending upon which of the three clefs is used and where it is placed. While treble and bass clefs are by far the most common in our notational system, followed by alto and tenor, there exist three other clefs which one might occasionally come across. They are the soprano clef, the mezzo-soprano clef, and the baritone clef. Each of these clefs is demonstrated below. Notice that there are two possible ways to write the baritone clef, but that the placement of notes on the staff is the same, regardless of which is used.

**EXAMPLE 8.2.1**

These clefs are most commonly found in old editions of sheet music and in the original notation of music composed before 1700. This may lead you to wonder why a contemporary musician would need to learn them.

Knowing all seven clefs is a valuable tool for transposition. If you can read all of the clefs fluently, then you can transpose any part to any key simply by visualizing it in the appropriate clef because any line or space can represent any note name. This method is more reliable than transposing each note as you go.

**EXAMPLE 8.2.2**

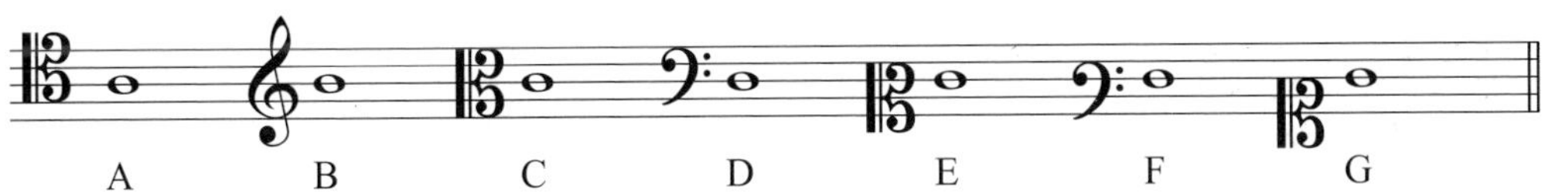


### Reading in the Soprano, Mezzo-Soprano, and Baritone Clefs

Just as with the treble and bass clefs, begin to develop reading fluency by selecting two or three lines to use as "reference points" on the staff. Relate other pitches to these reference points until you develop fluency reading all of the pitches on the staff.

## Assignments for Practice

1. Go back to the early chapters of this text and read each exercise as if it were written in any of the seven clefs. Figure out what transpositions you might be applying.
2. When practicing your instrument, play all exercises in the notated clef, then repeat in one or two of the other clefs. Get used to reading each clef on your instrument. Always start with your weakest clef.

## 8.3 Modulation to Closely Related Keys

### Facts You Need to Know

Modulation is the changing of tonal centers within a composition. It differs from tonicization in that it feels more permanent, usually because the new key is established through a strong cadence or by the length of time the music stays there.

The most frequent modulations are to closely related keys: those whose key signatures are the same or within one accidental of each other, or the keys of the major or minor triads found diatonically in the original key.

Modulation to a closely related key occurs through chromatically adjusting pitches in the original key so that they become the pitches that are unique to the new key. When starting in the major mode, the following alterations can yield modulation to the following key areas, if followed by an appropriately strong cadence:

1. **Supertonic**: raise scale degree 1 (e.g., C major to D minor).
2. **Mediant**: raise scale degree 2 (e.g., G major to B minor).
3. **Subdominant**: lower scale degree 7 (e.g., D major to G major).
4. **Dominant**: raise scale degree 4 (e.g., F major to C major).
5. **Submediant or relative minor**: raise scale degree 5 (e.g., E major to C♯ minor).

Here are the alterations when starting in the minor mode:

1. **Mediant or relative major**: use the subtonic instead of the leading tone (e.g., B minor to D major).
2. **Subdominant**: lower scale degree 2 and/or add the leading tone in the new key (e.g., A minor to D minor).
3. **Dominant**: raise scale degree 6 and/or add the leading tone in the new key (e.g., E minor to B minor).
4. **Submediant**: lower scale degree 2 (e.g., C minor to A♭ major).
5. **Subtonic**: raise scale degree 6 (e.g., F to E♭ major).

Notice that the chromatic alteration usually takes the form of a leading tone to the new tonic or a dominant chord seventh to the new scale degree 3.

You may at times find it easy to re-label a chord or scale degree that occurs in both keys. Find the new tonic, and then hear the music in relation to this new tonic.

When singing with a relative syllable system (movable-"do" or scale degree numbers), look for where the new leading tone or dominant chord seventh occurs and change your syllables or numbers to the new key at that note. This new syllable will usually be "ti" (7) or "fa" (4).

### Hearing

Listen first for the chromatic pitches that signal the shift in key. Note whether the chromatic pitch is a leading tone pointing toward the new tonic or dominant chord seventh pointing toward the new scale degree 3.

Determine the scale degree of the new tonic relative to the original key.

Hear the music in the original key up to the modulation and in the new key following the modulation. Note that you may have to work backwards to notate what happens after the modulation.

## Singing

Visually scan the music for indications of modulation. Look for accidentals that show up consistently following their first appearance. Determine the new tonic.

Alter the pitch in the scale that points to the new tonic. Determine the correct syllable or scale degree number to sing as it relates to the new key.

## Assignments for Practice

Practice singing a setup in the original key, then singing a scale or scale fragment that includes the chromatic alteration that results in a modulation to the new key. Sing a setup in the new key, then sing another scale or fragment that takes you back to the original key. The example below illustrates a modulation from a major key to the relative minor and back:

**EXAMPLE 8.3.1**

This example takes you from a major key to its dominant and back:

**EXAMPLE 8.3.2**

*Original Key Setup*

*Transition to the Dominant*

*Setup in the Dominant*

*Transition back to Original Key*

*Original Key Setup Again*

Come up with similar patterns for modulations to other closely related keys.

## Pitch Patterns

**PITCH PATTERN 8.3.1**

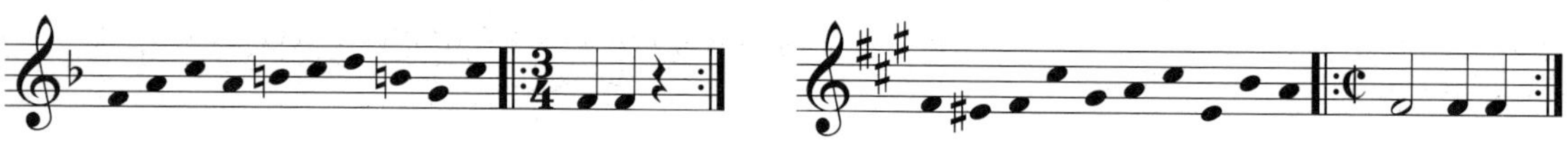

**PITCH PATTERN 8.3.2**

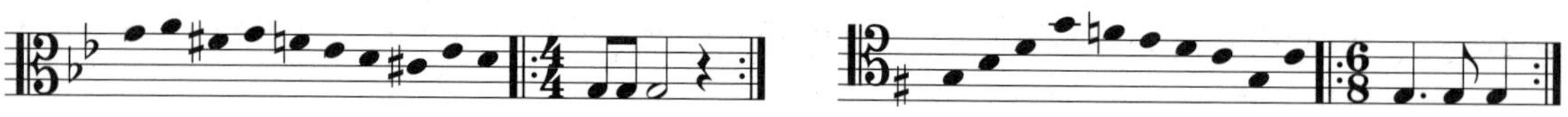

**PITCH PATTERN 8.3.3**

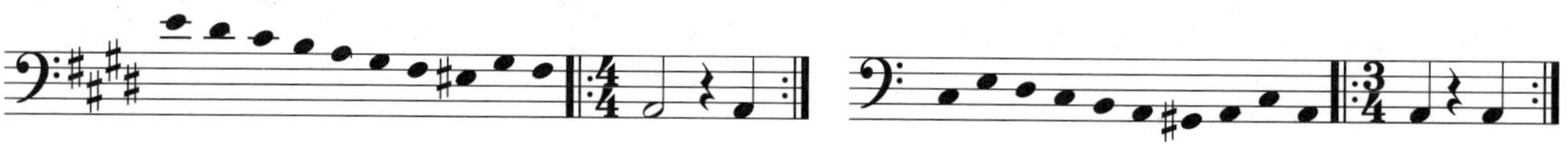

## Harmonic Progressions

1. I – ii – V – I – IV | ii – V – I
   VI – ii° – V – i – iv
2. I – vii° – I | vi – ii – V – I
   IV – V – I – ii
3. I – V – I – IV | ii – V – I
   I – ii – V – I – vi
4. i – iv – VII | i – ii° – V – i
   III – VI – ii° – V – i – iv
5. i – iv – VII | i – ii° – V – i
   V – I – IV – V – I – IV – vii° – iii

## Melodies

### MELODY 8.3.1

### MELODY 8.3.2

MELODY 8.3.3

MELODY 8.3.4

MELODY 8.3.5

MELODY 8.3.6

MELODY 8.3.7

## MELODY 8.3.8

## MELODY 8.3.9

## MELODY 8.3.10

**MELODY 8.3.11**

**MELODY 8.3.12**

**MELODY 8.3.13**

**MELODY 8.3.14**

**MELODY 8.3.15**

## Duets

### DUET 8.3.1

### DUET 8.3.2

**DUET 8.3.3**

## Chorale

**CHORALE 8.3**

### Self-Accompanied Melody

**SELF-ACCOMPANIED MELODY 8.3**

## 8.4 Diatonic Modulation to Distantly Related Keys

### Facts You Need to Know

Modulations to distantly related keys involve the changing of multiple accidentals from the original key. While some modulations might involve changing only two accidentals, others to more distant areas might involve altering six of the seven pitches in the scale!

More notes with different accidentals means that the chromatic pitch or pitches that introduce the modulation may be a variety of scale degrees in the new key, not just the new leading tone or dominant chord seventh.

## Hearing

Listen for the chromatic pitch or pitches that introduce the modulation. Retain your original tonic until you hear a confirming cadence in the new key, then compare the interval between the old and new key. Use this to determine the new key. Listen forward from the beginning up to the modulation to write the beginning of the music, then determine which scale degree the first pitch in the new key represents (or which Roman numeral of the chord if hearing a harmonic progression) to start hearing the music in the new key.

## Singing

Find the chromatic alteration that represents the modulation. Find the confirming cadence that follows it to determine what scale degree it represents in the new key. Sing up to this pitch in the original key, then re-label the first chromatic pitch or, if it makes musical sense, a different pitch nearby, in the new key. Be aware of the interval qualities and sizes as you sing scale degrees in the new key.

## Assignments for Practice

Give yourself two key names (like G major and B major) and see if you can figure out a smooth way to modulate back and forth between them.

### Pitch Patterns

#### PITCH PATTERN 8.4.1

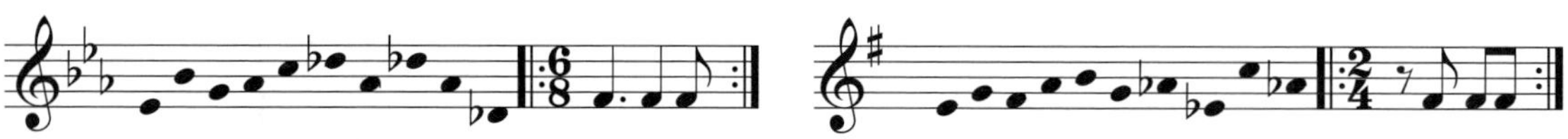

#### PITCH PATTERN 8.4.2

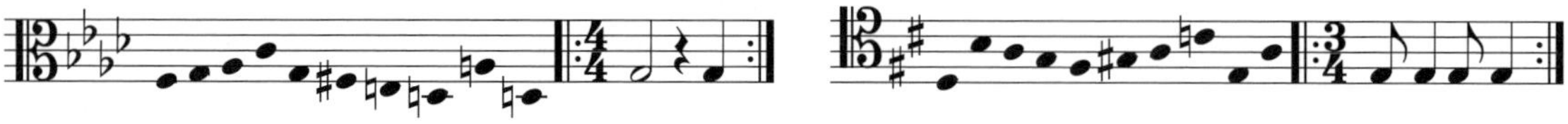

#### PITCH PATTERN 8.4.3

## Harmonic Progressions

1. I – IV – vii° – V
   IV – V – I – V – I
2. i – VI – iv
   iii – VI – ii – V – I
3. I – ii – V – vi – IV
   VII – iv – V – i

## Melodies

### MELODY 8.4.1

### MELODY 8.4.2

## MELODY 8.4.3

## MELODY 8.4.4

## MELODY 8.4.5

## MELODY 8.4.6

## MELODY 8.4.7

## MELODY 8.4.8

### MELODY 8.4.9

### MELODY 8.4.10

### MELODY 8.4.11

**MELODY 8.4.12**

**MELODY 8.4.13**

## MELODY 8.4.14

## MELODY 8.4.15

## Duets

### DUET 8.4.1

### DUET 8.4.2

## Chorale

### CHORALE 8.4

## Self-Accompanied Melody

### SELF-ACCOMPANIED MELODY 8.4

## 8.5 Music from the Literature

### EXAMPLE 8.5.1

*Piano Sonata in G Major*, Op. 79, II

Beethoven

### EXAMPLE 8.5.2

*Waltz*, Op. 39, No. 8

Tchaikovsky

### EXAMPLE 8.5.3

"Prelude No. 9 in E Major," from *The Well-Tempered Clavier*, Book I

J.S. Bach

**EXAMPLE 8.5.4**

*Sonata in C Major*, Pastorale

**EXAMPLE 8.5.5**

Aria from *Rodelinda, Regina de Longobardi*

**EXAMPLE 8.5.6**

From *Symphony No. 104*, "London," I

**EXAMPLE 8.5.7**

"Tuba Mirum," from *Requiem*, K. 626

m. 9–18 Mozart

**EXAMPLE 8.5.8**

"Fugue No. 4 in C-sharp Minor," from *The Well-Tempered Clavier*, Book I

m. 35–41 J.S. Bach

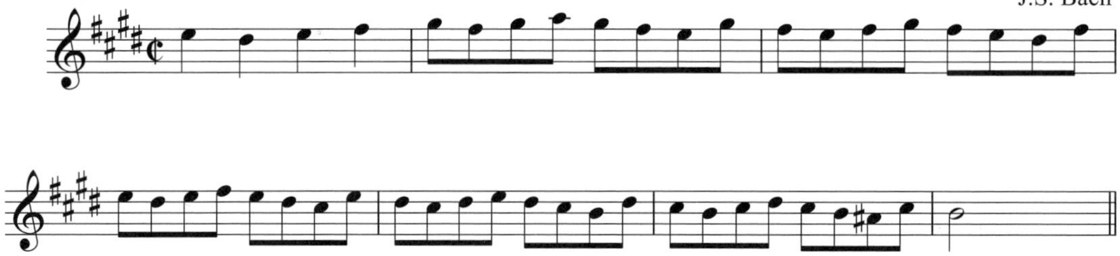

**EXAMPLE 8.5.9**

From *Symphony No. 5 in C Minor*, Op. 67, IV

m. 26–41 Beethoven

**EXAMPLE 8.5.10**

From *Impromptu in C Minor*, Op. 90, No. 1

m. 33–41 Schubert

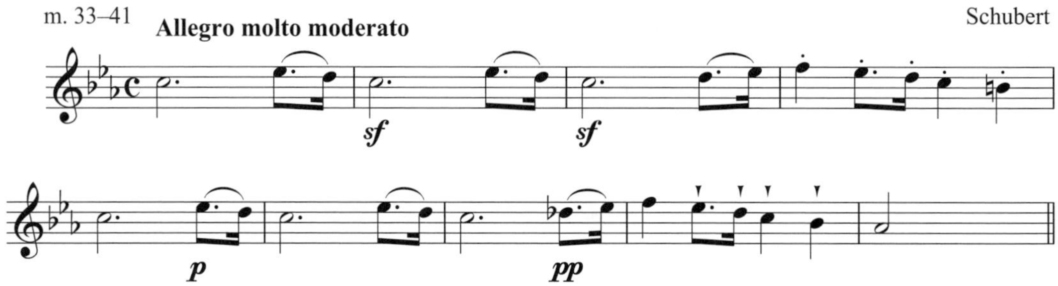

## Reflections: Performance Preparation

Popular culture usually gives the impression that musicians don't need to work hard to get ready for performance. In reality, every minute of performance results from hours of study and practice.

Performance preparation begins long before the actual performance date. As you learn new music, it is important to set a timeline for practice. Set specific goals for learning sections of music, working out technical and musical difficulties, and, if appropriate, memorizing. Learning music often requires "breathing time," time to consider, reconsider, and integrate ideas for communicating the music. The great Polish harpsichordist Wanda Landowska is reported to have described practice as "organizing the intuition." This suggests that although we approach music in an intuitive way, an effective performer doesn't leave the ultimate musical decisions to chance. The musical choices one makes are largely choreographed and selected ahead of time, sometimes through trial and error, but more effectively through careful consideration. On the other hand, some of the most electrifying performances occur when the performer suddenly has an epiphany about the piece (perhaps even mid-performance!). Be open to changes in your understanding of the music's story.

It is often a good idea to do periodic run throughs of your entire program. Every few weeks, play the entire program from start to finish in order to get a sense of where you need to focus in your work. Try as much as possible to follow your performance-day routines and habits, and allow unexpected mistakes to occur, so that you can practice adjusting to the inevitable unexpected moments that creep up in performance.

Recording practice sessions is also an excellent idea, as it allows you to spend time experiencing your program as an active listener. You might be amazed at how much you miss because of the technical distractions that are inherent in the act of performance.

As suggested above, it is a good idea to develop a routine for the time immediately preceding the performance. For some musicians, this "routine" starts a few minutes before the performance. Others start it the morning of the performance; yet others start it a week before. Most musicians use this short-term preparation time to take steps to reduce stress and anxiety. For example, many performers start to reduce the intensity of their practice sessions in the days immediately before a performance. Virtually all work to find a way to ensure a good night's sleep and adequate nourishment in the days before the performance. Many plan their travel schedules so that they arrive at the concert venue a day or two early.

As the concert approaches, be prepared to delegate the little details to someone else. Be prepared to "let go" of the little details so you can spend your time visualizing how you'd like your successful performance to sound.

Most of all, remember that you got into this business to have fun doing something that you love. Keep that in mind, visualize success, and trust in your preparation.

## 8.6 Dictation Materials

### I. Chord Identification

Your teacher will play several chords. Indicate the quality and inversion for each by using the correct figured bass symbol.

*Date:* ..............

1. ____ 2. ____ 3. ____ 4. ____ 5. ____ 6. ____ 7. ____ 8. ____

*Date:* ..............

1. ____ 2. ____ 3. ____ 4. ____ 5. ____ 6. ____ 7. ____ 8. ____

*Date:* ..............

1. ____ 2. ____ 3. ____ 4. ____ 5. ____ 6. ____ 7. ____ 8. ____

*Date:* ..............

1. ____ 2. ____ 3. ____ 4. ____ 5. ____ 6. ____ 7. ____ 8. ____

*Date:* ..............

1. ____ 2. ____ 3. ____ 4. ____ 5. ____ 6. ____ 7. ____ 8. ____

### II. Melodic and Rhythmic Dictation

Your teacher will play a short melody or rhythm. Notate it on the staves below. Be sure to adjust pitches using accidentals following modulations.

*Date:* ..............

*Date:* . . . . . . . . . . . . . .

*Date:* . . . . . . . . . . . . . .

*Date:* . . . . . . . . . . . . . .

*Date:* . . . . . . . . . . . . . .

## III. Harmonic Dictation

Write the soprano line, bass line, and provide a Roman numeral analysis (including inversional symbols) for the progression you hear on the grand staff below. Be sure to mark modulations.

*Date:* . . . . . . . . . . . . . .

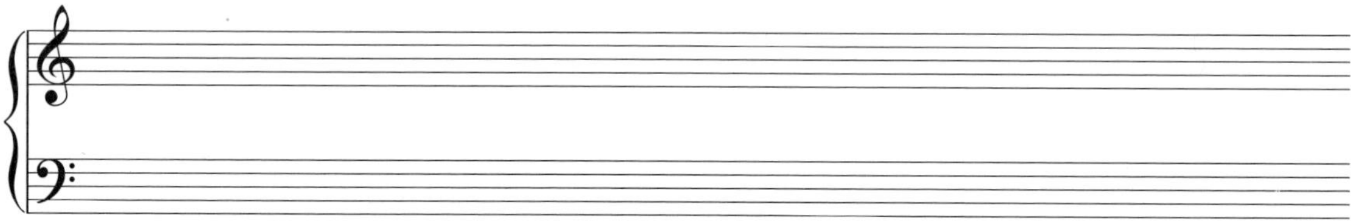

*Date:* . . . . . . . . . . . . . .

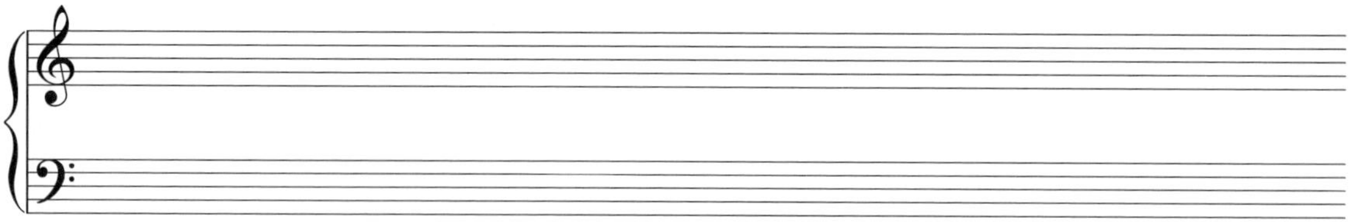

*Date:* . . . . . . . . . . . . . .

*Date:* . . . . . . . . . . . . . .

*Date:* . . . . . . . . . . . . . .

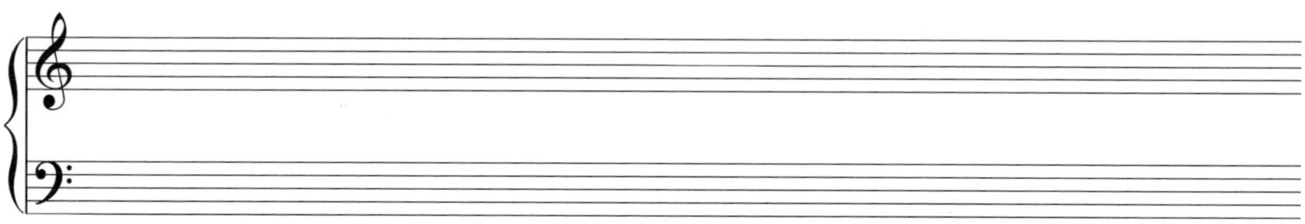

# Chapter 9

# Reading Complex Rhythms; More Complex Modulation

## 9.1 Reading Complex Rhythms

### Facts You Need to Know

Complex rhythms are those that utilize second division of the beat or greater, are permeated with syncopation or rests, and/or are written in less commonly used meters.

Visually, these rhythms may appear to be more difficult to read and perform, but, in essence, they simply require a strategy implemented consistently in order to execute them accurately and musically.

### Performing Complex Rhythms

When you encounter a rhythm you cannot perform intuitively, use these techniques to decipher it. Note that you may have used many of these techniques previously as you worked through the rhythm chapters of this text.

1. Determine the smallest note value you will count. For example, if the rhythm uses numerous 32nd and 64th notes, you may need to count 16th notes rather than quarters or eighths.
2. Draw lines or indicate beats and/or divisions with an "x" in the score; they will serve as a guidepost and allow your intuition to work with your intellect as you learn the rhythm, as shown in the example below:

EXAMPLE 9.1.1

3. If the rhythm has numerous ties, employ the above techniques, then practice the rhythm *without* the ties. Repeat immediately, with ties.
4. If the rhythm has numerous rests, mark beats. Practice by supplying sound where the rests occur in your inner hearing to ensure accuracy.

5. Practice the rhythm in small groups—one or two measures at a time, if necessary, and always practice to the first beat of the next measure so that you reinforce the crusis of the measure.
6. If the rhythm utilizes an irregular division you cannot feel intuitively, isolate it, practicing it individually, then surrounded by the division (or beat) from which it is derived, then put it in the context of the rhythm. This process is outlined in the example below:

**EXAMPLE 9.1.2**

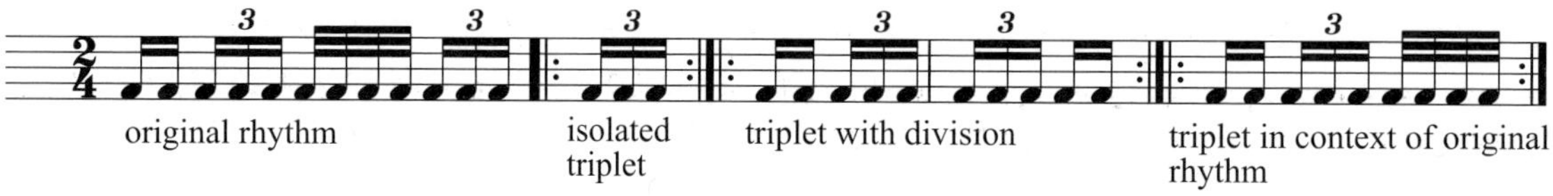


## Rhythms

**RHYTHM 9.1.1**

**RHYTHM 9.1.2**

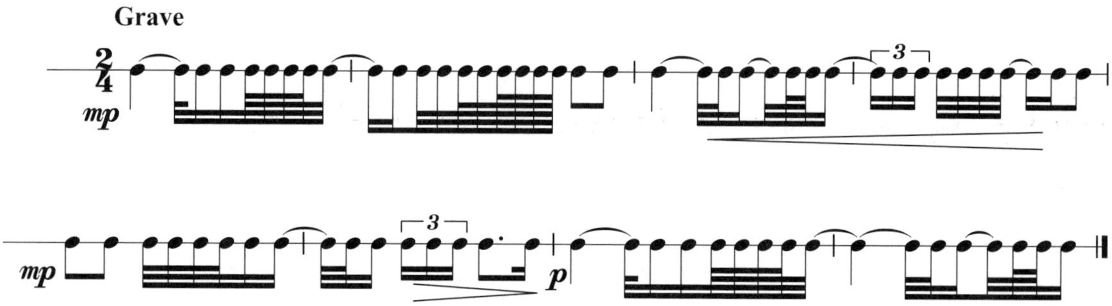


**RHYTHM 9.1.3**

RHYTHM 9.1.4

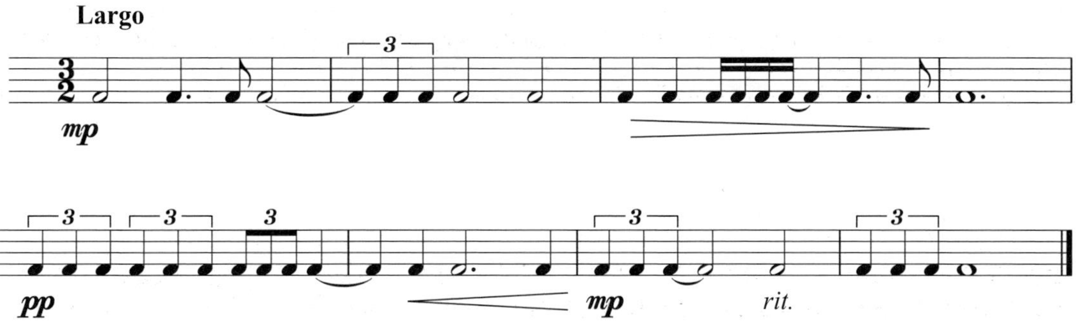


RHYTHM 9.1.5

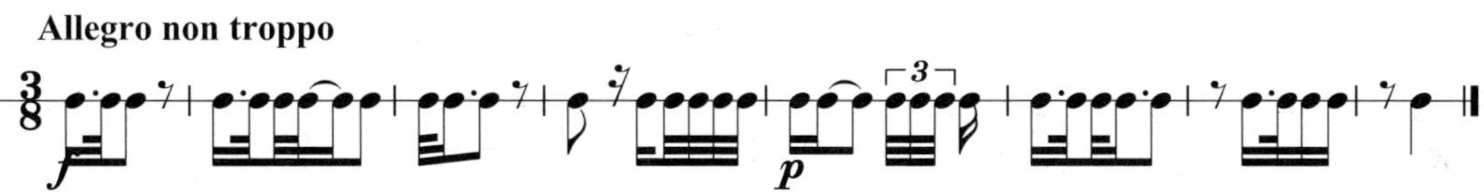


RHYTHM 9.1.6

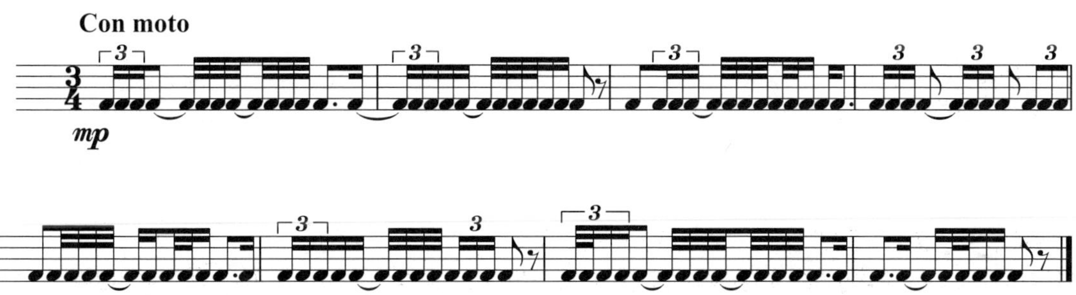


RHYTHM 9.1.7

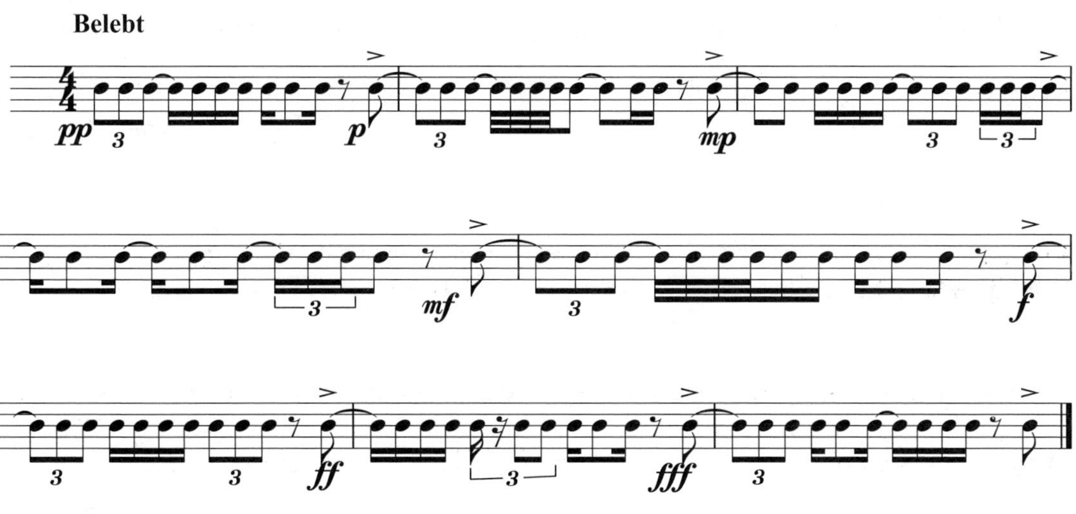

**RHYTHM 9.1.8**

**RHYTHM 9.1.9**

**RHYTHM 9.1.10**

**RHYTHM 9.1.11**

**RHYTHM 9.1.12**

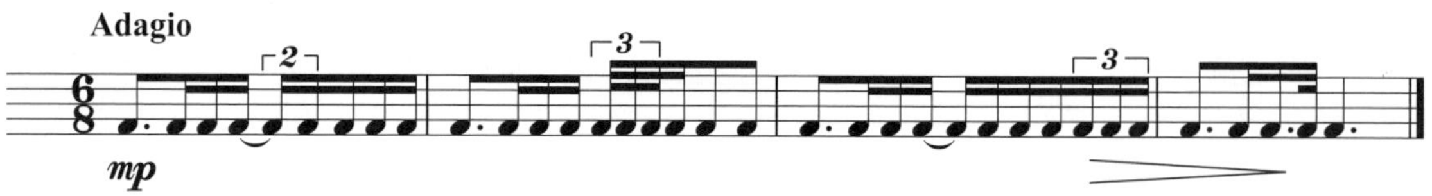

RHYTHM 9.1.13

RHYTHM 9.1.14

RHYTHM 9.1.15

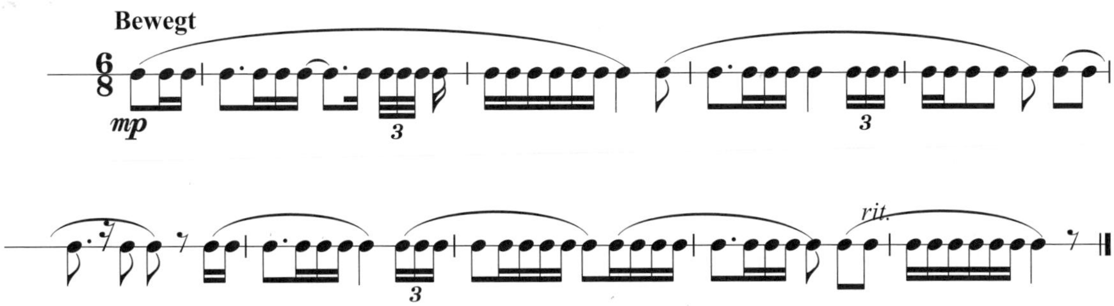


## 9.2 Direct, Chromatic, and Enharmonic Modulation

### Facts You Need to Know

A direct modulation is an unprepared modulation. They often happen at the beginning of phrases, but you may sometimes experience them within a phrase. Direct modulations require you to be able to sing the interval that separates the last note in the old and the first note in the new key, and then to quickly reorient yourself in the new key.

EXAMPLE 9.2.1

The modulations we have studied so far all rely on the recharacterization of elements (notes or chords) that are common to both the original key and the destination key. In a chromatic modulation, the transitional chord is chromatic in one of the two keys. This chromaticism may take the form of any of the chromatic structures you have studied, including secondary function or modal mixture.

**EXAMPLE 9.2.2**

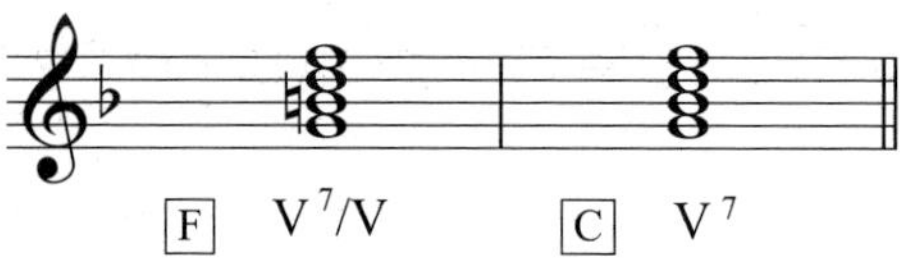


Enharmonic modulation relies on the same technique as most modulation—the recharacterization of an element that is common to both keys. In an enharmonic modulation, however, at least one of the common elements must be enharmonically respelled to lead to the new key. The most common enharmonic modulations involve:

1. Single pitches: a pitch is treated like its enharmonic equivalent.

**EXAMPLE 9.2.3**

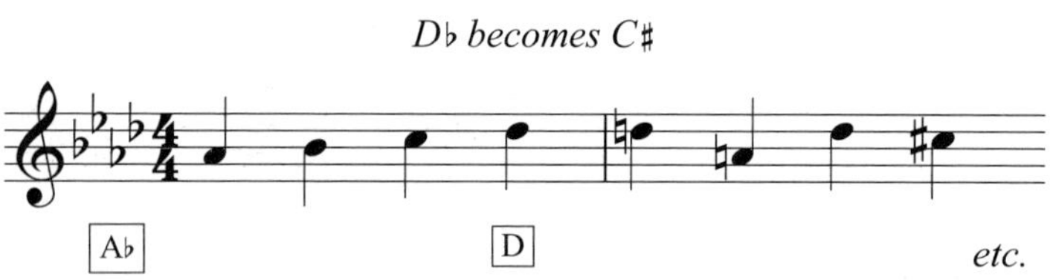


2. Fully diminished seventh chords: the interval structure sounds the same regardless of whether you treat the lowest pitch as the root, third, fifth, or seventh of the chord. You can modulate to keys a minor third or tritone above or below the original key.

**EXAMPLE 9.2.4**

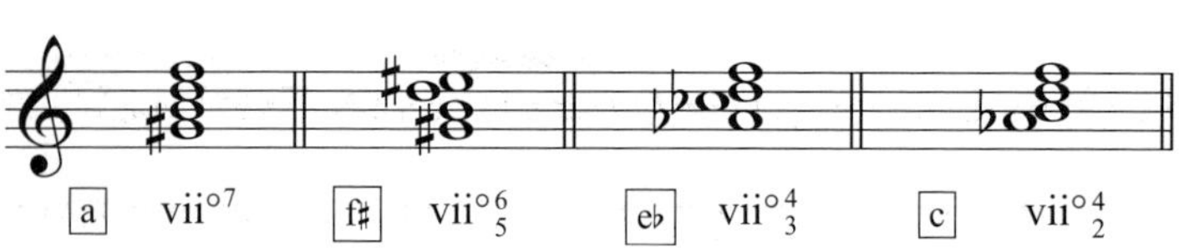


3. French augmented sixth chords: respelling this chord enharmonically creates a French augmented sixth in a key a tritone away.

**EXAMPLE 9.2.5**

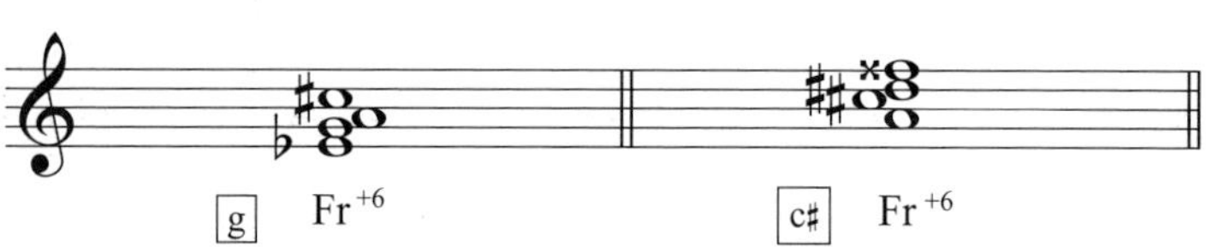

4. German augmented sixth chords: these chords have the same sound as dominant seventh chords and can be used to modulate to a key a half step above the original key.

**EXAMPLE 9.2.6**

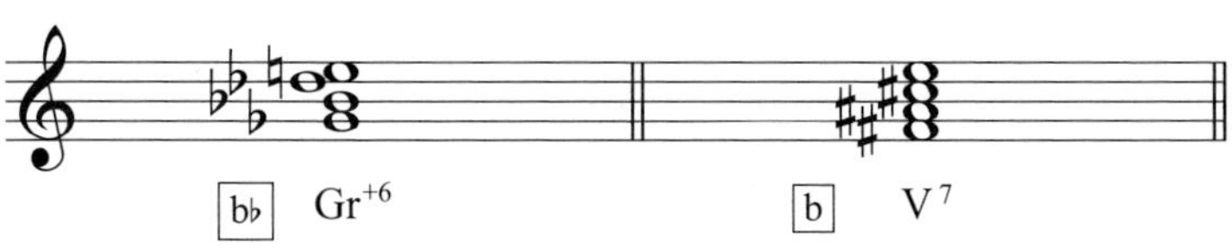


5. Dominant seventh chords: as stated above, these chords have the same sound as German augmented sixth chords and can be used to modulate to a key a half step below the original key.

**EXAMPLE 9.2.7**

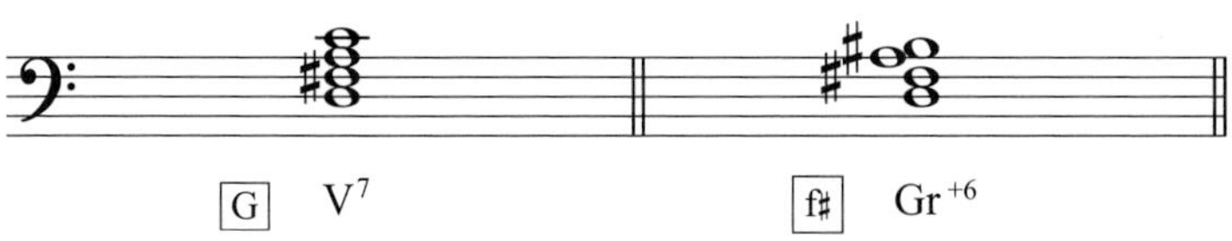


## Hearing

Listen for modulations that sound more abrupt than those you have previously studied. Listen for the context: Does the shift occur unexpectedly (direct)? Does the shift occur on a chord that sounds chromatic (chromatic)? Or does a seemingly "normal" chord resolve unexpectedly (enharmonic)? Determine the interval between the old and new keys, then work forward from the beginning and/or backward from the end to determine the harmonic and melodic content in the old and new key.

## Singing

Direct: determine the interval that separates the last note of the old key and the first note of the new key. Use your knowledge of intervals to sing the first note in the new key, then quickly reorient yourself in the new key.

Chromatic: use the same techniques (recharacterizing elements that are in common to both keys) to shift from the old to the new key. Be aware that what you recharacterize may be a chromatic pitch.

Enharmonic: use the same techniques to shift from the old to the new key.

## Assignments for Practice

Practice the following arpeggiated patterns for each of the enharmonic modulations below:

1. Renaming a root position fully diminished seventh chord into a first inversion diminished seventh chord:

**EXAMPLE 9.2.8**

2. Renaming a root position fully diminished seventh chord into second inversion:

**EXAMPLE 9.2.9**

3. Renaming a root position fully diminished seventh chord into third inversion:

**EXAMPLE 9.2.10**

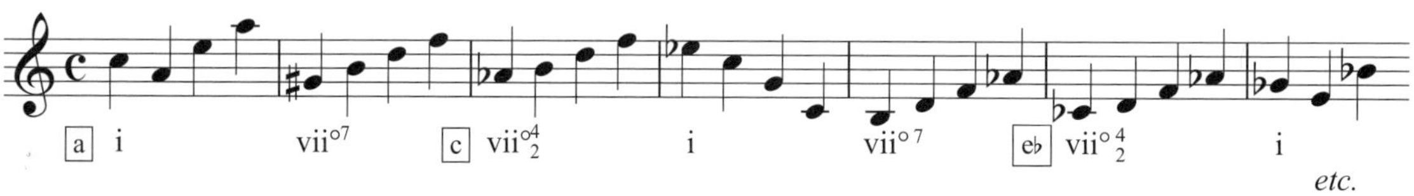


4. Renaming a dominant seventh chord as a German augmented sixth:

**EXAMPLE 9.2.11**

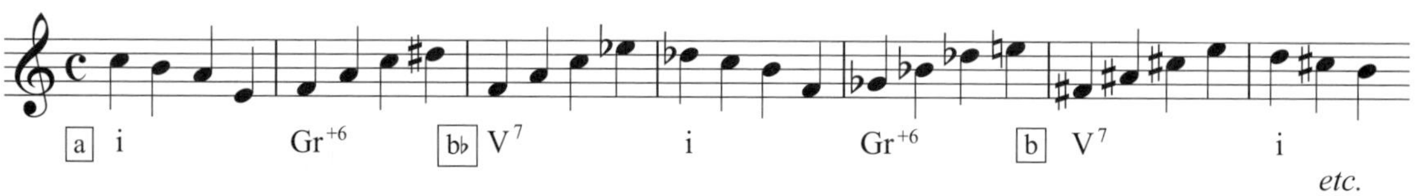


5. Renaming a German augmented sixth chord as a dominant seventh:

**EXAMPLE 9.2.12**

## Pitch Patterns

### PITCH PATTERN 9.2.1

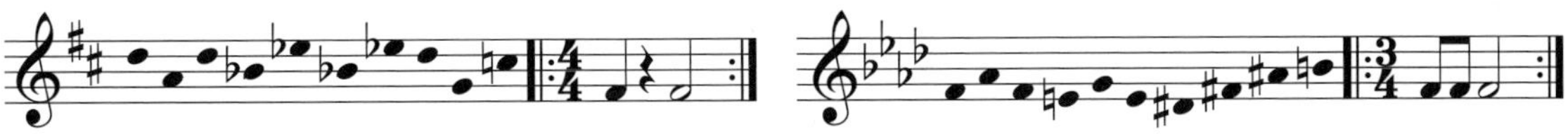

### PITCH PATTERN 9.2.2

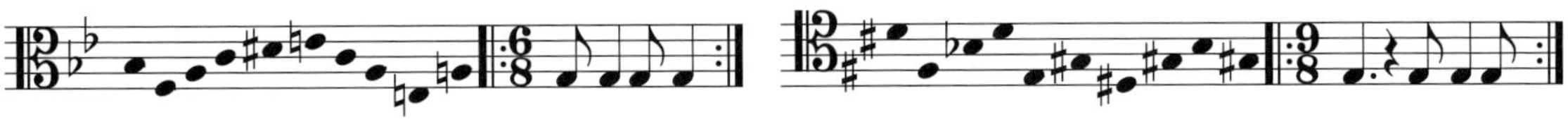

### PITCH PATTERN 9.2.3

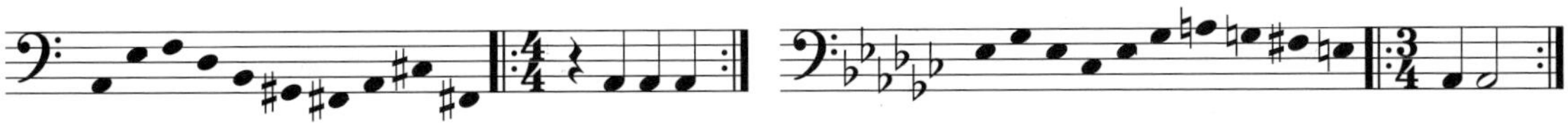

## Harmonic Progressions

1. i – VI – Gr$^{+6}$
   V$^{7}$ – i – iv – V – i
2. i – iv – vii°$^{7}$
   vii°* – i – iv – V – i

*You select the inversion.

3. i – VI – Fr$^{+6}$
   Fr$^{+6}$* – V – i

*Modulate to an enharmonic spelling of the augmented sixth chord.

## Melodies

### MELODY 9.2.1

### MELODY 9.2.2

### MELODY 9.2.3

### MELODY 9.2.4

MELODY 9.2.5

MELODY 9.2.6

MELODY 9.2.7

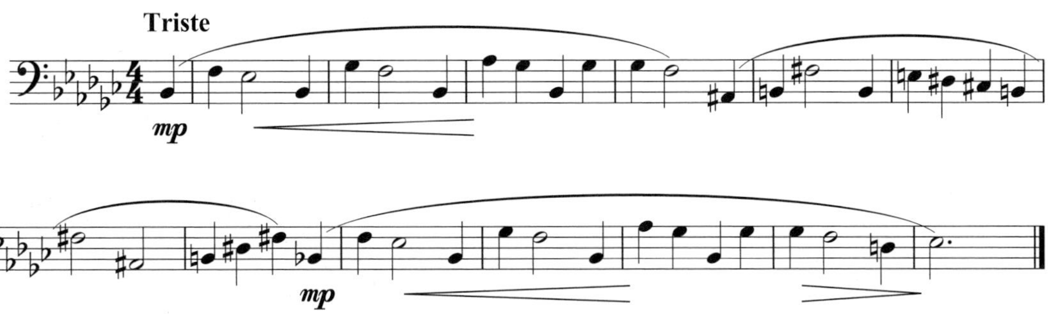

### MELODY 9.2.8

**Elegantly, relaxed**

### MELODY 9.2.9

**Somberly**

### MELODY 9.2.10

**Nicht zu schnell**

## MELODY 9.2.11

## MELODY 9.2.12

## MELODY 9.2.13

## MELODY 9.2.14

MELODY 9.2.15

## Duets

DUET 9.2.1

DUET 9.2.2

## Chorale

CHORALE 9.2

## Self-Accompanied Melody

### SELF-ACCOMPANIED MELODY 9.2

## 9.3 Rapidly Shifting and Unexpected Tonalities

### Facts You Need to Know

Some twentieth-century music retains its overall sense of common practice tonality but stretches the use of that musical language in unexpected ways. One of the common techniques used is that of placing unexpected harmonies or modulations within the music. This technique is called "wrong note technique" by some musicians, because the abruptness of the changes creates a very disjunct and jarring sound, much as when a person plays or sings a wrong note in a more traditional tonal piece of music. This name, however, ignores the fact that in many cases, using the "right" note(s) would rob the music of all of its individuality and interest.

### Hearing

Listen for a sound that is strikingly jarring, unexpected, and perhaps unsettling in the music. Usually it is a note or chord that is prepared in a traditional way, but the expected resolution created by that preparation does not appear. Work first on figuring out how the actual music varies from the expectation. Next, work on the music in sections, much as you would any modulating melody: start at the beginning or end and work on the parts that seem to "follow the rules" up to the unexpected element, and then following the unexpected element.

### Singing

Sing the majority of the excerpt as you would any piece of tonal music. Take extra time to figure out how the unexpected element works and why it sounds unexpected. Usually, this will involve the same techniques you used to navigate through direct, chromatic, and enharmonic modulations.

### Assignments for Practice

#### Pitch Patterns

PITCH PATTERN 9.3.1

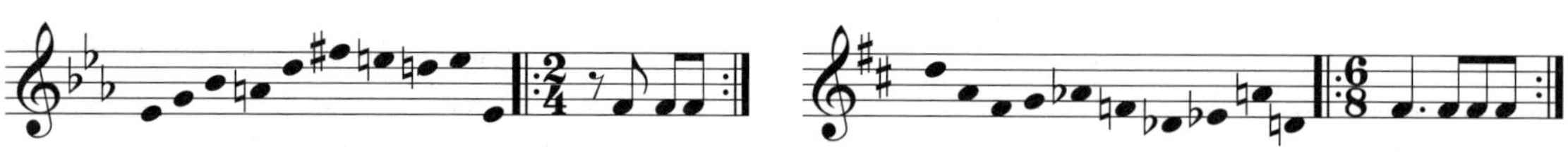

PITCH PATTERN 9.3.2

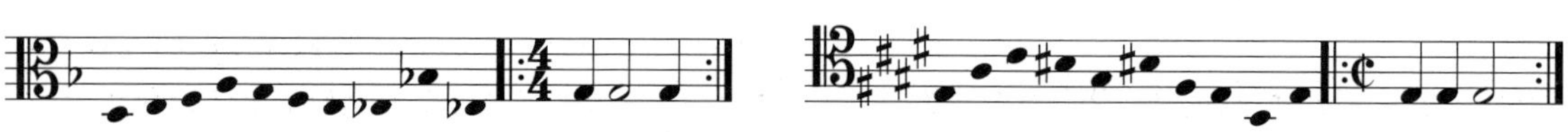

PITCH PATTERN 9.3.3

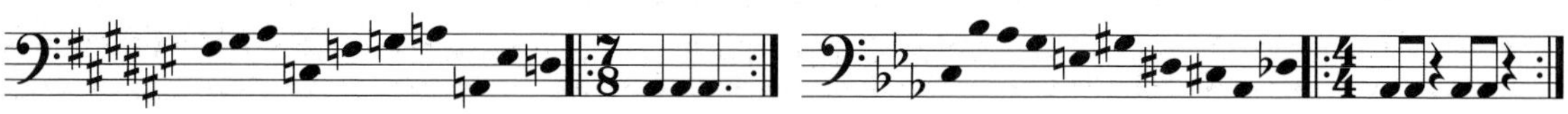

## Melodies

MELODY 9.3.1

MELODY 9.3.2

MELODY 9.3.3

MELODY 9.3.4

MELODY 9.3.5

MELODY 9.3.6

MELODY 9.3.7

## MELODY 9.3.8

## MELODY 9.3.9

## MELODY 9.3.10

## Duets

### DUET 9.3.1

### DUET 9.3.2

### DUET 9.3.3

## Chorale

### CHORALE 9.3

## Self-Accompanied Melody

### SELF-ACCOMPANIED MELODY 9.3

## 9.4 Music from the Literature

### EXAMPLE 9.4.1

*Sonata in G Major for Violin and Piano*, Op. 100, IV

**Allegro molto** Dvorak

### EXAMPLE 9.4.2

*Sonata in A Minor*, "Arpeggione," D. 821, II

m. 4–33 Schubert

**Adagio**

**EXAMPLE 9.4.3**

*Mai*, Op. 1, No. 2

m. 36-67

Fauré

**EXAMPLE 9.4.4**

*Scherzo*, Op. 99, No. 3

Joachim Raff

**Presto**

**EXAMPLE 9.4.5**

*Liebestraum No. 3 in A-flat Major*

m. 26–37

Liszt

**Più animato con passione**

**EXAMPLE 9.4.6**

*Impromptu in G-flat Major*, Op. 90, No. 3

m. 25–35

Schubert

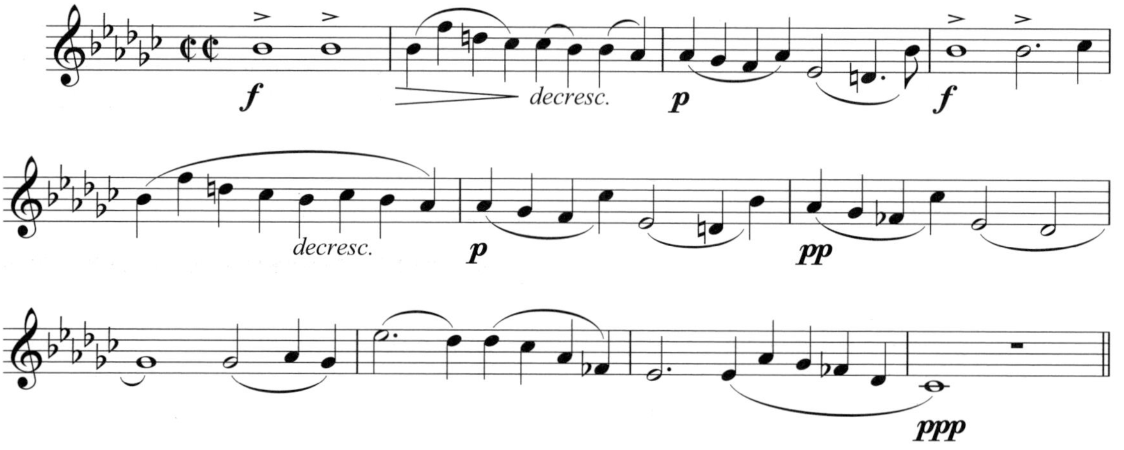


**EXAMPLE 9.4.7**

*Piano Sonata in E Minor*, Op. 90, II

m. 211–221

Beethoven

**Nicht zu geschwind und sehr vortragen**

**EXAMPLE 9.4.8**

*Piano Sonata in E Minor*, Op. 90, II

m. 114–130

Beethoven

**Nicht zu geschwind und sehr vortragen**

**EXAMPLE 9.4.9**

Gavotte, from *Symphony No. 1*, "*Classical*," Op. 25

## Reflections: Energy, Space, and Time

Time, space, and energy are the media through which music is created, transmitted, and sustained. In order to practice the right skills to make oneself an effective communicator of music, one must have some understanding of how music exists in these media.

At its most fundamental level, music is physical energy. Physicists refer to musical pitches in relation to the speed of these waves of energy. The term "A=440" refers to the fact that in order to create a pitch that sounds an A above middle C, one must start the air molecules vibrating at a speed of 440 cycles per second. A faster or slower rate of vibration creates respectively a higher or lower pitch, while more or less energy creates a louder or softer sound. As musicians, we learn to recognize subtle differences in the intensity and speed of musical energy.

Energy in music is more complex than just the physics of sound. Musical tension, created through techniques such as dissonance (melodic, harmonic, or metric), acts as a sort of potential energy, creating drive and desire toward a more consonant resolution. In this sense, musical energy is the psychological expectation of resolution. In the hands of a skilled composer, this creation of musical energy is a beautiful and compelling dramatic device.

Space implies distance, whether physical or imagined. It also implies a relationship between two or more objects. As such, it is fundamentally relative. Like energy, space manifests itself in music in multiple ways. A single beat is undefined. A second beat creates an expectation of the amount of time between beats. After the second beat, we can expect a third beat to occur at the same temporal distance from the second as the second was to the first.

Pitches, chords, and phrasing also manifest space. We describe pitches as being higher or lower than each other. Chords and keys are closer to or more distant from each other. In short, any musical structure that is measurable or that can be compared to another structure is a manifestation of musical space.

Like energy, space has a significant psychological component. In order to project resolution on a sound, we require an understanding of how music works as a *system*. We learn early on that pitches, rhythms, and chords behave in certain ways because we learn what our musical system demands of these structures, and we learn within a single composition to listen to its beginning more carefully because in that exposition lie the clues to understanding that music's particular establishment of artistic space.

Music is both sustained and nourished by its existence in time. Although the passage of time is constant, we see it only through its "shadows," or its effects on the tangible world in which we move. We see the growth or decay of a living thing, we see the changing of a picture's colors as it fades in the sunlight, and we hear the growth and decay of a musical sound. We only sense time through noticing how our physical world changes in it. Time is *change* itself, and the only way that we sense its passing is through our ability to remember how something once was and how it has changed. We sense a crescendo by remembering the intensity of a sound as it first began, and then by comparing the present perception of it.

Time has properties that seem to contradict each other. Time resembles space because it is both measurable and precise. Yet time's passage is often perceived unevenly. While constantly flowing in a single direction, it is at once fluid and unpredictable—it is the possibility of future becoming rather than the unfolding of a predetermined event. Although we might know what to expect when we hear a performance because we have heard that piece before, there is always the possibility of the unexpected—a missed note, a subtly changed rhythm of phrasing, that creates the intensity and excitement of live performance. Veteran concertgoers who have seen the same great performer multiple times often comment on being surprised by how the music always sounds fresh and new. Such surprise, and the fun and excitement of that experience and discovery, is the magic that drew many of us to a career in music. It is the sustaining and nourishing aspect of this perceived time—the time not of precision but of unexpected becoming, that creates the magic of music.

This isn't to say that "spatialized" time, the time of precision, is unnecessary. On the contrary, it is essential for a musician to master. We often describe a performer whose rhythmic presentation of time seems to be a bit "off" as either "rushing" or "dragging," creating an unsettling and unpleasant musical experience, while other performers effectively manipulate time through the technique of *rubato* with little or no complaint, and often even praise, from an audience. How can two very different expressions and experiences explain the same phenomenon?

Because this sort of time is measurable, it is also quantifiable. That is, we need to be able to measure out, divide, subdivide, and place musical events on a "timeline." If one isn't good at this, he or she is often described as being "early" or "late" in the presentation of his or her musical content. Because it is easily quantifiable, it is easily used as the basis for making objective judgments about the ability of a performer.

The time of experience, however, is very different yet equally important. It is the time of change and of memory. It is how music creates a narrative or story and how the listener, composer, and performer make sense of the sounds that they hear. It is the time of hearing and recognizing musical structures as they change throughout the course of a composition. This is the time of aesthetics, where meaning is communicated to the listener through the music.

## 9.5 Dictation Materials

### I. Chord Identification

Your teacher will play several chords. Indicate the quality and inversion for each by using the correct figured bass symbol.

*Date:* . . . . . . . . . . . . . .

1. ____ 2. ____ 3. ____ 4. ____ 5. ____ 6. ____ 7. ____ 8. ____

*Date:* . . . . . . . . . . . . . .

1. ____ 2. ____ 3. ____ 4. ____ 5. ____ 6. ____ 7. ____ 8. ____

*Date:* . . . . . . . . . . . . . .

1. ____ 2. ____ 3. ____ 4. ____ 5. ____ 6. ____ 7. ____ 8. ____

*Date:* . . . . . . . . . . . . . .

1. ____ 2. ____ 3. ____ 4. ____ 5. ____ 6. ____ 7. ____ 8. ____

*Date:* . . . . . . . . . . . . . .

1. ____ 2. ____ 3. ____ 4. ____ 5. ____ 6. ____ 7. ____ 8. ____

### II. Melodic and Rhythmic Dictation

Your teacher will play a short melody or rhythm. Notate it on the staves below. Be sure to adjust pitches using accidentals following modulations.

*Date:* . . . . . . . . . . . . . .

*Date:* . . . . . . . . . . . . . .

*Date:* . . . . . . . . . . . . . .

*Date:* . . . . . . . . . . . . . .

*Date:* . . . . . . . . . . . . . .

### III. Harmonic Dictation

Write the soprano line, bass line, and provide a Roman numeral analysis (including inversional symbols) for the progression you hear on the grand staff below.

*Date:* . . . . . . . . . . . . . .

*Date:* . . . . . . . . . . . . . .

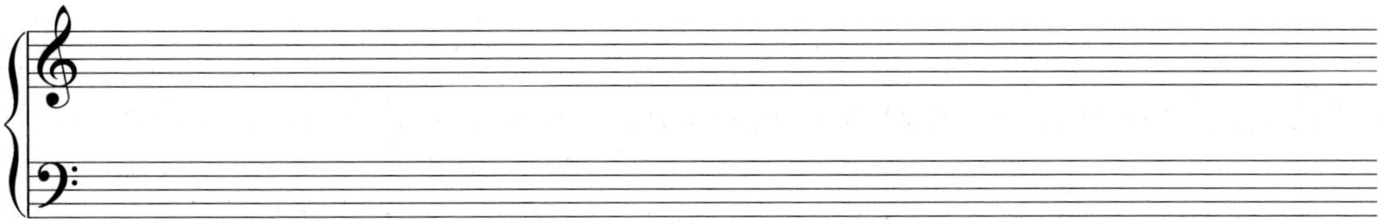

*Date:* . . . . . . . . . . . . . .

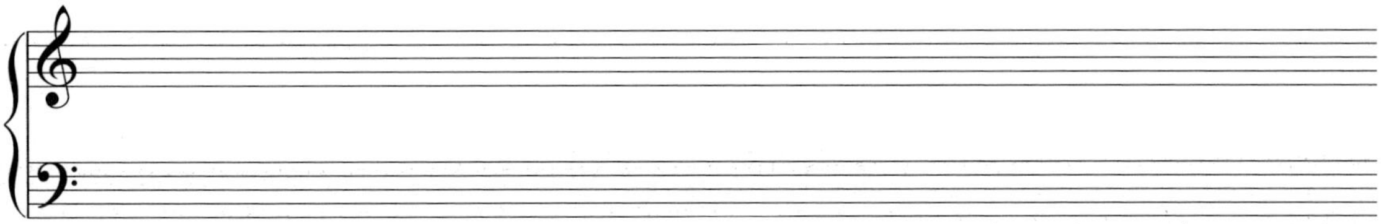

*Date:* . . . . . . . . . . . . . .

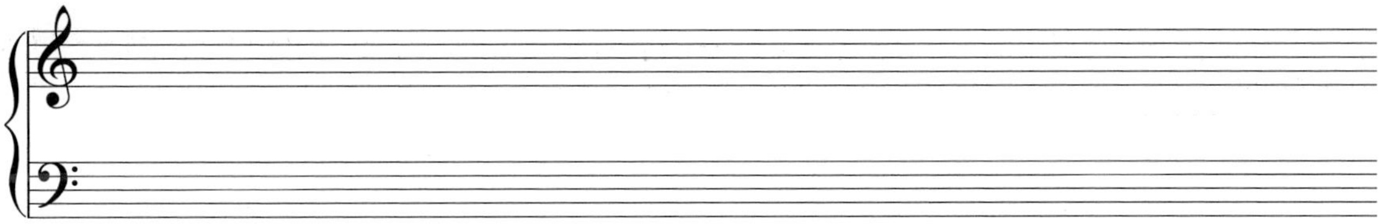

*Date:* . . . . . . . . . . . . . .

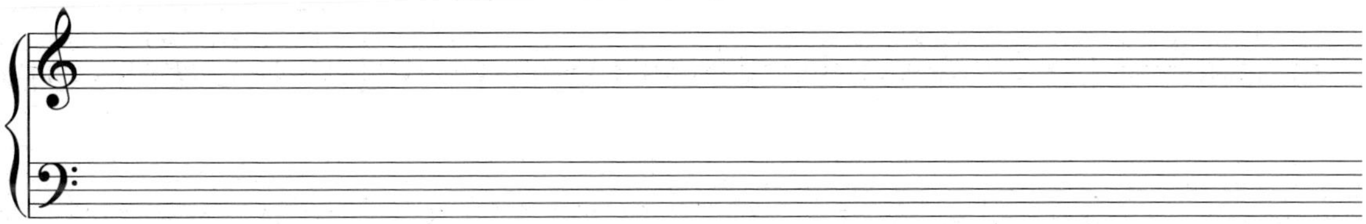

# Chapter 10

# Twentieth-century Rhythmic Techniques

## 10.1 Changing Meter II: Complex Changing Meter

### Facts You Need to Know

Complex changing meter occurs when the beat structure changes from simple to compound, or vice versa, within a meter change. The number of beats in a measure may or may not change.

Some examples of complex changing meter include $\frac{3}{4}$–$\frac{6}{8}$ (simple triple to compound duple), $\frac{9}{8}$–$\frac{2}{4}$ (compound triple to simple duple) and $\frac{4}{4}$–$\frac{6}{8}$ (simple quadruple to compound duple).

#### Performing Complex Changing Meter

In simple changing meter, the speed of the beat and the divisions remains constant through the meter change; the length of the measure expands or contracts. For example, when changing from $\frac{2}{4}$ to $\frac{3}{4}$, the measure is longer, but the tempo of the beat (quarter note) and divisions (eighth note) remains the same from one meter to the next.

In complex changing meter, the relationship from one meter to the next is more intricate. As you move between metric structures, a composer indicates whether the speed of the beat or the divisions will remain constant; the other will change.

Imagine you encounter a passage in which the meter changes from $\frac{2}{4}$ (a simple duple meter) to $\frac{6}{8}$ (a compound duple meter), as in the example below. In the top voice, you see divisions, in the bottom, the beats. Above the barline, you see the indication ♪ = ♪; this means that the speed of the eighth note will remain constant when the meter changes.

EXAMPLE 10.1.1

To execute a changing meter passage in which the division remains constant:

1. Clap eighth notes while articulating the top voice. Your hands and voice should be doing the same thing, and the tempo of the eighth notes should be the same throughout. Although the tempo of the eighth notes is steady, their character should change as you traverse from one meter to the next. If you have difficulty performing this accurately, practice with a metronome.
2. Perform the example again, this time clapping the beats (lower voice) while you articulate divisions. Notice that the beat slows down in the $\frac{6}{8}$ measure; this is because the compound beat has to expand in order to accommodate its three divisions. Conversely, notice that the simple beat feels faster, because you are fitting only two divisions in each beat.

Examine the example below.

**EXAMPLE 10.1.2**

The note values you see are exactly the same as in the original example, but now you see the notation ♩ = ♩. above the staff. This indicates that the speed of the beat will remain the same when the meter changes. In this case, the quarter note in $\frac{2}{4}$ will be performed at the same tempo as the dotted quarter in $\frac{6}{8}$.

To execute a changing meter passage in which the beat remains constant:

1. Clap the beat while articulating the bottom part. Your hands and voice should be in unison and the speed of the beat should be the same in both meters.
2. Without looking at the example, clap a beat. As you clap, articulate groups of two divisions, then groups of three divisions, and notice the difference in tempo between the two.
3. Return to the example. Clap the bottom voice and articulate the top voice. Your hands will remain steady throughout, but the speed of the divisions will change as you move from $\frac{2}{4}$ to $\frac{6}{8}$. Though the speed of the divisions in $\frac{6}{8}$ will be exactly the same as a simple meter triplet, the character is completely different.

The essence of performing complex changing meter passages lies in meticulously portraying the character of each meter. By nature, simple meters are more angular; compound meters rounded with a sense of sway. Accentuating the character of individual meters adds vitality and interest to a performance.

## $\frac{3}{4} = \frac{6}{8}$

Changing meter from $\frac{3}{4}$ to $\frac{6}{8}$ deserves special mention. A primary characteristic of music from Latin America, it is a relationship that appears frequently in music.

$\frac{3}{4}$ and $\frac{6}{8}$ have a significant characteristic in common—they share the same number of divisions. Because each has six divisions, they can be superimposed, and thus composers will often change between these meters without actually notating the change. Some argue that keeping the division constant when changing from $\frac{3}{4}$ to $\frac{6}{8}$ does not constitute a meter change at all, but rather, it is simply a change in emphasis within the meter, or a hemiola.

## Complex Changing Meter Preparatory Exercises

The following exercises focus on keeping the division constant between two meters. Practice each two ways: first by clapping the divisions (so that they act as a guide), then by clapping the beat while you articulate.

**EXAMPLE 10.1.3**

The following exercises focus on keeping the beat constant between two meters. Practice each, first with a metronome, then without. Try to hear the speed of the division before you actually have to change meter—always be aware of 2:3.

**EXAMPLE 10.1.4**

## Rhythms

### RHYTHM 10.1.1

### RHYTHM 10.1.2

### RHYTHM 10.1.3

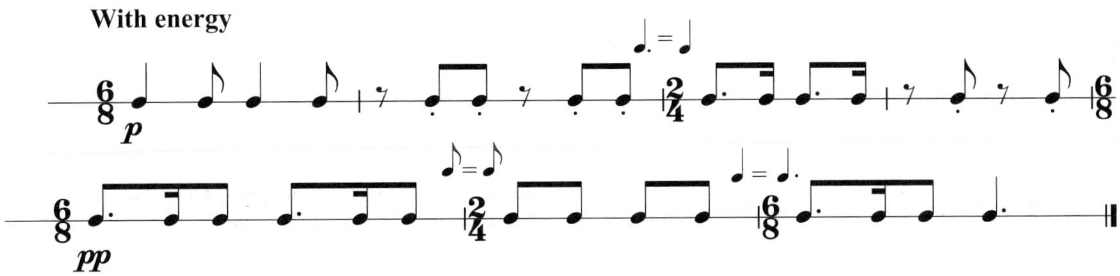


### RHYTHM 10.1.4

RHYTHM 10.1.5

RHYTHM 10.1.6

RHYTHM 10.1.7

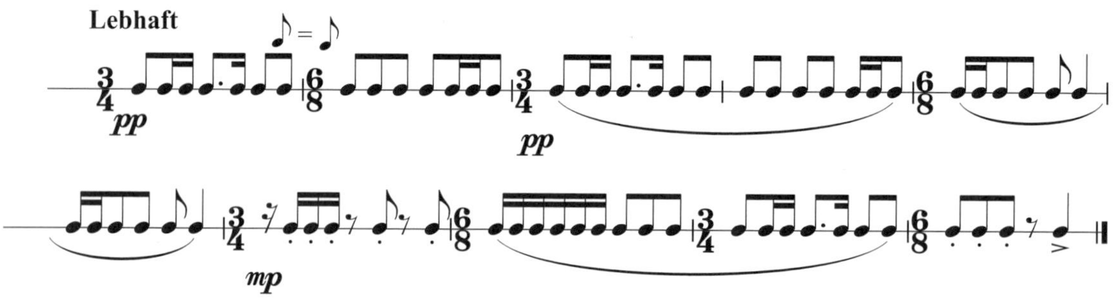


RHYTHM 10.1.8

RHYTHM 10.1.9

RHYTHM 10.1.10

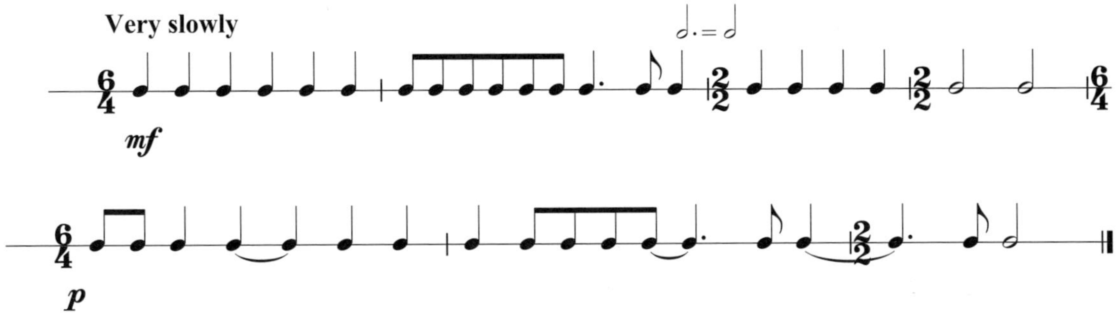


RHYTHM 10.1.11

RHYTHM 10.1.12

**RHYTHM 10.1.13**

**RHYTHM 10.1.14**

**RHYTHM 10.1.15**

**RHYTHM 10.1.16**

### RHYTHM 10.1.17

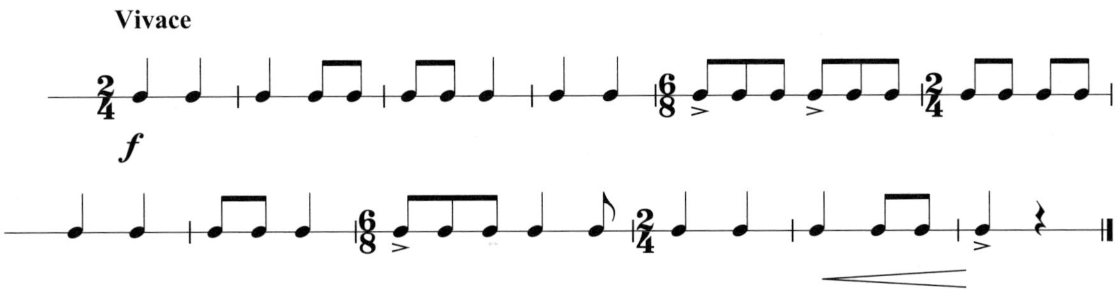


## Two-part Rhythms

### TWO-PART RHYTHM 10.1.1

### TWO-PART RHYTHM 10.1.2

### Three-part Rhythm

#### THREE-PART RHYTHM 10.1

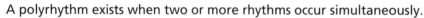

## 10.2 Polyrhythms

### Facts You Need to Know

A polyrhythm exists when two or more rhythms occur simultaneously.

When a polyrhythm involves superimposing two meters on each other, it is considered a polymeter. Polymeters are also called "cross-rhythms" because they pit indivisible numbers of beats against each other. Polymetric rhythms create metric ambiguity and tension in music because the regular beat and metric structure is completely obscured.

By definition, a polyrhythm exists between two voices. Percussionists, pianists, and other keyboard players need to master the skill of performing both voices of a polyrhythm simultaneously. Other instrumentalists need to be able to perform a single voice of a polyrhythm while hearing and feeling the other voice internally.

### Types of Polyrhythm

This example shows the most common polyrhythms; though not all-inclusive, it is comprehensive.

EXAMPLE 10.2.1

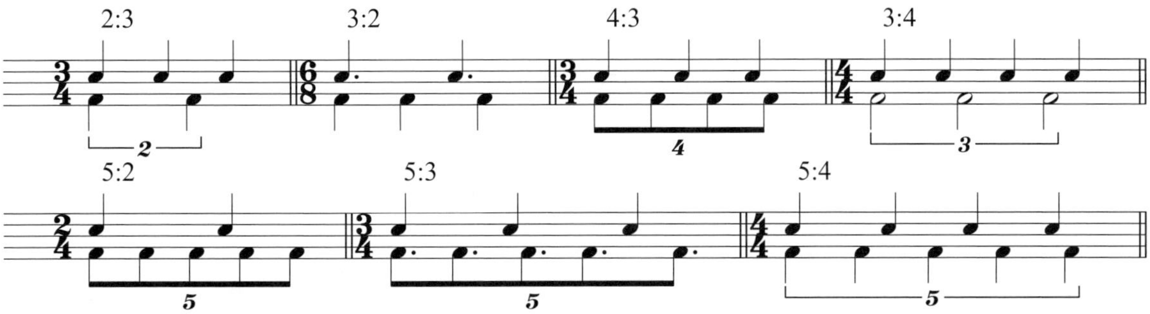


## Performing Polyrhythms

There are two approaches to learning to perform polyrhythms accurately. Experiment with each to determine which will work best for you.

### Method One: Using "Misplaced" Accents

In any polyrhythm, find the lowest common denominator between the two meters. For example, 2:3 has three quarter-note beats against two dotted-quarter beats; each meter has six divisions.

Look at the beaming in the $\frac{3}{4}$ example below. In measure one, the stems going up show the grouping in $\frac{3}{4}$; the stems going down show $\frac{6}{8}$. The beats of each meter are indicated with an "x."

EXAMPLE 10.2.2

Measure two uses of accents to indicate the two beats of $\frac{6}{8}$. To learn to perform 2:3:

1. Clap the three beats of $\frac{3}{4}$ while articulating the six divisions, intentionally stressing the first and fourth divisions, which represent the two beats of $\frac{6}{8}$. You are "misplacing" the natural stresses in $\frac{3}{4}$, replacing them with the $\frac{6}{8}$ beats.
2. Repeat, alternating between clapping the beats of $\frac{3}{4}$ and $\frac{6}{8}$. Continue to hear all six divisions in your head.
3. Repeat again, clapping in $\frac{3}{4}$ while articulating in $\frac{6}{8}$.

To perform 3:2, repeat the process, this time using the two beats of $\frac{6}{8}$ as your guide; you will "misplace" the stresses to find the three beats, as shown in the example below.

EXAMPLE 10.2.3

Use the same process for learning 3:4 and the reverse, as well as any other polyrhythm. Simply find the lowest common number of divisions, superimpose the two meters, then articulate with the misplaced accents. Look at 3:4 in the example below; here, the lowest common denominator is 12. The polyrhythm is shown using $^{12}_{8}$ (four dotted-quarter beats) against $^{3}_{2}$ (two half-note beats).

**EXAMPLE 10.2.4**

Finally, 4:3:

**EXAMPLE 10.2.5**

### Method Two: Using Composite Rhythms

In this method, you will focus on the beats of each meter.

In any polyrhythm, you can superimpose the beats of each meter (or rhythm) to create a new rhythm called a composite rhythm. The composite rhythm is how the two meters sound when performed as a single voice.

To discover a composite rhythm, superimpose the divisions in each meter, find the beats, then determine the length of notes between beats. Choose one meter in which to write the rhythm. (It is generally easier to write the rhythm in the meter with the greater number of beats.) The example below shows the composite rhythm for 2:3.

**EXAMPLE 10.2.6**

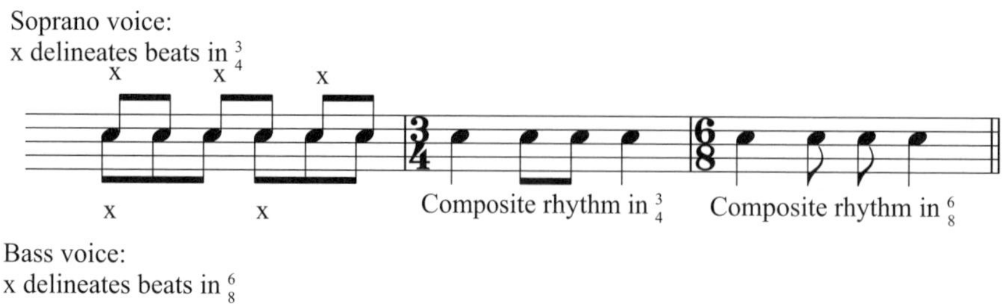


Notice that the composite rhythm in $^{12}_{8}$ and $^{3}_{2}$ look exactly the same. The rhythm *is* the same; the metric stresses are different. Also notice that this (and all) composite rhythm is a retrograde of itself; it is exactly the same forward and backward. This phenomenon is true for any composite rhythm. The composite rhythms for 2:5, 3:5, and 4:5, respectively, are below.

EXAMPLE 10.2.7

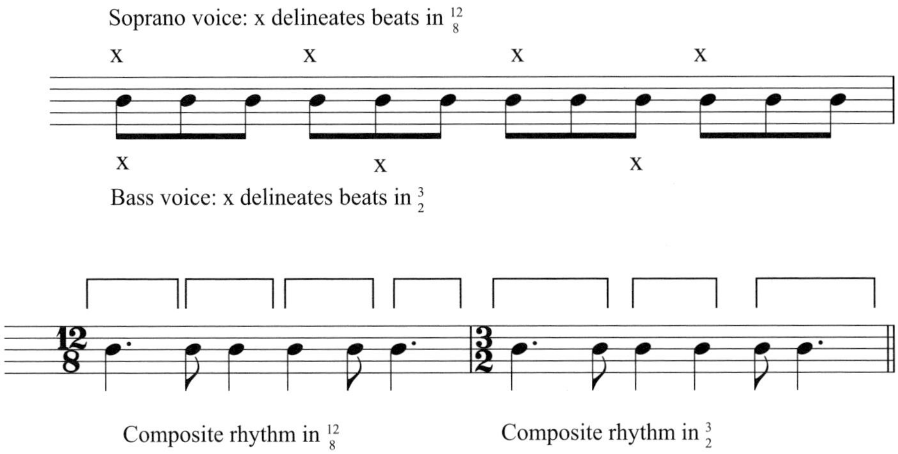


EXAMPLE 10.2.8

## Rhythms

RHYTHM 10.2.1

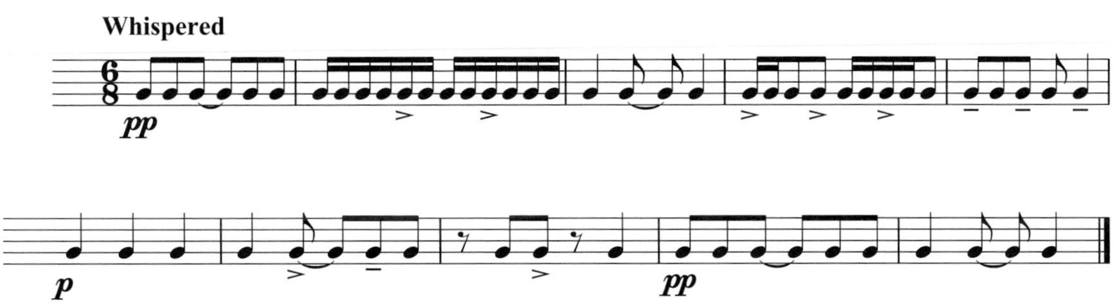


RHYTHM 10.2.2

RHYTHM 10.2.3

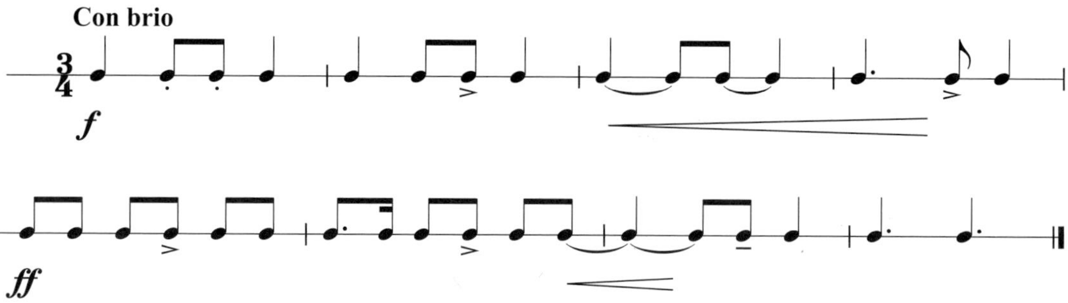


RHYTHM 10.2.4

RHYTHM 10.2.5

RHYTHM 10.2.6

RHYTHM 10.2.7

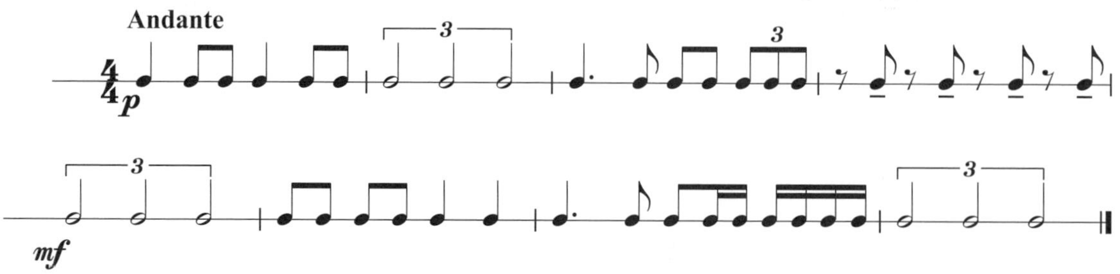

RHYTHM 10.2.8

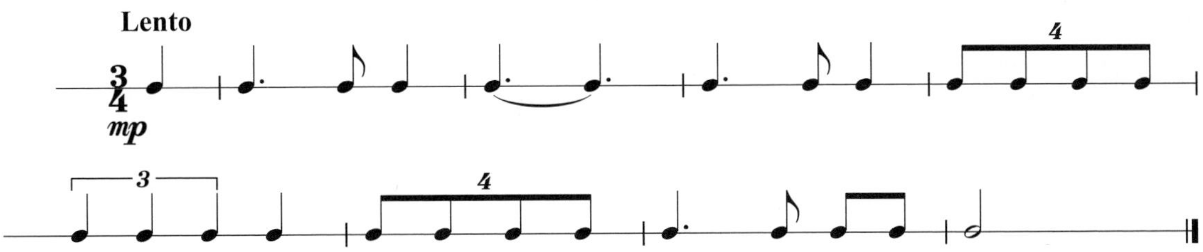


RHYTHM 10.2.9

RHYTHM 10.2.10

RHYTHM 10.2.11

## RHYTHM 10.2.12

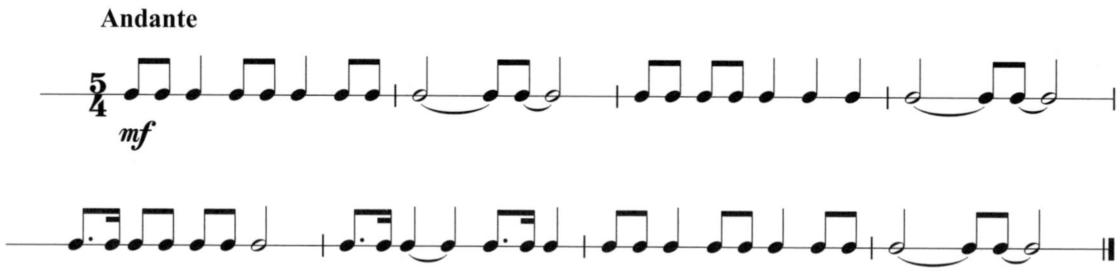


## RHYTHM 10.2.13

## RHYTHM 10.2.14

## RHYTHM 10.2.15

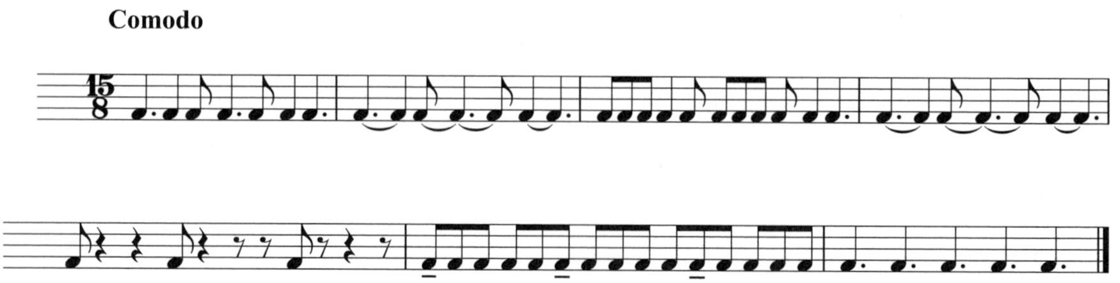

RHYTHM 10.2.16

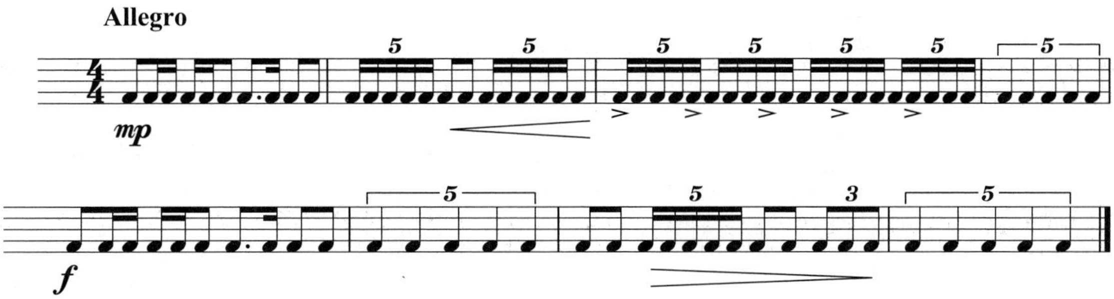


RHYTHM 10.2.17

## Two-part Rhythms

TWO-PART RHYTHM 10.2.1

TWO-PART RHYTHM 10.2.2

### TWO-PART RHYTHM 10.2.3

### TWO-PART RHYTHM 10.2.4

## Three-part Rhythm

### THREE-PART RHYTHM 10.2

## 10.3 Asymmetric Meters

### Facts You Need to Know

An asymmetric meter is one that uses any combination of groupings of 2, 3, and 4 divisions of a beat in a given measure. Beats do not occur at regular intervals, as they do in simple and compound meter, but are of unequal length; the duration of the beat expands and contracts within a measure.

In simple and compound meters, beats and divisions are divided and multiplied, resulting in 2:1 or 3:1 relationships within beats. In asymmetric meters, beats become longer or shorter by adding or subtracting divisions within them. Thus, asymmetric beat structures can be considered to use additive rhythms. Additive rhythms occur with great frequency in the traditional music of India.

Asymmetric meters are also referred to as unequal beats, complex meter, or composite meters.

Though the most prevalent usage of asymmetric meters in classical music occurs in music of the twentieth century and beyond, notable examples occur in music of the Common Practice period, including Tchaikovsky's *Sixth Symphony* and Mussorgsky's *Pictures at an Exhibition*.

### Performing Asymmetric Meters

The most common asymmetric meters include $\frac{5}{8}$, $\frac{7}{8}$, and $\frac{8}{8}$, though *many* other asymmetric meters exist. Within each asymmetric meter, various permutations may occur. For example, $\frac{5}{8}$ may be manifested as either $\frac{2+3}{8}$ or $\frac{3+2}{8}$. For this reason, composers sometimes indicate the groupings specifically in the time signatures. See the examples below.

EXAMPLE 10.3.1

If the beat groupings are not indicated in the time signature, the performer must ascertain the groupings by looking at how notes are beamed. Bear in mind that the groupings could shift within a piece to add interest and ambiguity. The time signature in the example below is $\frac{7}{8}$; the beams show that the grouping of measure one is $\frac{2+2+3}{8}$, measure two, $\frac{3+2+2}{8}$, measure three, $\frac{2+3+2}{8}$, and the last measure, $\frac{4+3}{8}$.

EXAMPLE 10.3.2

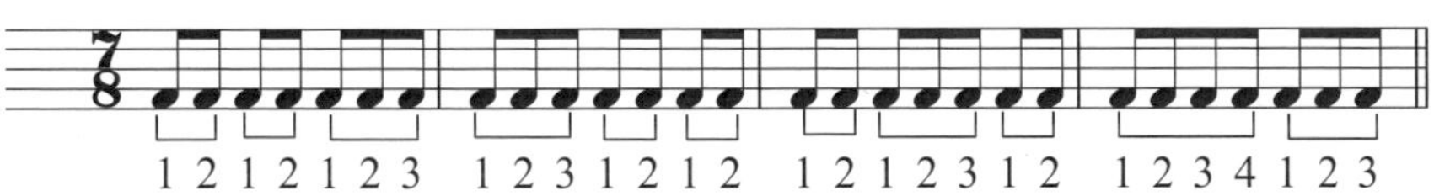


Example two also shows the easiest way to count in asymmetric meters. Simply counting the number of divisions in each groups is uncomplicated and allows a performer to see the difference in character of each group as it expands and contracts.

## Asymmetric Rhythm Reading

### Rhythms

#### RHYTHM 10.3.1

#### RHYTHM 10.3.2

#### RHYTHM 10.3.3

#### RHYTHM 10.3.4

RHYTHM 10.3.5

RHYTHM 10.3.6

RHYTHM 10.3.7

RHYTHM 10.3.8

## RHYTHM 10.3.9

## RHYTHM 10.3.10

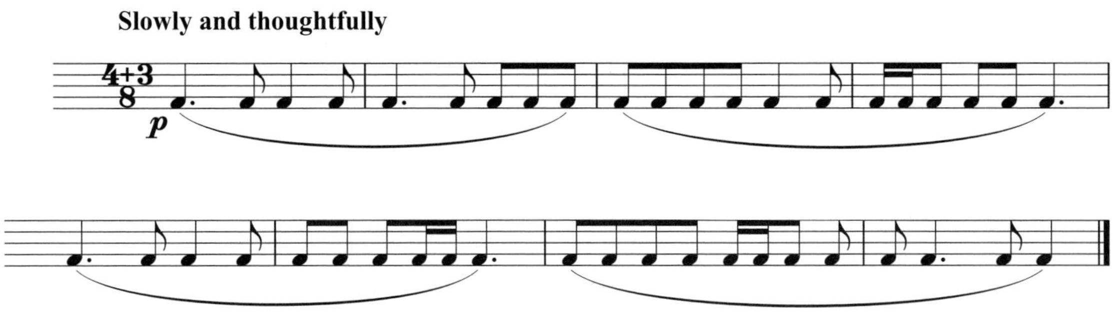


## RHYTHM 10.3.11

## RHYTHM 10.3.12

### RHYTHM 10.3.13

### RHYTHM 10.3.14

## Two-part Rhythms

### TWO-PART RHYTHM 10.3.1

### TWO-PART RHYTHM 10.3.2

### Three-part Rhythm

#### THREE-PART RHYTHM 10.3

## Reflections: Understanding and Appreciating Twentieth-century Music

Many people, music students included, are "turned off" when listening to music of the most recent century. They often have difficulty hearing what is beautiful or even fun about much of this music. Few musicians will have the luxury of being able to avoid twentieth-century music altogether throughout their careers. Most will have to perform it, or elements derived from it, at one point or another during their career. Here are some things to keep in mind as you learn how to approach this literature:

1. There is a tremendous variety of musical and compositional styles and languages used in twentieth-century music. Saying that you don't like one says nothing about how you might like the rest of it.
2. The twentieth century was, by and large, an era of experimentation with the setting of new "rules" for how music might sound. It was an era when composers weren't afraid to ask, and in many cases were even encouraged to ask "what if?" in regard to their compositional language.
3. Music of the twentieth century is often very personal, intimate, and emotional. The notion of music (and all art, for that matter) as being representative of beauty was replaced in the minds of many composers by the idea that music and art should represent "truth," whether beautiful or not.
4. Even though it might not sound like it, much twentieth-century music is extremely organized. Conversely, some of it relies on chance and the lack of organization. Try to understand how the music is put together. This will help you to understand how to present it.

5. In general, because no single musical language dominated the twentieth century, and because Common Practice tonality was abandoned or purposely avoided in much of it, this music requires extra care, rehearsal, and thoughtfulness to prepare. It is generally not music that sounds good when it is thrown together. Listen to groups or soloists who specialize in performing literature from this era to get its sound in your ear.
6. While many elements of traditional tonal music were altered or thrown out, many other elements were not. Use what is familiar to your ear (be it rhythm, meter, phrasing, timbre, pitch, etc.) to guide your decisions as to how this music will be performed.
7. In the end, it's OK to dislike this literature, but be thoughtful and specific about why. Keep in mind that much of this literature, like most music composed in every style period throughout the history of music, will not "survive the test of time" to be performed in our current century.
8. Above all, try to find a part of this literature that appeals to you, and have fun exploring the possibilities for expression and communication within it.

## 10.4 Dictation Materials

@

*Note:* This dictation chapter focuses on extra practice for the skills you have already learned.

### I. Chord Identification

Your teacher will play several chords. Indicate the quality and inversion for each by using the correct figured bass symbol.

*Date:* . . . . . . . . . . . . . .

1. ____ 2. ____ 3. ____ 4. ____ 5. ____ 6. ____ 7. ____ 8. ____

*Date:* . . . . . . . . . . . . . .

1. ____ 2. ____ 3. ____ 4. ____ 5. ____ 6. ____ 7. ____ 8. ____

*Date:* . . . . . . . . . . . . . .

1. ____ 2. ____ 3. ____ 4. ____ 5. ____ 6. ____ 7. ____ 8. ____

*Date:* . . . . . . . . . . . . . .

1. ____ 2. ____ 3. ____ 4. ____ 5. ____ 6. ____ 7. ____ 8. ____

*Date:* . . . . . . . . . . . . . .

1. ____ 2. ____ 3. ____ 4. ____ 5. ____ 6. ____ 7. ____ 8. ____

## II. Melodic and Rhythmic Dictation

Your teacher will play a short melody or rhythm. Notate it on the staves below. Be sure to adjust pitches using accidentals following modulations.

*Date:* . . . . . . . . . . . . . .

*Date:* . . . . . . . . . . . . . .

*Date:* . . . . . . . . . . . . . .

*Date:* . . . . . . . . . . . . . .

*Date:* . . . . . . . . . . . . . .

## III. Harmonic Dictation

Write the soprano line, bass line, and provide a Roman numeral analysis (including inversional symbols) for the progression you hear on the grand staff below.

*Date:* . . . . . . . . . . . . . .

*Date:* . . . . . . . . . . . . . .

*Date:* . . . . . . . . . . . . . .

*Date:* . . . . . . . . . . . . . .

*Date:* . . . . . . . . . . . . . .

## IV. Identification of Polyrhythms

You will hear several polyrhythms, either as single-line rhythms in a particular meter or as composite rhythms. Identify the polyrhythm that you hear. Your choices are:

2:3 3:2 4:3 3:4 5:2 5:4

*Date:* . . . . . . . . . . . . . .

1. ____ 2. ____ 3. ____ 4. ____ 5. ____ 6. ____ 7. ____ 8. ____

*Date:* . . . . . . . . . . . . . .

1. ____ 2. ____ 3. ____ 4. ____ 5. ____ 6. ____ 7. ____ 8. ____

*Date:* . . . . . . . . . . . . . .

1. ____ 2. ____ 3. ____ 4. ____ 5. ____ 6. ____ 7. ____ 8. ____

*Date:* . . . . . . . . . . . . . .

1. ____ 2. ____ 3. ____ 4. ____ 5. ____ 6. ____ 7. ____ 8. ____

*Date:* . . . . . . . . . . . . . .

1. ____ 2. ____ 3. ____ 4. ____ 5. ____ 6. ____ 7. ____ 8. ____

## V. Rhythmic Dictation

Notate the rhythms you hear on the staves below:

*Date:* . . . . . . . . . . . . . .

*Date:* . . . . . . . . . . . . . .

*Date:* . . . . . . . . . . . . . .

*Date:* . . . . . . . . . . . . . .

*Date:* . . . . . . . . . . . . . .

# Chapter 11

# Twentieth-century Material based on Tonal Models

## 11.1 Pentatonic and Blues Scales

### Facts You Need to Know

Pentatonic scales contain five notes separated by major seconds and minor thirds. The arrangement of these intervals is what differentiates the various forms of the pentatonic scale. The two most common pentatonic scales are the major pentatonic and the minor pentatonic scales. The major pentatonic scale is a major scale with scale degrees 4 and 7 removed.

**EXAMPLE 11.1.1**

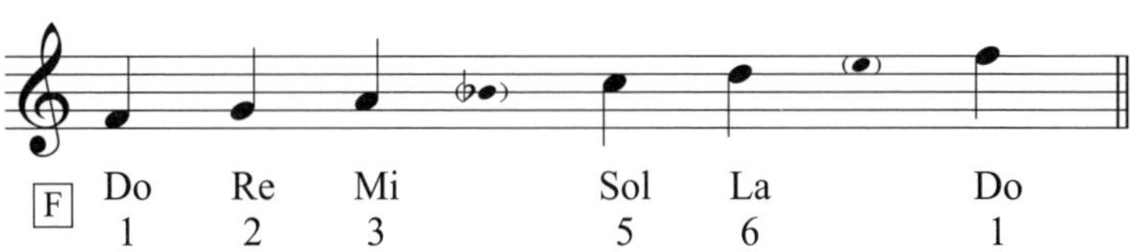


The minor pentatonic scale is a natural minor scale with scale degrees 2 and 6 removed.

**EXAMPLE 11.1.2**

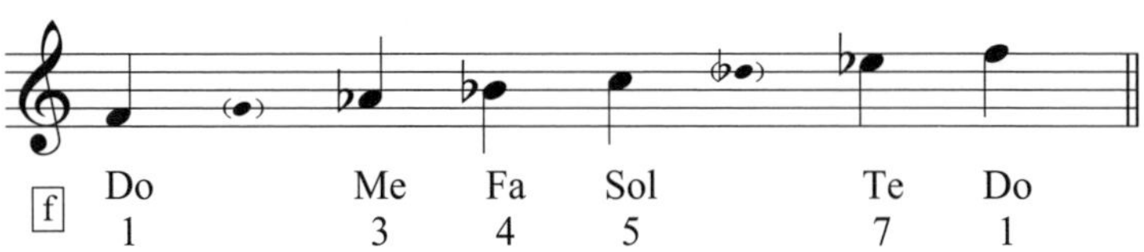


Other pentatonic scales can be heard as a major scale or natural minor scales that are missing two scale degrees:

**EXAMPLE 11.1.3**

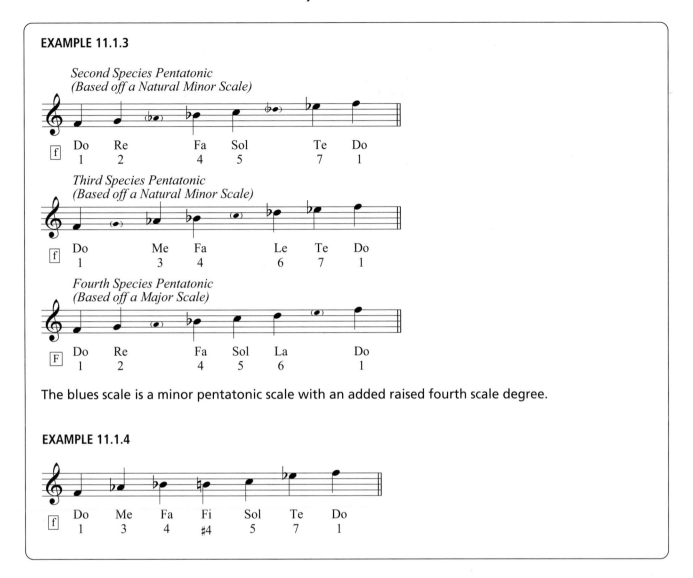

*Second Species Pentatonic*
*(Based off a Natural Minor Scale)*

*Third Species Pentatonic*
*(Based off a Natural Minor Scale)*

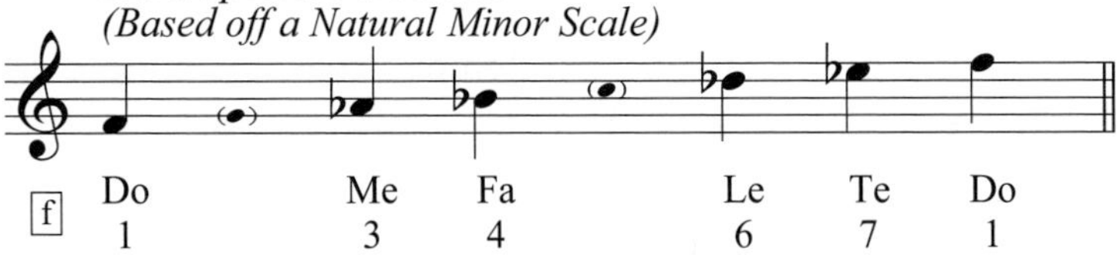


*Fourth Species Pentatonic*
*(Based off a Major Scale)*

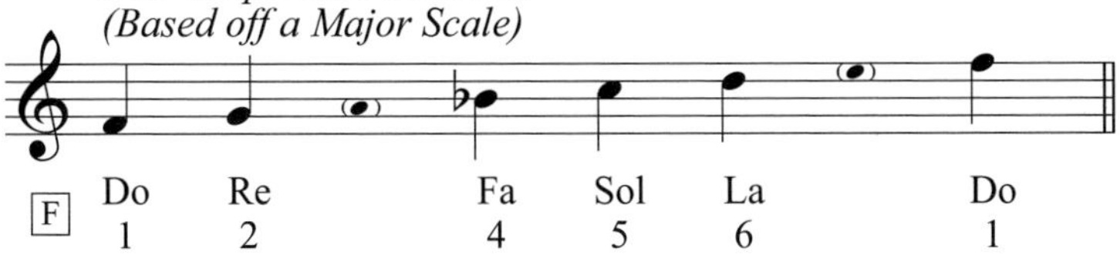


The blues scale is a minor pentatonic scale with an added raised fourth scale degree.

**EXAMPLE 11.1.4**

## Hearing

Use the following steps to identify scale types and music written from them:

1. Identify tonic and whether the scale sounds like it is closer to a major scale, a minor scale, or an atonal scale by listening specifically for the quality of scale degree 3. The major and fourth species pentatonic scales will have a major sound. The minor, second species, third species, and blues scale will have a minor sound.
2. Count the number of notes used in the scale. This may be difficult if only part of the scale is being used. Pentatonic scales will sound as if they have six notes (five unique pitches and an octave duplication). The blues scale sounds as if it has seven notes, with the added note sounding like a chromatic passing tone between scale degrees 4 and 5.
3. Listen for the approach to tonic from below. In most scales, this is an important identifying feature. The most common approaches from below are leading tones (m2), subtonics (M2), or minor thirds. No

pentatonic scales use leading tones. The minor, second, and third species and the blues scale have a subtonic. The major and fourth species pentatonics have a minor third below tonic.

4. Listen for altered scale degrees or other identifying characteristics. In the case of pentatonic scales, listen for the notes that seem to be "missing" from the major or minor scale. In the case of the blues scale, listen also for the added chromatic tone between scale degrees 4 and 5.

## Singing

Use the major or minor scale as your basis for singing pentatonic scales. Remove the appropriate scale degrees. Consult the chart below for determining which scale (major or minor) to use for each pentatonic scale, and which scale degrees to leave out.

| *Scale* | *Basis* | *Leave Out* |
|---|---|---|
| Major pentatonic (1st species) | Major scale | 4 and 7 |
| Minor pentatonic (5th species) | Minor scale | 2 and 6 |
| 2nd species pentatonic | Natural minor scale | 3 and 6 |
| 3rd species pentatonic | Natural minor scale | 2 and 5 |
| 4th species pentatonic | Major | 3 and 7 |
| Blues | Natural minor scale | 2 and 6, add a #4 |

## Assignments for Practice

### Pitch Patterns

#### PITCH PATTERN 11.1.1

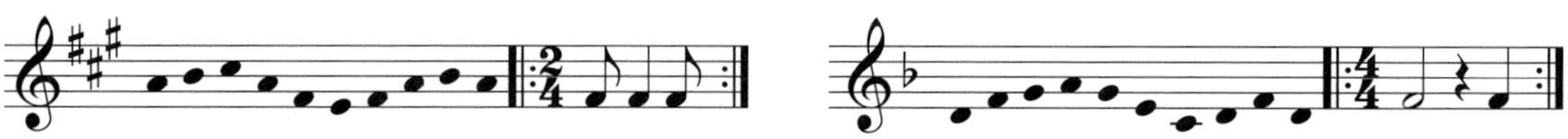

#### PITCH PATTERN 11.1.2

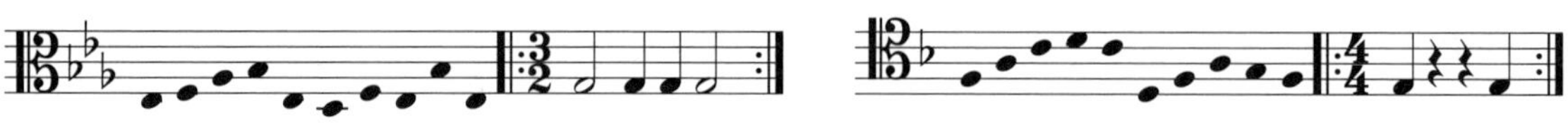

#### PITCH PATTERN 11.1.3

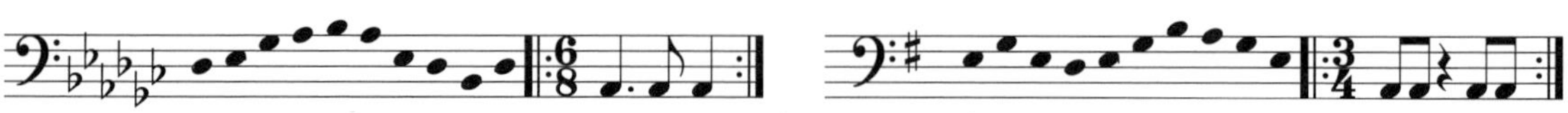

## Melodies

### MELODY 11.1.1

### MELODY 11.1.2

### MELODY 11.1.3

### MELODY 11.1.4

**MELODY 11.1.5**

**MELODY 11.1.6**

**MELODY 11.1.7**

**MELODY 11.1.8**

**MELODY 11.1.9**

**MELODY 11.1.10**

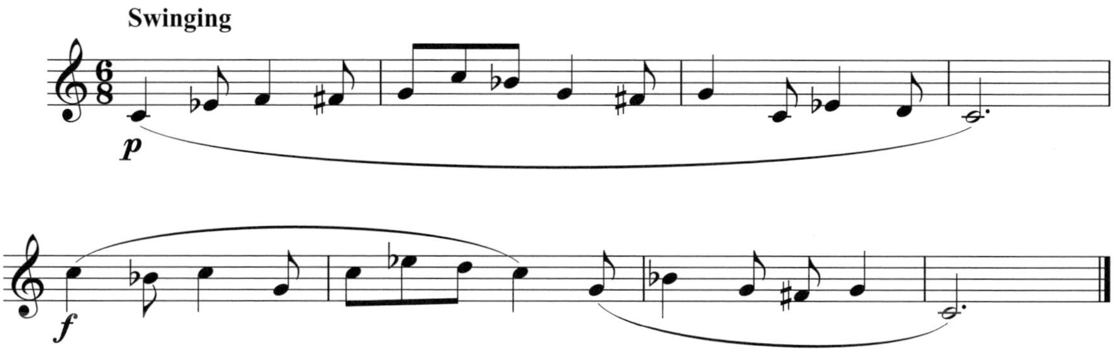


**MELODY 11.1.11**

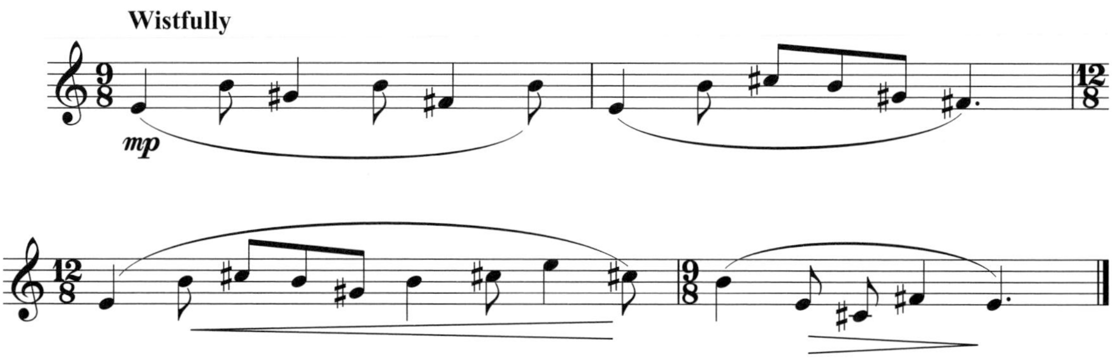


**MELODY 11.1.12**

### MELODY 11.1.13

### MELODY 11.1.14

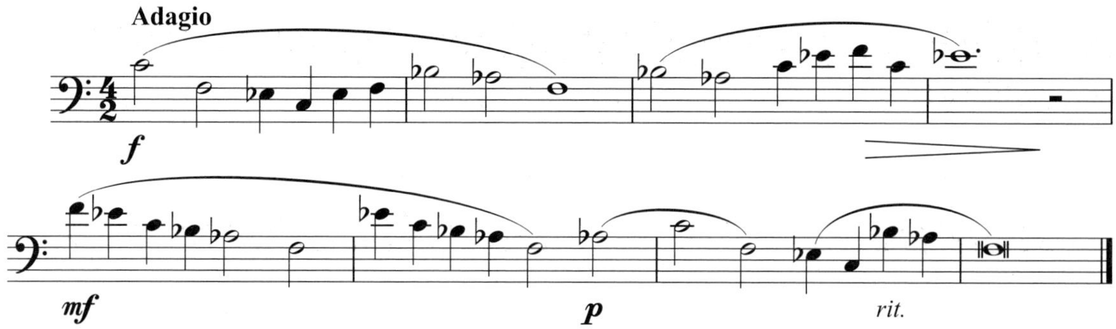


### MELODY 11.1.15

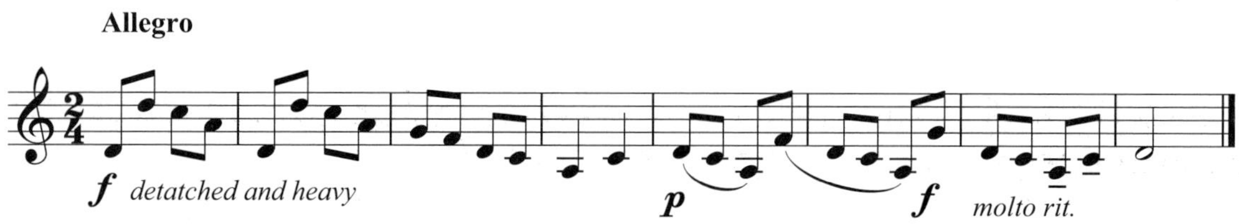


## Duets

### DUET 11.1.1

DUET 11.1.2

DUET 11.1.3

## Chorale

### CHORALE 11.1

## Self-Accompanied Melody

### SELF-ACCOMPANIED MELODY 11.1

## 11.2 The Ecclesiastic Modes

### Facts You Need to Know

Modes are scale formations that were the basis of most Western music until the creation of major and minor scales. While the pre-tonal use of modes is very different from our concept of scales, modern modes are generally treated as major or minor scales with one or more altered pitches.

Modes returned to somewhat common use in the twentieth century as a means of evoking an "old" sound and as an aid for improvising in jazz music.

The original modal system was based on the natural or "white" keys on the keyboard (a Dorian mode consists of all the natural notes starting on D, Phrygian starting on E, etc.). Like scales, modes are fully transposable, so it is best to memorize them as major or minor scales with altered scale degrees. Memorize the chart of the modes below:

**EXAMPLE 11.2.1**

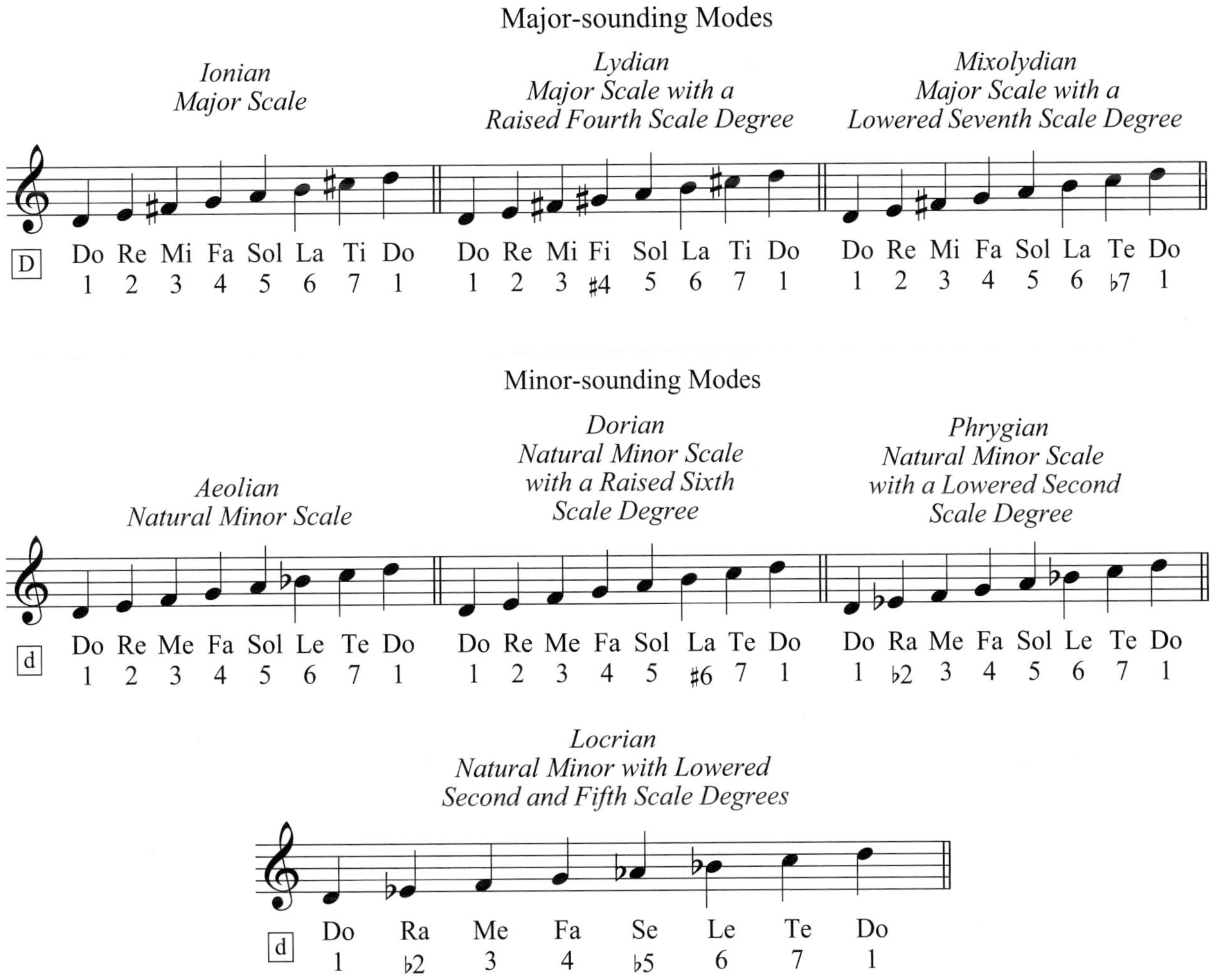

## Hearing

Like all scales, listen for 1) the modality (major or minor), 2) the number of pitches (all modes sound as if they have 8 pitches), 3) the approach to tonic from below, and 4) other identifying characteristics. See the chart on p. 487 for each mode's identifying characteristics.

## Singing

When singing any of the modes:

1. Know which scale serves as the basis for the mode you are singing. Set yourself up in a key using that scale.
2. Know the chromatic alterations that you need to apply to your scale.
3. Repeat your scale with the appropriate alterations.

## Assignments for Practice

1. Practice singing all modes in rapid succession from a given pitch. Change the order in which you sing the modes.
2. Improvise using the modes. Figure out how to take advantage of the "altered" scale degree that gives each mode its unique sound. Focus on presenting this scale degree.

### Pitch Patterns

PITCH PATTERN 11.2.1

PITCH PATTERN 11.2.2

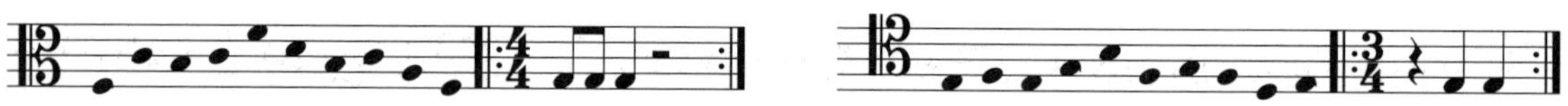

PITCH PATTERN 11.2.3

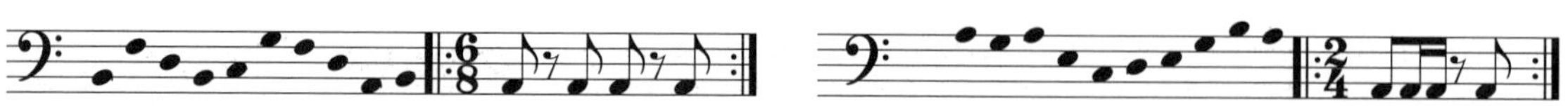

## Melodies

### MELODY 11.2.1

### MELODY 11.2.2

### MELODY 11.2.3

## MELODY 11.2.4

## MELODY 11.2.5

## MELODY 11.2.6

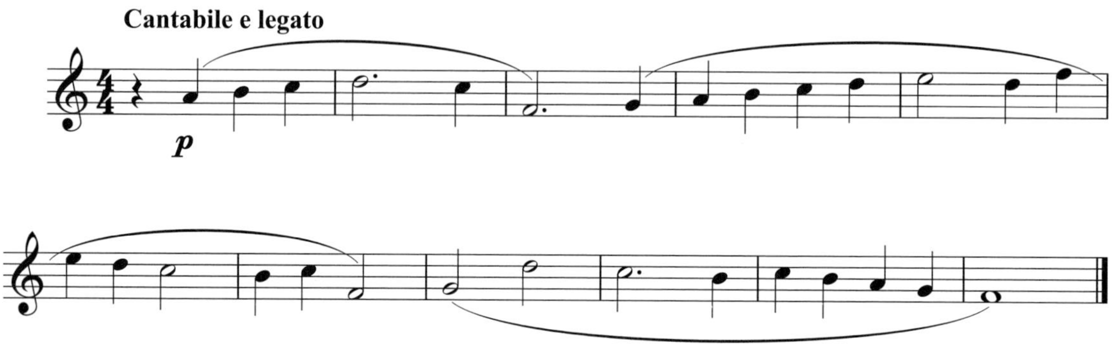


## MELODY 11.2.7

MELODY 11.2.8

MELODY 11.2.9

MELODY 11.2.10

MELODY 11.2.11

MELODY 11.2.12

MELODY 11.2.13

MELODY 11.2.14

### MELODY 11.2.15

## Duets

### DUET 11.2.1

### DUET 11.2.2

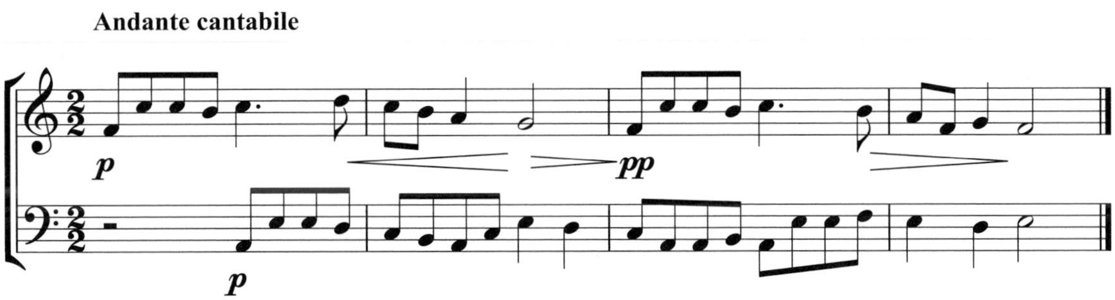


### DUET 11.2.3

## Chorale

### CHORALE 11.2

## Self-Accompanied Melody

### SELF-ACCOMPANIED MELODY 11.2

## 11.3 Other Scales

### Facts You Need to Know

There are hundreds of ways of arranging the 12-note octave into interesting and exotic-sounding scales. Like modes, most retain a basic major or minor sound and rely on altered or added scale degrees to give them a unique character.

Many "exotic" scales have ethnic names. Often these names have little to do with their country of origin. Other scales have descriptive names that can help you to figure out their pitch content. Some of the more common named scales appear below. Note that the chart below represents a fraction of the scale possibilities. Many other "unnamed" scales exist and can be used to create a unique sound in a piece of music.

**EXAMPLE 11.3.1**

*Overtone Scale*
*Lydian-Mixolydian Scale*
*(Major with raised 4 and lowered 7)*

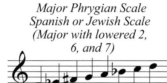

*Major Phrygian Scale*
*Spanish or Jewish Scale*
*(Major with lowered 2, 6, and 7)*

*Gypsy Minor Scale*
*Hungarian Minor Scale*
*(Harmonic minor with raised 4)*

*Major Locrian Scale*
*Arabic Scale*
*(Major with lowered 5, 6, and 7)*

*Dorian-Phrygian Scale*
*Javanese Scale*
*(Natural minor with lowered 2 and raised 6)*

*Dominant Bebop Scale*
*(Major with added lowered 7)*

Notice that the labeling of these scales is not standardized. As a result, it is often better to learn and refer to these scales as alterations of either the major or the minor scale.

### Hearing

As with all scales, follow these steps for identification:

1. Listen for tonic.
2. Listen for modality. Does it sound major or minor?
3. Listen for the number of pitches.
4. Listen for the approach to tonic, especially from below.
5. Listen for added or altered scale degrees.

## Singing

Know the identifying characteristics of the scale you are going to sing. Establish tonic and the scale's modality.

Find diatonic "waypoints" in your scale. For example, a perfect fifth above the tonic or a major or minor third scale degree are excellent places to check the integrity of your scale.

Sing the scale as major or minor with added or altered scale degrees.

## Assignments for Practice

1. Practice singing scales and then altering one or more scale degrees.
2. Improvise using a scale before singing a melody. Notice how its unique characteristics affect the sound of the music.

### Pitch Patterns

#### PITCH PATTERN 11.3.1

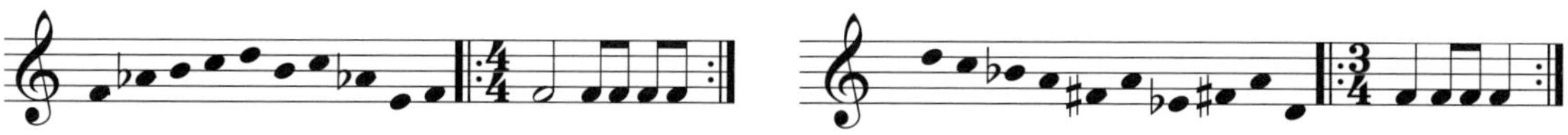

#### PITCH PATTERN 11.3.2

#### PITCH PATTERN 11.3.3

### Melodies

#### MELODY 11.3.1

**MELODY 11.3.2**

**MELODY 11.3.3**

**MELODY 11.3.4**

**MELODY 11.3.5**

MELODY 11.3.6

MELODY 11.3.7

MELODY 11.3.8

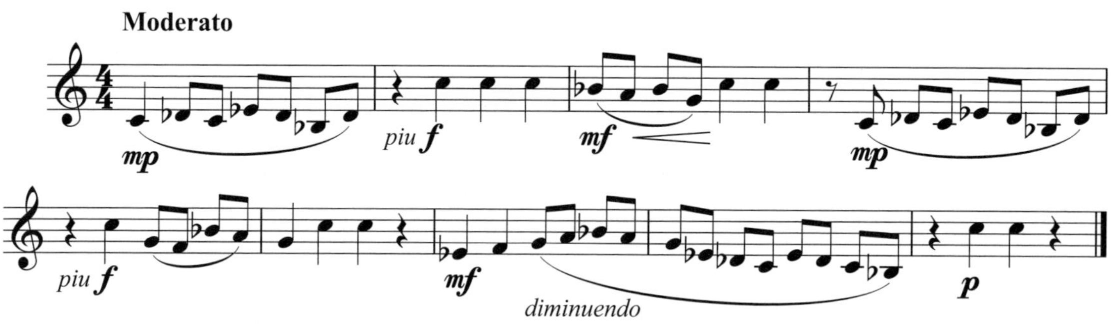


MELODY 11.3.9

**MELODY 11.3.10**

**MELODY 11.3.11**

**MELODY 11.3.12**

**MELODY 11.3.13**

MELODY 11.3.14

MELODY 11.3.15

## Duets

DUET 11.3.1

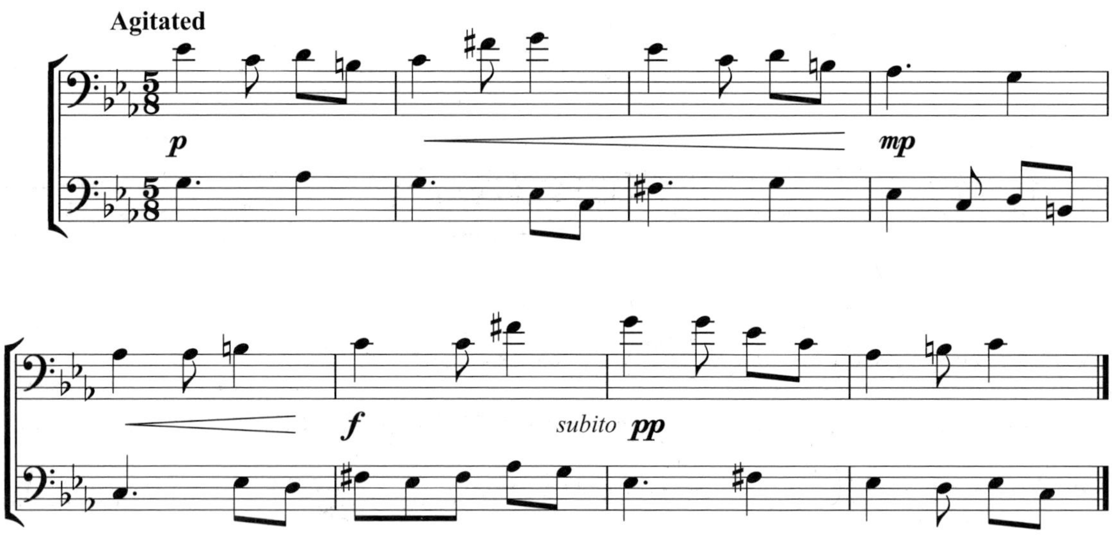

DUET 11.3.2

DUET 11.3.3

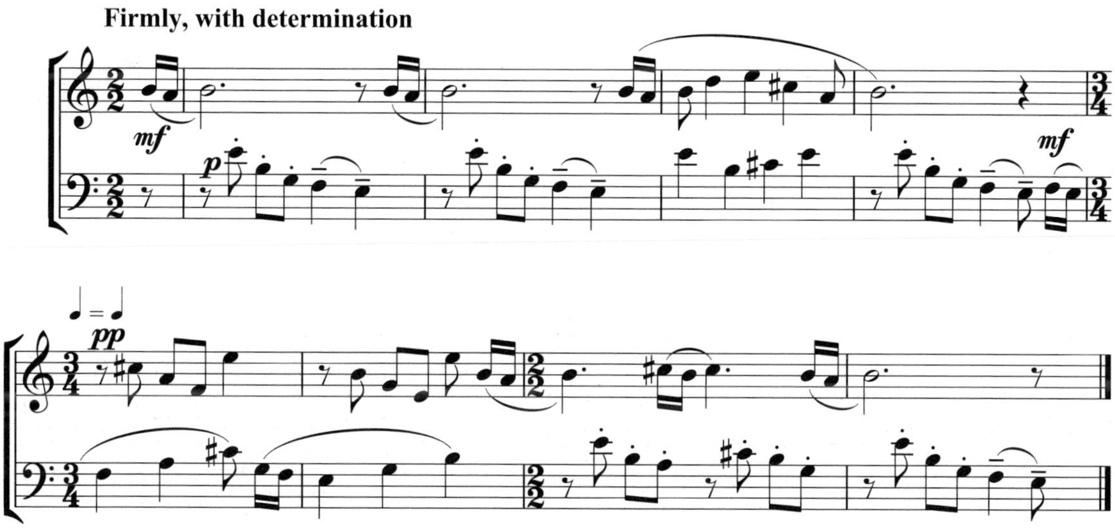

## Chorale

### CHORALE 11.3

## Self-Accompanied Melody

### SELF-ACCOMPANIED MELODY 11.3

## 11.4 Polytonality and Polymodality

### Facts You Need to Know

Polytonality and polymodality occur when two or more elements of a piece of music appear in different keys or modes simultaneously.

The elements that occur in different keys or modes are usually separated by timbre, texture, or register.

Each separate element typically presents a single key or mode in a very clear way.

### Hearing

1. Listen for the separation of elements by register and/or timbre.
2. Listen for the "clash" of sounds between the keys that are used in each separate voice.
3. Listen and write the musical element that you hear most clearly. This may be either melodic or harmonic in nature.
4. Listen for the other musical elements and write them down.
5. Listen for how the separate elements interact. Is it a largely consonant or dissonant interaction? What intervals can you hear between the two voices?

### Singing

1. Polytonality and polymodality require that more than one musical voice be sounding at the same time.
2. Focus on the integrity of your musical part. Retain your own sense of tonic, and hear all of your pitches in relation to this tonic.
3. As you perform, listen for the interaction between your part and all other parts. Listen for the consonances or resonances that result from the sounding of the musical lines together. Listen for the integrity of the intervals or chords.

### Assignments for Practice

With a friend, sing parallel scales starting on different pitches. Be careful to maintain the integrity of both scales.

## Duets

### DUET 11.4.1

### DUET 11.4.2

### DUET 11.4.3

**DUET 11.4.4**

**Stately**

**DUET 11.4.5**

**Moderate and unfettered**

**DUET 11.4.6**

**Happily, with a hint of silliness**

**DUET 11.4.7**

**DUET 11.4.8**

**DUET 11.4.9**

## Chorale

### CHORALE 11.4

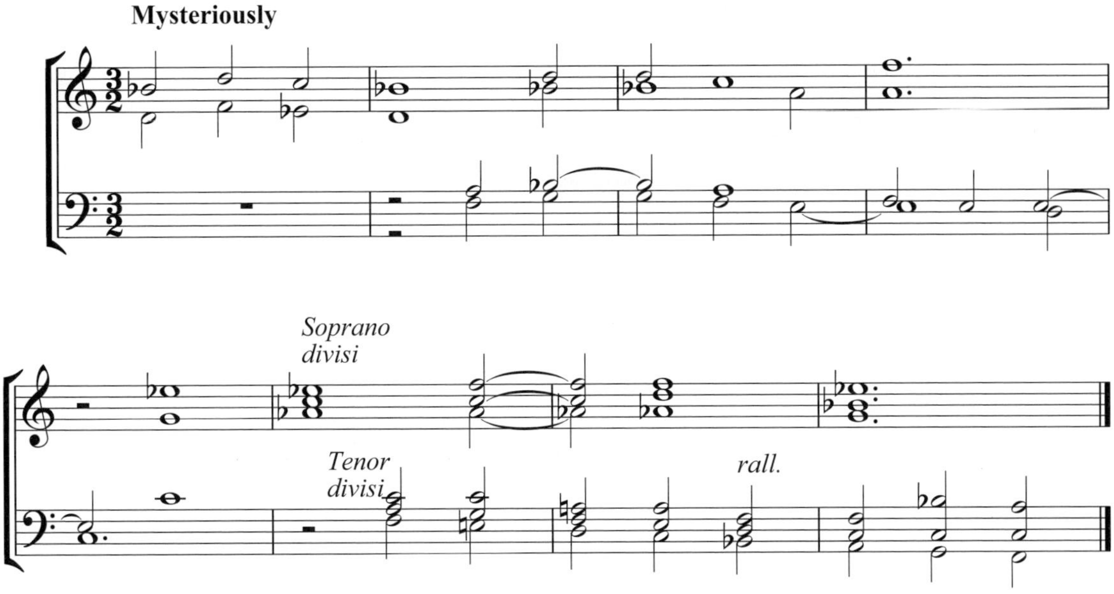


## Self-Accompanied Melody

### SELF-ACCOMPANIED MELODY 11.4

## 11.5 Music from the Literature

### EXAMPLE 11.5.1

"Bruyères," from *Preludes pour Piano*, Book II

**Calme, Doucement expressif**

Debussy

### EXAMPLE 11.5.2

"Laideronnette, Impératrice des Pagodes," from *La Mère l'Oye*

m. 105–134

Ravel

**Mov't de Marche**

### EXAMPLE 11.5.3

*The Cherry Tree Carol*

**Gently**

Kentucky

### EXAMPLE 11.5.4

"Passepied," from *Suite Bergamasque*

m. 3–10

Debussy

**EXAMPLE 11.5.5**

*Helft mir Gott's Güte preisen*

J.S. Bach

**EXAMPLE 11.5.6**

**EXAMPLE 11.5.7**

**EXAMPLE 11.5.8**

"Es ist genug, so nimm, Herr," from *Cantata No. 60*

J.S. Bach

**EXAMPLE 11.5.9**

"Pagodes," from *Estampes*

m. 33–37

**Sans lenteur**

Debussy

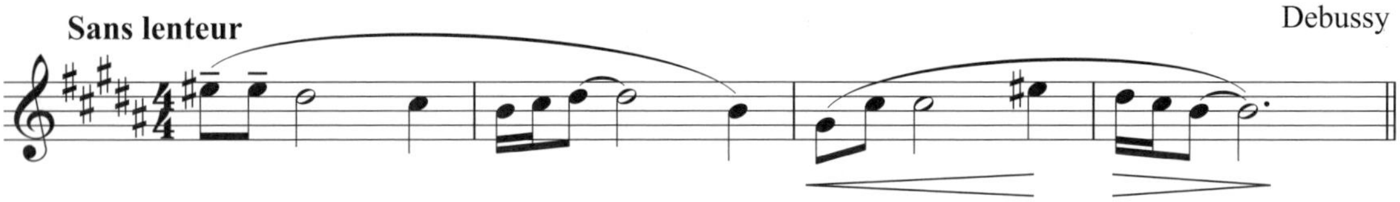

**EXAMPLE 11.5.10**

"Christus, der uns selig macht"

J.S. Bach

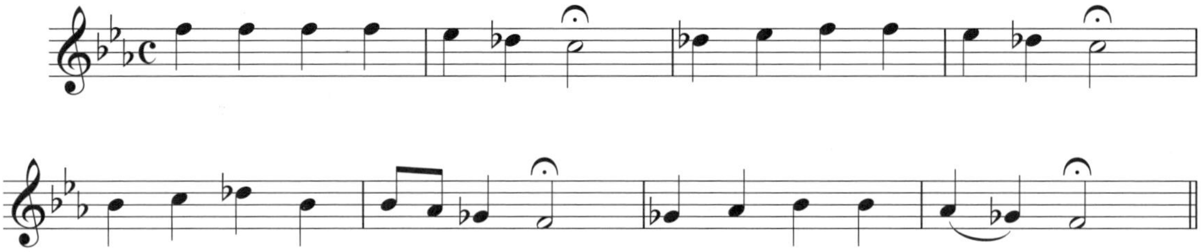

**EXAMPLE 11.5.11**

*Mazurka*, Op. 41, No.1

**Maestoso**

Chopin

**EXAMPLE 11.5.12**

*O Virgo Splendens*

Anonymous, fourteenth-century Spain

## 11.6 Non-Western Music from the Literature

Folk music from non-Western cultures provides a large body of music that utilizes non-traditional scales. The folk songs below provide a sampling of the diverse sounds and scale structures available to musicians. As with all music that uses non-traditional scales, begin by figuring out the scale and its important characteristics. Sing that scale and get used to its sound. See how that sound helps to tell the musical story in each song.

### Music from Africa

**EXAMPLE 11.6.1**

*Ngoma Kurila* (A Lament)

**EXAMPLE 11.6.2**

*Woza* (Come)

African Song

**EXAMPLE 11.6.3**

*Amampondo* (Pondo Man)

African Song

**EXAMPLE 11.6.4**

*Kwaheri*

Traditional Kenyan Song

## Music from Australia

### EXAMPLE 11.6.5

*The Green New Chum*

Australian Bush Song

### EXAMPLE 11.6.6

*Where's Your Licence?*

Australian Bush Song

### EXAMPLE 11.6.7

*Farewell to the Ladies of Brisbane*

Australian Bush Song

## Music from Japan

**EXAMPLE 11.6.8**

*Hotaru Koi*

3-part round

Traditional Japanese Song

## Music from China

**EXAMPLE 11.6.9**

*Hua Ku Ka* No. 2 (The Flower Drum)

Chinese Song

**EXAMPLE 11.6.10**

*Ch'u T'ou Ko* (Farmer's Song)

Chinese Song

**EXAMPLE 11.6.11**

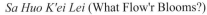

*Sa Huo K'ei Lei* (What Flow'r Blooms?)

Chinese Song

## Jewish Folk Music

**EXAMPLE 11.6.12**

*Die Alte Kashe*

Jewish Folk Song

**EXAMPLE 11.6.13**

*Mi Y'malel*

Chanukkah Song

**EXAMPLE 11.6.14**

*Ruchot Hayam*

Jewish Folk Song

## Native American Music

**EXAMPLE 11.6.15**

*Haliwa-Saponi Canoe Dance*

Native American

**EXAMPLE 11.6.16**

*Song to the Four Directions*

Native American

**EXAMPLE 11.6.17**

*Basket Dance*

Native American

## Reflections: Being an Advocate for Music

Many music students enter college with a view that music is the vehicle that will provide them with a career, and possibly even fame and fortune. Most of us entered this field at least partly because of the "rush" we felt as an audience clapped for a performance—for *our* performance. Being a musician, however, is both a privilege and a responsibility. Success in the field of music also requires one to be an effective advocate for one's art. In order for music to continue to be the vehicle through which we develop our careers, every musician must also "give back" to the field through effective arts advocacy, training the next generation of musicians, and insisting on the continued improvement and development of music as an art. It is only through these actions that we will be able to demonstrate the importance of live and new music as a cornerstone of our culture, build and retain audiences for our craft, and demonstrate the relevance of what we do. If we fail to do these things, then we imperil the future of the very thing that we ask to sustain us.

Being an advocate for music involves demonstrating the importance of live and new music in the life of our culture. We do this through demonstrating professionalism and, more importantly, excellence in our craft. We do what we do not only because we love it but also because it is not something that everybody can do. Part of artistry is the goal of inspiring awe on the part of our audience, so that they too can aspire to greatness through our example.

Music advocacy also involves promoting new music. Musicians who only perform music from the "standard repertory" risk becoming living museums—a window only into our culture's past and not fully connected to the intellectual and artistic life of our time. To do this effectively, however, one must insist not only on excellence (there's that word again) but also on the development of a strong sense of aesthetic discrimination. We are the agents who create, discover, and select the master works of our time. It is, along with training the next generation of musicians, our gift to the future.

Finally, music advocacy involves insisting that what we do is important. Music, as all art, has the ability to elevate humankind above the mundane and ordinary. It has the capacity to ask questions and reveal truths that may take science generations to uncover. Musicians must insist that they have a value to society that goes far beyond economics.

As you develop your skills and embark on your career, pay attention to how your attitude toward and relationship with music is likely to change. Whereas many music students come to college thinking that music will serve them, the most successful ones leave considering how they can serve the art.

## 11.7 Dictation Materials

### I. Scale Identification

Your teacher will play melodies based on exotic scales. For each, begin by determining the number of notes that comprise the scale. Next, determine its modality (major or minor). After that, listen for the approach to tonic from below—it will most commonly be a leading tone (minor second), subtonic (major second), or minor third. Next, listen for altered scale degrees. Finally, if the scale used in the melody has a name, provide it. Otherwise, create a name that describes what you hear (for example, a harmonic minor scale with a raised fourth scale degree).

*Date:* . . . . . . . . . . . . . .

**TABLE 11.1**

| No. of Notes | Modality | Approach to Tonic | Altered Scale Degrees | Scale Name |
|---|---|---|---|---|
| | | | | |
| | | | | |
| | | | | |
| | | | | |

**TABLE 11.2**

| No. of Notes | Modality | Approach to Tonic | Altered Scale Degrees | Scale Name |
|---|---|---|---|---|
| | | | | |
| | | | | |
| | | | | |
| | | | | |

**TABLE 11.3**

| No. of Notes | Modality | Approach to Tonic | Altered Scale Degrees | Scale Name |
|---|---|---|---|---|
| | | | | |
| | | | | |
| | | | | |
| | | | | |

**TABLE 11.4**

| No. of Notes | Modality | Approach to Tonic | Altered Scale Degrees | Scale Name |
|---|---|---|---|---|
| | | | | |
| | | | | |
| | | | | |
| | | | | |

**TABLE 11.5**

| No. of Notes | Modality | Approach to Tonic | Altered Scale Degrees | Scale Name |
|---|---|---|---|---|
| | | | | |
| | | | | |
| | | | | |
| | | | | |

## II. Melodic and Rhythmic Dictation

Your teacher will play a short melody or rhythm. Notate it on the staves below. Remember to write the rhythm first. Next try to determine what scale is being used. Remember to add in the appropriate accidentals to stay in the scale.

*Date:* . . . . . . . . . . . . . .

*Date:* . . . . . . . . . . . . . .

*Date:* . . . . . . . . . . . . . .

*Date:* . . . . . . . . . . . . . .

*Date:* . . . . . . . . . . . . . .

## Chapter 12

# Twentieth-century Material based on Non-Tonal Models

## 12.1 Whole-tone, Octatonic, and other Non-Tonal Scales

### Facts You Need to Know

A whole-tone scale is a six-note scale consisting entirely of whole steps.

**EXAMPLE 12.1.1**

An octatonic scale is an eight-note scale that alternates whole steps and half steps. Octatonic scales can begin with a half step (0–1 octatonic) or a whole step (0–2 octatonic).

**EXAMPLE 12.1.2**

(Because both scales are constructed to avoid tonicizing any particular pitch, note that the top number refers to the scale degree of each pitch, while the bottom number indicates the number of semitones above the starting pitch—a numbering system called integer notation. Integer notation will be explained more fully in Chapter 12, Section 2, Atonality.)

## Hearing

Because these scales symmetrically divide the octave, there is no built-in drive towards any particular pitch as being tonic. As a result, these scales have an indeterminate sound that is often described as "floaty," "ethereal," or "dream-like." As with all scales, begin by counting pitches, listening for tonal center and modality. If no tonal center is apparent, listen for the presence or absence of minor seconds.

## Singing

Begin singing both scales by dividing them into three-note segments. Each of these segments individually suggests a recognizable tonal structure:

Whole-tone scale: first three pitches of a major scale
0–2 octatonic scale: first three pitches of a minor scale
0–1 octatonic scale: scale degrees 3–4–5 in the major mode

**EXAMPLE 12.1.3**

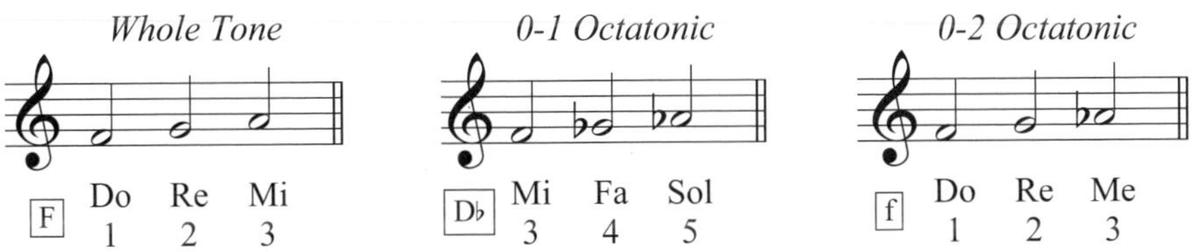


When you reach the end of each three-note segment, treat the last pitch as the starting point for the next three-note segment. Repeat until you reach the octave.

**EXAMPLE 12.1.4**

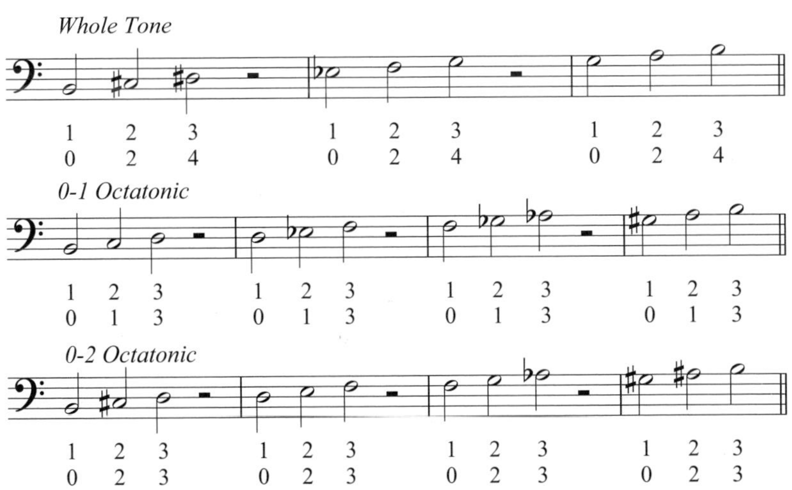

Once you feel comfortable singing the three-note segments individually, try singing the scale without pausing to "reset" your tonal center.

## Assignments for Practice

### Pitch Patterns

#### PITCH PATTERN 12.1.1

#### PITCH PATTERN 12.1.2

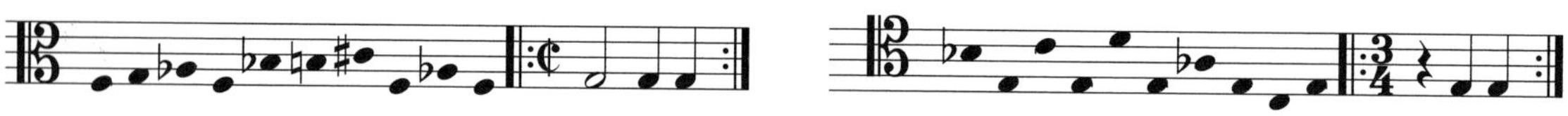

#### PITCH PATTERN 12.1.3

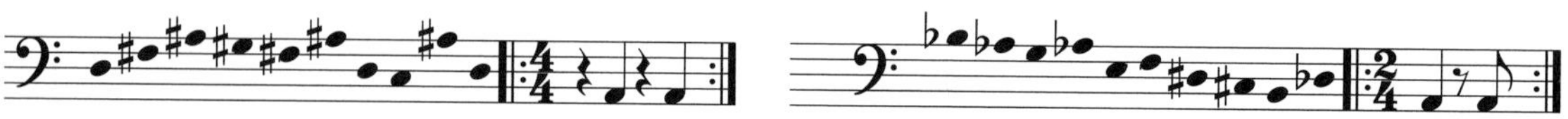

### Melodies

#### MELODY 12.1.1

#### MELODY 12.1.2

MELODY 12.1.3

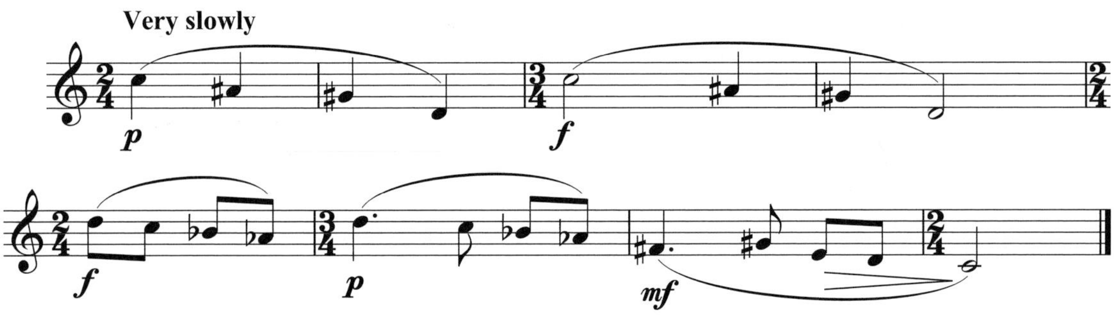


MELODY 12.1.4

MELODY 12.1.5

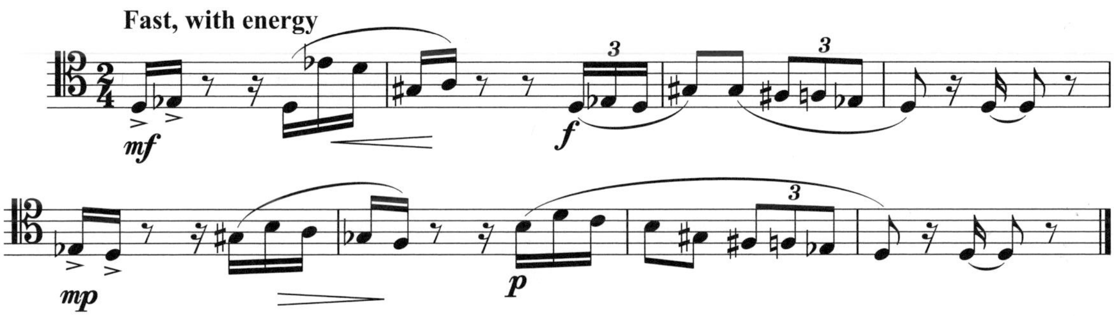


MELODY 12.1.6

MELODY 12.1.7

MELODY 12.1.8

MELODY 12.1.9

MELODY 12.1.10

## MELODY 12.1.11

## MELODY 12.1.12

## MELODY 12.1.13

## MELODY 12.1.14

### MELODY 12.1.15

## Duets

### DUET 12.1.1

### DUET 12.1.2

DUET 12.1.3

## Chorale

CHORALE 12.1

## Self-Accompanied Melody

### SELF-ACCOMPANIED MELODY 12.1

## 12.2 Atonality

### Facts You Need to Know

Atonal music seeks to avoid establishing a hierarchy of pitches.

The syllable system you have used up to now has been based in tonal relationships. When music purposefully avoids establishing a tonal center, these labels become meaningless. A different labeling system is commonly used to show relationships in atonal music. This system labels the lowest pitch in a structure as "0." Other pitches are labeled based on the number of semitones between it and the lowest pitch. The table below shows the integer equivalent of the common interval names:

| | |
|---|---|
| Perfect Unison | 0 |
| Minor Second | 1 |
| Major Second | 2 |
| Minor Third | 3 |
| Major Third | 4 |
| Perfect Fourth | 5 |

| | |
|---|---|
| Tritone | 6 |
| Perfect Fifth | 7 |
| Minor Sixth | 8 |
| Major Sixth | 9 |
| Minor Seventh | 10 |
| Major Seventh | 11 |
| Perfect Octave | 12 |

There are three common techniques for hearing and singing atonal music. You should learn and practice all three. While you will probably rely more on one than the others, you will most likely need to employ a combination of the three to effectively hear and sing atonal music.

### Method 1: Sing Intervals

When singing tonal music, you were specifically instructed to sing scale degrees instead of intervals. Since atonal music is constructed using a different set of "rules," and, as a result of continuing to practice your intervals, you either have achieved (or will achieve) a high level of proficiency singing and recognizing intervals, you may choose to figure out parts of melodies by dealing exclusively with their interval content. Note that most professional musicians who regularly perform atonal music state that this is the method they use least frequently.

### Method 2: Find Small Intervals

Even in the most disjunct and angular atonal melodies, some pitches will end up repeating others or being immediately next to others. Find these relationships and use them to retain the integrity of pitch in the melody.

### Method 3: Rapidly Shifting Tonic

From the beginning, the method this textbook employs has been based on the idea that people hear tonally. If this is true, atonal music presents a serious problem. Some musicians deal with this by figuring out how to hear atonal music in short tonal segments that rapidly shift. This method requires thorough study of the score and planning of one's tonal shifts.

## Preliminary Melodies

The following melodies are specifically designed to practice Method 2, finding small intervals above. Each is constructed from two or more chromatic lines that are intertwined. Begin by finding and singing the notes of one line at a time, leaving space (rest) for the pitches in the other melodic line(s). Once you are comfortable with each line individually, then try singing them together, keeping track of how each line moves individually. Listen for "friendly" intervals (such as perfect octaves, fourths, or fifths) between the lines that can help you determine whether you are maintaining the integrity of the pitches.

**PRELIMINARY MELODY 12.2.1**

**PRELIMINARY MELODY 12.2.2**

**PRELIMINARY MELODY 12.2.3**

**PRELIMINARY MELODY 12.2.4**

**PRELIMINARY MELODY 12.2.5**

**PRELIMINARY MELODY 12.2.6**

**PRELIMINARY MELODY 12.2.7**

**PRELIMINARY MELODY 12.2.8**

## Pitch Patterns

### PITCH PATTERN 12.2.1

### PITCH PATTERN 12.2.2

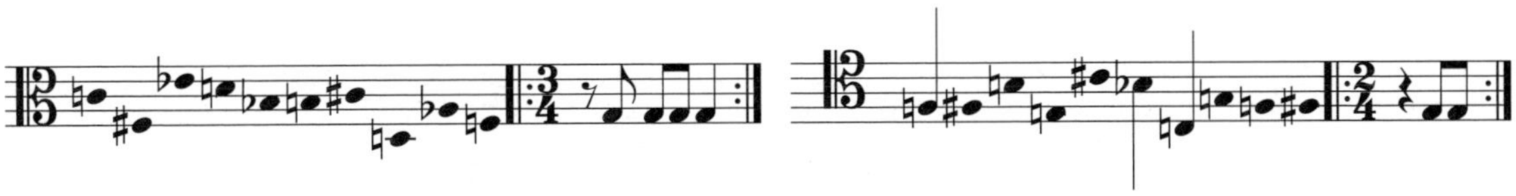

### PITCH PATTERN 12.2.3

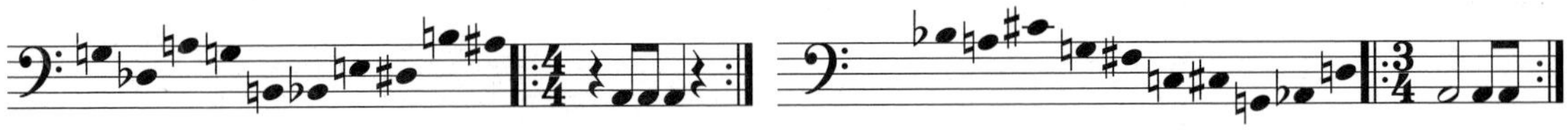

## Melodies

### MELODY 12.2.1

### MELODY 12.2.2

MELODY 12.2.3

MELODY 12.2.4

MELODY 12.2.5

MELODY 12.2.6

### MELODY 12.2.7

### MELODY 12.2.8

### MELODY 12.2.9

### MELODY 12.2.10

## Duets

### DUET 12.2.1

Adagio

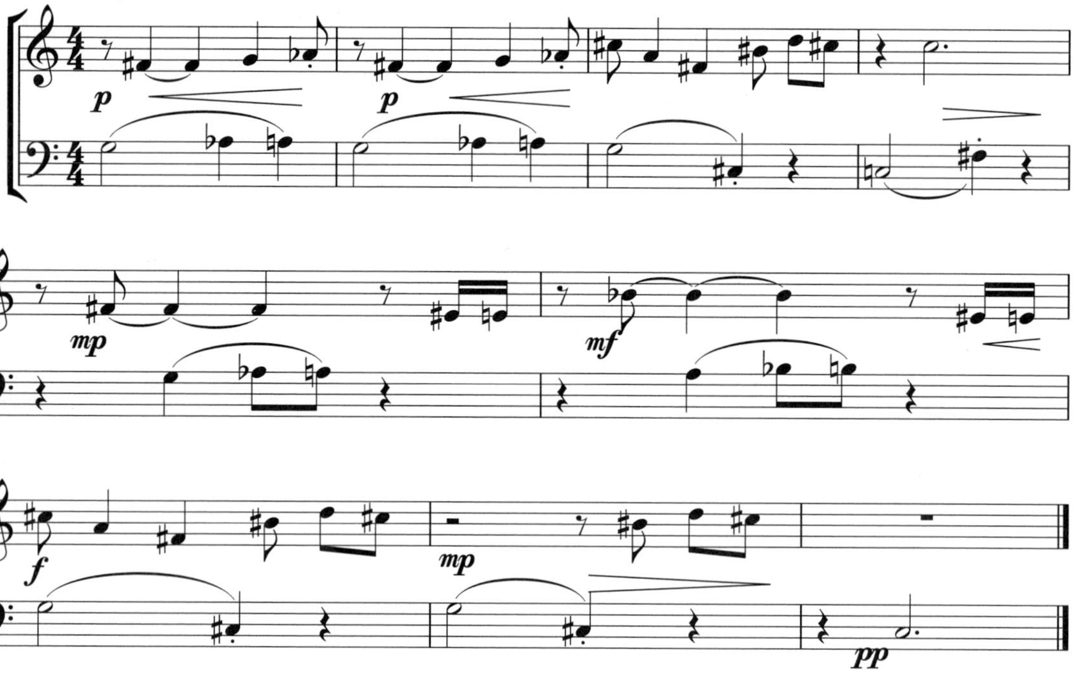

### DUET 12.2.2

Vif

**DUET 12.2.3**

## Chorale

**CHORALE 12.2**

## Self-Accompanied Melody

### SELF-ACCOMPANIED MELODY 12.2

## 12.3 Atonal Trichords and Manipulating Atonal Sets

### Facts You Need to Know

One way of organizing and explaining musical structures is through the use of set theory. Set theory, originally developed by and borrowed from the field of mathematics, is based on the idea that it is easier to make meaningful descriptions of and comparisons between things if they are placed into logical, small groups.

When applied to music, set theory usually involves the placing of pitches into these groups. Comparing the properties of these groups can reveal whether certain combinations of pitches or intervals (the spaces between the pitches) appear with regularity or in a pattern.

One easy group of musical sets to memorize and manipulate are trichords. There are only twelve possible combinations of intervals formed when three unique pitches are grouped together in a set. The chart below describes these twelve sets. Each box contains:

1. The Forte number: where this set exists in a numbering system developed by the noted music theorist Allen Forte.
2. The prime form of the set: the most compact statement of the three pitches with the smallest intervals appearing closer toward the lowest pitch, which is labeled as "0."

3. The inverted form of the set: the most compact statement of the three pitches with the smallest intervals appearing closer toward the highest pitch. Notice that sets in the top row of the chart do not have inverted forms.
4. The interval content of the set.

You should memorize all information in this chart:

| | | | |
|---|---|---|---|
| 3–1<br>012<br>Two minor seconds<br>One major second | 3–6<br>024<br>Two major seconds<br>One major third | 3–10<br>036<br>Two minor thirds<br>One tritone | 3–12<br>048<br>Two major thirds<br>One minor sixth |
| 3–2<br>013<br>023<br>One minor second<br>One major second<br>One minor third | 3–7<br>025<br>035<br>One major second<br>One minor third<br>One perfect fourth | 3–11<br>037<br>047<br>One minor third<br>One major third<br>One perfect fifth | |
| 3–3<br>014<br>034<br>One minor second<br>One minor third<br>One major third | 3–8<br>026<br>046<br>One major second<br>One major third<br>One tritone | | |
| 3–4<br>015<br>045<br>One minor second<br>One major third<br>One perfect fourth | 3–9<br>027<br>057<br>One major second<br>One perfect fourth<br>One perfect fifth | | |
| 3–5<br>016<br>056<br>One minor second<br>One perfect fourth<br>One tritone | | | |

Musical sets are commonly manipulated in a few ways. Notice that none of these change the interval content of the set. Even though the pitches may be different, the set, and its characteristic sound, remains the same.

1. Reordering: the exact same pitches appear in a different order. (For the six possible orderings of trichords, see Section 1.10, Major Triads in Root Position.)

**EXAMPLE 12.3.1**

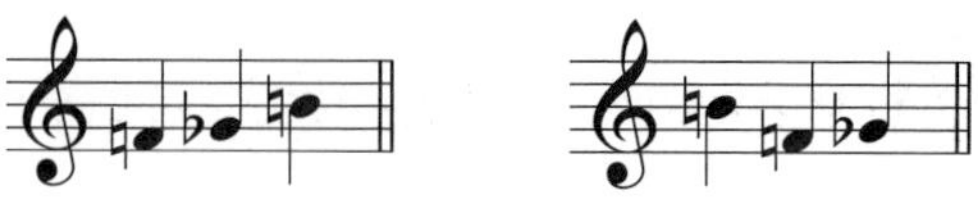

2. Pitch displacement: one or more of the pitches are displaced by an octave, resulting in a different musical contour.

**EXAMPLE 12.3.2**

3. Transposition: all of the pitches are moved by the same interval.

**EXAMPLE 12.3.3**

4. Inversion: the intervals of the set are placed in reverse order.

**EXAMPLE 12.3.4**

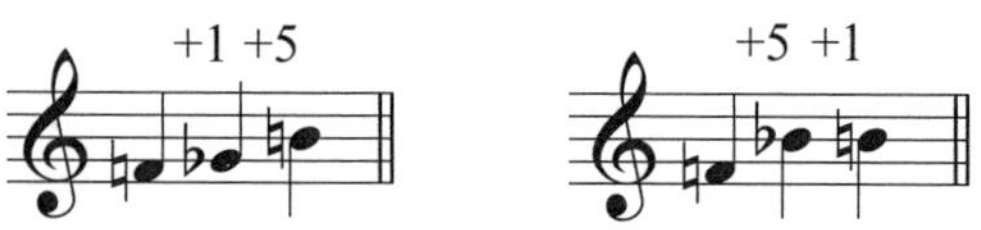


Notice that multiple operations may be performed on a set at the same time.

## Hearing

### Trichords

1. To identify trichords, begin by reordering the pitches from low to high, in your head if necessary.
2. Determine the interval formed by the boundary pitches of the set (the lowest and highest).
3. Next, listen for the placement of the interior pitch. Determine the interval either above the lower or below the higher boundary pitch. Use your knowledge of intervals (and math!) to determine the remaining interval.

4. Use your knowledge of the interval content of each trichord (from the chart above) to determine the correct trichord.

### Set-based Melodies

1. Begin as you would any melodic dictation: figure out the rhythm and starting pitch.
2. Listen for the first statement of the set—it will usually appear prominently at the beginning of the piece.
3. Listen for identifying characteristics of the set. For example, if the set utilizes a semitone, listen specifically for instances of that semitone throughout the melody. Mark them.
4. Use your techniques for hearing atonal melodies (see Chapter 12, Section 2, Atonality) to fill in the remaining pitches.

## Singing

### Trichords

1. Begin by singing the boundary pitches of the set.
2. Place the remaining pitch above the lower boundary pitch (if in prime form) or below the upper boundary pitch (if in inverted form).
3. Perform other operations such as reordering or displacement.

### Set-based Melodies

Use your techniques for singing atonal melodies described in Section 12.2. Be aware of identifying characteristics of the set (such as an identifying interval) that you can use to maintain the integrity of the melody.

## Assignments for Practice

### Pitch Patterns

**PITCH PATTERN 12.3.1**

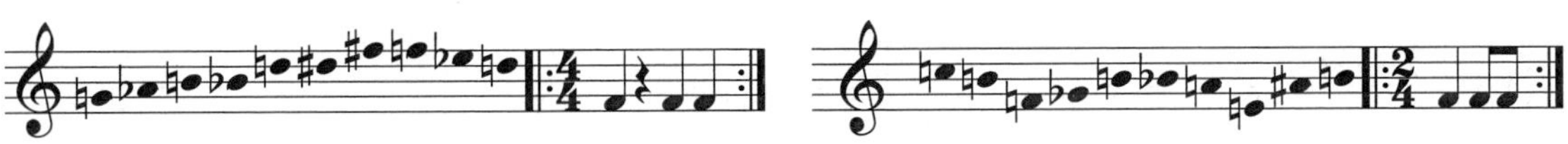

**PITCH PATTERN 12.3.2**

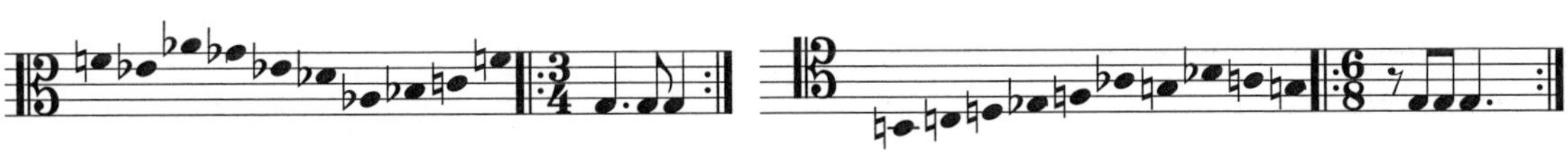

**PITCH PATTERN 12.3.3**

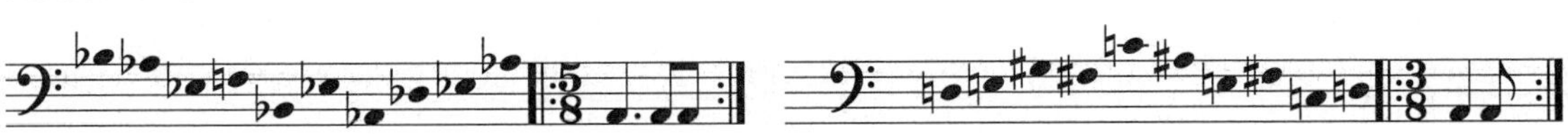

## Melodies

### MELODY 12.3.1

### MELODY 12.3.2

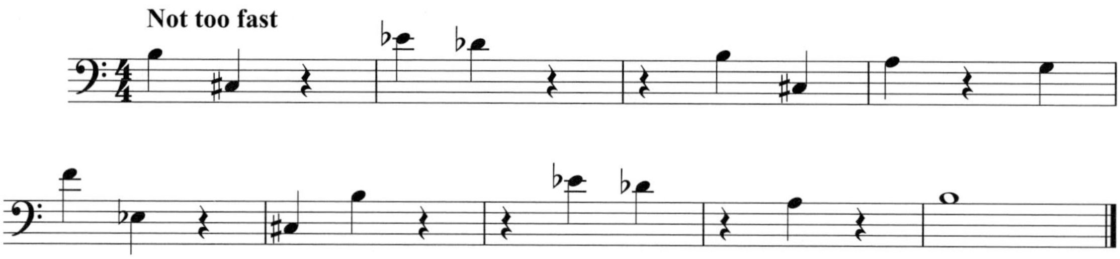


### MELODY 12.3.3

### MELODY 12.3.4

**MELODY 12.3.5**

**Allegro**

**MELODY 12.3.6**

**Feroce**

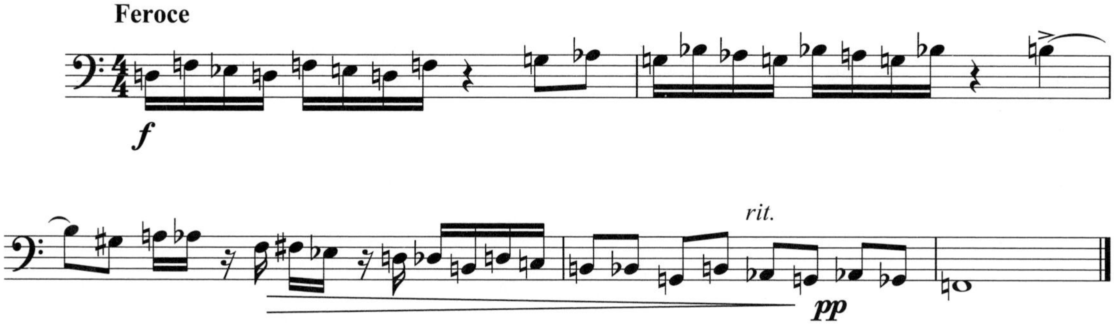


**MELODY 12.3.7**

**Moderato**

**MELODY 12.3.8**

**Schnell**

**MELODY 12.3.9**

**Tango**

## MELODY 12.3.10

## MELODY 12.3.11

## MELODY 12.3.12

## MELODY 12.3.13

## MELODY 12.3.14

### MELODY 12.3.15

## Duets

### DUET 12.3.1

### DUET 12.3.2

### DUET 12.3.3

## Chorale

### CHORALE 12.3

## Self-Accompanied Melody

### SELF-ACCOMPANIED MELODY 12.3

## 12.4 Larger Atonal Sets and Serial Music

### Facts You Need to Know

Set-based atonal music can utilize groups of notes of any size. The techniques for organizing this music and manipulating these sets remain the same.

In atonal music, the ordering of the pitches in the set is not important to the organization of the music. In serial music, the ordering is essential. All the pitches in the set must appear before the set can repeat in either its original or a modified form. The most common form of serial music involves cycling through all twelve chromatic pitches.

These organizational schemes do not significantly impact upon the sound of the music. You can still rely on the techniques you have already learned for singing and hearing atonal music.

### Hearing

Use the same techniques for hearing atonal music that you learned earlier in this chapter.

### Singing

Use the same techniques for singing atonal music that you learned earlier in this chapter.

### Assignments for Practice

#### Melodies

**MELODY 12.4.1**

**MELODY 12.4.2**

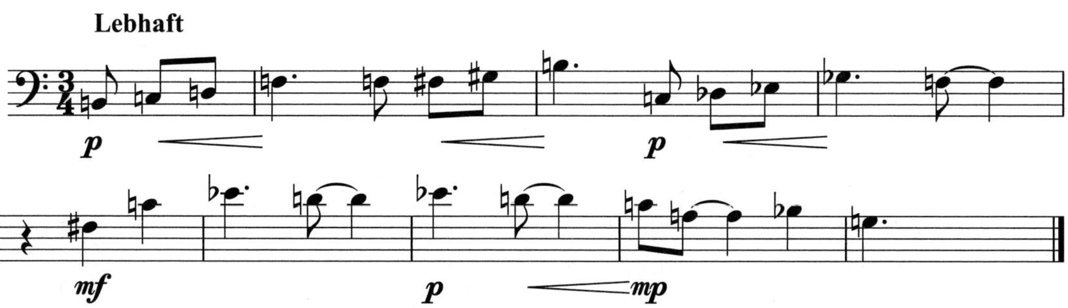

### MELODY 12.4.3

### MELODY 12.4.4

### MELODY 12.4.5

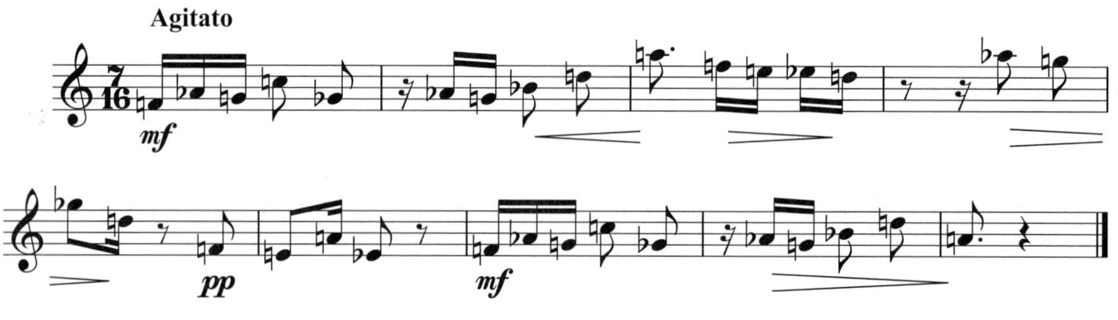


### MELODY 12.4.6

MELODY 12.4.7

MELODY 12.4.8

MELODY 12.4.9

MELODY 12.4.10

**MELODY 12.4.11**

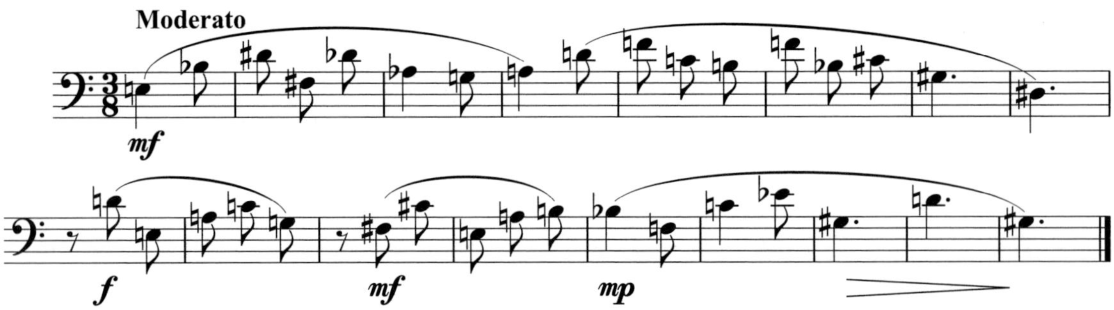


**MELODY 12.4.12**

**MELODY 12.4.13**

**MELODY 12.4.14**

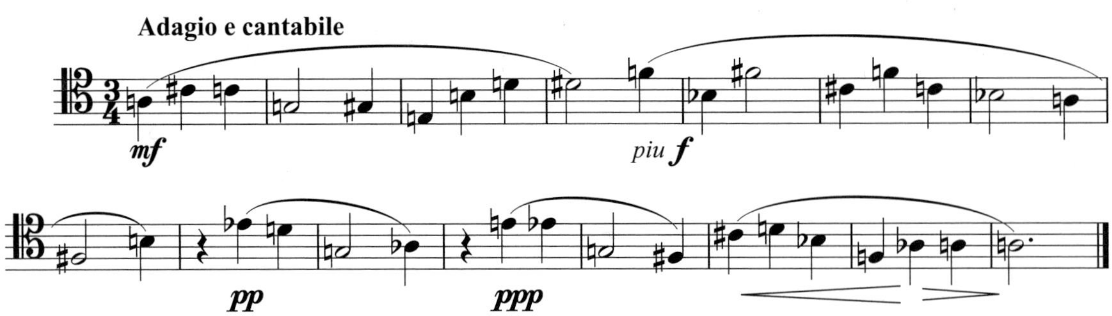

**MELODY 12.4.15**

**Allegro leggiero**

## Duets

**DUET 12.4.1**

**Moderately fast**

**DUET 12.4.2**

**March tempo**

DUET 12.4.3

## Chorale

CHORALE 12.4

## Self-Accompanied Melody

### SELF-ACCOMPANIED MELODY 12.4

## 12.5 Music from the Literature

### EXAMPLE 12.5.1

"Free Variations," from *Mikrokosmos*, No. 140

Bartok

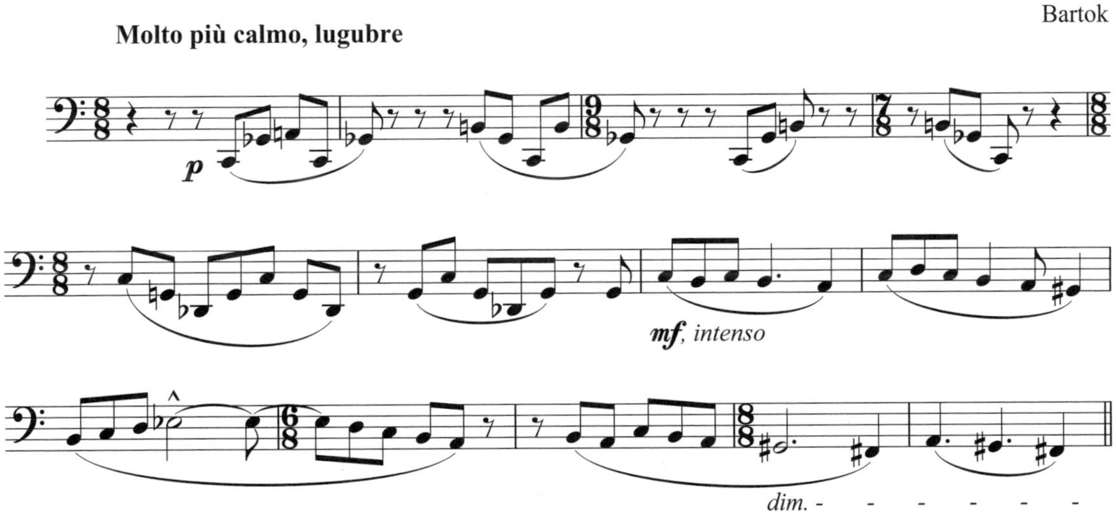

**EXAMPLE 12.5.2**

*The Cage*

Charles Ives

**EXAMPLE 12.5.3**

"Whole Tone Scale," from *Mikrokosmos* No. 136

m. 1–12, left hand

**Andante**

Bartok

**EXAMPLE 12.5.4**

"Nacht," from *Seven Early Songs* (1907)

Alban Berg

**Sehr langsam**

**EXAMPLE 12.5.5**

"Sleep," from *Six Elizabethan Songs*

Dominick Argento

**Lentamente**

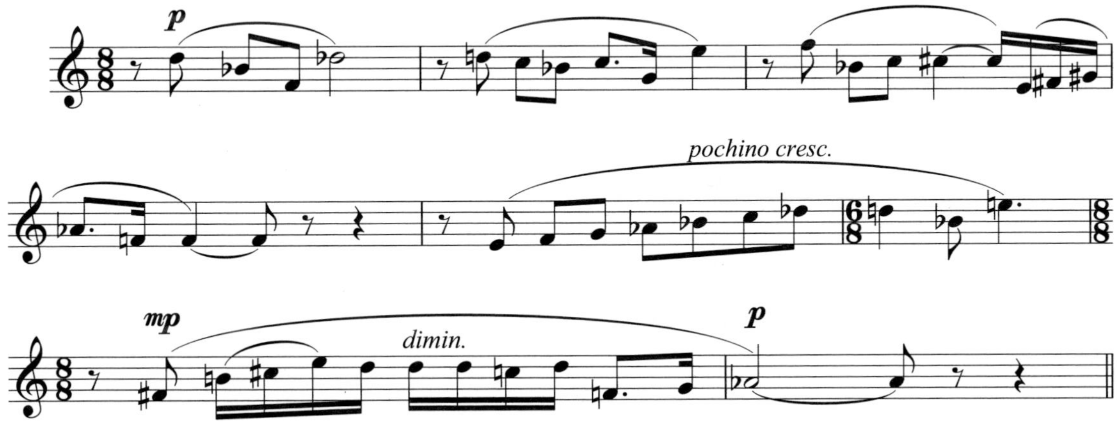

**EXAMPLE 12.5.6**

From *Piano Variations* (1930)

m. 12–20

**Grave**

Aaron Copland

**EXAMPLE 12.5.7**

"Voiles," from *Préludes pour Piano*, Book I

m. 10–21

Debussy

**Modéré**

**EXAMPLE 12.5.8**

From *La Lugubre Gondola*, II

m. 23–32

**Andante mesto, non troppo lento**

Liszt

**EXAMPLE 12.5.9**

"Tot," from *Three Songs*, Op. 48

**Etwas langsam** Arnold Schoenberg

**EXAMPLE 12.5.10**

Prelude 4, from *Five Preludes*, Op. 15

**Lent, vague, indécis** Alexander Scriabin

**EXAMPLE 12.5.11**

"Thema," from *Variations for Orchestra*, Op. 31,
Cello line

m. 34–50

Arnold Schoenberg

Used by permission of Belmont Music Publishers.

**EXAMPLE 12.5.12**

"Galop," from *Souvenirs*, Op. 28

Samuel Barber

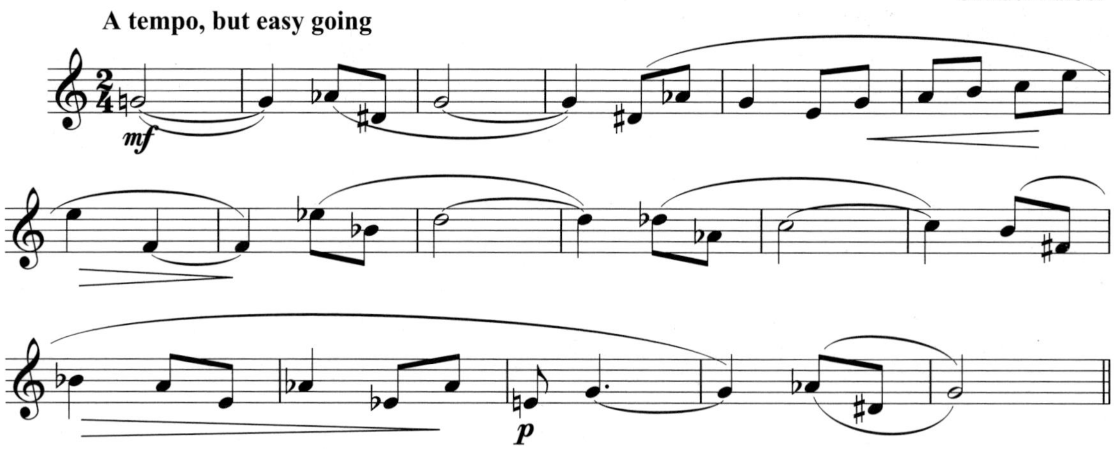

## Reflections: A Life of Solfège

So you're just about to finish your last aural skills test. No more stressing out over identifying intervals or chords. No more writing down or figuring out melodies. Think back on where you were two years ago when you first started taking your aural skills courses. Do you remember how there were a lot of things that you could tell sounded "right" or "wrong," but you couldn't say why? Do you remember how you discovered that feeling of incompleteness when a phrase ended on scale degree two instead of one? Do you remember your first awkward attempts at improvising tonic harmony? Take a look back at the melodies and chapters in the first units of this book. Those chapters almost certainly look a lot easier now. You may not even have stopped to realize it, but you probably don't hear music the same way that you did when you first started aural skills two years ago. You have certainly come a long way!

Let's consider how your ear got to where it is today. Basic concepts were laid down, and then each new structure was related to those basic concepts. Each time you undoubtedly had to practice, but as the individual musical topics got more complex, the things that you had already learned probably seemed to become easier. Some of this newer material could sure use some extra time to sink in, so it's too bad that this class is over. Or is it?

You became good at solfège through practice. If you're like most people, you probably feel that you could become even better with more practice. You've probably found yourself starting to apply some of the things you have learned in this class to practice on your instrument or learning music for a solo recital or ensemble performance. The truth is, solfège is one of the basic sustaining skills of every professional musician. The strength of your ear and your musical mind is the basis for your career, and it only stays strong (or gets stronger) through continued daily practice.

So, although your aural skills class might be over, your time practicing and improving your aural skills certainly isn't. The big difference is that now you are on your own. As you encounter musical problems in your career, think back on the skills and approaches you used in this class. Practice adapting them to your current situation.

Music acts like a language in many ways. One cannot achieve or maintain fluency in a language without regularly speaking and interpreting it. The same is true for music. Also, the characteristic that separates the successful professional musician from the amateur is one's sensitivity to sound. This is a skill that can never be overly developed, and increasing one's sensitivity to what he or she hears also increases one's enjoyment of music. Every performance has the opportunity to be a completely surprising and transformational experience.

So keep practicing, work to be a better musician today than you were yesterday, and remember to always seek out the joy of immersing oneself in music.

## 12.6 Dictation Materials

@

### I. Interval Identification

Identify each interval you hear using integers instead of traditional names. Be sure to use the plus or minus sign to indicate direction.

*Date:* . . . . . . . . . . . . . .

1. ____ 2. ____ 3. ____ 4. ____ 5. ____ 6. ____ 7. ____ 8. ____ 9. ____ 10. ____

*Date:* . . . . . . . . . . . . . .

1. ____ 2. ____ 3. ____ 4. ____ 5. ____ 6. ____ 7. ____ 8. ____ 9. ____ 10. ____

*Date:* . . . . . . . . . . . . . .

1. ____ 2. ____ 3. ____ 4. ____ 5. ____ 6. ____ 7. ____ 8. ____ 9. ____ 10. ____

*Date:* . . . . . . . . . . . . . .

1. ____ 2. ____ 3. ____ 4. ____ 5. ____ 6. ____ 7. ____ 8. ____ 9. ____ 10. ____

*Date:* . . . . . . . . . . . . . .

1. ____ 2. ____ 3. ____ 4. ____ 5. ____ 6. ____ 7. ____ 8. ____ 9. ____ 10. ____

### II. Trichord Identification

You will hear several three-note sets (trichords). Begin by determining the interval content of the set. Provide either the prime form of the set or its Forte number, as requested by your teacher. If the set is inverted, place a letter "I" after your answer. Beware of set reorderings and pitch displacements!

*Date:* . . . . . . . . . . . . . .

1. ____ 2. ____ 3. ____ 4. ____ 5. ____ 6. ____ 7. ____ 8. ____ 9. ____ 10. ____

*Date:* . . . . . . . . . . . . . .

1. ____ 2. ____ 3. ____ 4. ____ 5. ____ 6. ____ 7. ____ 8. ____ 9. ____ 10. ____

*Date:* . . . . . . . . . . . . . .

1. ____ 2. ____ 3. ____ 4. ____ 5. ____ 6. ____ 7. ____ 8. ____ 9. ____ 10. ____

*Date:* . . . . . . . . . . . . . .

1. ____ 2. ____ 3. ____ 4. ____ 5. ____ 6. ____ 7. ____ 8. ____ 9. ____ 10. ____

*Date:* . . . . . . . . . . . . . .

1. ____ 2. ____ 3. ____ 4. ____ 5. ____ 6. ____ 7. ____ 8. ____ 9. ____ 10. ____

## III. Set Relationships

You will hear several pairs of sets. Determine if each pair is related (the same prime form or Forte number) and, if so, how they are related. Possible answers are:

T—Related by transposition
I—Related by inversion
X—No relationship; the two sets have different prime forms
D—Related by pitch displacement
R—Related by reordering

*Date:* . . . . . . . . . . . . . .

1. ____ 2. ____ 3. ____ 4. ____ 5. ____ 6. ____ 7. ____ 8. ____ 9. ____ 10. ____

*Date:* . . . . . . . . . . . . . .

1. ____ 2. ____ 3. ____ 4. ____ 5. ____ 6. ____ 7. ____ 8. ____ 9. ____ 10. ____

*Date:* . . . . . . . . . . . . . .

1. ____ 2. ____ 3. ____ 4. ____ 5. ____ 6. ____ 7. ____ 8. ____ 9. ____ 10. ____

*Date:* . . . . . . . . . . . . . .

1. ____ 2. ____ 3. ____ 4. ____ 5. ____ 6. ____ 7. ____ 8. ____ 9. ____ 10. ____

*Date:* . . . . . . . . . . . . . .

1. ____ 2. ____ 3. ____ 4. ____ 5. ____ 6. ____ 7. ____ 8. ____ 9. ____ 10. ____

## IV. Melodic and Rhythmic Dictation

Your teacher will play a short melody or rhythm. Notate it on the staves below. Remember to write the rhythm first. Listen specifically for pitches that return or are near to each other (pitch affinity), recurring intervals, short fragments of tonality, and "friendly" intervals.

*Date:* . . . . . . . . . . . . . .

*Date:* . . . . . . . . . . . . . .

*Date:* . . . . . . . . . . . . . .

*Date:* . . . . . . . . . . . . . .

*Date:* . . . . . . . . . . . . . .

# Appendix A: Glossary of Musical Terms

**a tempo** (It.) return to the previous tempo
**abschwellen** (Ger.) getting softer
**accelerando** (accel.) (It.) gradually getting faster
**adagietto** (It.) slightly faster than adagio; with ease
**adagio** (It.) slowly, with ease
**affretando** (It.) hurrying
**agitato** (It.) agitated
**alla** (It.) in, in the style of . . .
**allargando** (It.) growing slower
**allegretto** (It.) moderately fast
**allegro** (It.) fast
**allegro ma non troppo** (It.) fast, but not too fast
**andante** (It.) moderately slow, walking tempo
**andantino** (It.) moderately slow
**animato** (It.) lively, with spirit
**animé** (Fr.) animated, lively
**ardent** (Fr.), **ardente** (It.) fiery
**assai** (It.) very
**assez** (Fr.) rather, enough
**aufhalter** (Ger.) slowing down (*see also* **ritard**)
**ausdruck** (Ger.) with heartfelt expression
**avec** (Fr.) with

**behaglich** (Ger.) easily
**belebt** (Ger.) animated, brisk
**bene** (It.) well (**ben marcato**—well marked)
**bewegt** (Ger.) moved, agitated
**bewegter** (Ger.) getting faster
**breit** (Ger.) broad, stately

**calando** (It.) "decreasing," gradually becoming softer
**calcando** (It.) "pressing," hastening the tempo
**cantabile** (It.) in a singing style
**cèdez** (Fr.) go slower
**chaleur** (Fr.) warmth
**comodo** (It.) easy, leisurely, at a convenient pace
**con** (It.) with

**con brio** (It.) "with noise," spiritedly
**con caloroso** (It.) with warmth
**con forza** (It.) with force, energy
**con fuoco** (It.) with fire
**con moto** (It.) with motion
**crescendo** (cresc.) (It.) gradually growing louder

**decrescendo** (decresc.) (It.) gradually growing softer
**deficiendo** (It.) dying away
**diminuendo** (dim.) (It.) gradually growing softer
**dolce** (It.) sweetly and softly
**dolente** (It.) doleful, plaintive, sad, sorrowful
**douce(ment), doux** (Fr.) sweetly

**einfach** (Ger.) with simplicity
**en dehors** (Fr.) to bring out (a melody or voice)
**espressivo** (espr.) (It.) with expression
**etwas** (Ger.) rather, somewhat

**facile** (Fr.) easily
**feuerig, mit feuer** (Ger.) fiery

**gedehnt** (Ger.) sustained, prolonged, slow, stately
**gefällig** (Ger.) pleasing, graceful
**gemächlich** (Ger.) easy, comfortably
**gemessen** (Ger.) held back, sustained
**geschwindt** (Ger.) swiftly, rapidly
**getragen** (Ger.) sustained
**giocoso** (It.) playfully, merrily
**grave** (It.) heavy, slow, ponderous in movement
**grazioso** (It.) gracefully, elegantly

**immer** (Ger.) always

**l'istesso tempo** (It.) the same tempo; return to tempo
**langsam** (Ger.) slowly
**largamente** (It.) "largely," broadly, characterized by a sustained sound
**larghetto** (It.) slowly, but somewhat faster than largo
**largo** (It.) slowly, broad
**lebhaft** (Ger.) animated, lively
**legato** (It.) smoothly and connected
**léger** (Fr.) light
**leggiero, leggero** (It.) light, airy
**leicht** (Ger.) light, brisk
**lente** (Fr.) slowly
**lento** (It.) slowly

**lourd** (Fr.) heavy
**luftig** (Ger.) lightly

**maestoso** (It.) majestically, dignified
**marcato** (It.) "marked," with distinctness and emphasis
**mässig** (Ger.) moderately
**meno** (It.) less; not so . . .
**meno mosso** (It.) less motion
**misterioso** (It.) mysteriously
**mit** (Ger.) with
**mit wärme** (Ger.) with warmth
**moderato** (It.) moderately
**modéré** (Fr.) moderately
**molto** (It.) very, much
**morendo** (It.) dying away

**nicht** (Ger.) not
**nicht zu schnell** (Ger.) not too fast
**non** (It., Fr.) not

**ohne** (Ger.) without

**pensieroso** (It.) pensive, thoughtfully
**pesante** (It.) heavy
**peu, peu à peu** (Fr.) little; little by little
**più** (It.) more
**più mosso** (It.) more motion, becoming faster
**plus** (Fr.) more
**poco, poco a poco** (It.) little; little by little
**presses** (Fr.) accelerate, growing gradually faster
**prestissimo** (It.) very fast
**presto** (It.) very fast

**quasi** (It.) as if; nearly
**quelque peu** (Fr.) somewhat

**rallentando** (rall.) (It.) growing slower and slower
**rasch** (Ger.) fast, rapid, swift
**retenu** (Fr.) holding back
**ritard, ritardando** (rit.) (It.) growing slower and slower
**ritenuto** (It.) held back; at a slower rate of speed
**rubato** (It.) "robbed," lengthening certain notes while shortening others
**ruhig** (Ger.) calmly

**sans** (Fr.) without
**scherzando** (It.) lightheartedly, jestingly; as a tempo, fast

**schnell** (Ger.) fast, quick, rapid
**schneller** (Ger.) getting faster
**sehr** (Ger.) very
**semplice** (It.) with simplicity
**sempre** (It.) always
**senza** (It.) without
**slentando** (It.) growing slower
**smorzando** (It.) dying away
**sostenuto** (It.) sustained, often implying a broadening of the tempo
**soutenu** (Fr.) held, sustained
**stretto** (It.) pressed, hurried
**stringendo** (It.) hastening, accelerating, often with a crescendo
**subito** (It.) suddenly
**süss** (Ger.) sweetly

**tempo primo** (It.) play at the original tempo
**toujours** (Fr.) always
**tranquillo** (It.) tranquilly
**traurig** (Ger.) sadly
**très** (Fr.) very

**vershwindend** (Ger.) vanishing, dying away
**viel** (Ger.) much, great
**vif** (Fr.) lively
**vite** (Fr.) fast
**vivace** (It.) lively, animated, brisk
**vivo** (It.) lively, spirited

**wenig** (Ger.) little
**wuchtig** (Ger.) weighty, ponderously, with emphasis

**zart(lich)** (Ger.) tenderly
**ziemlich** (Ger.) somewhat, rather
**züruckhaltend** (Ger.) holding back, gradually becoming slower

# Appendix B: Syllable Systems

Syllable systems have been a standard component of musical instruction since the beginnings of solfège study in seventeenth-century Italy. The consistent use of a syllable system seeks to accomplish one or more of the following goals:

1. Recognition of notes and harmonic structures
2. Understanding of musical relationships within a key
3. Practice in observing multiple aspects of a musical sound
4. Providing a musical sound on which to sing each pitch

Each syllable system emphasizes one or two of these characteristics over the others. As such, the system you will be asked to use will be determined by the characteristics that your teacher values the most from the list above. All syllable systems have merit and can be used effectively. It is important that you spend time learning and practicing the system that you are required to use.

### Common Syllable Systems

#### Fixed-Do

The fixed-do syllable system uses traditional French or Italian names for pitches and emphasizes musical sound and mastery of note reading and harmonic structures. Students must name the pitches they sing, albeit in a different language than they would use in normal conversation. As such, the ability to competently read all of the standard clefs is emphasized. Students must also know the notes that go into each structure (in every key) in order to sing the correct syllables. This reinforces the spelling of chords, scales, and other structures taught through harmony. In addition, the use of French or Italian pitch names provides syllables on which it is easier to make musical sounds.

In most English-language fixed-do systems, chromatic alterations on pitches are ignored, so all pitches with the same letter name (D-flat, D-natural, etc.) would receive the same syllable.

**TABLE B.1**

| *Pitch* | *Syllable* | *Pitch* | *Syllable* |
|---|---|---|---|
| C, C-sharp, C-flat | Do | G | Sol |
| D, D-sharp, D-flat | Re | A | La |
| E, etc. | Mi | B | Si |
| F | Fa | | |

Perhaps most importantly, a fixed-do system teaches sensitivity to sound. Students who learn solfège using this system often report that over time, they develop a sense of the uniqueness of discrete pitches, chords in particular keys, and even the individual keys themselves sound. As such, fixed-do solfège seeks to instill a very strong and precise sense of relative pitch.

### Letter Names

A variation of the fixed-do system is the use of English letter names. Like traditional fixed-do solfège syllables, reading of pitches and spelling of harmonic structures are reinforced. Many teachers feel that the English letters have a less musical sound than the traditional solfège syllables, but they allow the student to sing in his or her "native" language. When this system is used, alterations to pitches are often omitted, just as in fixed-do solmization. Therefore, G-flat, G-natural, and G-sharp would all be sung as simply "G."

### Moveable-Do

In any moveable-do system, a solmization syllable replaces the scale degree number of the indicated pitch. Therefore, scale degree 1 in any major or minor key is typically replaced with the syllable Doh. Chromatically altered pitches are accommodated in this system by altering the vowel sound of the diatonic syllable. A list of the complete system with chromatic alterations appears below:

**TABLE B.2**

| *"Flatted" notes* | | *"Natural" notes* | | *"Sharped" notes* | |
|---|---|---|---|---|---|
| *Scale degree* | *Syllable* | *Scale degree* | *Syllable* | *Scale degree* | *Syllable* |
| ♭1 | — | ♮1 | Do | #1 | Di |
| ♭2 | Ra | ♮2 | Re | #2 | Ri |
| ♭3 | Me | ♮3 | Mi | #3 | — |
| ♭4 | — | ♮4 | Fa | #4 | Fi |
| ♭5 | Se | ♮5 | Sol | #5 | Si |
| ♭6 | Le | ♮6 | La | #6 | Li |
| ♭7 | Te | ♮7 | Ti | #7 | — |

Thus, a major and a natural minor scale (in any key) side by side would have the following syllable sequences:

**TABLE B.3**

| *Scale degree* | | | | | | | | |
|---|---|---|---|---|---|---|---|---|
| *Scale* | 1 | 2 | 3 | 4 | 5 | 6 | 7 | 1 |
| *Major* | Do | Re | Mi | Fa | Sol | La | Ti | Do |
| *Natural Minor* | Do | Re | Me | Fa | Sol | Le | Te | Do |

Moveable-do systems emphasize relationships within a key and as such are extremely effective at building a very strong sense of tonal direction and function. A Do-minor system places an emphasis on the parallel relationship between a major key and a minor key starting on the same tonic pitch.

### La-Minor Moveable-Do

A variant of the system above is a La-minor moveable-do system. In this system, major key syllables are identical to those used in Do-minor moveable-do. In minor keys, however, the tonic pitch receives the syllable La. This system emphasizes the relative instead of the parallel relationship between major and minor keys, as well as the consistency of syllable sounds (no syllable sounds have to be altered to sing a natural minor scale).

Thus, the major and minor scales placed next to each other would have the following syllable sequences:

**TABLE B.4**

*Scale degree*

| | | | | | | | | |
|---|---|---|---|---|---|---|---|---|
| *Scale* | 1 | 2 | 3 | 4 | 5 | 6 | 7 | 1 |
| *Major* | Do | Re | Mi | Fa | Sol | La | Ti | Do |
| *Natural minor (La-minor)* | La | Ti | Do | Re | Mi | Fa | Sol | La |

The advantage of a La-minor moveable-do system is in the ease of dealing with chromatically altered pitches, such as scale degrees 6 and 7 in the melodic minor scale. All raised pitches will share the same vowel sound ("i" pronounced "ee" as in "Fi–Si–La").

### Numbers

Like letter names, English scale degree numbers may be used instead of solfège syllables. These make a more direct connection between sung pitches and scale degree function, but many teachers feel they have a less musical sound and they can add to confusion when harmonic structures labeled with numbers are used (teachers tend to say things like "Sing 3, 5, and 1 for a I chord in 6–3 position!"). The syllable for scale degree 7 is often shortened to "sev" for ease of singing.

### Which System is Best?

No single system yet developed accomplishes all four goals outlined above. As a result, most effective solfège classes utilize a combination of systems so that the best aspects of each may be emphasized, depending on the pedagogical need. For example, a class that uses fixed-do will often use scale degree numbers simultaneously to strengthen the students' sense of harmonic function within a key. Many moveable-do classes will use letter names when teaching clef-reading. Note that most combinations mix solfège syllables with English names so that potential confusion between systems is minimized. Many variations on these systems are used in schools of music across the country. Usually these variants serve to enhance one of the four goals stated above. Whatever system is used, it is important to emphasize consistency, accuracy, and musicality, and to keep the goal of using syllables in mind.

# Appendix C: Using Your Voice

Proper singing consists of three elements:

1. Posture
2. Breathing
3. Vocalization

**Posture.** When water flows through a pipe, it moves fastest and with the least resistance when its path is straight and the pipe is secured to a stable base. Think of your body as a pipe through which musical energy flows. It flows on the breath, and you need to make a straight, unimpeded, and secure path for it. This is accomplished through using good posture. At first, when you are building the habit of standing with good posture, methodically go through the following checklist that takes you from the floor or seat to your head.

Check that . . .

1. Your feet are on the floor and that your body weight is evenly distributed but leaning just slightly forward, toward the balls of your feet. Make sure your knees are not locked. If seated, make sure your legs are bent at a comfortable angle and your feet are resting comfortably on the floor.
2. Your body is centered above your hips.
3. Your back is comfortably straight, your shoulders are relaxed but not sagging, and your arms are hanging comfortably but not pulling your shoulders down.
4. Your head is centered over your neck, your eyes are looking straight ahead, and your chin is at a level position.

**Breathing.** Effective singing starts with effective deep breathing. When inhaling, begin by opening your mouth (we take in air more efficiently through the mouth instead of the nose) and relaxing your oral cavity and throat so that they feel relaxed and open. Think of expanding your rib cage upward and outward and relaxing your abdominal muscles so that your diaphragm (a muscle between your chest cavity and abdominal organs) descends. In essence, you are, in a very relaxed way, expanding your chest cavity, which draws air into your lungs. Relaxation is key: keep your shoulders and arms hanging and relaxed.

When exhaling, keep your oral cavity in its open, and relaxed state. Begin to contract your chest cavity by raising the diaphragm and bringing the chest down and in. Let the air flow naturally through your relaxed throat and mouth and out of your body.

Remember that musical phrasing happens on the air stream. As a result, try to have the intensity of your exhalation match the musical contour of the phrase you are singing. Also, be aware of exhaling enough air so that you can follow it with a deep inhalation that brings in fresh air to replace it. Finally, allow yourself enough time to take a relaxed, deep, and effective breath before the next musical phrase, and make sure that you think of this breath as a part of the musical fabric. Make the use of air and breath as musical as you can so that it will support the pitches, dynamics, articulation, etc. Think of the breath as part of the music, not as something that interrupts or happens between moments of music.

To feel if you are breathing correctly, lie down on your back and notice how you breathe. When you stand up again, try to replicate that same feel. Wind instrumentalists should notice that the breathing process feels very similar to the one you use for playing your instrument.

**Vocalization.** A good way to begin to vocalize is to hum. When humming, start with a good breath. Try to make your mouth cavity a large but comfortable size by lowering your tongue and lifting the back of your throat (the soft palate). For most people, the sound will be very muffled and feel as though it is being created near the bottom of the throat. Imagine moving that sound forward in your mouth to your teeth. As you start to imagine the sound moving, you should start to feel a tickling sensation in your nose. As the sound approaches the teeth and lips, that tickling sensation should strengthen. This sensation is an indication that you are producing sound correctly.

Listen for the steadiness of the pitch. Even though your sound is being created by the vocal cords, do not try to control the pitch and steadiness of the sound by tightening your throat. Instead, try to relax the throat and control the volume and steadiness of the sound by controlling your exhalation.

Once your pitch is steady and established, open your mouth to create the syllable "ma." When you open your mouth, be very aware that the things you did to create the hum do not change. Is your air flowing steadily? Does it feel as if the note is being produced up near your teeth instead of in your throat? Is the pitch steady? Energizing the muscles in your face and eyes helps to create a more interesting sound. One way to do this is to smile while you sing.

Especially for beginning singers, you need not sing loudly. Have your first sounds be of a moderate volume, and then practice making your sound softer without changing pitch or noticeably reducing the amount of air you use. As you begin, it will be easier to tune and blend these softer sounds. After you have learned to control these, then begin to push your dynamic range toward louder sounds.

Good singers learn to recognize and manipulate many little details about their breath control, oral cavity, and mental approach to consistently produce the best sound. If you are a vocalist, practice your singing technique in your solfège exercises. If you are an instrumentalist, practice the techniques detailed above and challenge yourself to make as beautiful and musical a sound as you can.

# Index of Musical Examples